*A*way for the
WEEKEND
S O U T H E A S T

Away for the WEEKEND

S O U T H E A S T

Great Getaways for
Every Season in
Alabama
Georgia
North Carolina
South Carolina
Tennessee

ELEANOR BERMAN

Crown Trade Paperbacks
New York

Published by Crown Trade Paperbacks, 201 East 50th Street, New York, New
York 10022. Member of the Crown Publishing Group.

Random House, Inc. New York, Toronto, London, Sydney, Auckland

Crown Trade Paperbacks and colophon are trademarks of Crown Publishers, Inc.

Manufactured in the United States of America

Library of Congress Cataloging-in-Publication Data

Berman, Eleanor
     Away for the weekend, Southeast : great getaways for every season
  in Alabama, Georgia, North Carolina, South Carolina,
  Tennessee / Eleanor Berman. — 1st ed.
        p.   cm.
     Includes index.
     1. Southern States—Tours.   I. Title.
  F207.3.B47   1994
  917.504′43—dc20   93-24158
                                                            CIP

ISBN 0-517-88052-0

10   9   8   7   6   5   4

Acknowledgments

It would take a whole book to thank all the individuals who helped me at every stop during my long research travels around five states. But a few who must be singled out for their guidance, assistance, and friendship are the wonderful tourism people in each of the states. Patti Culp Mullen and Patty McDonald of the Alabama Travel Council, Karin Koser in Georgia, Rebecca Moore in North Carolina, Cherie Had in South Carolina, and Mark Forester in Tennessee have shown me the real meaning of Southern hospitality. Special thanks, too, to Lee Sentell, president of the Alabama Travel Council, who so generously shared valuable research from his own excellent recent guide on the state. Finally, thanks to my editor, Shirley Wohl, who manages to find fresh enthusiasm for each project and makes my work so much more rewarding with her support and encouragement.

Contents

Introduction

From the misty ridges of the Great Smoky Mountains to the white sands of the Atlantic, from the skyscrapers of Atlanta to the Colonial charm of Charleston, the Southeastern states are filled with travel treasure. Antebellum mansions and cozy log cabins, spectacular gardens, fast horses and lazy rivers, mountain crafts and modern art, the Appalachian frontier and the frontiers of outer space—all of these await in this beautiful and bountiful region.

With so much to choose from, the problem is where to begin. Should it be the mountains of North Carolina, Tennessee, Alabama, or Georgia? The beaches of the Outer Banks, the Grand Strand, or the Gulf Shore? The eighteenth century in Winston-Salem, the Old South in Macon, or the future in Huntsville?

Away for the Weekend®: Southeast invites you to try them all, one at a time, as memorable weekend getaways.

Unlike most guides, this book is not divided into individual states, but samples the best of five states: Alabama, Georgia, North Carolina, South Carolina, and eastern Tennessee. It offers change of pace and a recharge of spirits for every mood and interest around the calendar.

The organization of each trip suggests a weekend itinerary that brings together all the attractions within easy reach of each destination, so that you won't go home and find you've missed something special just a few miles out of your way.

Most of the trips are within an easy drive of Atlanta, the largest city in the region, and are conveniently accessible to other major cities such as Charlotte, Birmingham, and Nashville. Driving directions include instructions from Atlanta, but pinpoint destinations to make it easy to plot a course from any direction, and mileages are given for the closest cities.

Because the region is large, some of the very best places—the coasts of both Carolinas and the tip of eastern Tennessee, for example—are long drives from many metropolitan areas, but they are well worth the trip. Consider these for long weekends, or check the public transportation information in each chapter to take advantage of convenient flights that make it possible to go farther for a weekend adventure.

The book is divided into four seasonal sections to allow you to make the most of each time of year. That means, for example, the best gardens and house tours for spring, beach and mountain escapes in summer, autumn foliage routes, and special Christmas festivities. Reading ahead allows you to take advantage of special events, planning a relaxing and leisurely weekend and reserving the best of local lodging.

Don't be bound by the calendar, however. Many of these destinations are equally appealing and less crowded when nothing special is happening. Mild Southern weather invites off-season jaunts that are easy on the budget and a special delight because you can have busy destinations almost to yourself. The information listings at the end of each chapter are appropriate no matter in what season you make the trip.

It should be noted from the start that this is a personal and selective guide. Instead of listing every possibility in each state, I've selected what I feel are the cream of the weekend destinations. Nor is every single sightseeing attraction, lodging, and restaurant in each location included. I've limited the listings to places I've visited myself or that were recommended by knowledgeable local sources and frequent visitors to these areas—people whose opinions I respect.

Since Southern inns and resorts are very special places, many are prominently mentioned and some become destinations in themselves. However, this is primarily a guide to destinations and events, not to lodgings. Where motels are the only accommodations available, the lists reflect this. The final chapter of the book, "The Last Roundup," covers resorts that did not fit into the destinations in other chapters.

Registry listings and free state guides listed in the information pages at the end of this Introduction will widen your options for bed-and-breakfast accommodations.

HOW TO USE THIS BOOK

Like its predecessors for the New York area, New England, the mid-Atlantic, and northern California, *Away for the Weekend®: Southeast* assumes you have a normal two-day weekend to spend, arriving on Friday night and leaving on Sunday. Each trip suggests activities for a two-day stay, with added attractions to accommodate varying tastes and time schedules. I've included what I hope is just enough history and background to make each area more interesting without bogging you down in lengthy detail. If you become intrigued and want more information, you can get it on the spot.

When there is enough to do to warrant a long stay, a symbol at the start of each trip will tell you so. When you do have more than a weekend to spend, use these symbols as a cue, or use the maps at the end of the book to combine nearby weekends to fill out an extended stay. Mountain destinations in northeast and northwest Georgia, and the South Carolina coast from Charleston to Myrtle Beach, are examples of places that can easily be combined for a longer tour.

The following letter codes indicate trips that seem appropriate for children, though you are the best judge of what your family might enjoy:

C = recommended for children

L = recommended for long weekends

Lodging prices are for a double room; dining prices indicate main entrees only, rather than an entire meal, since many people do not choose to order two or three courses with every meal.

I (inexpensive)   = under $70

M (medium)   = $71 to $100

E (expensive)   = $101 to $135

EE (extra expensive) = over $135

When meals are included in the rates, these letters are used:

   CP = continental plan (breakfast only)

MAP = modified American plan (breakfast and dinner)

   AP = American plan (all three meals)

Dining prices are coded as follows:

   I = most entrees under $12 per person

   M = most entrees between $12 and $18

   E = most entrees between $18 and $25

EE = most entrees over $25 (or, when indicated, a prix-fixe menu)

When prices bridge two categories, a combination of letters is used.
Since AAA, Mobil, and other, similar guides do so well by motel ratings, I've omitted motels here unless they are the only available lodgings or have a special appeal. You can always get a listing of motels and hotels by writing to the local tourist office noted at the end of each chapter.

Camping information is not included here, but the state listings include state park information numbers.

Admission prices to sightseeing attractions use dollar signs to indicate price categories, as follows:

   $ = under $2
   $$ = $2–$4.99
   $$$ = $5–$10
   $$$$ = over $10

Rates increase steadily, often before a book makes it from author to publisher to bookstore. Rates given here are as accurate as could be determined at the time of publication, and are included as a general indication of what to expect. Please use them just that way, as a generalguide *only*. Always use the telephone numbers included to check for current prices when you plan your trip. It is a good idea to verify current hours and holiday closings, as well.

When it comes to restaurants and lodgings, remember that a new owner or chef can make a big difference, and changes and closings cannot always be predicted. If you find that any information here has become seriously outdated, that a place has closed or gone downhill, I hope that you will let me know by writing to me in care of Clarkson N. Potter, Inc., 201 East 50th Street, New York, NY 10022, so that the entry can be corrected. If you discover new places or know some appealing ones that I have missed, I hope you will let me know about these as well.

The maps in this book are simplified to highlight locations of suggested destinations. They are not necessarily reliable as road maps. You can get an excellent overall map free from the tourism offices listed below.

One last tip: Reserve well ahead of time if you want to stay in country inns or visit beach resorts or Great Smoky Mountain National Park and other foliage meccas in autumn. Most lodgings offer refunds on deposits if you can cancel with reasonable notice, so plan ahead and take your pick, instead of settling for leftovers.

For this native Southerner who has lived in the Northeast for many years, the year and a half spent researching this book was truly a joy. Though I have returned frequently to visit family, my trips seldom allowed time for exploring. I have been reminded anew of the pleasures found everywhere in the Southeast: the haunting beauty of the mountains, the glorious gardens, the beaches beyond compare. Everywhere the special history and flavor of the past continue to make this one of America's most uniquely interesting and colorful regions. My waistline has felt the effects of the wonderful cuisine, from low-country shrimp and grits to flaky fried chicken and fresh-caught mountain trout.

I was delighted to see the remarkable progress that has transformed so many Southern cities, particularly my hometown of Birmingham.

I hope that my very real enthusiasm for these places and pleasures comes through, inspiring both Southerners and more of my Northern neighbors to share these discoveries—and to make some of their own.

State Tourist Information

Write to or telephone any of these state tourist offices for free maps and literature on attractions throughout their states. Those marked with an asterisk also publish a directory of bed-and-breakfast listings:

Alabama Bureau of Tourism and Travel*
401 Adams Avenue, P.O. Box 4309
Montgomery, AL 36104
(800) ALA-BAMA

Georgia Tourism Division*
P.O. Box 1776
Atlanta, GA 30311
(404) 656-3590

North Carolina Division of Travel and Tourism
430 North Salisbury Street
Raleigh, NC 27603
(800) VISIT-NC

South Carolina Division of Tourism*
1205 Pendleton Street
Columbia, SC 29201
(803) 734-0235

Tennessee Department of Tourism
P.O. Box 23170
Nashville, TN 37202
(615) 741-2158

State Parks

For camping, lodging, and recreation information, contact the following:

Alabama State Parks
Department of Conservation and Natural Resources
64 North Union Street
Montgomery, AL 36130
(205) 242-3333 or (800) ALA-PARK

Georgia State Parks and Historic Sites
1352 Floyd Tower East
205 Butler Street, Atlanta, GA 30334
(404) 656-3530 or (800) 342-7275 in GA
(800) 342-7275 out of state

North Carolina Division of Parks and Recreation
512 North Salisbury Street
Raleigh, NC 27611
(919) 733-4181

South Carolina Division of State Parks
1205 Pendleton Street
Columbia, SC 29201
(803) 734-0156

Tennessee State Parks
L and C Tower, 401 Church Street
Nashville, TN 37243
(615) 532-0001 or (800) 421-6683

BED-AND-BREAKFAST LISTINGS

Write to the following for directories of bed-and-breakfast accommodations in their areas:

Bed & Breakfast Birmingham
(and Alabama)
Route 2, Box 275
Leeds, AL 30594
(205) 699-9841

Bed and Breakfast Atlanta
1801 Piedmont Avenue, NE, Suite 208
Atlanta, GA 30324
(404) 875-0525 or (800) 967-3224

Georgia Bed & Breakfast
(Atlanta)
2472 Lauderdale Drive
Atlanta, GA 30345
(404) 493-1930

Quail Country Bed & Breakfast
1104 Old Monticello Road
Thomasville, GA 31792
(912) 226-7218

R.S.V.P. Georgia and Savannah
417 East Charlton Street
Savannah, GA 30410
(912) 232-7787 or (800) 729-7787

Savannah Historic Inns & Guest Houses
Reservation Service
147 Bull Street
Savannah, GA 31401
(800) 262-4667 or (800) 262-4667

North Carolina Bed & Breakfast Association
P.O. Box 1077
Asheville, NC 28802
(800) 849-5392

South Carolina Bed and Breakfast Association
1705 Bay Street
Beaufort, SC 29902
(803) 522-1122

Tennessee Bed & Breakfast Innkeepers Association
3313 South Circle
Knoxville, TN 37920
(615) 579-4508

Spring

Harbour Town, Hilton Head. Photo courtesy of Sea Pines Plantation, South Carolina

Making the Pilgrimage to Eufaula

It was noon on a sunny April day in 1865 when a messenger came racing over the hill to report that a regiment of Union cavalry was on the way to Eufaula, Alabama. Though the Civil War had officially ended two weeks earlier at Appomattox, General Benjamin H. Grierson was demanding further "truce."

Knowing the fate of other towns that had been burned down by the enemy, the mayor and other local dignitaries rode out personally to escort the general and his staff into town and entertain them at dinner. Southern charm prevailed, and Eufaula was spared.

Today it is a showcase of "high cotton days," the good years before the war, when the "white gold" of the Old South enriched this small town on the Chattahoochee River with a treasury of lovely homes. The Seth Lore and Irwinton Historic District includes more than 700 architecturally significant structures dating back as early as 1836. Set among tall trees draped with Spanish moss, they make for a pretty picture.

The annual spring Eufaula Pilgrimage draws hundreds for the chance to tour some of these homes, many still furnished with family heirlooms. This is Alabama's oldest house tour and one of its finest, a tradition since 1966. Favorite features are the evening candlelight tours, each led off by a wine-and-cheese party at the town's showplace Shorter Mansion.

The weekend also includes a prestigious annual antique show at the old National Guard Armory, and an outdoor art exhibit of works from throughout the Southeast. An encampment of authentically clad Confederate re-enactors brings to life the town's early days, including that fateful day when the Yankees came to town.

Add the color of azaleas and dogwoods in the early spring, and the beauty of the Southern belles in period hoop skirts serving as hostesses at the homes and gardens on the tour, and there's every good reason to plan a Eufaula visit.

For a change of pace, spend some time at a neighboring state resort park on Lake Eufaula, the body of water formed by the construction of the Walter F. George Lock and Dam on the Chattahoochee River. Or do some bird-watching at the Eufaula National Wildlife Refuge, a haven for waterfowl.

The name Eufaula comes from one of the Indian tribes found living beside the river when early settlers arrived in 1823. The streets of the oldest part of town were laid out by Captain Seth Lore, and the initial letters of their names spell out his surname—Livingston, Orange, Randolph, and Eufaula. The town changed its name briefly to Irwinton in 1823 to honor General William Irwin, the largest slave and land owner in the state, who used his influence in the legislature to create a steamboat landing in town. His name remains in the title of the historic district, along with Lore's.

Eufaula prospered, both from its cotton plantations and from the commerce brought by the boats that steamed in to the dock to take on bales of cotton. The walking-driving tour of the historic district, available from the Chamber of Commerce or at the Shorter Mansion, leads down streets such as Eufaula, lined with stately, pillared Greek Revival homes such as the 1863 Raney Taylor house, the 1854 Couric-Smith House, and the 1848 Drewry-Moorer house with its fancier Italianate columns.

Fendall Hall, built in 1856–60 and renovated in the 1880s, is one of the most beautiful of the Italianate structures, with fine marble floors and stenciled walls. It offers the chance to see a restoration in progress, a look at what it takes to return a historic home to its original state. It is open by appointment only, except during Pilgrimage days.

Another town showplace is the Tavern, Eufaula's oldest frame structure, built in 1837 on the bluffs as a riverside inn, amid ancient, moss-draped trees. Now a private home and photographer's studio, it is often included on Pilgrimage tours.

Some of the old homes have new uses. The Chamber of Commerce is located in the town's oldest residence, the 1837 Sheppard Cottage, and the Historic Chattahoochee Commission has quarters in the Greek Revival–style Hart House, built in the early 1800s. Both are open to visitors on weekdays, free of charge.

The Shorter Mansion, headquarters of the Eufaula Heritage Association, is also open for tours. Built in 1884 by a wealthy cotton planter, and remodeled in 1906, when 17 Corinthian columns were added, the home is lavishly furnished with period pieces, thanks to an appropriation from the Alabama legislature. It includes a "Governor's Parlor," honoring six Alabama governors who came from Barbour County.

Eufaula has several fine early churches as well as homes, and a stroll down Broad Street, the commercial center of town, reveals more history, since many current businesses are housed in nineteenth-century buildings. Broad Street rates its own printed walking-tour guide. On this street also is Kendall Manor, an Italianate home with a cupola that is now a spectacular bed-and-breakfast inn. St. Mary's, a more modest 1850 home once used as a church retreat, is also open to guests.

Eufaula's Pilgrimage events can easily fill a weekend, but you might choose to save Sunday for the out-of-doors and Lakepoint Resort State Park. The 85-mile lake, on the Alabama-Georgia border, is famous for its large catches of bass, but the park offers more than fishing. The grounds include a lakeside beach, a marina, an 18-hole golf course, tennis courts, picnic grounds, a nature center, and, in season, a pool for guests who stay in the park's modern motel rooms or cabins. The attractive lodge dining room offers lake views.

Even if you're not a fisherman, you'll likely enjoy a visit to Tom Mann's Fish World Aquarium, a 38,000-gallon tank filled with bass and other native fish and billed as the world's largest freshwater bass aquarium. Phone to find out hours when the fish are fed; the mad rush for food is a sight to behold. The aquarium is adjacent to the plant where Tom Mann produces lures that are legendary among bass fishermen. There's a monument here to the late Leroy Brown, the fish that Mann swore by as a tester for his lures. If Leroy bit, Tom knew he had a winner. The aquarium is located on Route 431 north of Eufaula, on the way to the state park.

If you have still more time, you can cross the Georgia border to Lumpkin and see the restored village of Westville and the amazing formations of Providence Canyon State Park (see page 146).

There's plenty to do and see in the area, but none of it compares to the simple pleasure of a stroll through Eufaula, a return to the best of the Old South.

Area Code: 334

DRIVING DIRECTIONS   Eufaula is located on U.S. Routes 431 and 82 in southeast Alabama, near the Georgia border. From Atlanta, follow I–85 to I–185 south to U.S. 431, about 167 miles. From Birmingham, Take I–65 south to Montgomery, then U.S. 82 east to U.S. 431 south, about 169 miles.

ACCOMMODATIONS   *St. Mary's Bed & Breakfast,* 206 Rivers Avenue, 36027, 687–7195, I-CP ● *Kendall Manor,* 534 W. Broad Street, 36072, 687–8847, M, CP ● *Lakefront Resort State Park,* P.O. Box 267, 36072, 687–8011 or (800) 544-LAKE; central reservation service 800-ALA-PARK, 101 motel rooms, I; 29 cabins, I-E ● *Best Western Eufaula Inn,* 1337 S. Eufaula Avenue, 36072, 687–9300, I ● *Holiday Inn,* E. Barbour Street, 36072, 687–2021, I.

DINING   *The Dogwood Inn,* 214 N. Eufaula Avenue, 687–5629, 1905 former Victorian boardinghouse, Southern specialties, I-M. *Lakefront Resort State Park* (see above), I-M.

SIGHTSEEING   *Eufaula Pilgrimage,* Eufaula Heritage Association, P.O. Box 486, Eufaula 36072, 687–3793. Three days of tours by day and by candlelight, held the first weekend in April. Phone for current rates ● *Shorter Mansion,* 340 N. Eufaula Avenue, 687–3793. Hours: Monday to Saturday 10 A.M. to 4 P.M.; Sunday from 1 P.M.; $$ ● *Fendall Hall,* 917 West Barbour Street. By appointment; check with Chamber of Commerce ● *Tom Mann's Fish World,* U.S. 431 North, 687–7044. Hours: daily 7 A.M. to 6 P.M., $$ ● *Lakepoint Resort State Park,* off U.S. 431, 7 miles north of Eufaula, P.O. Box 267, Eufaula, 687–6676, daylight hours, park free, fees for golf and other activities ● *Eufaula National Wildlife Refuge,* off state road 165, Box 97-B, Eufaula, 687–4065. Hours: daily during daylight hours, free ● *Ante-Bellum Tours,* P.O. Box 655, 687–4340. Guided tours can be arranged in Eufaula whenever you visit; phone for details.

INFORMATION   Eufaula/Barbour County Chamber of Commerce, Sheppard Cottage, 504 E. Barbour Street, Eufaula, AL, 687–6664.

Welcoming Spring in Wilmington

Azaleas light up the spring landscape all over the South, but nowhere are they more bountiful or beautiful than in Wilmington, the home of the annual North Carolina Azalea Festival. Not only do billions of blossoms turn the whole city into a garden, but the many plantations nearby are also in their glory.

It's the state's premier celebration of spring, and a perfect time to discover a delightful Colonial port city. To make things even nicer, April is warm along the Cape Fear coast, and the white sands of Wrightsville Beach are just 15 miles away.

Saturday is the big day for the festival, which celebrated its forty-fifth anniversary in 1992. The Azalea Queen's parade is in the morning, followed by the opening of a lavish two-day street fair along River Front Park.

Saturday evening brings a free street dance downtown, or you can attend the Queen's gala Coronation Pageant. The Azalea Queen each year is a popular entertainer, her court a retinue of local beauties. Big-name entertainment is also a traditional feature of the weekend.

In between the hoopla, take time for a walk through North Carolina's largest urban historic district, armed with the free map available from the Visitors Bureau. The main sights are near the center of town. If you can join the Wilmington Adventure walking tour, you'll not only learn a lot of history from Bob Jenkins, the colorful guide with the hat and cane, but have a very good time sharing his knowledge. Among the tidbits, you'll find out why North Carolinians are known as Tarheels.

The town's wide streets remain as they were laid out in 1734. The city was incorporated in 1739, named for the royal governor, the Duke of Wilmington. Prosperity came quickly from two sources, the Cape Fear River and the pine tree.

The river was the deepest in the colony, and the only one leading directly into the Atlantic Ocean. It helped Wilmington thrive as an export center for cotton and for the rice that was grown on dozens of area plantations.

The name Fear (from *fere*, Latin for "danger") was inspired by the tricky shoals offshore, easy for the natives to maneuver, but perilous for any ship whose pilot was unfamiliar with local tides and currents. Local pilots helped blockade runners evade the Union Navy during the Civil War. Fort Fisher, which guarded the entrance to the river, held out against Union assault until a major sea battle in 1865.

The pine forests found in abundance in the area were a valuable source of the desirable products known as naval stores. Tough heart of pine could be used for shipbuilding, and pine resin could be reduced to the pine tar necessary to coat ships' bottoms and ropes. With a rich supply of pine and an easy route for shipping, this region was America's largest supplier of naval stores until the twentieth century. It was pine tar that inspired the nickname "Tarheels."

Like many early ports, Wilmington languished over time, until a strong preservation movement began in the 1960s. A town survey identified more than 200 historic blocks. Many of these sites are now occupied by businesses and offices. Walk into downtown buildings such as the Cafe Atlantique, and you can still see the original brick and heart-of-pine walls erected in 1840.

The spirit of revival has transformed the waterfront, and turned old waterfront warehouses such as Chandler's Wharf and the Cotton Exchange into atmospheric shopping and dining enclaves.

These changes have attracted many new young residents to Wilmington, a number of them living in apartments over shops in the downtown area, just as merchants did in colonial times.

Many of the earliest buildings were lost to a fire in 1840, so most of those still standing were built after that year. An exception is the Burgwin Wright House, circa 1770, a Colonial gentleman's town house with lovely parterre gardens and a three-story outside kitchen. General Cornwallis used it as his headquarters during the American Revolution. The triple-tier porches are typical of early coastal Carolina architecture.

Watch for plaques marking the sites of buildings that were lost before the preservation movement took hold. Among them is one for the home of Whistler's mother, the subject of the famous painting by James Whistler.

The columned Zebulon Latimer House, Wilmington's second showplace, was built in stately Italianate style in 1852 by a wealthy merchant and remained in the Latimer family until 1963, when it was restored as headquarters for the local historical society.

Wilmington is known as "the city of churches," and many are well worth noting. The standout is St. James Episcopal Church at 1 South Third Street, a Gothic Revival building erected in 1840 for a congregation dating to 1781. Among the many fine details are the carved wooden ceiling and the rose window.

St. Paul's Evangelical Lutheran Church, at 603 Market Street, has stained-glass windows thought to have been created by Tiffany. The Moorish-style Temple of Israel, at 1 South Fourth, is the oldest Jewish synagogue in the state, completed in 1876.

Two museums downtown also merit a visit. The Cape Fear Museum opened its new home in 1992, telling of the area's history and heritage with life-size dioramas and interactive displays. When you try to stir a paddle through sticky pine tar, you'll understand why it was so valuable as protection for ships.

St. John's Museum of Art, a complex of three restored buildings, has a major collection of the work of Mary Cassatt and a big selection of Jugtown pottery, one of North Carolina's time-honored crafts. The museum also shows work by many state artists.

The final historic attraction not to be missed is Thalian Hall, part of the 1855–58 City Hall building. This theater, built when Wilmington was the largest city in the state, was grand, and a major stop on the traveling theatrical circuit. In the years following the Civil War, it played host to the likes of Lillian Russell, "Buffalo Bill" Cody, and John Philip Sousa.

Recently restored and expanded, the elegant hall now hosts more than 600 performances every year in three theater spaces. Check for the current offerings.

These days, Wilmington has another star on the entertainment scene. Carolco Studios, located on North 23rd Street, is one of the largest motion picture and television production facilities east of Hollywood, and a host of TV and feature films have been produced here since 1984, from "The Young Indiana Jones Chronicles" to *Teenage Mutant Ninja Turtles*.

One of Wilmington's most popular attractions is the USS *North Carolina* Battleship Memorial. Board the river taxi shuttle for a chance to tour the ship that took part in every major Pacific naval battle during World War II. During the summer, it is the scene of a spectacular outdoor sound-and-light show. Sightseeing cruises on the water are also available via riverboat.

Antiquers should pick up the current shopping guide. There are more than two dozen antique shops in town, many located on Front Street, with more clustered north of town on Market Street.

No spring stay in Wilmington is complete without a tour of nearby plantations and gardens. Orton Plantation is an example of the eighteenth-century rice plantations that were once common in the area. The ricefields and marshes are now a wildfowl refuge. The 1725 main house is private, but 20 acres of beautiful gardens are open to the public.

History buffs may want to make a detour from Orton to the nearby Brunswick Town Historic Site, the excavated remains of the oldest colonial settlement on the Cape Fear coast.

Poplar Grove, once a peanut plantation, is the place to tour an antebellum mansion. The plantation house now features demonstrations of old-time crafts such as weaving and blacksmithing.

Airlie Gardens, famous for its five miles of azaleas, is privately owned and open for touring only while the azaleas are in bloom. The estate's spacious lawns, serene lakes, rare plantings, majestic, moss-draped live oaks, and views of Wrightsville Sound are an unforgettable backdrop for the brilliant color of the flowers.

Greenfield Gardens is another spring spectacle, with a five-mile scenic drive surrounding a lake. It was to raise funds for this city park that the Azalea Festival was born.

When you've had your fill of festivals and flowers, Wrightsville Beach beckons, only about 15 minutes east via U.S. 74. This small island community is a longtime family resort with miles of sand for sunning and quiet walks. There are lodgings such as the Blockade Runner right on the beach, making for a nice counterpoint to the attractions of Wilmington. If the weather is right, Wrightsville may well tempt you to extend your stay.

Area Code 919

DRIVING DIRECTIONS   U.S. Routes 74, 421, 17, and 117 all lead into Wilmington. From Raleigh, take I–40 to U.S. 17 west, 123 miles; from Charlotte, follow U.S. 74 east to Route 17, 203 miles. From Atlanta, take I–20 east to I–95 north, then U.S. 74 east, approximately 413 miles.

ACCOMMODATIONS   *Graystone Inn,* 100 South Third Street, Wilmington 28401, 763–2000, E, CP ● *The Inn at St. Thomas Court,* 101 South Second Street, Wilmington 28401, 343–1800 or 800–525–0909, M, CP ● *Five Star Guest House,* 14 North Seventh Street, Wilmington 28401, 763–7581, I-M, CP ● *McKay-Green Inn,* 312

South Third Street, Wilmington 28401, 762–4863, M, CP • *Stemmerman's*, 130 South Front Street, Wilmington 28401, 763–7776, efficiency suites, M, CP • *Murchison House*, 305 South Third Street, Wilmington 28401, 343–8580, I, CP • *Worth House*, 412 South Third Street, Wilmington 28401, 762–8562, M, CP • *Hilton Hotel*, 301 North Water Street, Wilmington 28401, 763–5900, M • *Blockade Runner*, 275 Waynick Boulevard, Wrightsville Beach 28480, 256–2251 or 800–541–1161, oceanfront hotel and adjoining inn, M-E • *Shell Island*, 2700 North Lumina Avenue, Wrightsville Beach 28480, 256–5050, oceanfront suites, E.

DINING   *Cafe Atlantique*, 10 Market Street, 763–8100, French, widely considered best in town, E • *Ferrovia*, 502 Nutt Street, 763–6677, restored warehouse, Italian menu, jazz on weekends, I-M • *Pilot House*, 2 Ann Street, Chandler's Wharf, 343–0200, restored 1870 quarters on the river, M • *Elijah's*, 2 Ann Street, Chandler's Wharf, nautical decor, river view, informal, seafood specialties, I-M • *Crooks*, 138 South Front Street, 762–8898, Southern specialties, like its Chapel Hill counterpart, M • *Oceanic*, 703 S. Lumina Avenue, Wrightsville Beach, 256–5551, I-M • *Blockade Runner* (see above), M • *Bridge Tender*, Airlie Road at Wrightsville Beach Bridge, 256–4519, seafood, view of Intercoastal Waterway, M-E • For breakfast or lunch, a best bet is *Nuduls and Strudels*, 505 Nutt Street, 343–1520, I; for barbecue, try *Skinner & Daniels*, 5214 Market Street, 799–1790, I.

SIGHTSEEING   *North Carolina Azalea Festival*, P.O. Box 51, Wilmington 28402, 763–0905. Three-day weekend held in early April; check for current dates and events • *Wilmington Adventure Tour Company*, 763–1785. Hours: walking tours meet at the Foot of Market Street daily April through October at 10 A.M. and 2 P.M., $$$ • *USS North Carolina Battleship Memorial*, junction of U.S. 74/76, 17, and 421, also reachable by ferry from Wilmington, 251–5797, $$ • *Cape Fear Museum*, 814 Market Street, 341–4350. Hours: Tuesday to Saturday 9 A.M. to 4 P.M.; Sunday 2 P.M. to 5 P.M.; donation • *St. John's Museum of Art*, 114 Orange Street, 763–0281. Hours: Tuesday to Saturday 10 A.M. to 5 P.M.; Sunday 12 noon to 4 P.M.; free • *Burgwin Wright House*, 224 Market Street, 762–0570. Hours: Tuesday to Saturday 10 A.M. to 4 P.M., $$ • *Zebulon Latimer House*, 126 S. Third Street, 762–0492. Hours: Tuesday to Friday 10 A.M. to 4 P.M.; Saturday 10 A.M. to 3 P.M.; $$ • *Cape Fear Riverboats*, P.O. Box 1881, 343–1661 or 800–676–0162: *Henrietta II* paddleboat cruises, river taxi to Battleship Memorial, sightseeing tours. Phone for current schedules and rates ● *Plantations and gardens: Orton Plantation Gardens,* NC route 133, 18 miles south of Wilmington, 371–6851. Hours: 8 A.M. to 6 P.M. March through August; to 5 P.M. September through November; $$$; *Poplar Grove Historic Plantation,* U.S. 17, 9 miles north of Wilmington, 686–9518. Hours: Monday to Saturday 9 A.M. to 5 P.M., Sunday 12 noon to 5 P.M., February through December; $$; *Airlie Gardens,* Airlie Road, 8 miles east on U.S. 74/76, 763–9991. Hours: daily 8 A.M. to 6 P.M. during spring azalea season only, $$$ ● *Greenfield Gardens,* U.S. 421, 2.5 miles south, 341–7855. Hours: daily, daylight hours, free.

INFORMATION Cape Fear Coast Convention & Visitors Bureau, 24 North Third Street, Wilmington, NC 28401, 341–4030 or 800–222–4757.

Tapping the Waters Near Cave Spring

Northwest Georgia is full of discoveries, refreshing places that are off the usual tourist track.

Take Cave Spring, for example. With a population of 905, it is only a hamlet, yet it boasts 90 buildings and sites on the National Register of Historic Places—not to mention an abundance of choice antiques and talented craftspeople. And don't forget the wonder that inspired the town's name, a spring hidden in a cave that flows at an amazing three to four million gallons a day.

Then there is Oak Hill, the antebellum mansion and magnificent gardens that were home to Martha Berry. She founded a remarkable school in a log cabin nearby, and it grew into one of the largest college campuses in the world. It's right across the street from Oak Hill, a testament to Berry's achievements.

And what about Barnsley Gardens, not far away, near Adairsville? They were begun by an Englishman in the 1840s and completed by a German prince in the 1990s to show off, among other beautiful blooms, more than 180 varieties of pre–Civil War roses. The ruins of the house are romantic, and the newly revived gardens grow more beautiful by the year. Late spring, when the roses are at their peak, is just the right time to pay a call.

The closest town of any size in this area is Rome, which offers motel accommodations. But there are more unusual choices, depending on your tastes and the temperature.

Red Top Mountain State Park, on Lake Allatoona, is an ideal gateway to the area, allowing you to add the great outdoors to your agenda. The recently built 33-room park lodge and 18 two-bedroom cabins are modern, with many rooms offering lake views. Opportunities abound for hiking, biking, swimming, and picnicking; there are many ranger-led walks; and boats can be rented to take advantage of the 11,860-acre lake.

At mealtime, the big picture window in the lodge's dining room gives a close-up view of deer and other animals at feeding troughs just a stone's throw away. The feeding area is lit at night.

Bed-and-breakfast fans may prefer the historic Hearn Academy Inn in Cave Spring, a modest but nicely restored nineteenth-century building that is filled with antiques and warmth. It serves as headquarters for the Cave Spring Historical Society. Adairsville offers Old Home Place, an 1855 country house on six acres, and those who admire the Craftsman style of the early 1900s will find it at Stoneleigh in Calhoun.

Wherever you stay, allow plenty of time for shopping and meeting the creative folks in Cave Spring. Driving into town is taking a step back in time. The tiny green, surrounded by old-fashioned shops, might well have been lifted from a painting. Inside those shops are some very interesting wares.

Antiques and curios of all kinds are found around the square, on Broad Street, and on US 411/State Route 53, which bends at a right angle near the center of town and takes two different names, Alabama Street and Rome Road. The biggest selection of wares is found at the Country Roads Antique Mall on Rome Road, where there are 30 dealers.

The most interesting shops are those with talented shopkeepers who create their own collectibles. At Christa's, for example, the owner's specialties include hand-fringed lampshades and hand-appliquéd jackets and bags.

Country Craftsman, on Cedartown Road, offers handcrafted furniture by father-and-son artisans, and Kudzu Pottery Farm, north of town on state route 100, has pottery mugs with whimsical animal faces, as well as clay baskets featuring delightful renderings of kudzu, a pesky Southern plant not often afforded such artistic treatment. Other local finds include paintings, custom-designed signs, and carousel horses.

Pick up a shopping guide in any of the stores for the full listing—and don't forget a stop at Martha Jane's, as famous for her fudge as for antiques. For still more variety, come for the annual arts festivals held the second weekend in June and the fourth weekend in September.

Turn off the square to Rolater Park and you'll spy people lined up with bottles and jugs, scooping up the cool, crystal-clear water produced by the abundant spring. Guided tours are offered through the big limestone cave that is the spring's source. Some of the water is bottled and distributed commercially, but there is easily enough left over to supply the two-and-a-half-acre town swimming pool.

The park grounds were once the campus of the Manual Labor School, founded in 1839. Two of the original buildings and the church are being restored, and the original student lodging has been turned into the Hearn Academy Inn. Other lodging options in town are of the motel or rustic-lodge variety.

Cave Spring has been home to the Georgia School for the Deaf since 1846; that is the reason why you may see many local residents fluent in American Sign Language. The original administration building served as a field hospital during the Civil War. The school is now located on a more modern campus on the edge of town.

From Cave Spring, the next stop is Rome, about 18 miles north on state route 53, on the Coosa River. You'll find a nicely revitalized downtown and riverfront and a couple of interesting galleries.

The 28,000 acres of Rome's Berry College are impressive, but its history and purpose rather than its size are what make this school unique.

A Sunday in the late 1890s was the fateful day when Martha Berry looked out the window of her log playhouse on the grounds of Oak Hill to see a group of mountain children watching her read. She invited them in to listen to Bible stories. Soon she was teaching Sunday school to these neglected but eager students. Next she started a day school and finally the "Berry Schools," which grew into a college on 83 acres of land that Miss Berry inherited from her father. It provided a chance for youngsters who would otherwise have had no hope of getting an education.

The first stop for visitors is the Martha Berry Museum and Art Gallery, constructed in Greek Revival style to complement the columns of nearby Oak Hill. The film shown here, telling her story, is quite moving. Adjacent, in its original setting, is the modest cabin that was the school's birthplace.

The next stop is Oak Hill, the mansion that remains as it was when ③ Miss Berry lived here. It is surrounded by the giant oaks and formal gardens that were the family's pride.

Finally, with the map guide available at the museum, drive across the road to see what Miss Berry accomplished. The older campus is Georgian in design. A large and rather opulent English Gothic complex, added in the 1920s, was a gift from Henry Ford, who was not noted for philanthropy, but who was mightily impressed with Miss Berry's goals and accomplishments.

Drive into the Log Cabin Area to the first location of the Martha Berry School for Girls, a pioneer in education for women.

Rome's other attraction will draw those who are interested in the story of the Cherokee Indians who once called this land home. The Chieftain's Museum, once the residence of the Cherokee leader Major

Ridge, is far different from most visions of Indian dwellings. It is a fine house, part of a plantation that included a ferry landing and a trading post, reflecting the prosperity of the nation that was broken apart by the removal of the Cherokees from their land.

This museum is a stop on the Chieftain's Trail, which explores the history of the Native Americans of northwest Georgia. Another nearby site is the Etowah Indian Mounds, southwest of Cartersville.

The most important site is in Calhoun. Here you'll see a reconstruction of the New Echota Cherokee Capital as it looked in 1825, when it was the seat of government for the nation that once covered northern Georgia and parts of four other southeastern states. It includes the Supreme Court building, the print shop where the Cherokee newspaper was produced, a tavern, and the home of a Christian missionary. The more one learns about the Cherokees, the sadder becomes the story of their removal.

From Rome, those interested in folk art will surely want to drive 26 miles north to Summerville and the studio of Howard Finster, a former minister now approaching age 80, who has become one of America's best-known unschooled artists. Just ask anyone in town where he lives. It is worth the trip just to see the ''Paradise Garden'' that Finster spent more than 20 years creating outside of his studio, an indescribable mélange of three-dimensional constructions, paintings, and writings inspired by his visions of other worlds. Finster's wooden cutouts and some of his paintings are on sale here for prices far below those asked by city galleries. Come to visit on Sunday afternoon, and you'll find the artist himself, ready to chat nonstop about his views of the world, earthly and heavenly. He'll sign his work for you.

If you prefer flowers to folk art, head straight for Barnsley Gardens. It was in the 1840s that Godfrey Barnsley, an English immigrant who made a fortune on Georgia cotton, created an Italian-style villa in the mountains for his Savannah-born wife. The 26-room house was reputed to be the first home away from the East Coast that had hot and cold running water, indoor toilets, and gaslights. Barnsley called it Woodlands.

Legend has it that a Cherokee chief had warned Barnsley that harm would come to his family if he built on the crest of a hill that the Indians considered sacred. Whatever the cause, Julia Barnsley did not live to see the home completed. Her brokenhearted husband planted the gardens in her memory.

Though the house survived the Civil War, Barnsley's bad luck continued. He was financially ruined by the war. Two of his sons died, and a daughter's husband was killed in an accident just as he was beginning to restore the estate. In the early 1900s a tornado took the roof off the house. The place was all but forgotten, the house picked over by looters, the gardens overrun with kudzu, when Prince Hubertus Fugger and his wife, Princess Alexandra, came to the rescue.

The wealthy Bavarian prince, it seems, had always had a romanti(dream of owning a Southern plantation, and had hired real-estate agents to scout one out for him. In 1988 he bought the Barnsley property sight unseen for a reported $3.5 million. No one has recorded his reaction when he first laid eyes on his purchase, but he and the princess were intrigued with the history of the estate and determined to restore the gardens to their former grandeur.

Grand they were when they opened in 1991, with swans gliding on the ponds and more than 141,000 plantings, including an entire slope of rhododendrons, a hillside with over 50,000 naturalized daffodils, a new wildflower meadow, and a 120-foot perennial border that is in almost constant bloom.

Loveliest of all are the antique roses seen everywhere, trained along wooden rail fences and growing against the buildings and in the flower borders. The gardens have been designated a national historic landmark.

Fugger did not try to restore the mansion, finding it more romantic as a ruin. One wing is now a small museum with a pictorial history of the Barnsley family and a video giving the history of Woodlands. A gift shop, snack bar, and garden shop have also been added.

The Barnsley Gardens are not huge or famous, and for that very reason a visit is personal and satisfying. The same might be said of all the pleasures of this special corner of Georgia.

Area Code: 706

DRIVING DIRECTIONS   Cave Spring is at the intersection of U.S. 411 and state Route 100. From Atlanta, take U.S. 278 west to state Route 100 north, about 75 miles. From Birmingham, take I–59 east to U.S. 411 east, about 100 miles. For Red Top Mountain State Park, take I–75 north from Atlanta to exit 123, Cartersville, and drive 2 miles east.

ACCOMMODATIONS   *Hearn Academy Inn,* P.O. Box 715, Cave Spring 30124, 777–8865, I, CP ● *Cedar Creek Lodge,* P.O. Box 345, Cave Spring 30124, 232–3239, chalets along Little Cedar Creek, I, CP ● *Creekside Inn,* 2 Rome Street, Cave Spring 30124, 777–0826, basic motel, I ● *Red Top Mountain Lodge,* 653 Red Top Mountain Road S.E., Cartersville 30120, 975–0055, lodge rooms and cottages, I ● *Old Home Place,* 764 Union Grove Church Road, SE, Adairsville 30103, 625–3649, I, CP ● *Stoneleigh,* 316 Fain Street, Calhoun, 629–2093, I, CP ● *Holiday Inn–Sky Top Center,* U.S. 411, Rome, 295–1100, I.

DINING   *Todd's Country Kitchen,* Cedartown Street, Cave Spring, 777–8327, no frills, bountiful buffet Sunday through Friday, I ●

Shumate's Diner, on the square, Cave Spring, 777–3766, basic fare, I
● *Adairsville Inn,* 100 South Main Street, on the square, Adairsville,
773–2774, steaks, seafood, great homemade yeast rolls, I ● *Tiberio,*
201 Broad Street, Rome, 291–2229, restored bank building, Rome's
best, M ● *Malone's,* River Place, Rome, 234–5092, informal, riverside
location, I-M ● *Partridge Cafe,* 330 Broad Street, Rome, hearty
Southern cooking in a restored movie theater, I ● *Schroeder's,* 406
Broad Street, Rome, 234–4613, informal, jazz on weekends, I-M ●
Country Gentleman, GA Route 27 north, Rome, 235–2108, Greek and
Middle Eastern, I-M.

SIGHTSEEING *Barnsley Gardens,* 597 Barnsley Gardens Road,
Adairsville, 773–7480. Hours: March 1 to November 15, Tuesday to
Saturday 10 A.M. to 6 P.M., Sunday from 12 noon; rest of year to 4:30
P.M.; \$\$\$ ● *Chieftain's Museum,* Riverside Parkway between state
route 53 spur and U.S. 27, Rome, 291–9494. Hours: Tuesday to Friday
11 A.M. to 4 P.M.; Sunday 2 P.M. to 5 P.M.; \$\$ ● *Etowah Creative Arts
Council,* 11 Wall Street, Cartersville, 382–8277. Hours: Tuesday to
Friday 10 A.M. to 4 P.M.; Saturday 10:30 A.M. to 2:30 P.M.; free ● *Etowah
Indian Mounds,* 813 Indian Mounds Road SW, Cartersville, 387–3747.
Hours: Tuesday to Saturday 9 A.M. to 5 P.M.; Sunday 2 P.M. to 5:30 P.M.
● *New Echota Cherokee Capital,* GA Route 225, Calhoun, 629–8151.
Hours: Tuesday to Saturday 9 A.M. to 5 P.M.; Sunday 2 P.M. to 5:30 P.M.
● *Oak Hill and Martha Berry Museum,* Berry College, Martha Berry
Boulevard (U.S. 27), Rome, 291–1883. Hours: Tuesday to Saturday 10
A.M. to 5 P.M.; Sunday from 1 P.M.; \$\$ ● *Red Top Mountain State Park,*
781 Red Top Mountain Road, Cartersville, 975–4203. Hours: daily,
daylight hours. Car fee, \$.

INFORMATION *City of Cave Spring,* P.O. Box 365, Cave Spring,
GA 30124, 777–3382 ● *Cartersville-Bartow County Tourism Council,*
16 W. Main Street, Cartersville, GA 30120, 387–1357 ● *Chieftain's
Trail Council,* P.O. Box 5823, Rome, GA 30161, 295–5576.

Having a Ball at Hilton Head

Name your favorite sports target—golf ball or tennis ball. Or maybe
it's a beach ball you'd rather bounce around. Whatever your game, you
can indulge it to your heart's content on Hilton Head Island, where
more than 20 golf courses and over 200 tennis courts beckon.

This is also the place to watch the pros put the ball into play in some very prestigious tournaments each spring, and to sign on for top-notch instruction to improve your own strokes.

It's hard to believe, but South Carolina's prime resort island used to be a remote, sparsely settled place. Twelve miles long and up to four miles wide, it is rimmed with beaches for almost its entire length, with lush palms and palmettos growing right up to the sand.

Hilton Head was named for Sir William Hilton, the English explorer who sailed into Port Royal harbor in 1663. Early settlers prospered by establishing plantations growing indigo, a plant that produces blue dye valued for its intense color. When plantation life ended with the Civil War, Hilton Head slumbered.

Then, in the 1950s, a bridge was completed connecting Hilton Head to the mainland, and the word *plantation* took on a new meaning, as the Sea Pines Plantation began development on the southern tip of the island. It was a fresh concept at the time, a limited-access residential community with golf courses, bike paths, marinas, and beaches, all carefully planned and placed so as to retain as much of the surrounding natural environment as possible. Over 600 acres were left as a forest and nature preserve.

Sea Pines flourished, and pretty soon there were other posh "plantations" all over the place—Shipyard, Port Royal, and Hilton Head, for example—each with a private gate guarding its villas, beach, golf courses, and other recreational facilities. Some have resort hotels within their property. These plantations now occupy two-thirds of the island. Many of their facilities are open to the public.

As a result of all this development, there are nearly 25,000 permanent residents and almost 1.5 million visitors each year—far too many to suit a lot of people who knew the island in its early days. Visitors now arrive via a busy divided highway lined with shops, restaurants, and outlet stores. The stretch of beach along Forest Beach Drive has become motel-condo row.

So don't look for solitude on Hilton Head—but you'll have to look far to find a better place for sports or beaching. It's a great family vacation haven, with accommodations in a wide enough range to suit any budget. You'll see families all over, happily pedaling along the island's miles of bike paths. And there are still a few carefully guarded nature preserves to show you why people loved Hilton Head in the first place. Since the climate is semitropical, the weather is conducive to sports most of the year, allowing you to take advantage of lower off-season rates.

Despite the competition, Sea Pines remains the largest of the plantations, with 5,000 acres, and the most popular, as you can deduce from the big Welcome Center building at the gate. For those who want to tour or dine in the plantation, day passes are available here for a small fee.

Beyond the gates are winding lanes of villas tucked among the moss-draped trees, many of them adjoining one of the three golf courses, including the famous Harbour Town links, home of the MCI Heritage Classic in April. The Harbour Town Clubhouse is worth visiting just to see the original oil paintings showing the Classic winners over the last 20-plus years, a "who's who" of the golfing world. A wide range of instruction is available at the Sea Pines Academy of Golf.

The Sea Pines Racquet Club hosts the Family Circle Cup women's tournament, which has brought top names to the area in April annually for over 20 years. Resident tennis pro Stan Smith also often appears in exhibition matches. Instruction includes clinics and lessons for all levels, from tots to almost-pros. Smith has his own weekend and week-long clinics.

The Wildlife and Forest Preserve offers seven miles of groomed trails. You can take guided tours on foot or on horseback from Lawton Stables, or take it easy on a hayride or horse-drawn carriage tour through the forest.

Favorite activities also include cycling on 15 miles of paved bicycle paths, with rentals available at the Sea Pines Sports and Conference Center. Many bikers enjoy taking a spin on the hard-packed beach.

Almost everyone who comes to Hilton Head visits Sea Pines at least for a meal and a stroll in Harbour Town, where the lighthouse and a marina full of sleek yachts make for the island's most picturesque scene, especially at sunset.

South Beach, at the very tip of South Sea Pines Drive, has its own marina and village, and an inn with a look that is more Cape Cod than South Carolina.

The scene is quite different just north of the Sea Pines gate. Adjoining the public Coligny Beach Park area are South and North Forest Beach roads, wall-to-wall with more-modest villas and motels. This stretch has the largest concentration of people—and some of the most reasonable rates. If you choose to stay here, you can still play golf for a fee at many of the private courses, including Harbour Town, as well as at many fine public links such as the Hilton Head National. The island's largest public tennis facility is the 24-court Van Der Meer Tennis Center, where excellent instructional tennis weeks and clinics are held.

Continuing north brings you to Shipyard Plantation, 800 acres including 27 holes of golf, another Racquet Club, and the Holiday Inn Crowne Plaza Resort.

Palmetto Dunes ranks after Sea Pines in size, and its 2,000 acres include both the fancy Hyatt Regency and the less expensive Mariner's Inn. Facilities are lavish, including three golf courses, the Tennis Racquet Club, and Shelter Cove Harbour, a yacht basin with restaurants and shops.

Folly Field, the second public beach area, is a little less manicured than the rest of the island, and has its own moderately priced motels and villas.

The final major plantation is the Port Royal Resort, at the north-eastern corner of Hilton Head, the location of the upscale Westin Resort.

Tennis buffs can get inspiration at the free exhibitions usually held at the Racquet Clubs at Sea Pines, Palmetto Dunes, and Shipyard on Mondays at 5:30 P.M.; at Port Royal on Tuesdays at 6 P.M.; and at the Van der Meer Tennis Center on Sundays at 6 P.M. A call to verify current times is a good idea. With so many options for instruction, there's no better place to brush up on your game.

When you're not swinging at a ball or watching one whiz by, you can explore some of the natural beauty that remains on the island. The Museum of Hilton Head holds interpretive beach walks on Tuesdays and Fridays at low tide, and guided tours of Tupelo Swamp on Fridays at 10 A.M. You can also join the guided walks at Sea Pines Plantation, which take in a waterfowl pond, a freshwater fishing pond, and an ancient Indian "shell ring." Pinckney Island National Wildlife Preserve, on an island between the two bridges connecting Hilton Head to the mainland, offers 4,000 unspoiled acres with paths for hiking and biking and great opportunities for bird-watching. A variety of boat trips take you into some of the backwater creeks and salt marshes that are the unique beauty of the low country.

If none of that appeals to you, you can rent a sailboat, sign on for a catamaran sail, or take a Zodiac cruise to spot dolphins and marine life. Or take a ferry over to Daufuskie Island and explore an island where autos have yet to arrive. If the unthinkable happens and it rains, you can always check out the art galleries and dozens of shops on the island.

With all the activity available on Hilton Head, you have only yourself to blame if you don't have a ball.

Area Code: 803

DRIVING DIRECTIONS Hilton Head Island is located along the southernmost point on the South Carolina coast, 95 miles south of Charleston and 45 miles north of Savannah, Georgia. From the north, take I–95 to exit 28 (Coosawhatchie) and head east on S.C. route 462 until it merges with U.S. 278. Follow 278 into Hilton Head. From the south, take I–95 exit 5 and follow the signs to Hilton Head. It is 292 miles from Atlanta, 262 miles from Charlotte, 164 miles from Columbia.

PUBLIC TRANSPORTATION Hilton Head has its own airport, or you can fly to Savannah, less than one hour away. Limos bring passengers from Savannah to Hilton Head; taxis and rental cars are available at both airports.

ACCOMMODATIONS Rates vary with seasons and proximity to the beach; villa rates given are for one bedroom. Ask about golf and tennis packages at all resorts. *Sea Pines Plantation,* P.O. Box 7000, 29938, 800–845–6131, villas, M-EE • *Palmetto Dunes Resort,* P.O. Box 5606, 29938, 800–845–6130 (in South Carolina, 785–1161), villas or hotel-type rooms with daily maid service, E-EE • *South Beach Marina Inn,* South Beach, Sea Pines Plantation, 29938, 800–367–3909, M-EE • *Hyatt Regency,* P.O. Box 6167, Palmetto Dunes, 29938, 785–1234, EE • *Hilton Resort,* 23 Ocean Lane, Palmetto Dunes Resort 29938, 842–8000, M-EE • *Crystal Sands,* 130 Shipyard Drive, Shipyard Plantation 29938, 842–2400 or 800-HOLIDAY, EE • *Westin Resort and Villas,* 2 Grasslawn Avenue, Hilton Head Plantation, 29928, 800–228–3000 or 681–4000, EE • *Adventure Inn,* South Forest Beach Drive, P.O. Box 5646, Hilton Head 29938, 800–845–9500 (in South Carolina, 800–785–5151), efficiency rooms and villas on the beach, M-E • *Sea Side Villas,* 4 Forest Beach Drive 29938 800–487–9246 (in South Carolina, 842–7453), on the beach, M-E • *Days Inn,* 2 Tanglewood Drive (off South Forest Beach Drive) 29938, 842–6662, across the road from the beach, good value, I-M • *Hilton Head Island Beach & Tennis Resort,* 40 Folly Field Road 29938 800–777–1700 or 842–4402, I-E • *Best Western Oceanwalk Suites,* 33 South Forest Beach Drive 29938, 800–528–1234, 842–3100, suites M-E, motor inn, I-M.

CENTRAL RESERVATION SERVICES With so many options, many services provide advice and reservations anywhere on the island. This is a sampling; write for complete list. *Hilton Head Central Reservations,* 800–845–7018 or 785–9050 • *Hilton Head Travel Directory,* 800–521–7262 or 671–7262 • *Hilton Head Vacation Rentals and Sales,* 800–346–0426 or 785–4487 • *Hilton Head Island Realty & Rentals,* 800–845–5552 or 842–2424 • *Vacation Villa Rentals,* 800–654–7101 • *Vacations on Hilton Head,* 800–232–2463 • *PMA of Hilton Head,* Golf packages, 800–767–0277 • *TEE-TIMES,* Golf packages, 800–562–5532.

DINING *Gaslight,* 303 Market Place, 785–5814, French cuisine, candlelight, M-E • *Truffles,* Sea Pines Center, 671–6136, interesting menu, grill specialties, I-M • *South Seaport Cafe,* South Beach Marina Village, Sea Pines Plantation, 671–7327, varied menu, emphasis on seafood, waterfront and marsh views, screened porch, M ● *CO's Harbour Town*, Sea Pines Plantation, 671–2779, varied menu, casual, long-time favorite, M ● *Cafe Europa*, Harbour Town, 671–3399, varied menu, super view, M ● *Crazy Crab*, 2 locations, Harbour Town, 363–2722 or U.S. 278, Jarvis Creek, 681–5021, seafood, steamed, boiled or fried, I-M ● *La Maisonette*, Craig Building, Pope Avenue, 785–6000, formal French, EE prix-fixe ● *Harbourmaster's*, off U.S. 278 on Shelter Cove, 785–3030, overlooking the harbor and marshes, M-E ● *Topside at the Quarterdeck*, Harbour Town, 671–2222, pastas and seafood, harbor views, informal, M ● *Damon's*, Village at Wexford, U.S. 278, 785–6677, known for ribs and onion ring loaf, I-M ● *Remy's Restaurant*, Arrow Road and Dunnagan's Alley (near Sea Pines Circle), 842–3800, locals' favorite for generous portions and low prices, I-M ● *Fitzgerald's*, Adventure Inn (see above), 785–5151, nothing fancy, more good food at moderate prices, I-M ● *Salty Dog Cafe*, South Beach Marina, 671–2233, great for lunch on the docks, try the crab salad, I.

ACTIVITIES (Check for current schedules and prices.) *Beach walks: Museum of Hilton Head*, 800 Plantation Center, 842–9197 ● *Bicycle rentals: Harbour Town Bikes*, 785–3546; *Fish Creek Landing*, 785–2021; *Pedaling Pelican*, 785–5470; *South Beach Cycles*, 671–2453; *The Fun Center*, 5 locations: Holiday Inn, 785–5517; Adventure Inn, 842–2453; Hilton Head Beach & Tennis, 689–2453; Daddy Zacks, 785–2150; Palmetto Bay Marina, 686–4555 ● *Boat cruises: Adventure Cruises*, 785–4558; *Daufuskie Seafari*, 785–5654; *Vagabond Cruises*, 842–4155 ● *Canoe rentals: Fish Creek Landing*, Palmetto Dunes, 785–2021 ● *Daufuskie Island Ferry Service*, Shelter Cove Marina, 785–4558 ● *Horseback riding: Lawton Stables*, Sea Pines Plantation, 671–2586; *Waterside Rides*, Jonesville Road off Spanish Wells Road, 689–3423 ● *Nature cruises: Adventure Kayak Tours*, 842–8378; *Skimmer Nature Cruises*, Shelter Cove Marina, 842–7001 ● *Nature preserves: Pinckney Island National Wildlife Refuge*, 785–3673; *Sea Pines Forest Preserve*, 671–6486 ● *Sailing: Cheers*, Harbour Town Yacht Basin, 671–1800; *Island Water Sports*, South Beach Marina, 671–7007; *The Flying Circus* catamaran cruises, Palmetto Bay Marina, 785–7131 ● *Zodiac raft rides: Commander Zodiac*, South Beach Marina, 671–3344.

INFORMATION Hilton Head Island Chamber of Commerce, P.O. Box 5647, Hilton Head, SC 29938, 785–3673. Ask for Hilton Head Island Vacation Planner.

Arts and Flowers in Winston-Salem

Start with an eighteenth-century community famed for its Old World crafts skills. Combine with a twentieth-century manufacturing center whose benevolent business tycoons strongly support the arts.

The result: Winston-Salem, North Carolina, a surprising city. Known best for history and its textile and tobacco industries, Winston-Salem is gaining an equal reputation as a Southern center for the arts.

The original community, known as Old Salem, remains the most popular of the city's visitor attractions, but it now has strong competition. Two art showplaces are in former mansions of industrial magnates. The R. J. Reynolds home, Reynolda, has become a noted house-museum of American art. The Hanes mansion is now part of the Southeastern Center for Contemporary Art (SECCA), the region's foremost showcase for cutting-edge modern art.

The Museum of Early Southern Decorative Arts, a division of Old Salem, is an underpublicized treasure of period rooms and galleries, featuring the decorative arts of seven Southern states from 1690 to 1820. Decorative arts of the future are being influenced by students at the Sawtooth Center for Visual Design, located in a converted 1910 textile mill. The school houses three art galleries with rotating presentations by local artists.

Winston-Salem is also the home of the North Carolina School of the Arts, the first state-supported school of arts in the United States, nurturing young talent in music, drama, dance and art. The school offers a wealth of concerts and performances at the handsome Roger L. Stevens Center, a renovated movie palace.

The best place to start a visit is where the town began. Tucked away in the shadow of downtown, Old Salem is one of the most authentic restorations in America, with some 90 buildings from the eighteenth and nineteenth centuries. Visit in spring for garden tours, an annual crafts festival, and a treasured tradition, the Moravian Easter sunrise service which attracts more than 30,000 worshippers.

Salem was founded by Moravians, a German-speaking Protestant sect based in what is now Czechoslovakia. Fleeing religious persecution in Europe in the mid–1700s, members established missions in various parts of the world. Their first American settlement was in Pennsylvania; the second was in North Carolina. The communities and their missionary work were supported by making and selling high-quality handicrafts.

Established in 1766, Salem, like all Moravian communities, was under the control of the church. Residents lived in "choirs" according to age, sex, and marital status. Skilled work and worship were stressed, and religious music was an important part of life.

Salem ceased to be a church-owned town in the mid-nineteenth century, but remained an active community until it was merged with the larger and more prosperous industrial city of Winston in 1913. After World War II, when the old buildings were threatened with demolition, Old Salem was formed to preserve the unique heritage.

When you enter Old Salem today, there's a sense of life and continuity that is missing in many such restorations. This is partly because it shares a green with the architecturally compatible buildings of Salem College, a liberal arts school for women, and Salem Academy, a girls preparatory school, first established in 1772. The first boarding school building, dating to 1805, still serves as a college dorm.

Each Moravian family not only had a garden for its needs but was assigned a lot outside town where field crops like corn, wheat, pumpkins, and sweet potatoes were grown and the family cow was pastured. Over 30 gardens have been reconstructed, using plants documented as the same varieties cultivated 200 years ago. Most of the historic brick and clapboard houses in the historic area are now private residences.

The dozen Old Salem buildings that are open to the public run along Main Street. The self-guided tour is almost like dropping in on a town two centuries ago. Cooking, baking, sewing, tinsmithing, pewter making, blacksmithing, weaving, and dyeing are some of the crafts you might see demonstrated by costumed residents re-creating the life of an earlier day. On Monday, you may encounter a woman carrying a 25-pound bucket of water in each hand to wash the linens. Return on Tuesday to find her pressing them, using a six-pound iron heated in front of the fire.

Most of the artisans are found in the largest restored building, the Single Brothers House, a 1769 half-timbered structure with a brick addition. Boys were required to live here from the age of 14 while they learned a trade from one of Salem's renowned craftsmen.

Other stops include individual shops where a shoemaker may be cutting out leather, a potter turning his wheel with a foot treadle, and a joiner showing off his fine carpentry skills.

So highly regarded were these artisans that the town tavern thrived simply by accommodating customers who came to purchase local products. The original tavern remains furnished as it was in the past.

The new Salem Tavern is the place to stop for a wonderful lunch, especially the flaky pot pies and homemade rolls. For dessert, you won't do better than the Winkler Bakery, where goodies such as Moravian sugar cake are baked in a wood-fired oven and sold to the public. It is the most crowded of all the exhibit buildings.

At the end of Main Street is the Museum of Early Southern Decorative Arts (MESDA), a one-of-a-kind showcase that merits full attention, so try to get there before your energy is spent, or come back the next day. Tickets can be purchased separately or in combination with an Old Salem visit.

Nineteen fully furnished rooms show different aspects of the South before 1820, an unrivaled display of the talent of the region's early craftsmen. From a Palladian manor on Virginia's James River to a log house from the Carolina back country, each room is filled with furnishings of its time and place.

The core of the materials is from the private collections of Frank L. Horton and his mother, Theo L. Taliaferro, who also endowed the institution. The museum serves an important role as a center for the study of early Southern arts.

The other "must" attraction in Winston-Salem is Reynolda House, a treasury of American art in an exquisite setting. This was the country home built between 1914 and 1917 by Richard J. Reynolds, the founder of the enterprise that became the largest tobacco company in the world. The white columned, bungalow-style 100-room mansion with a low-hanging green roof is surprisingly livable, grand yet comfortable at the same time.

Unfortunately, both Reynolds and his wife, Katherine, died not many years after the house was completed. Their daughter, Mary, acquired the property in 1934 and lived there with her husband, Charles Babcock. They were responsible for opening the house to the public in 1967 as a museum of American art and culture.

The distinguished collection spanning the years from 1755 to the present is a significant survey of American art from Copley and Peale to O'Keeffe and Calder. An outstanding example of the Hudson River School is Frederic E. Church's masterpiece, *The Andes of Ecuador*.

A very human side of the family can be seen on the third floor, where clothing worn by members of the Reynolds family is displayed, dating from 1905. Included is the outfit hand-sewn by Mrs. Reynolds for her wedding; she was a local girl of modest means who married the boss.

Downstairs, indoor amusements for the family, such as a glass-enclosed indoor swimming pool, squash courts, a bowling alley and a shooting gallery, give an idea of their lavish lifestyle.

The grounds were also planned for recreation, including polo, golf, and tennis. The fine gardens were located so that they could be enjoyed by the public without impinging on the family's privacy. They make for a glorious spring stroll.

Reynolda was planned as a model farm and village as well as a private estate. It had its own telephone and power systems, post office, school, church, and staff residences. The stables, barn, workshops, and homes of workmen living on the property, all done with the same white walls and green roofs as the main house, are now Reynolda Village, one of Winston-Salem's most attractive shopping and dining complexes.

Beyond is the 340-acre Reynolda campus of Wake Forest University. Founded in the town of Wake Forest in 1834, the school was relocated in 1956 to this site, thanks to the generosity of the A. Smith Reynolds Foundation and the Reynolds family, who donated 300 acres of land for the campus and an annual grant of $500,000. With their aid, the campus has grown in less than 40 years from an original 14 structures to more than 40 major buildings.

Stop at the Welcome Center at the Reynolda Road entrance for a map. Besides admiring the expansive modern campus, you can visit the Museum of Anthropology, displaying objects from around the world, including materials collected by Moravian missionaries.

Across the road from the Reynolda mansion is a must for anyone who wants to know what is happening now in the world of modern art. The modernistic galleries of the Southeastern Center for Contemporary Art (SECCA) are a startling contrast from their entrance, the 1929 stone mansion of the late textile magnate James G. Hanes, the original building on the 32-acre site.

A prime mission of SECCA is to bring artists and the public together in a dialogue about modern art. The changing shows each year are an unpredictable variety of styles and media. Guided art walks by the staff help visitors understand the concept of the exhibitions and allow them to ask questions. Some pieces you may like, some you may hate, but all will likely arouse your interest. As the brochure promises, you'll be seeing the future of art.

Contemporary crafts also can be seen in the making in small studios along Trade Street, a downtown area becoming known as "Salem SoHo." The Studios, 560 North Trade, is the largest workshop, home to a pottery studio, three jewelers, a calligrapher, and the Artworks Gallery, a co-op of visual artists.

Add to Winston-Salem's artistic list Piedmont Craftsmen, an organization representing over 300 top Southeast artisans, who must meet juried standards to join. Their works in a variety of media are on display in a gallery on Reynolda Road.

While you are in this part of the state, you may want to take time out to take advantage of another North Carolina specialty, furniture bargains. It is just 19 miles to the dealers in High Point or 70 miles to Hickory's vast Furniture Mart, the largest manufacturers' outlet in the country selling directly to the public, with dozens of showrooms, including quality manufacturers such as Drexel-Heritage and Henredon.

Another possibility is an hour's drive south to the North Carolina Zoo, near Asheboro. One of the country's largest animal parks, comprising some 1400 acres, the zoo has many outstanding naturalistic displays, including African plains, chimpanzee and lion habitats, and the R. J. Reynolds Forest Aviary, a miniature jungle that is home to more than 150 exotic birds.

If the day is fine, you can also enjoy the outdoors closer to town at Tanglewood Park, located about 15 minutes west of Winston-Salem. This was the estate of William Neal Reynolds, another heir to the tobacco fortune, who willed it to the county. Now it is a forested playground that includes picnic grounds, nature trails, a wildlife park where deer and peacocks stroll, lakes, a pool, tennis courts, stables, and 54 holes of golf, including the challenging Robert Trent Jones course that is the site of the Vantage Championship, one of the richest Senior PGA golf tournaments. The park is the setting for many other special events, from concerts to steeplechase races, an annual Chili Cookoff to a dazzling display of Christmas lights.

It's just one more example of the variety that beckons in Winston-Salem.

Area Code: 919

DRIVING DIRECTIONS   Winston-Salem is reached via I–40 from east or west, or via U.S. 52 from north and south. From Atlanta, take I–85 east to I–77 north, then I–40 east, 340 miles; from Charlotte take I–77 north to I–40, 81 miles.

PUBLIC TRANSPORTATION   The closest major airport is Greensboro, about half an hour away. A car is necessary to see the sights.

ACCOMMODATIONS   *Brookstown Inn,* 200 Brookstown Avenue, Winston-Salem, 27101, 725–1120, M-E, CP ● *Manor House,* Tanglewood Park, Highway 158 (off I–40), Clemmons 27012, 766–0591, M-E, CP; Lodge (motel rooms), I ● *Augustus Zevely House,* Blum and Main streets, Old Salem 27108, historic home turned bed and breakfast, phone Old Salem for information ● *Downtown hotels* (ask for weekend package rates): *The Marque,* 460 N. Cherry Street 27101, 725–1234, EE; *Stouffer Winston Plaza,* 425 N. Cherry Street 27101, 722–6475, EE ● *Bed-and-breakfast homes: Colonel Ludlow Inn,* Summit and West Fifth streets, Winston-Salem, 27101, 777–1887, M-E, CP; *Lady Anne's Bed & Breakfast,* 612 Summit Street, Winston-Salem, 27101, 724–1074; *Mickle House Bed & Breakfast,* 927 West Fifth Street, Winston-Salem, 27101, 722–9045, CP.

DINING   *Bistro 900,* 900 South Marshall Street, 721–1336, I-M ● *Cafe Piaf,* 410 West Fourth Street, 750–0855, French, convenient for

Stevens Center, I-M ● *La Chaudiere,* 120 Reynolda Village, 748–0269, fine dining, E ● *Daryl's 1880 Restaurant,* 4625 Brookstown Avenue, 748–1880, handsome quarters for the popular chain, lively, I-M ● *Leon's Cafe,* 924 South Marshall Street, 725–9593, eclectic interesting menu, excellent, make reservations, M-E ● *Michael's,* 848 West Fifth Street, 777–0000, steak and seafood, M-E ● *Rose & Thistle,* 107 Lockland Avenue, 725–6444, casual, I ● *Salem Tavern,* 736 South Main Street, Old Salem, 748–8585, great food and ambience, don't miss the pot pie, lunch, I, dinner, M-E ● *Southern Lights Bistro and Bar,* Newtown Square, 420 Jonestown Road, 659–8062, trendy, M ● *Zevely House,* 901 West Fourth Street, 725–6666, dining in an 1815 landmark with fireplace and patio, M-E ● *Lunch and light fare: West End Cafe,* 878 West Fourth Street, 723–4774, I; *Rainbow News and Cafe,* 712 Brookstown Avenue, 723–0858, I ● For barbecue lovers, the place is *Pig Pickins of America,* 615 Deacon Boulevard, 777–0105, or drive half an hour south to Lexington, a town wall-to-wall with barbecue restaurants.

SIGHTSEEING *Old Salem,* 600 South Main Street, 721–7300 or 800–441–5305. Write for calendar of special events. Hours: Monday to Saturday 9:30 A.M. to 4:30 P.M.; Sunday from 1:30 P.M.; $$$ ● *Museum of Early Southern Decorative Arts,* 924 South Main Street, Old Salem, 721–7360. Hours: Monday to Saturday 10:30 A.M. to 4:30 P.M.; Sunday from 4:30 P.M.; $$$ ● *Reynolda House Museum of American Art,* Reynolda Road, 725–5325. Hours: Tuesday to Saturday 9:30 A.M. to 4:30 P.M.; Sunday from 1:30 P.M.; $$$ ● *Wake Forest Museum of Anthropology,* P.O. Box 7267, Reynolda Station, Wake Forest University, 759–5282. Hours: Tuesday to Friday 10 A.M. to 4:30 P.M.; weekends from 2 P.M.; modified hours in summer; donation ● *Where to see contemporary art: Southeastern Center for Contemporary Art* (SECCA), 750 Marguerite Drive (off Reynolda Road), 725–1904. Hours: Tuesday to Saturday 10 A.M. to 5 P.M.; Sunday from 2 P.M.; $$. *Sawtooth Center for Visual Design,* Winston Square, 226 North Marshall Street, 723–7395. Hours: Monday to Friday 9 A.M. to 9 P.M.; Saturday to 6 P.M., free. *Piedmont Craftsmen,* 1294 Reynolda Road, 725–1516, Hours: Tuesday to Saturday 10 A.M. to 6 P.M.; Sunday 1 P.M. to 5 P.M.; free. *Urban Artware Gallery,* 600 Trade Street, 723–5277. Hours: Tuesday to Friday 10 A.M. to 5 P.M.; Saturday 11 A.M. to 3 P.M.; free ● *Other diversions: North Carolina Zoological Park,* N.C. route 159, 6 miles southeast of Asheboro, 879–7250. Hours: Daily 9 A.M. to 5 P.M. April to October; to 4 P.M. rest of year; $$$ ● *Tanglewood Park,* U.S. 158 (off I–40), Clemmons, 766–0591. Hours: daily, dawn to dusk. Admission to grounds, $ ● *Furniture shopping: Hickory Furni-*

ture Mart, 2220 U.S. 70, exit 125 from I–70, Hickory, 800–462–MART, largest showroom in the Southeast; for High Point shopping information, contact High Point Convention & Visitors Bureau, 300 South Main Street, P.O. Box 2273, High Point, NC 27261, 884–5255.

INFORMATION *Winston-Salem Convention & Visitors Bureau,* P.O. Box 1408, Winston-Salem, NC 27102, 725–2361 or 800–331–7018. Visitor Center is at 601 N. Cherry Street, 777–3796 or 800–331–7018.

 # Mr. Callaway and Mr. Roosevelt of Pine Mountain

A textile mogul and founder of Callaway Mills, Cason J. Callaway was known as a man who believed that the most interesting ideas were "conceived in superlatives." But even his wife, Virginia, was surprised back in the 1930s when she asked for a magnolia tree for her birthday, and a truckload of 5,000 trees arrived.

Those trees were a harbinger of what was to come. They can still be seen in full bloom each spring at what is now Callaway Gardens, the family's superlative legacy to the South. The gardens they grace today comprise 14,000 acres of horticultural displays, as well as the largest conservatory in North America for colorful butterflies that are aptly described as "flowers on the wing."

Mr. Callaway was not the only prominent man who influenced this region, whose scenery surprises many who do not expect mountains in central Georgia. The ridgetop Pine Mountain Trail traverses land that once belonged to Franklin Delano Roosevelt, whose Little White House may be visited in Warm Springs, 11 miles from Callaway Gardens. When you see the natural beauty of the area, you'll understand why two powerful men came to love it.

One of the nation's major floral attractions came into being almost by accident when the Callaway family took a drive in the country and discovered a spot near Hamilton called Blue Spring. On a walk in the woods, Cason picked a sprig of a bright red wild azalea for his wife, who loved wildflowers. She identified it as a prunifolia or plumleaf, a species so rare it was on the verge of extinction. Callaway reacted by buying up 2,500 acres to save the shrubs. The family built a compound that became their treasured weekend getaway, Blue Spring Farm.

A heart attack in 1948 caused Cason Callaway to change his priorities. He and Virginia divided their land among their four children and deeded a fifth portion to the Ida Cason Callaway Foundation, named for his mother. That last portion became their focus. According to a biographer, the Callaways determined to create "one corner of Georgia in which every sight was beauty."

Callaway Gardens, which opened to the public in 1952, was the fulfillment of that mission. It is a showcase for the world's largest display of hollies, more than 700 kinds of azaleas, and endless varieties of wildflowers. Mr. Cason's Vegetable Garden, a seven-and-a-half-acre showplace where more than 400 varieties of vegetables, fruits, and herbs are grown, uses many of the growing techniques developed at Blue Spring Farm. The grounds also include a wildlife sanctuary and a 3,000-acre protected wilderness area.

The gardens can be seen via walking trails, as well as a 13-mile paved drive and a ten-mile biking trail. Stops along the way allow for visiting each of the special gardens. The Azalea Trails are in their glory from March to May, accented with dogwoods, rhododendrons, and a rainbow of wildflowers.

Callaway's attractions continue to grow. The Ida Cason Callaway Memorial Chapel was dedicated in 1962. The English Gothic church is a favorite setting for weddings and is noted for its organ, whose music may be heard outside the church through the louvered tower.

In 1984 the John A. Sibley Horticultural Center added a dramatic five-acre greenhouse complex featuring a two-story waterfall and year-round floral displays.

Most spectacular of all is the Cecil B. Day Butterfly Center, a 15,000-square-foot garden enclosed by soaring glass walls, where more than 1,000 exotic butterflies are allowed to fly free. These graceful, airy creatures are given their bold colors by nature as protection; the bright hues and bold patterns signal predators that these butterflies are not good to eat. However, these same brilliant shades are an endless delight for humans, who rarely get such a close-up vantage point for admiring nature's palette. Some of the fluttering beauties are so tame they will light on your hand.

The center was opened in 1988, a gift from Deen Day Smith in honor of her late husband Cecil Day, the founder of Days Inns of America.

Callaway Gardens attracts more than 750,000 visitors yearly, popularity that has helped develop the little town of Pine Mountain, a few miles away on U.S. 27. Here are dining places, and several antique shops and galleries. The Anne Tutt Gallery is of interest for its paintings of Callaway landscapes by Alexander Kalinin. The Pine Mountain Antique Mall on Main Street has 50 dealers and holds auctions on the second and fourth Saturday nights each month.

An unusual stop is the Pine Mountain Wild Animal Park, where 300 kinds of exotic animals, from alligators to zebras, can be seen via "safari bus." There's also a petting zoo for the very young.

The Callaway Gardens Country Store is the place to pick up traditional Southern foods, including the store's own muscadine products, and to have substantial Southern breakfasts and lunches at the Country Kitchen, overlooking the valley.

Right across the road from the store begins the Pine Mountain Trail, an outstanding hiking trail. Since 1975, volunteers young and old have worked to build and maintain the spectacular 23-mile footpath along the mountain ridge. An inexpensive map is available at the FDR State Park Welcome Center.

As noted, much of the land this trail traverses was owned by Franklin Roosevelt. Roosevelt was a young attorney in New York in 1924, in despair over the polio that had seemingly ended a promising career, when he heard about a Georgian with the same disease who had regained sensation in his legs after bathing in the bubbling hot waters at Warm Springs.

Those close to Roosevelt claimed that his spirits revived along with the sensation in his numbed limbs as he swam in the Warm Springs pool. Here he also regained his drive and ambition, and went on to become the president who led the nation to recovery from the Depression and to victory in World War II.

Roosevelt loved Warm Springs, where he spent many of his happiest days, fishing, riding, and enjoying country life in spite of his disability. In 1932 he built a six-room white clapboard house with Southern-style pillars on a site above a deep wooded ravine, the home that would become known as the Little White House. He became a familiar figure in the area, cruising the country roads in a runabout convertible specially fitted with hand controls, stopping to chat with anyone he spotted in a front yard. Two of his 1938 roadsters are on display at his home.

Many historic decisions were made at Warm Springs, and it was here that Roosevelt died on April 12, 1945, while posing for a portrait, seated in his favorite brown leather chair.

The house remains just as he left it, with the unfinished portrait still on the easel. The modest pine-paneled rooms, fieldstone fireplace, shelves of books, and comfortable furnishings are a contrast to Roosevelt's formal public life. The house is filled with the ship models and maritime paintings he admired.

FDR's wife was rarely among the guests at Warm Springs, according to local gossip. It was his longtime friend Lucy Mercer who was with him when he suffered his fatal stroke in 1945, a side of his life only recently made public. This is not discussed at the home, which is now a State Historic Site.

On the grounds is a museum telling the story of his life and of his battle with polio. A film showing a laughing Roosevelt romping with children in the pool and picnicking in the nearby woods reveals a playful side of the great man that is seldom seen. Here he even allowed photographers to show his shrunken legs, usually so carefully hidden from the public.

With polio conquered, Roosevelt's original foundation encountered funding difficulties, and in 1974 it was sold to the state for one dollar. It has since become a state rehabilitation facility serving people with a wide variety of physical disabilities. The original springs and outdoor pools have been maintained as an historic attraction.

The land the president loved to roam has become Georgia's largest state park, with a special marking at Dowdell's Knob, the point overlooking Pine Mountain Valley that was FDR's favorite picnic retreat. The park's stone swimming pool and stone and log buildings were built as part of Roosevelt's Civilian Conservation Corps program.

The village of Warm Springs, which had declined over the years, was rediscovered and restored by private developers in 1983. With its quaint turn-of-the-century structures transformed into shops and cafés, it is now ideal for strolling. The old hotel is once again receiving visitors.

This is just one of several lodging options in the area. For bed-and-breakfast lovers there is Wedgwood, an 1850s home in Hamilton, six miles south of Callaway Gardens. Two rustic resort retreats that take advantage of the mountain scenery are Pine Mountain Club Chalets on a private lake and Mountain Top Inn and Resort, with log cabins and a lodge on a secluded ridge adjoining the wilderness of the state park. Both offer pools and tennis. Cabins are also available within the Franklin D. Roosevelt State Park, where amenities include two lakes, the pool, 30 miles of hiking trails, and horseback riding.

Those who choose to stay at Callaway Gardens can take advantage of even more extensive resort facilities, such as 63 holes of golf, 17 lighted tennis courts, indoor racquetball courts, bicycle and jogging paths, a 1,000-acre hunting preserve with skeet and trap ranges, and 13 man-made lakes for swimming, waterskiing, fishing, boating, or just reflecting on the lovely reflections.

Lodgings range from 345 hotel-style rooms in a wing adjoining the main lobby and dining rooms to cottages and luxurious villas.

If you can't afford the tab at on-site lodgings, not to worry. Most of Callaway's sports facilities, including golf and tennis, are available to all, for a fee.

Area Code: 706

DRIVING DIRECTIONS Callaway Gardens is about 85 miles south of Atlanta. From Atlanta, take I–85 to I–185, continue 7 miles farther to U.S. 27 south, and proceed 11 miles to the gardens. From Birmingham, take I–20 east to I–85. From Nashville, take I–75 south to I–85, and follow directions above. For Warm Springs, take I–75 to state Route 85W. Georgia Route 190 is a scenic connector between Callaway Gardens, on U.S. 27, and U.S. 27A leading to Warm Springs.

ACCOMMODATIONS   *Callaway Gardens & Resorts,* Pine Mountain, 31822, 800–282–8181, Gardens Inn I-E, cottages E-EE, villas EE • *Mountain Top Inn & Resort,* Ga. Route 190 and Hines Gap Road, P.O. Box 147, Pine Mountain, 31822, 663–4858 or 800–533–6376, lodge rooms I-M, log cabins E, both CP • *Pine Mountain Club Chalets,* Ga. route 18, Pine Mountain, 31822, 663–2211 or 800–535–7622, M • *Wedgwood Bed & Breakfast,* U.S. 27, P.O. Box 115, Hamilton, 31811, 628–5659, I-M • *Hotel Warm Springs,* P.O. Box 351, Warm Springs, 31850, 655–2114, I, CP • *Franklin D. Roosevelt State Park,* 2970 Ga. route 190, Pine Mountain, 663–4858, rustic cabins, I.

DINING   *Cricket's Restaurant,* Ga. Route 18, Pine Mountain, 863–8136, excellent menu with a Cajun touch, I-M • *Bon Cuisine Restaurant,* 113 Chipley Square, Pine Mountain, 663–2019, French cuisine and wild game specialties, M-E • *Oak Tree Victorian Restaurant,* U.S. 27, Hamilton (5 miles south of Callaway), 628–4218, French, E • *Callaway Gardens dining places: Plantation Dining Room,* Southern-style buffets, all three meals, dinner I-M, Friday seafood buffet E; *Georgia Room,* candlelight and continental cuisine, prix-fixe, EE; *Veranda Room,* Italian cuisine, views of the golf course, I-M; *Gardens Restaurant,* casual, I-M; *Country Kitchen,* bountiful breakfast or lunch with panoramic view, I.

SIGHTSEEING   *Callaway Gardens,* U.S. 27, Pine Mountain, 663–2281 or 800–282–8181. Hours: daily 8 A.M. to 5 P.M., $$$ • *Little White House Historic Site,* Ga. route 1, P.O. Box 10, Warm Springs, 655–3511. Hours: daily 9 A.M. to 5 P.M., last admission 4 P.M., $$ • *Franklin D. Roosevelt State Park,* 2970 Ga. route 190, entrances on U.S. 27 and Ga. route 190, 663–4858. Hours: daily 7 A.M. to 10 P.M., $ • *Pine Mountain Wild Animal Park,* 1300 Oak Grove Road, Pine Mountain, 663–8744 or 800–367–2751. Hours: daily 10 A.M. to 5 P.M., last tickets sold 4 P.M., $$$.

INFORMATION   *Pine Mountain Tourism Association,* Inc., P.O. Box 177, Pine Mountain, GA 31822, 663–4338 or 800–441–3502.

Making the Most of Montgomery

Montgomery is going to surprise you. With a population of 200,000, this is not a huge city, yet it is chock-full of Southern history and alive with arts. Civil War and civil rights, Hank Williams and Zelda Fitzgerald, Shakespeare, Greek sculpture and American art—all of these are part of the unexpected mix that makes up Alabama's varied and vital capital.

This is an excellent destination for families, with lots of attractions to please kids. If you come in early spring, you can add to your agenda the oldest and largest rodeo east of the Mississippi. Wait until Memorial Day and you can enjoy parades, a boat regatta, fireworks, and the Alabama Folklife Festival, a chance to see and hear musicians, storytellers, and craftspeople re-create tradition of all regions of the state.

Begin with a visit to the Thompson Mansion, an 1850s columned beauty that serves as the visitors center for the city. Pick up maps and information here, watch a video on Montgomery's highlights, and you're ready to explore the sights. One good plan is to cover nearby downtown, then move on to the many outlying attractions.

As with many cities these days, Montgomery's center is no longer the shopping heart of the city, and it can't be called scenic, but it does hold many sightseeing treasures.

One of the most instructive is Old Alabama Town, a three-block complex just behind the Thompson Mansion that shows how people lived in central Alabama from 1800 to 1900. More than 30 restored buildings interpret changing lifestyles in the state. Lucas Tavern, the reception center, is where the first pioneers socialized when they came into the territory in 1817. An audio tape by Alabama's favorite storyteller, Kathryn Tucker Windham, serves as a colorful guide while you stroll through the rest of the town. Among the stops are a log cabin, a one-room school, a grocery, and a doctor's office. Grandest of all is the Ordeman-Shaw home, a circa-1850 town house filled with antiques of the period. Interpreters are on hand to tell about life for the Ordeman family and the rising middle class before the Civil War.

The Drugstore Museum and Rose House Craft Center, located around the corner on Columbus Street, also are worth a stop. At the Craft Center you will find artisans in action, spinning, weaving, woodcarving, and building musical instruments.

Montgomery was founded in 1818, when two smaller settlements merged and named their town for a Revolutionary War hero, Brigadier General Richard Montgomery. It prospered as a cotton market and transportation center and, with the promise of a privately financed capitol building atop Goat Hill, replaced Tuscaloosa as the state capital in 1846. When the first capitol was lost to fire, a second went up in 1851.

In 1861 this building served as the first capitol of the Confederacy. Thousands celebrated in front of the capitol portico on February 16, 1861, as Mississippian Jefferson Davis was inaugurated as president of the Confederate States. Alabama governors are still sworn in with the Bible that Davis used.

The capitol building is fresh from extensive restorations and is now a combination working capitol and museum. It is beautiful to see, and full of Southern history.

Another interesting place to see downtown is the White House of the Confederacy, the 1835 home where Jefferson Davis and his family lived while in Montgomery.

Montgomery recovered quickly from the Civil War. By the 1880s it was prospering once again as a railroad center, and downtown boasted the nation's first electric trolley system, called the "Lightning Route" for its amazing speed of six miles an hour.

Visitors today can ride a re-creation of the Lightning Route trolley for just 25 cents. It leaves from Old Alabama Town and makes stops at most of the historic downtown sites.

Not far away is a monument to a different period in Montgomery's history. The city's Civil Rights Memorial was designed by Maya Lin, creator of the Vietnam Veterans Memorial in Washington, D.C. Like her earlier creation, this one is moving in its simplicity. It is a curved circular black granite table with the names of 40 martyrs of the Civil Rights Movement radiating from the center, like the hands of a clock. Water flows from the center across the surface. On the wall behind are the words of Dr. Martin Luther King, Jr.: "We will not be satisfied until justice rolls down like waters and righteousness like a mighty stream."

Dr. King became the minister of the nearby Dexter Avenue Baptist Church in 1954. It was the focal point for meetings of blacks who organized an 18-month bus boycott that eventually resulted in the Supreme Court decision outlawing segregation on public transportation. It set in motion the Civil Rights Movement of the later 1950s and 1960s. Dr. King went on to win the Nobel Peace Prize for his work. A folk mural in his former church depicts King's work.

Not far from the church is Centennial Hill, a prominent black residential area developed in the 1870s, with fine homes along Jackson and Union streets. At 1524 St. John Street is the more modest Cole-Sanford House, the birthplace of singer Nat "King" Cole.

A much-visited shrine to another famous Montgomery entertainer is the grave of country music great Hank Williams. Williams is buried on a hilltop in the Oakwood Cemetery Annex, just north of the state capitol, with a granite ten-gallon hat as a memorial. A life-size statue of the singer stands across from City Hall.

Having traced the past of Montgomery, it's time to see its vibrant present, the Wynton Blount Cultural Park, where the Alabama Shakespeare Festival Theater and the Montgomery Museum of Fine Arts face each other across a serene pond populated by majestic swans.

The elaborate red brick theater does not try to emulate Stratford, but the Bard would no doubt be pleased if he could see the handsome quarters where his works are staged by a 200-member repertory company. The theater holds two stages, and contemporary works are also on the program. This is one of the largest and most productive regional theaters in the country, and it attracts more than a quarter-million visitors each year.

The $21-million gift by former U.S. Postmaster General Blount and his former wife to rescue a struggling Anniston, Alabama, Shakespeare troupe and build its new home in Montgomery was the largest single contribution ever made to a U.S. theater.

The imposing Museum of Art, built in a style to complement the theater, holds another Blount contribution, his significant collection of American art ranging from colonial times to the present, from John Singer Sargent to Georgia O'Keeffe.

One of the most impressive parts of the museum is its Artworks, a hands-on gallery and studio introducing art to children.

This arts-conscious town also has a number of art galleries, including the Alabama Artists Gallery, operated by the Arts Council of Alabama. Some galleries specialize in "outsider" art, works by talented but unschooled artists who are gaining national renown.

Off U.S. 231, north of Montgomery, is Jasmine Hill, which should delight both art and flower fanciers. The gardens were conceived by Benjamin and Mary Fitzpatrick, an Alabama couple who spent their lives establishing a successful chain of stores in the South, sold out just before the Depression, then retired to their hilltop estate to create a living memorial to ancient Greece. They made more than 20 trips to Greece to study the sculpture and to purchase exact copies of the greatest art of ancient Greece, pieces such as the Venus de Melos, the Lions of Delos, and the remains of the Temple of Hera at Olympia.

Fans of F. Scott Fitzgerald should not miss the home where he and his wife Zelda lived in the fashionable Cloverdale suburb in 1931. Zelda Sayre, daughter of an Alabama Supreme Court judge, was born in Montgomery in 1900. Fitzgerald met her at a dance while he was stationed at nearby Camp Sheridan, and they returned to the city for a time after Zelda suffered her first mental breakdown in 1930. The house is filled with memorabilia, photos, and Zelda's paintings and poignant letters, both hopeful early love letters and later ones written during her bouts with mental illness.

This is one of several older neighborhoods on the National Register of Historic Places that make for a pleasant driving tour. Others include the Garden District and Cottage Hill. Check a local map or ask for directions at the Information Center.

If you've brought kids along, perhaps you'd rather head for the zoo, which has recently been enlarged and modernized to the tune of $6 million. A fun way to see it all is aboard the Montgomery Express, a miniature train that traverses the grounds.

Finally, about that rodeo. For more than 35 years the Southeastern Livestock Exposition has been held in early spring to promote Alabama's cattle and livestock industry and the Alabama Agricultural Center. The proceeds, more than $1 million to date, help fund youth activities. The event includes a livestock and horse show and the rodeo, with more than 400 cowboys and cowgirls showing off at bareback riding, barrel racing, and bronco busting. It's a taste of the Old West—just one more unexpected pleasure in Alabama's surprising capital city.

Area Code: 334

DRIVING DIRECTIONS Montgomery is at the intersection of I–65 and I–85. From Atlanta, direct access is via I–85 west, 175 miles; from Birmingham, via I–65 south, 95 miles.

PUBLIC TRANSPORTATION Montgomery is served by Delta and American Eagle airlines and Amtrak trains. Downtown transportation weekdays and Saturday is via Lightning Route Trolleys, replicas of the city's 1886 streetcars.

ACCOMMODATIONS *Clarion Riverfront Inn,* 200 Coosa Street, 36104, 834–4300, renovated railroad depot, the most interesting lodging in town, I • *Madison Hotel,* 120 Madison Avenue, 36104, 264–2231, pick of the downtown locations, I-M • *Governor's House,* 2705 South Boulevard, 36104, 288–2800, I-M • *State House Inn,* 924 Madison Avenue, 36104, 265–0471, I • *Holiday Inn East, Holidome,* Eastern Boulevard at I–85, 36117, 272–0370, convenient for Shakespeare Festival, I-M • *Red Bluff Cottage,* 551 Clay Street, Montgomery 36101, 264–0056, charming bed-and-breakfast convenient to downtown, I, CP • *Bed & Breakfast Montgomery,* P.O. Box 1026, Montgomery 36101, 264–0056.

DINING *The Bistro,* 1059 Woodley Road, 269–1600, continental with a Cajun accent, good revues, M • *Panache at Rose Hill,* 11250

Highway 80 East, 277–7620, historic plantation house, upscale Southern menu, EE prix-fixe ● *Chantilly,* 1931 Vaughn Road, 271–0509, elegant home, continental menu, E-EE prix-fixe ● *Kat & Harri's Nice Place,* 1061 Woodley Road, 834–2500, casual bistro, Cajun dishes, I-M ● *Vintage Year,* 405 Cloverdale Road, 264–8463, attractive arty decor, Italian menu, I-M ● *Sahara,* 511 East Edgemont Avenue, 262–1215, handsome decor, longtime local favorite, excellent seafood, I-E ● *Plaza Cafe & Grill,* 5040 Vaughn Road, 271–3663, casual, American plus Cajun and Creole, I ● *Jubilee Seafood,* 1057 Woodley Road, 262–6224, I-M ● *Tony's Pizza and Pit,* 1985 Bell Street, 264–7081, steaks, salads, pizza—you name it and it is well prepared, I-M ● *Farmers Market Cafeteria,* 315 North McDonough, 262–9163, generous and delicious Southern fare for breakfast and lunch, I ● *Bates House of Turkey,* 1060 East Boulevard, 279–9775, turkey every way imaginable, good lunch spot, I ● *Joe's Delicatessen,* 2960A Zelda Road, Zelda Place Shopping Center, 244–0440, another best bet for breakfast or lunch, I ● *Sassafras Tea Room,* 532 Clay Street, 265–7277, Queen Anne home on the Alabama River, delightful place for lunch, I ● *Country Barbecue,* 1740 East South Boulevard, 284–1411, the locals' choice; other locations at 5335 Atlanta Highway, 270–0126, and 2610 Zelda Road, 262–6211, I ● *McNeal's Barbecue,* 4250 Wetumpka Highway, 277–5515, another favorite, I.

SIGHTSEEING *Alabama State Capitol,* Capitol Hill, east end of Dexter Avenue, 242–3184. Hours: Monday to Friday 9 A.M. to 5 P.M., tours on the hour, free ● *Executive Mansion,* 1142 South Perry Street, 834–3022. Monday to Friday 8 A.M. to 4:30 P.M.; weekends and holidays from 9 A.M.; tours by appointment, free ● *First White House of the Confederacy,* Washington Avenue, 242–1861. Hours: Monday to Friday 8 A.M. to 4:30 P.M.; Saturday and Sunday from 9 A.M.; free ● *Montgomery Museum of Fine Arts,* Wynton M. Blount Cultural Park, off Woodmere Boulevard, 244–5700. Hours: Tuesday to Saturday 10 A.M. to 5 P.M.; Thursday to 9 P.M.; Sunday 1 P.M. to 5 P.M.; free ● *Alabama Shakespeare Festival,* Wynton M. Blount Cultural Park, off Woodmere Boulevard, 277-BARD. Phone for current programs and prices ● *Scott and Zelda Fitzgerald Museum,* 919 Felder Avenue, 264–4222. Hours: Wednesday to Friday 10 A.M. to 2 P.M.; Saturday and Sunday 1 P.M. to 5 P.M.; donation ● *Jasmine Hill Gardens & Outdoor Museum,* off U.S. 231 North on Jasmine Road, 567–6463. Hours: March through September, 9 A.M. to 5 P.M., $$ ● *Old Alabama Town,* 310 North Hall Street off Madison Avenue, 263–4355. Hours: Monday to Saturday, 9:30 A.M. to 3:30 P.M.; Sunday from 1:30 P.M.; $$$ ● *Montgomery Zoo,* 329 Vandiver Boulevard, 240–4900. Hours: daily

A.M. to 5:30 P.M. May through September; to 4:30 P.M. the rest of ear; $$ ● *Alabama Archives and State History Museum,* 624 ington Avenue, 242–4363. Hours: Monday to Friday 8 A.M. to 5 P.M.; Saturday and Sunday from 9 A.M.; free ● *Dexter Avenue King Memorial Baptist Church,* 454 Dexter Avenue, 263–3970. Hours: Monday to Friday 9 A.M. to 12 noon; 1 P.M. to 4 P.M.; Saturday 10 A.M. to 2 P.M.; donation ● *Art Galleries: Alabama Artists Gallery,* 1 Dexter Avenue, 242–4076. Hours: Monday to Friday 8 A.M. to 5 P.M. *Sac's Gallery,* 1033 South Hull Street, 265–9931. Hours: Monday to Saturday 10 A.M. to 4 P.M. *Armory Gallery,* 1018 Madison Avenue, 241-ARTS. Hours: daily 8 A.M. to 5 P.M. "Outsider" art galleries by appointment only, Marcia Weber, 262–5349; Anton Haardt, 263–5494.

SPECIAL SPRING EVENTS *Southeastern Livestock Exposition,* Garrett Coliseum, 265–4011, usually held during school spring break week. Check current schedules ● *Jubilee and Alabama Folklife Festival,* usually three days over Memorial Day weekend. For information, phone the Center for Traditional Culture, 834–5200, or the State Council on the Arts, 242–4076.

INFORMATION *Montgomery Area Chamber of Commerce, Convention & Visitor Division,* P.O. Box 79, Montgomery, AL 36101, 834–5200.

Back to the Past in Rugby

An unsuspecting traveler happening upon Rugby, Tennessee, could hardly be faulted for thinking he had encountered a mirage. After all, who would expect to find an English Victorian village alive and well on a sparsely settled back road in northeastern Tennessee?

In its heyday, Rugby was the biggest town in three counties, populated with the cream of British society. Today it gives the visitor a chance to step back in time, strolling along unpaved lanes past quaint wooden cottages rich with gingerbread trim, while learning about one of the most unusual settlements in America.

Adding to the pleasure of the trip is the timeless beauty of the Cumberland Plateau region, including the rugged Big South Fork National River and Recreation Area nearby.

The idea for "New Rugby" originated with Thomas Hughes, an

English social reformer and the author of *Tom Brown's School Days.* He founded the colony in 1880 out of concern for England's "second sons," young men from wealthy families who were denied inheritance of the family fortune by the law of primogeniture, according to which the entire estate passed to the eldest son.

Hughes bought 75,000 acres of wilderness on the Cumberland Plateau, offering it as a haven for such young men, most of them cultured and well educated. His goal was "to plant on these highlands a community of ladies and gentlemen." In his utopian dream, all would work cooperatively for the good of the town.

Things went well at the start. By 1884 there were 450 residents and more than 70 buildings. A resort hotel went up to accommodate visitors, and Rugby was the scene of sporting events and fancy balls; formal teas were served at 4 P.M. each day.

But Rugby was not meant to be. Misfortunes beset the town, from a typhoid epidemic to drought to fire, and many of the original settlers moved on. By the 1920s, Rugby had dwindled to a small farming community of about 125 people. But many of the original buildings remained, and in 1964 a 16-year-old resident, Brian Stagg, began a one-man campaign to bring his historic hometown back to life. Mustering support in the community, Stagg became director of the Rugby Restoration Association, attending college only every other semester in order to carry out his work.

Rugby received Historic Landmark designation in 1976, but restoration money remained scarce and the obstacles were many. After Brian Stagg's untimely death at age 28, his sister Barbara took over the fight.

Some 20 buildings have been restored and the town is being rediscovered. As many as 70,000 visitors now come each year for tours and to attend special weekends such as the annual spring Music and Craft Festival, the Rugby Pilgrimage in fall (the only time that private homes are open for touring), and Christmas at Rugby, held early in December. The Harrow Road Cafe was built in 1985 to provide dining facilities.

Whenever you come, a visit begins at the restored 1907 schoolhouse, now converted into a Visitor Center, where you'll learn a little about Rugby's unusual history. Daily guided tours take in three important sites.

The first is the town church. With its peaked roof and tiny belfry, it is a charming example of Carpenter Gothic design. The original bell still calls worshipers to church.

Hughes's own cottage, Kingstone Lisle, is the second stop. Many original Rugby pieces are among the furnishings, showing what early life was like in the colony.

The final stop will please devotees of Victoriana. The Thomas Hughes Free Public Library, little changed from its 1882 appearance, is stocked with 7,000 volumes donated by publishers, showing the reading tastes of the late Victorian era.

All of these buildings are on Central Avenue, once a dirt road with wooden boardwalks but now the main highway running through town. To really get the feel of the past, head down the still-unpaved lanes to the rear of town, where small wooden cottages with names like Wren's Nest and Martin Roost are tucked into the trees. Most of these are privately owned, but you can learn about their histories with the self-guiding tour available at the Visitor Center.

Save time for browsing in Rugby's two intriguing stores. The Commissary, a reconstruction of the original village cooperative, is filled with traditional mountain crafts, from handmade dulcimers to cornhusk dolls. The Board of Aid Bookshop is the place to find rare Rugby and area history and a nice stock of books on the Victorian period.

If the weather is fine, buy a sandwich and dessert for a picnic and spend the afternoon by the river.

Follow the loop to the left of the town cemetery, and you'll see the parking area and trailhead sign for the Gentlemen's Swimming Hole. A quarter-mile walk through the forest brings you down the gorge to the Clear Fork River, with huge boulders along the bank. It is a spot to appreciate the natural beauty that drew Hughes to this area. To the left you'll come to the Swimming Hole, no longer only for gentlemen. It is a scenic spot for relaxing, even if the weather doesn't make you want to take a plunge. Go a mile farther to the right and you'll come to the "Meeting of the Waters," where the Clear Fork and White Oak Creek converge, another nice picnicking spot.

The 1880 Newbury House and the Pioneer Cottage in Rugby's historic district have been restored as inns for modern visitors. Guests are treated to breakfast at the Harrow Road Cafe.

Or you can stay a mile down the road at Grey Gables, a new inn built in the style of a Victorian farmhouse, with an 80-foot wraparound porch for taking in the views. Antiques and family mementoes throughout the inn give a warm feeling. Hostess Linda Brooks Jones serves her delicious meals family-style so that guests can socialize at dinner.

Linda and her husband also run the R. M. Brooks General Store, built by her grandfather, just down the road on Route 52. The center of commerce after the Rugby Colony's decline, it still looks much like a country store of yore, with a pot-bellied stove, and the old post office tucked in a corner. Although filled with memorabilia, it continues as an operating business and a local lunch favorite for bologna sandwiches and stick candy. In the back of the store the Joneses have installed Granny's Attic Crafts and Gifts, selling work by mountain artisans.

You'll pass the store if you take a drive along the South Fork Heritage Trail, a route from Rugby that offers views of the great natural beauty of this region and a couple of sightseeing stops as well. Driving west, detour one mile off state route 52 for Colditz Cove, a heavily wooded area where 60-foot Northrup Falls tumbles off the high cliffs. An easy walking loop leads through the area.

At U.S. 127, you may want to turn south briefly for Highland Manor, Tennessee's only winery. Turning north on 127 will bring you to the Sergeant Alvin C. York Mill and Grave, a small and moving memorial to one of America's most decorated heroes of World War I. The York Grist Mill and Dam is across the road.

Come back to the junction of 154 and turn east to the Big South Fork National River and Recreation Area. Located 35 miles from Rugby, the area was recently acquired by the National Park Service. It encompasses more than 100,000 acres on the Cumberland Plateau, straddling the Kentucky-Tennessee border, including the Big South Fork of the Cumberland River, with more than 80 miles of navigable water. This is great territory for fishermen, and for canoers, kayakers, and white-water rafters.

It takes a little effort to fully appreciate the beauty of the area; except for one overlook at the East Rim, near park headquarters, most of the spectacular gorge views and rock formations are not accessible by car. Guided horseback rides are available from the stables at Bandy Creek, and there are 150 miles of marked hiking trails in the dense and beautiful woodlands. The Slave Falls Trail is a moderate 1.2-mile walk leading to waterfalls, bluffs, rock shelters, and the Needle Arch, one of the natural rock bridges in the park.

Nature lovers can stay amid the tall trees at Charit Creek Lodge, a collection of log cabins accessible only by horse or on foot. There is no electricity; cabins are lit by kerosene lanterns. But there's no lack of comfort, and guests are treated to simple, hearty dinners and country breakfasts in the main lodge, a weathered building dating from 1817. The shortest way in is under one mile. The most scenic route is the Twin Arches Trail, 1.8 miles, leading past towering Twin Arches, the most famous of the area's rock formations. Mere humans look like pinpoints beside it.

A wonderful detour awaits heading south from Rugby, off I–75 north of Knoxville. The Museum of Appalachia is a loving and authentic presentation of pioneer life. It includes a village of some 30 authentic log structures moved to this site and one of the largest collections of frontier and pioneer memorabilia to be found anywhere. What sets the exhibit buildings apart is their personal approach, using photos tracing actual families and the things they created and used.

Unlike Rugby's pioneers, these simple, hardy people tamed the frontier and survived, leaving a rich legacy for all of us who came behind.

Area Code: 615

DRIVING DIRECTIONS   Rugby is located on Tenn. Route 52, 16 miles southeast of Jamestown, 35 miles from I–40 or I–52. It is about 300 miles from Atlanta, 125 miles northeast of Nashville, and 70 miles northwest of Knoxville.

ACCOMMODATIONS   *Newbury House* and *Pioneer Cottage,* c/o Historic Rugby, Inc., P.O. Box 8, Rugby 37733, 628–2441, I, CP ● *Grey Gables,* P.O. Box 5252, Highway 52, Rugby 37733, M, MAP ● *Charit Creek Lodge,* c/o 250 Apple Valley Road, Sevierville, TN 37862, 429–5704, M, MAP.

DINING   *Harrow Road Cafe,* Rugby, 628–2350, informal dining, the only choice in town, I.

SIGHTSEEING   *Historic Rugby,* P.O. Box 8, Rugby, 628–2441. Tours available February 1 to December 31, Monday to Saturday 10 A.M. to 4:30 P.M.; Sunday from 12 noon; admission, $$ ● *Big South Fork National River and Recreation Area,* open year round. Information available from Superintendent, Big South Fork NRRA, Route 3, Box 401, Oneida, TN 37841, 879–3625 ● *Museum of Appalachia,* off I–75, P.O. Box 359, Norris, 494–7680. Hours: April to October, daily 9 A.M. to dark; rest of year, 9 A.M. to 5 P.M. $$.

INFORMATION   *Middle East Tennessee Tourism Council,* P.O. Box 19806, Knoxville, TN 37939, 584–3553.

Thinking Pink in Macon

Move over, Washington, D.C. The title of Cherry Blossom Capital belongs to Macon, Georgia, where the spectacular blooms of 170,000 Yoshino cherry trees crown the town each spring in clouds of pink. Macon has many more trees than the nation's capital—more, in fact, than in any single town in Japan.

When all those pink blossoms become a backdrop for Macon's famous antebellum white columns, it's a glorious time to pay a call on the South's nineteenth-century "inland queen." Diverse attractions nearby add to the springtime scenery, and you can drive home via the Peach Blossom Trail.

Macon owes its extraordinary spring show to the generosity of the late William A. Fickling, who planted the first trees. The festival was launched in his honor in 1982. His family has continued the tradition of planting as many as 10,000 new trees in a single year, so that the blooming season grows ever more beautiful.

A festival takes place during the peak bloom in late March, with parades, fashion shows, polo matches, riding exhibitions, art and antique shows, and big name entertainment. There are 200 events in all, including tours through the town's loveliest residential sections. Homeowners celebrate the season by festooning doors, mailboxes, streetlights, and even automobiles with pink bows, flags, and cherry-blossom sprays.

Between festival events, you can get acquainted with Georgia's third largest city, one that has prospered from its founding in 1823. Cotton, the Ocmulgee River, and the railroad accounted for the trade that made fortunes in Macon's nineteenth-century heyday. Antebellum mansions and Victorian cottages built by wealthy planters and businessmen remain to delight visitors today. The city has six districts on the National Register of Historic Places, and hundreds of buildings dating from the 1820s. The film at the Macon Heritage Foundation provides a good background before you set out to see the sights.

A stop at the Welcome Center, in the handsomely restored Terminal Station on Cherry Street, will arm you with a printed walking-tour guide, or you may sign up for one of Sidney's Old South Historic Tours, which leave from the center, led by a guide dressed like native poet Sidney Lanier. Corny perhaps, but you'll pick up a lot of entertaining local lore as you admire the splendid homes of the Old South.

The most lavish of the homes is the Hay House, a domed, red brick, 24-room Italian Renaissance palace completed in 1860 for Macon entrepreneur William Butler Johnston. The home is not only an architectural masterpiece, but was noted for such innovations as indoor plumbing, walk-in closets, and a sophisticated ventilation system, amenities that were far ahead of their time.

Other showplaces include the Old Cannonball House and Confederate Museum, built in 1853 and best known for the cannonball that struck it during a Union attack in 1864. The cannonball still sits at the landing.

Follow the ''White Columns'' walking tour to see more stately homes in the historic district on the hill high above the city. Stroll Georgia Avenue to admire sites such as the Carmichael House, a national landmark built in 1840, with a free-standing, three-story spiral staircase. On College Street, one of the classic homes is now the 1842 Inn, the city's finest lodging. The Woodruff House on Bond Street, an 1836 Greek Revival Mansion on the hill overlooking Macon, was built for one of the South's wealthiest cotton planters and has been beautifully restored by Mercer University.

Washington Park, on Magnolia Street, where natural springs once supplied water for the town, is a fine starting place for a tour of Victorian Macon. The street has several vintage cottages as well as the site of Macon's first water works building (circa 1850), now a gift shop. Paralleling Washington is High Street, with the 1840 cottage that was the birthplace of the poet Sidney Lanier. It is now headquarters for the Middle Georgia Historical Society, displaying period furnishings and Lanier memorabilia.

A downtown tour includes several points of interest. Macon's showplace, the Grand Opera House, was built as an Academy of Music in 1883–84 and restored in 1969 as the entertainment center of the city. It boasts one of America's largest stages, almost seven stories high, where legendary performers such as Sarah Bernhardt and Will Rogers once appeared.

The 1836 City Hall was the temporary capitol of Georgia from 1864 to 1865, and the Municipal Auditorium, constructed in 1925, boasts one of the world's largest copper-covered domes and a mural inside depicting Macon's history from DeSoto's visit in 1540 to World War I.

Also downtown are some outstanding houses of worship, such as the 1858 First Presbyterian Church; Temple Beth Israel, built in 1902, with a singular dome lined with stained glass; and Macon's oldest church, the 1825 Christ Episcopal, where Sidney Lanier was married in 1867. The upstairs office where Lanier practiced law with his father and uncle before turning to poetry is at 336–48 Second Street.

In 1993, ground was broken next to the restored Terminal Station for Macon's newest attraction, the Georgia Music Hall of Fame. It's an appropriate location, since so many of the state's best-known performers are Macon natives. The list includes Little Richard, Otis Redding, James Brown, and Lena Horne. Macon-based Capricorn Records boasted the Allman Brothers Band as its most famous artists. The recording studio put the city at the center of the music industry for nearly a decade.

Macon's Pleasant Hill Historic District was one of the first black neighborhoods to be listed on the National Register of Historic Places. The Harriet Tubman Historical and Cultural Museum features the African-American history and culture of Macon and the nation, and has a striking wall mural, *From Africa to America,* by a local artist, Wilfred Stroud.

One of the most fascinating historic tales is told at the Ocmulgee National Monument—the most extensively excavated of the South's major Indian sites—where 12,000 years of Southeastern Indian cultures are documented. Six temple mounds, a burial mound, and a ceremonial earth lodge remain of a ceremonial center on the Macon Plateau dating to about A.D. 900. An excellent film, ''People of the Macon Plateau,'' is shown every half hour.

There's plenty to keep you busy in Macon, especially during festival time, but you might want to allow time for a day south of the city, where more attractions await.

Warner Robins Air Force Base is home to one of the top three most visited museums in Georgia, boasting the biggest and best displays of aircraft south of the Smithsonian's National Air & Space Museum. With a recent major addition, the museum offers more than 70 aircraft in its collection, tracing the history of flight from the first gliders to the fighters used in the Operation Desert Storm attack on Iraq in 1990.

Massee Lane Gardens in Fort Valley, the home of the American Camellia Society, has nine acres of display gardens, at their peak in winter and very early spring. The museum here also contains the world's largest collection of Edward Marshall Boehm porcelain, exquisite, lifelike re-creations of flowers and birds that are worth a trip even when the gardens are not in bloom.

The pretty little town of Perry is the center of this region, located about midway between Fort Valley and Warner Robins. It will appeal to antiquers both for the shops in town and for the Antiques and Collectibles Market that is featured the last weekend of every month at the Georgia State National Fairgrounds and Agricenter. The fairgrounds also host the Georgia Folk Festival in June, the Georgia National Fair in October, and the Georgia National Stock Show and Rodeo in early spring.

Twice a year, one of Georgia's most outstanding folk and crafts events, the Mossy Creek Barnyard Arts and Crafts Festival, is held in a wooded country setting three miles from town. There's no better place to see nationally acclaimed artists and artisans demonstrate crafts from decoy carving to dulcimer making; to hear folk songs and stories; to watch cloggers in action; and to take your own turn to a country music band.

You'll have to come back to catch Mossy Creek in action, and for many of the fairground events, but March is just the right time to head north on U.S. 341 and 41 from Perry, back toward Atlanta along the Peach Blossom Trail. Cherry blossom time coincides with the period when the orchards are showing off their delicate spring blossoms, a sight guaranteed to send you home with your spirits abloom.

Area Code: 912

DRIVING DIRECTIONS   Macon is at the intersection of I–75 and I–16. From Atlanta, follow I–75 south about 84 miles.

ACCOMMODATIONS   *1842 Inn,* 353 College Street, Macon 31201, 741–1842 or 800–336–1842, elegant columned mansion, best in town, M, CP ● *Macon's Downtown Hotel,* 108 First Street, Macon

31202, 746–1461, high-rise in town center, pool, M • *Best Western Riverside,* 2400 Riverside Drive, 31204, 743–6311, motel, I • *Swift Street Inn,* 1204 Swift Street, Perry 31069, 987–3428, 1837 plantation-style home, I-M, CP.

DINING *Beall's 1860,* 315 College Street, 745–3663, 1860 Greek Revival mansion, American menu, M • *Green Jacket,* 325 Fifth Street, 746–468, steaks and seafood, salad bar, M • *Natalia's,* 2720 Riverside Drive, Riverside Plaza, 741–1380, northern Italian, M-E • *Len Berg's,* Post Office Alley, 742–9255, Southern specialties, I • *Fresh Air Barbecue,* 3076 Riverside Drive, Northgate Shopping Center, 477–7229, oldest barbecue restaurant in Georgia, I • *Leo's,* 558 Mulberry Street, 742–2769, intimate cafe, M • *Jim Shaw's Restaurant,* 3040 Vineville Avenue, 746–3697, seafood, I • For lunch in a quaint antique shop, visit Sassafras Tea Room, 2242 Ingleside Avenue, 746–3336.

SIGHTSEEING *Hay House,* 934 Georgia Avenue, 742–8155. Hours: Monday to Saturday 10 A.M. to 5 P.M.; Sunday from 1 P.M.; $$ • *Old Cannonball House and Macon Confederate Museum,* 856 Mulberry Street, 745–5982. Hours: Tuesday to Friday 10 A.M. to 1 P.M. and 2 P.M. to 4 P.M.; Saturday and Sunday 1:30 P.M. to 4:30 P.M.; $$ • *Grand Opera House,* 651 Mulberry Street, 749–6580. Hours: Tours Monday to Friday, 10 A.M., noon, 2 and 3 P.M., $ • *Harriet Tubman Historical and Cultural Museum,* 340 Walnut Street, 743–8544. Hours: Monday to Friday, 10 A.M. to 5 P.M.; Saturday from 2 P.M.; free • *Ocmulgee National Monument,* 1207 Emery Highway (U.S. 80, 2 miles east of Macon), 752–8257. Hours: daily, 9 A.M. to 5 P.M., free • *Sidney's Old South Historic Tours,* Macon-Bibb County Convention & Visitors Bureau, Inc., 200 Cherry Street, 743–3401. Hours: Monday to Saturday 10 A.M. and 2 P.M., $$$ • *Museum of Aviation and Georgia Aviation Hall of Fame,* Robins Air Force Base, Warner Robins, 926–6870. Hours: daily 10 A.M. to 5 P.M., free • *Massee Lane Gardens,* One Massee Lane, Fort Valley, 967–2358. Hours: November to March, Monday to Saturday 9 A.M. to 5 P.M., Sunday from 1 P.M.; rest of year, Monday to Friday 9 A.M. to 4 P.M.; $ • *Georgia National Fairgrounds and Agricenter,* 401 Golden Isles Parkway, Perry, 987–2774. Write for current schedule of horse shows, Georgia Folk Fair, Georgia National Fair, Georgia National Stock Show and Rodeo • *Mossy Creek Barnyard Arts & Crafts Festival,* Ga. route 96, 3 miles from Perry, held late April and mid-October annually. For current dates, write to 106 Anne Drive, Warner Robins, 31093, 922–8265.

INFORMATION *Macon-Bibb County Convention & Visitors Bureau, Inc.,* Terminal Station, 200 Cherry Street, Macon, GA 31204, 743–3401.

On the Green in Pinehurst

Entrepreneurs, who tend to be optimists by nature, often see possibilities that the rest of the world cannot.

Take James Walker Tufts, for example. A Massachusetts man who made a fortune as one of the first American designers and manufacturers of soda fountains, Tufts was considered something of a fool when he paid one dollar an acre in 1885 for 5,890 acres of land in central North Carolina. The land had been stripped of its timber and abandoned. The useless sandy terrain had caused the region to be called the Sandhills.

But Tufts had a vision: a health retreat where Northerners would flock to enjoy the mild winter climate. Ignoring the skeptics, he hired Frederick Law Olmsted, the landscape architect famed for his design of New York's Central Park, to lay out a new village with "open park spaces and winding streets that attain their usefulness by following lines of beauty."

Olmsted did not disappoint. One year and some 222,000 trees later, Tufts had a charming retreat with a circular village green and streets sweeping from it in concentric circles. By 1896 the village he dubbed Pinehurst had a general store, a dairy, a boardinghouse, 20 cottages, a horse-drawn trolley car, and a hotel, the 45-room Holly Inn.

No one scoffed anymore. Guests arrived in growing numbers to play at Pinehurst, and they have been coming ever since, enjoying their games against a backdrop of lush pines, hollies, and magnolias that grow lovelier by the year. Most beautiful of all are the tall and stately longleaf pines, with slim needles over a foot long, growing in clusters like delicate flowers on the boughs. The pines, whose fresh scent fills the air, account for the town's name and have become its trademark.

Even Tufts, who was a visionary, could not have predicted that Pinehurst would achieve its greatest fame from golf. The sandy terrain turned out to be perfect for golf courses, drying quickly even after heavy rains. Today there are an amazing 35 courses in the area, attracting ever-growing numbers of golfing retirees as well as tourists. If you are good at the game, the challenge is legendary. If you are thinking of taking up golf, Pinehurst instruction is superb, and you can attend golf schools for a weekend as well as a week.

But this is an equally fine destination if your game is tennis or trapshooting, croquet or canoeing—or if all you want to do is get away to a gracious slice of yesterday. The delightful village beckons with tempting shops along its brick sidewalks. The flat terrain is ideal for biking beneath the pines; ask at the visitor center for the bike-tour brochure called "Tour Moore." Old-fashioned carriage rides are another popular way to see the area; they seem perfectly at home in this quaint setting.

The neighboring town of Southern Pines adds nature preserves, gardens, steeplechase racing, and carriage parades to the list of area activities, and Pinehurst supplies its own horsey flavor with polo games on Sunday afternoons in spring and fall. April is the month when the biggest and most colorful equestrian events are scheduled.

Excellent nearby excursions from Pinehurst will surely tempt you to make this a long weekend, allowing time for antiquing, visiting the traditional pottery village of Seagrove, or talking to the animals at the North Carolina Zoo.

When you stop in at the PGA/World Golf Hall of Fame, you'll quickly realize the importance of golf to the area. The long history of golf, dating from the 1300s, is fascinating even if you don't play the game. Women may be particularly interested in the distaff side of the exhibits, starting with Mary, Queen of Scots, who was the first recorded female golfer, back in the 1500s. You'll also discover how profoundly this small Southern town affected the growth of the game in America.

According to local legend, the first Pinehurst golf course came about in 1898 when a workman complained to James Tufts that guests were disturbing the dairy cows with the little white balls they were hitting around the fields. Tufts had a rudimentary course laid out for this pastime, then newly imported from England.

In 1901, when the grand Carolina Hotel (now the Pinehurst Hotel) was built, a young Scottish professional named Donald Ross was hired to direct golf operations. Ross remained for the next 47 years and became the foremost architect of American golf, designing more than 400 courses throughout North America.

At Pinehurst, he expanded the original No. 1 Course to 18 holes and eventually added three more courses. His crowning achievement was the No. 2 Course, which became and remains one of the best known in the country. Pinehurst has hosted scores of tournaments, including the PGA tour championships in 1991 and 1992.

The Pinehurst Hotel is still *the* place to stay in town. The white, pillared building, topped with a cupola and wrapped with canopied porches, has been fondly dubbed the "White House of Golf." It retains an Old World aura and tradition that newer resorts simply cannot match.

The golf courses now number seven. Other facilities include 24 tennis courts, croquet, lawn-bowling, five swimming pools, a 200-acre man-made lake where boats and windsurfers can be rented, and the Gun Club, where Annie Oakley was once the resident instructor, with trap and skeet shooting.

If you can't afford the tab at the Pinehurst, at least have a drink, inspect the memorabilia in the Ryder Cup bar, and stay for the multicourse dinner served beneath sparkling chandeliers.

Two other golf resorts, in nearby Southern Pines, are also well worth considering, each offering tennis, a pool, and a Donald Ross course to tempt golfers.

Mid-Pines, a stately, Southern-style hotel built in 1921, has warm wood paneling, a charming garden dining room, and a gracious setting on 250 acres. Pine Needles, a rustic resort with a chalet-like feeling, is owned by the family of noted golfer Peggy Kirk Bell, a founder of the LPGA tour. Bell herself teaches at the resort's Golfari schools. Programs are available for ladies only, for couples, for adults, and for children age 10 to 18.

Those who prefer smaller inns have several choices. Still very much at the center of things in the village is the original rambling wooden Holly Inn, now with 77 rooms and nicely updated while retaining its turn-of-the-century feel. The Pine Crest Inn is another old-timer, a homey hotel dating from 1913. The dining room and piano bar are local favorites.

Knollwood House, a 1927 mansion in Southern Pines, has the air of an English manor, and rooms and suites that are elegant indeed. The lawn rolls down to the Mid-Pines golf course. All inns offer packages for golfers.

After you've traced the history of the game at the Golf Hall of Fame, you can learn more about Pinehurst at the Tufts Archives at the Given Memorial Library, a collection of letters, photos, news stories, and memorabilia dating back to 1895.

If shopping is on your agenda, the Sandhill Women's Exchange is the place to find handicrafts and a little lunch room, all under the low ceilings of an 1810 log cabin. Within the nearby village circle, all manner of clothing and gift shops await, including a variety of shops and a cafe housed in a former movie theater.

Midland Road, once the route of the trolley that brought guests to Pinehurst from the train depot in Southern Pines, stretches for six scenic miles between the towns, with august rows of tall pines on either side and in the median. Along this road is the area's outstanding shop, Midland Crafters, a fine arts gallery with an outstanding collection of contemporary American crafts.

Southern Pines presents more shopping possibilities along an old-fashioned main street that runs on either side of the railroad tracks. The town remains an Amtrak stop on the run from the Northeast to Florida.

Drive out Connecticut Avenue to see some of the cultural and equestrian heritage of Southern Pines. Weymouth Center, listed on the National Register of Historic Places, was the home of author and publisher James Boyd, and is now a gracious setting for lectures and concerts. Across the way, the Campbell House, a handsome Georgian home occupied by the Moore County Arts Council, has a gallery showing local art.

Farther out along this same road is Stoneybrook Farm, home of the steeplechase race that annually launches the spring season on the second Saturday in April. Now past its forty-fifth anniversary, the event draws as many as 40,000 spectators, who enjoy elaborate tailgate picnics as well as the excitement of the race.

Stoneybrook is one of more than 80 farms in this area where racehorses are bred and trained. Make a right turn onto sandy, unpaved Old Mail Road to see some of the loveliest of these farms, and signs reading "Slow, Horse and Dog Crossing." The Southern Pines Horse Farm Tour in April is a favorite event, featuring a traditional hunt breakfast at one of the stops.

Two other major April horse happenings include an international carriage-driving competition held in the open fields along Old Mail Road and an annual Spring Carriage Drive, a parade from Southern Pines through Pinehurst of beautifully groomed, high-stepping horses pulling shiny carriages, with drivers dressed in fancy period attire. It's a fantastic show.

The horsey side of Pinehurst centers around the Harness Track, a major training center for harness racers. Come over any morning, fall through spring, to watch the trotters and pacers working out, and return on Sunday afternoon for polo matches held on the track grounds.

Flower fanciers will want to visit the Sandhills Horticultural Gardens, featuring the largest holly collection on the East Coast, a specialized conifer garden, and the Sir Walter Raleigh Garden, a formal acre-and-a-half English garden. The gardens are maintained by horticultural students at the Sandhills Community College.

Those who want to get out and breathe the pine-scented air will find peaceful nature trails at Weymouth Woods, a 571-acre preserve in Southern Pines. Nature programs are offered on Sunday in spring and summer.

The only problem you may encounter is fitting in all of this and still finding time for the nearby attractions. Ten miles away, just off U.S. 1 in the tiny town of Cameron, is a host of antique stores in quaint nineteenth-century quarters, and two delightful stops for lunch, the Dewberry Deli in the old hardware store and Miss Bell's Antiques and Tea Room.

The 45-minute drive to the village of Seagrove, via N.C. route 211 west to N.C. route 705 north, allows you to visit the shop-studios of more than 40 potters who live and work in a community where the pottery-making tradition dates back to the 1700s. Some of the young potters are the ninth generation of their families to ply this craft. Watch for the shops of the Coles, Owens, Cravens, Lucks, and Teagues, the earliest families in the area.

Just a few miles north of Seagrove, in Asheboro, is the superb and still growing North Carolina Zoo. This 1,448-acre sanctuary is one of the first American zoos built around the natural-habitat philosophy, a revolutionary vision that would most certainly have appealed to that other nature lover and visionary, Mr. James Walker Tufts of Pinehurst.

Area Code: 919

DRIVING DIRECTIONS   Pinehurst is located on U.S. 15/501, U.S. 1, and N.C. Routes 2, 211, and 5. From Raleigh-Durham, follow U.S. 1 south to U.S. 15/501, 70 miles; from Charlotte, follow U.S. 74 east to U.S. 1 north, 104 miles. From Atlanta, take I–85 to Charlotte, exit at Brookhaven Expressway southbound, watch for connection to U.S. 74, and follow Charlotte directions above, about 352 miles. From Columbia, South Carolina, take I–20 east to U.S. 1 north, about 130 miles.

PUBLIC TRANSPORTATION   USAir has commuter service directly to Pinehurst from Charlotte, and Amtrak serves Southern Pines, 6 miles away. Raleigh-Durham International Airport is 70 miles from Pinehurst, a drive of about an hour and 15 minutes; transportation is available from the airport.

ACCOMMODATIONS   Area rates are highest in spring and fall, but considerably lower in winter, when the weather is often mild enough for sports. All lodgings offer special golf packages. *Pinehurst Resort and Country Club,* Carolina Vista, P.O. Box 4000, Pinehurst, 28374, 295–6811 or 800-ITS-GOLF, EE, MAP ● *Mid Pines Resort,* 1010 Midland Road, Southern Pines, 28387, 692–4615 or 800–323–2114, M-E or EE, MAP ● *Pine Needles Resort,* P.O. Box 88, Southern Pines, 28387, 692–7111, EE, MAP ● *Holly Inn,* Cherokee Road, P.O. Box 2300, Pinehurst, 28374, 295–2300, M-E ● *Pine Crest Inn,* Dogwood Road, P.O. Box 879, Pinehurst, 28374, 295–6121, E-EE, MAP ● *Knollwood House,* 1495 West Connecticut Avenue, Southern Pines, 28387, 692–9390, M-E, CP ● *Area motels: Days Inn,* 1420 U.S. 1, Southern Pines, 28387, 692–7581, I; *Hampton Inn,* 1675 U.S. 1, Southern Pines, 28387, 692–9266, I; *Holiday Inn,* U.S. 1 at Morganton Road, Southern Pines, 28387, 692–8585, I.

DINING   Reservations required for resort dining rooms. *Carolina Dining Room,* Pinehurst Resort (see above), EE prix-fixe ● *Donald Ross Grill Room,* Pinehurst Resort Country Club, 295–6811, lunch daily, I; dinner Thursday to Saturday, M-E ● *Midpines Resort* (see above), E ● *The Holley Inn* (see above), M-E ● *Pinecrest Inn* (see above), very popular, M-E ● *Magnolia Inn,* Magnolia Road, Pinehurst, 295–6900, quaint turn-of-the-century inn in the village, M-E ● *The Coves,* Market Square, Pinehurst, 295–3400, informal, nautical decor, I-M ● *Sleddon's Restaurant,* South Bennett Street, Southern Pines, 692–4480, pleasant dining room in an old home, M-E ● *Whiskey McNeill's Restaurant,* Northeast Broad Street, Southern Pines, 692–5440, informal, I.

SIGHTSEEING   *PGA/World Golf Hall of Fame,* PGA Boulevard off the traffic circle, Pinehurst, 295–6651. Hours: March through December 15, daily 9 A.M. to 5 P.M., $$ ● *Sandhills Horticultural Gardens,* Sandhills Community College, Airport Road, Pinehurst, 692–6185. Hours: daily, daylight hours, free ● *Tufts Archives,* Given Memorial Library, Pinehurst, 295–3642. Hours: Monday to Friday 9:30 A.M. to 12:30 P.M. and 2 P.M. to 5 P.M.; Saturday 9:30 A.M. to 12:30 P.M.; free ● *Weymouth Center,* East Vermont Extension off Connecticut Avenue, Southern Pines, 692–6261. Hours: Monday to Friday 10 A.M. to noon, 2 P.M. to 4 P.M., free ● *Weymouth Woods Nature Preserve,* 400 Fort Bragg Road, Southern Pines, 692–2167. Hours: Monday to Saturday 9 A.M. to 5 P.M.; Sunday noon to 5 P.M., free ● *Campbell House Galleries,* Connecticut Avenue, Southern Pines, 692–4356. Hours: Monday to Friday 9 A.M. to 5 P.M., free ● *North Carolina Zoological Park,* N.C. route 159, 6 miles south of U.S. 64 and 220 intersection, Asheboro, 879–7000. Hours: April to October, Monday to Friday 9 A.M. to 5 P.M.; weekends 10 A.M. to 6 P.M.; rest of year, daily 9 A.M. to 4 P.M.; $$ ● *Carriage rides: Candlewood Carriage,* Southern Pines, 692–3447; *Pinehurst Livery Stable,* 295–6811 ● *Polo games: Pinehurst Race Track,* 949–2106. Hours: April through June, Sundays at 2 P.M.; check for fall schedule; free ● For current dates of steeplechase, carriage competitions, and carriage drive, contact the Pinehurst Area Convention and Visitors Bureau below.

SPORTS   *Bicycle rentals: Rainbow Cycles,* Southwest Broad Street, Southern Pines, 692–4494 ● *Tennis: Lawn and Tennis Club of North Carolina,* One Merrywood, Pinehurst, 692–7270; for locations of public courts, phone Moore County Parks and Recreation Department, 947–2504 ● *Trap and skeet shooting: Pinehurst Gun Club,* Gun Club Road, Pinehurst, 295–6811, ext. 7404.

INFORMATION   *Pinehurst Area Convention and Visitors Bureau,*
1480 U.S. 15/501, Southern Pines, NC 28388, 962–3300 or 800–346–
5362. Events line, 692–1600.

Humming Along in Nashville

Andrew Jackson must have been a man of amazing foresight. At the
Hermitage, the gracious home of our seventh president, just outside of
Nashville, is a driveway in what seems unmistakably to be the shape of
a guitar.

How could Jackson have known that a century and a half later his
hometown would be best known as Music City, U.S.A., the home of
the guitar-picking, toe-tapping Grand Ole Opry?

Guitars are now in evidence all over Nashville, which has become
the ultimate destination for lovers of country music. But don't be
fooled into thinking that this is a one-note city.

The flip side of Nashville is a landscape of green hills, Southern
mansions, and gracious gardens, some of them dating back to Jackson's day. Before music stole the spotlight, Nashville was known as
"the Athens of the South" for the many colleges established here.
Hidden on one of the smaller campuses is a prize private art collection,
among several displays in the city that will surely please art lovers.

As the state capital, Nashville also boasts more than its share of
history, centered in the capitol building and state museums in the heart
of the city. Along the downtown riverfront, turn-of-the-century warehouses are blossoming into a lively center for dining and nightlife
known as "The District."

In fact, Nashville is a city with so many facets you can have a
wonderful time even if you don't care a hoot for Hank or Dolly or
Garth. So unless country is the reason for your visit, plan a weekend
with the dial first tuned elsewhere, thereby discovering sides of the city
that many visitors overlook.

This was rugged frontier country when the first settlers arrived at the
Cumberland River on a frosty Christmas Eve in 1799. A reconstruction
of their log fort stands on the riverbank downtown to remind the visitor
of what things were like. Those brave first arrivals fought off the
Indians, raised racehorses, traded with the rest of the world via
riverboat, and explored what was then considered the West.

To see how quickly the early settlers prospered and created an oasis
of culture in the wilderness, drive a few miles south of town to
a restoration of the historic Travellers' Rest, built in 1799 by

John Overton, Andrew Jackson's law partner. The house was enlarged in 1808 and again in 1828, and is a chronicle of changing decorative arts.

It will set the stage for Jackson's Hermitage, the 1821 Greek Revival home that the president built for his young bride, the one place he most wanted to return to after his illustrious military and political careers. This is one of the most personal of all the presidential homes, furnished almost entirely with the family's own belongings. The self-guided cassette tour, with dramatized narratives by various "family members," gives insight into "Old Hickory," the tough hero of the War of 1812 and the tender husband who never stopped grieving for his wife, Rachel, after her sudden death in 1828. He and his wife are buried together in a corner of her beloved garden, kept just as it was designed for her in 1819.

A vintage mansion telling a different kind of Nashville tale is Belle Meade Plantation, considered the "queen of Tennessee plantations" and once one of the finest thoroughbred breeding farms in the country. The mansion is fine, the racing history is fascinating, and the big carriage house and stables hold one of the largest antique carriage collections in the South.

While you are in the Belle Meade neighborhood, drive around to admire Nashville's best addresses in one of the most magnificent residential sections to be found in any Southern city.

Not too far away is a third mansion not to be missed. The Cheekwood estate includes the Tennessee Botanical Gardens on its 55 acres. The Georgian-style main house is now a Fine Arts Center, a lovely home setting for American art and collections of decorative arts that include Worcester porcelain and Old Sheffield silver. The grounds are a showplace of gardens that include boxwood, wildflowers, a Japanese garden, and changing displays of seasonal blooms. Walking trails lead through native trees and shrubs, past cascading streams and quiet pools. There's also a Botanic Hall with a tropical atrium, sculptured fountains, and changing exhibits.

A virtual garden is the campus of Vanderbilt University, a 75-acre site not far from the city center that is also an arboretum boasting more than 60 species of trees. Outdoor sculptures are artistically placed among them.

The school was built with a gift of $1 million, a vast sum when it was given in 1873 to a city never seen by the donor, Cornelius Vanderbilt. Vanderbilt's Southern wife had some knowledge of Nashville through her connection with a local minister. She convinced her husband that it was crucial for the South to have centers of learning if it was to come back after the Civil War. Though a statue honors him, Vanderbilt never came to see the college he helped to create.

Stop at Kirkland Hall at the main campus entrance for a self-guiding map to the lovely Victorian campus, and stop in the Fine Arts Gallery in the historic Old Gym to see changing exhibits from the Vanderbilt Art Collection.

Not far from Vanderbilt is Nashville's most unusual art venue, the Parthenon, a full-scale replica of the Greek original down to the smallest detail, with a re-creation of the 42-foot-tall statue of Athena as a focus. Built for the 1897 Tennessee Centennial Exposition, it was kept as a museum, showing the Cowan Collection of American art as well as changing exhibits.

The true art treasure of the city is in far more modest surroundings. Fisk University, founded in 1866, is one of the oldest black colleges in America. Along with Meharry Medical College, which opened in 1876, it made Nashville a leader in education for blacks after the Civil War. Here again, the city benefited from a donor who had never visited. Because of her association with Carl Van Vechten, a New York writer and critic with a strong interest in Fisk, artist Georgia O'Keeffe in 1949 presented to this modest campus a major portion of the important art collection of her late husband, Alfred Stieglitz, who was not only a brilliant photographer but a noted patron of the arts.

O'Keeffe did come to Nashville personally to oversee the installation in a small red brick building that was once the school gymnasium, now called the Carl Van Vechten Gallery of Fine Arts. Included are more than 100 paintings by such artists as Cezanne, Picasso, Renoir, Toulouse-Lautrec, John Marin, George Grosz, Diego Rivera, and O'Keeffe herself, along with some 18 fine Stieglitz photographs and a selection of African sculptures. The Aaron Douglas gallery, on the third floor of the Fisk Library, is another worthwhile stop, highlighting works by African-American artists.

Having seen some of the fine homes and fine arts of the city, head downtown for the historic 1859 state capitol building. Still the active seat of state government, the building's handsome chambers, fine details, and ceiling frescoes have been restored to their original nineteenth-century appearance. Outside are a statue of Andrew Jackson and the grave of Tennessee's second president, James K. Polk.

The Tennessee State Museum is also interesting, tracing the state from prehistoric times to the early 1900s, with a separate building set aside for military history. The museums are high on a hill among a stately complex of government buildings. Below is the nicely land-scaped Church Street, which leads past the city's enclosed Marketplace, a mall of small shops, and on to the riverfront and the boutiques and lively cafes of "The District." Pick a restaurant with a view, or board a riverboat for a cruise, and you're back to the river where Nashville began.

Now it's time to liven your stay in Nashville with a chorus of country. The Country Music Hall of Fame and Museum honors the greats from Hank Williams to Johnny Cash, and tells the tale of how "hillbilly" music captured the heart of city folk when the Grand Ole Opry was first broadcast on WSM radio in 1943. It is the heart of the area known as Music Row, which includes several "museums" devoted to individual country stars such as Barbara Mandrell and Hank Williams, Jr. They are as much gift shops as museums.

Near Music Row, you can tour RCA's historic Studio B, where some of the greatest country hits were recorded. You'll also see the headquarters of the many recording companies that now operate out of Nashville. Commercial studios on Music Row and at Opryland offer the chance to star on your own record, singing against a prerecorded background.

It's often possible to attend tapings of cable TV shows like "Nashville Now" on TNN, the Nashville Network at Opryland; phone 883–7000 for schedules.

Walk down Broadway to get a feel for the old days in Nashville. You'll see an unbelievable array of glitzy guitars at Gruhns Guitar, find just about every country music record imaginable at the Ernest Tubb Record Shop, and see a lot of glitter at Robert's Rhinestone Western Wear. Don't miss the whimsical, oversize, junk-metal cowboy sculptures lounging around at 404 Broadway.

Printer's Alley, the area of Church Street between Third and Fourth avenues, is an entertainment center, and the singing starts by 11 A.M. at Tootsie's Orchid Lounge, on the corner of Broadway and Fifth Avenue. Tootsie's is a bit down at the heels, but remains a nostalgic favorite because so many of the country greats hung out here between sets at the nearby Ryman Auditorium. Tours are offered at the Ryman, where the Grand Ole Opry was performed until 1974.

That's when the show moved to much grander quarters, about 20 minutes outside town. The fancy new auditorium boasts some of the floorboards from the old Ryman, just for luck. The theater adjoins Opryland, a 120-acre playland with rides and a host of musical performances ranging from rock to rockabilly. A country music museum was recently added, and there's another marvelous museum featuring over 1,000 guitars, the private collection of the late country star Roy Acuff.

Opryland has its own enormous, lavish hotel for those who want to be as close as possible to the park and the performances, but unless you are devoted to country music, you'd do better to stay in the city, where there is far more variety in dining and nightlife. Join the recording stars and record producers who stay at Loew's Vanderbilt Plaza Hotel, or take a nostalgia trip at the handsomely restored Union Station. Center-city hotels such as the Holiday Inn Crowne Plaza and the Stouffer Nashville are within walking distance of the capitol, the Tennessee Performing Arts Center, and The District.

In a town where almost everyone is or wants to be a music star, it's not surprising that you can hear some great music in local clubs. The queen of nightlife is the Blue Bird Cafe, about six miles west of town, but all you have to do is wander The District and you'll find live music at many of the local restaurants, from jazz to country, all of it a harmonious sampling of the Nashville sound.

Area Code: 615

DRIVING DIRECTIONS Nashville is at the intersection of I–40 east-west and I–24 and I–65 north-south. From Atlanta, follow I–75 north to I–24 north, about 250 miles. I–65 leads directly from Birmingham, about 192 miles.

PUBLIC TRANSPORTATION Nashville is a hub city for American Airlines, and is served by almost all major airlines. Downtown trolleys connect The District, Music Row, the Parthenon, and other downtown attractions.

ACCOMMODATIONS *Opryland Hotel,* 2800 Opryland Drive, Nashville 37214, 889–1000, EE ● *Loew's Vanderbilt Plaza Hotel,* 2100 West End Avenue, Nashville 37203, 320–1700, E-EE ● *Union Station,* 1001 Broadway, Nashville 37203, 726–1001 or 800–331–2123, M-EE ● *Holiday Inn Crowne Plaza,* 623 Union Street, Nashville 37219, 259–2000 or 800–447–9825, E ● *Stouffer Nashville,* 611 Commerce Street, Nashville 37203, 255–8400 or 800-HOTELS, EE ● *Holiday Inn Vanderbilt,* 2613 West End Avenue, Nashville 37203 or 800–777–5871, high-rise hotel, convenient location, reasonable rates, I.

DINING *Fine dining: Arthur's,* Union Station (see above), 255–1494, continental menu, EE, prix-fixe; *Mario's,* 2005 Broadway, 327–3232, northern Italian, E-EE; *Julian's,* 2412 West End Avenue, 327–2412, classic French, E-EE ● *Handsome restored quarters in The District: The Merchants,* 401 Broadway, 254–1892, M-E; *Mere Bulles,* 152 Second Avenue N, 256–1946, M-E ● *Other choices: Sunset Grill,* 2001 Belcourt Avenue, 386–3663, a current trendy favorite, M-E; *Amerigo,* 1920 West End Avenue, 320–1740, informal Italian, I-M; *Stock-Yard,* 901 Second Avenue N, 255–6464, steaks are the specialty, M-EE; *Loveless Cafe,* 2823 Nolensville Road, 254–9888, worth a drive, good Southern cooking and lots of it, legendary biscuits, country stars often on hand, great for all three meals, I; *Swett's Restaurant,* 2725 Clifton, 329–4418, more Southern specialties, cafeteria style, I.

NIGHTLIFE *Places to hear country music: Bluegrass Inn,* 184 Second Avenue, 244–8877; *Boots Randolph's,* 209 Printer's Alley, 256–5500; *Stock Yard Bull Pen Lounge,* 901 Second Avenue N and Stock Yard Boulevard, 255–6464; *Tootsie's Orchid Lounge,* 422 Broadway, 726–3739. A short drive from town: *Bluebird Cafe,* 4104 Hillsboro Road, 383–1461; *Nashville Palace,* 2400 Music Valley Drive, 885–1540; Station Inn, 402 12th Avenue S, 255–3307 ● *For jazz: Mere Bulles* and *The Merchants* (see restaurant listings).

SIGHTSEEING *The Hermitage,* 4580 Rachel's Lane, 889–2941. Hours: daily 9 A.M. to 5 P.M. except holidays and third week in January, $$$ ● *Belle Meade Plantation,* 5025 Harding Road, 356–0501. Hours: Monday to Saturday 9 A.M. to 5 P.M.; Sunday from 1 P.M.; $$$ ● *Historic Traveller's Rest,* 636 Farrell Parkway, 832–2062. Hours: June to August, Monday to Saturday 10 A.M. to 5 P.M.; Sunday from 1 P.M.; rest of year to 4 P.M. $$ ● *Cheekwood,* Tennessee Botanical Gardens and Fine Arts Center, 12000 Forrest Park Drive, 356–8000. Hours: Monday to Saturday 9 A.M. to 5 P.M.; Sunday from 1 P.M.; $$$ ● *The Parthenon,* West End and 25th avenues, Centennial Park, 862–8431. Hours: Tuesday to Saturday 9 A.M. to 4:30 P.M., $$ ● *Van Vechten Gallery,* Fisk University, 18th Avenue North, 329–8543. Hours: Tuesday to Friday 10 A.M. to 5 P.M.; Saturday and Sunday from 1 P.M.; $$ ● *Aaron Douglas Gallery,* Fisk University, Jackson Street, Third Floor Fisk Library, 329–8543. Hours: Tuesday to Friday 10 A.M. to 5 P.M.; Saturday and Sunday from 1 P.M.; $ ● *Tennessee State Museum,* 505 Deaderick Street, 741–2692. Hours: Tuesday to Saturday 10 A.M. to 5 P.M.; Sunday from 1 P.M.; free ● *Tennessee State Museum, Military History Branch,* War Memorial Building, 741–2692. Hours: Tuesday to Saturday 9 A.M. to 5 P.M.; Sunday from 1 P.M.; free ● *Vanderbilt Fine Arts Gallery,* 23rd and West End avenues, 322–2831. Hours: Monday to Friday 1 P.M. to 4 P.M.; Saturday and Sunday to 5 P.M.; free ● *Riverboat rides* (phone for current schedules): *Belle Carol Riverboat Company,* 106 First Avenue South, Riverfront Park, 244–3430; *The General Jackson Showboat,* 2802 Opryland Drive, 889–6611.

INFORMATION Nashville Convention & Visitors Bureau, 161 Fourth Avenue North, Nashville, TN 37219, 259–4700.

Plantation Pleasures
Near Charleston

Once upon a time, 20 lovely plantations stood along the Ashley River northwest of Charleston, South Carolina. Growing conditions were ideal here, not only for the rice and indigo that made planters rich, but for some of the first and most magnificent gardens in early America.

The Civil War banished this way of life. In fact, when the war was over, all but three of the 20 original plantation homes had been destroyed, a vivid testimony to the terrible toll that struggle exacted from the South.

Luckily for today's visitors, however, the gardens have proven more durable. The remaining plantations and their fabulous grounds are among the loveliest springtime sites in the Southeast. Many people make the trip out South Carolina route 61 and hurry through the plantations as part of a visit to Charleston, but these sites really deserve a weekend to themselves, with time to absorb their history, their haunting beauty, and the tales they tell of another era.

Each of these properties has something unique to offer. Drayton Hall, begun in 1738 and one of the earliest examples of Georgian-Palladian architecture in America, still looks remarkably as it did in the 1700s. It is the only plantation on the Ashley that survived the war intact. Some say the troops passed it by because they heard that smallpox victims were being treated there. The house remained in the Drayton family until 1974, used as a summer home only and kept in its original state, without plumbing or electricity.

Now maintained by the National Trust for Historic Preservation, Drayton Hall is shown without furnishings and is somehow all the more memorable with nothing to distract from the details of the workmanship, including the extraordinary sculpted plaster ceilings and hand-carved paneling and moldings.

Not far away is Magnolia Plantation and Gardens, a residence for other members of the Drayton family for ten successive generations. The original house, dating to the 1680s, was lost to fire; the replacement was burned by Union soldiers. The present modest home—occupied by the family until quite recently—is of interest mainly as an example of how plantation life changed after the Civil War.

The pride here is the large and lush garden, first planted in 1685 by Thomas Drayton. By the time Drayton died, in 1717, his small English garden had grown to ten acres. The earliest portion, still known as Flowerdale, remains virtually unchanged, but it is now part of 50 sumptuous acres of gardens overhung with Spanish moss romantically reflected in dark lakes that once nurtured rice fields. At night, softly lit for tours known as "Magnolia by Moonlight," the gardens are an unforgettable sight.

This is one of the nation's floral showplaces, resplendent in winter with 900 varieties of camellias and in spring with some 250 types of azaleas. Brick paths laid out centuries ago lead to a biblical garden, a topiary garden, a maze, and an herb garden.

Also on the property is the Audubon Swamp Garden, where boardwalks allow you to see alligators and the many varieties of birds that inhabit South Carolina's "Low Country."

The two Drayton properties will fill a day nicely; Middleton Place deserves a day on its own. This contains America's oldest formal landscaped gardens, laid out personally over 250 years ago by Henry Middleton, who became president of the First Continental Congress.

Creating the formal parterre lawn terraces leading up from the river, the butterfly lakes, and the many paths and geometric patterns required ten years of work by 100 Middleton slaves.

Middleton died in 1784, too soon to appreciate the additions made two years later by the French botanist André Michaux, who, according to family legend, planted exotic trees such as mimosa and ginkgo and brought as a gift the first four camellia bushes to be grown in America, three of which still bloom near the terraces.

In the nineteenth century winding walks in wooded settings and naturalistic plantings were added, a contrast to the formal early sections.

The main house was burned by Sherman's army in the 1860s; one wing was restored after the war to serve as a residence and is now a museum, where you can share the colorful history of the Middleton family, and see family collections of art, Charleston-made furniture, English silver, and a sampling of the library, which is said to have contained some 10,000 volumes in 1865.

The gardens languished until a Middleton descendant, J. J. Pringle Smith, and his wife came on the scene in the 1930s and began the daunting task of restoration. Today the gardens are as beautiful as ever, magnificent in every season.

The plantation stableyards have also been restored to show animals and early crafts, and workshops that re-create the era when plantations were self-sufficient. Also remaining is Eliza's House, built in 1870 as a two-family dwelling for the freed blacks who remained on the plantation.

One other attraction on this side of the river is Charles Towne Landing, the site of the original English settlement in South Carolina, founded in 1670. This is a state-owned nature preserve that brings to life the experience of the first settlers. A full-scale replica of the seventeenth-century trading vessel *Adventure* can be boarded, and there are replicas of buildings and crop gardens of the original town.

Also on the property is the Animal Forest, a 20-acre natural-habitat zoo.

Though you can easily stay in Charleston and enjoy plantation touring by day, there is one unusual inn on the Ashley, right in the midst of the attractions. Even though it is on an old plantation's grounds, Middleton Inn is starkly modern in style, and seems almost unattractive at first sight. Yet inside it is quite special, with handsome handmade furnishings and big windows with river views. The inn serves breakfast, and a short path along the river leads to the restaurant at Middleton Place, which specializes in Southern cooking for lunch or dinner. Horseback riding from Middleton Stables and miles of trails for nature walks are available, along with swimming and tennis.

One other appropriate choice, just over the bridge on the Charleston side of the Ashley River—closer to the plantations than downtown Charleston—is Loundes Grove Plantation, a magnificent 1786 home that is the only surviving plantation on this side of the peninsula. It is on the National Register of Historic Places. The home operates as a bed-and-breakfast inn, with five beautifully decorated guest rooms and a pool and Jacuzzi for guests.

If you have more time and want to complete a tour of area plantations and gardens, travel northeast across the Cooper, the river on the other side of Charleston, and follow U.S. 17 north to Boone Hall Plantation.

The classic columned mansion here is called America's most photographed plantation. The three-quarter-mile arching Avenue of Oaks approaching Boone Hall can be seen in countless illustrations. The oaks were planted in 1743 by Captain Thomas Boone, a descendant of the original settler, Major John Boone, who arrived to claim his land grant in 1681.

Boone Hall became a thriving cotton plantation, covering 17,000 acres in its heyday. The house itself was rebuilt in 1935, respecting the original 1750 Georgian architecture and using the original brick and woodwork.

The original "Slave Street," with nine brick slave cabins circa 1743, is one of the few such original quarters remaining in the Southeast.

The gardens at Boone Hall are loveliest in spring, when masses of bulbs add to the color of the azaleas and camellias.

Even more spectacular is Cypress Gardens, several miles farther north. Originally part of Dean Hall, one of the Cooper River's major rice plantations, the 163-acre swamp garden was once the center of the antebellum estate and was used as a reservoir to flood the surrounding rice fields. This blackwater swamp is now the center-piece of the gardens that were created by owner Benjamin Kittredge in the late 1920s. Three miles of walking paths lead through the plantings, but the best way to see the garden is to traverse the waters via flat-bottom boat.

Cypress Gardens suffered badly from the winds of Hurricane Hugo in 1989, losing many of its trees, but replanting is quickly returning the old beauty, and the increased sunlight has meant more blooming color, all the lovelier reflected in the water.

Like all of Charleston's centuries-old plantation gardens, this one will surely rise again.

Area Code: 803

DRIVING DIRECTIONS   See Charleston directions, page 227. From Charleston to the plantations, cross the Ashley River bridge and follow S.C. Route 61 north.

ACCOMMODATIONS   *Middleton Inn,* Ashley River Road (S.C. route 61), Charleston 29414, 556–0500, M-EE, CP ● *Loundes Grove Plantation,* 266 St. Margaret Street, Charleston 29403, 723–8438. Also see Charleston listings, page 228.

DINING   *Middleton Place Restaurant,* Ashley River Road, Charleston, 556–6020, I-M. Also see Charleston listings, page 228.

SIGHTSEEING   *Drayton Hall,* Ashley River Road (S.C. Route 61), Charleston, 766–0188. Hours: March to October, daily 10 A.M. to 5 P.M.; rest of year to 3 P.M.; $$$ ● *Magnolia Plantation and Gardens,* Ashley River Road (S.C. route 61), Charleston, 571–1266. Hours: daily 9:30 A.M. to 5 P.M., $$$ ● *Audubon Swamp Garden,* Magnolia Plantation, $$ ● *Middleton Place,* Ashley River Road (S.C. route 61), Charleston, 556–6020. Hours: daily 9 A.M. to 5 P.M., $$$ ● *Charles Towne Landing,* S.C. route 171, Charleston, 556–4450. Hours: daily 9 A.M. to 5 P.M.; until 6 P.M. June through August; $$$. *Boone Hall Plantation,* U.S. 17, Charleston, 884–4371. Hours: April through Labor Day, Monday to Saturday 8:30 A.M. to 6:30 P.M., Sunday 1 P.M. to 5 P.M.; rest of year, Monday to Saturday 9 A.M. to 5 P.M., Sunday 1 P.M. to 4 P.M.; $$$ ● *Cypress Gardens,* 3030 Cypress Gardens Road (off U.S. 17), Moncks Corner, 553–0515. Hours: daily 9 A.M. to 5 P.M., $$$.

INFORMATION   Charleston Trident Convention and Visitors Bureau, P.O. Box 975, Charleston, SC 29402.

Ambling Around in Atlanta

Old and New South meet head-on in Atlanta, Georgia.

Scarlett O'Hara, Atlanta's best-known fictional resident, would be dumbfounded if she could see the present-day skyline of the city that was burned to the ground during the Civil War. High-rise architecture, from John Portman's shiny hotel towers to the cupola of Philip Johnson's much-lauded IBM building, is an unmistakable monument to a metropolis on the rise, the major business center of the South.

Growth has spawned three distinct business areas—Downtown, Midtown, and the city's Perimeter—and has brought lavish shopping and dining and ever-spreading residential suburbs in four counties, all connected by a whizzing spaghetti maze of freeways.

Look beyond the flash and the freeways, however, and the grace of the older South remains. What Atlantans like best about their town is a lifestyle that mixes the modern with some of America's loveliest, leafiest residential neighborhoods. Come to visit in spring, when the dogwoods or magnolias are in bloom, and it's all but impossible not to fall under the city's spell.

Sightseeing begins Downtown, where Ted Turner's CNN Center in the Omni complex offers guided studio tours, plus a chance to shop for souvenirs at the Clubhouse Shop of Turner's Atlanta Braves. The stately halls of the state capitol are nearby.

An early downtown neighborhood of streets near the railroad terminal became a forgotten warehouse district after the roads were paved over by viaducts. But they have bloomed anew as Underground Atlanta, a lively shopping and entertainment complex that now extends to street level and offers 12 acres of shops, eateries, and clubs.

The New Georgia Railroad is still in business, running excursions around the city and to Stone Mountain.

Peachtree Fountain Plaza, the gateway to Underground Atlanta, is easy to spot with its showy ten-story light tower and cascading fountains. A dazzle of neon marks the area's most popular attraction, The World of Coca-Cola. A million patrons a year enjoy this slick, highly entertaining look at how Coke grew to become one of the world's best-known products.

Free soda samples are served at the end by a high-tech fountain of the future, which swirls the liquid ten feet into the air before pouring it neatly into a cup.

Atlanta's selection as the site for the one-hundredth anniversary of the modern Olympics, in 1996, has made major-league sporting facilities convenient for visitors. The Olympic Ring, an imaginary circle with a radius of one and a half miles of the Georgia World Congress Center, Atlanta's downtown convention facility, includes the

70,500-seat Georgia Dome, headquarters for Atlanta Falcons football, and the 85,000-seat Olympic Stadium, which will be home for Atlanta's beloved Braves baseball team. The Atlanta Hawks basketball team also plays downtown, at the Omni arena.

Take the MARTA subway system or drive north on Peachtree Street to Midtown to visit Richard Meier's striking High Museum of Art. It is part of the Woodruff Arts Center, the city's fine arts hub, where the Alliance Theatre Company and the Atlanta Symphony perform. Not far away is the unique Center for Puppetry Arts, America's most comprehensive complex of its kind, with four theaters and a museum. The Center offers the country's only series of puppetry performances specifically for adult audiences, with no one under age 14 admitted.

Other Midtown attractions include Scitrek, Atlanta's much-lauded interactive science and technology museum, and the elegantly restored Fox Theater, where *Gone With the Wind* had its worldwide premiere. It is now used for plays and concerts.

Piedmont Park, a 185-acre urban oasis, includes the city's Botanical Garden, with acres of woods and walking trails; perennial, herb, and rose gardens; and a striking indoor conservatory.

Wherever you are in Atlanta, rolling hills and lush greenery are only a block or two from even the busiest arteries. More sightseeing awaits in these sylvan neighborhoods.

Begin with a drive farther north to Buckhead and the long lineup of multimillion-dollar mansions on and around Paces Ferry Road, the city's most prestigious area. The governor's mansion is one of those along the way.

In the middle of the mansions is the Atlanta History Center, where you can tour one of the grandest of the homes, the Swan House, built and lavishly furnished in 1928 by Edward Hamilton Inman, heir to a cotton fortune.

After a guided tour of the house, admire the formal gardens and stroll among the stately trees of the 32 wooded acres. The grounds also include an 1840 farmhouse and outbuildings, showing what rural life was like before the Civil War.

The museum building, newly enlarged in 1993, is Georgia's largest urban-history museum and one of the largest of its kind in the nation. Exhibits trace the city from 1835 to the present. The museum houses several noted private collections, such as the DuBose Civil War Collection and the John A. Burrson Folklife Collection, as well as its own renowned assembly of costumes and textiles and *Gone With the Wind* memorabilia.

Buckhead is the place to sample the sophisticated shopping and dining that are Atlanta trademarks. The Lenox Square Mall is one of the largest in the south, and Phipps Plaza, across the street, offers elegant stores in a setting that looks more like a plush hotel lobby than a mall.

One of the city's posh antiques centers is at 2300 Peachtree Road in

Buckhead. For artier shopping, seek out Bennett Street, a side street off Peachtree Road at the southern end of Buckhead, where you'll find some 75 galleries, antique shops, and intriguing boutiques within a short stroll. Giant pinwheels out front mark the TULA Arts Complex, a former factory that now houses 45 galleries and working artists' studios.

There's a funkier scene in Virginia-Highlands, an older neighborhood being rediscovered by young Atlantans. Drive past the gracious homes beneath tall trees, then walk along Highland Avenue to see the blues bars, cafés, and offbeat galleries, such as the Modern Primitive Gallery, a folk art haven at 1402 North Highland Avenue.

Another area ripe for exploring is Druid Hills, whose gardenlike streets were the setting for the movie *Driving Miss Daisy*. They were laid out in 1893 by landscape architect Frederick Law Olmsted, who was also responsible for Piedmont Park.

One of the best ways to appreciate the beauty of Druid Hills is on the walking tours sponsored by the Atlanta Preservation Center. The Center offers other walks as well, which take in sights ranging from modern architecture to the Victorian beauties of Inman Park, the city's first garden suburb, which includes the homes of early Coca-Cola magnates Asa Candler and Ernest Woodruff.

Inman Park is where you will find the Carter Presidential Center and Museum of the Jimmy Carter Library, at Copenhill, the site from which General Sherman directed the battle of Atlanta. Set on 30 lush acres including lakes, a Japanese garden, and a waterfall, the library features a film showing how the president's role has changed under succeeding incumbents. Displays include a life-size replica of the Oval Office and exhibits reminding the visitor of Carter's accomplishments, including fostering peace between Israel and Egypt.

Auburn Avenue is where another famous Georgian, Martin Luther King, Jr., was born. It is the heart of an early progressive upper-class black community, known as ''Sweet Auburn'' for the good life it represented. America's Civil Rights Movement was born here, even before King became its leader. The National Park Service conducts tours through King's birthplace, and is slowly restoring the remaining buildings on the block. Also open to visitors is the Ebenezer Baptist Church, where Dr. King, following in the footsteps of his father and grandfather, was co-pastor from 1960 until 1968. His grave is nearby, at the Martin Luther King, Jr., Center for Nonviolent Social Change, an organization headed by Coretta Scott King and dedicated to her husband's goals.

Civil War buffs will want to pay a visit to the Atlanta Cyclorama, an enormous painting-in-the-round depicting the Battle of Atlanta. It is in Grant Park, which is also home to the Atlanta Zoo.

The famous mammoth carving on the mountain of Confederate leaders Davis, Lee, and Jackson can be seen at Stone Mountain State Park, 17 miles to the north. This wooded, 3,200-acre recreational area, a site for Olympic canoeing, cycling, rowing, and tennis events, can fill a day or more on its own with golf, tennis, lakes, and other recreational facilities. Gondola and steam-train rides and a paddlewheel steamboat are among the other diversions.

Those who want to stay here will find two attractive lodgings, the Stone Mountain Inn and the Evergreen Conference Center and Resort.

The Fernbank Science Center, on the city outskirts near Decatur, is the place to take a walk along a two-mile trail through one of the largest virgin forests in any U.S. metropolitan area. The center also boasts the Southeast's largest planetarium. The Fernbank Museum of Natural History, opened in 1992, is the largest natural history museum south of the Smithsonian. The spectacular Dinosaur Hall has seven life-size inhabitants; the Okefenokee Swamp gallery surrounds visitors with realistic sights and sounds of the swamp.

The best way to experience Atlanta's gracious lifestyle firsthand is to stay in a bed-and-breakfast home or an inn in one of the wooded residential areas.

When it comes to hotels, the Ritz Carlton properties, both downtown and at the five-star location in Buckhead, are acknowledged as tops for luxury lodging as well as dining in the city. Since Buckhead is convenient to shopping and many of the city's best restaurants, another good bet is the dramatic new Swissotel adjacent to the Lenox Square Mall. Days Hotel at Lenox is a Buckhead budget choice, but even the Ritz and Swissotel are bargains on the weekend.

Atlanta's trendy restaurants come and go, and there will undoubtedly be new stars by the time you read this. Those listed below have stood the test of time (at least up to the time of this writing). The Virginia-Highlands district has many of the current favorites of young Atlantans. The Peasant restaurants, with several locations, are popular moderately priced choices.

If Southern fried chicken is what you had in mind, join the long line at Mary Mac's Tearoom, which has been serving cafeteria style at the same stand for 42 years—proving that despite all that modern glitter, there's still a lot of the Old South left in new Atlanta.

Area Code: 404

DRIVING DIRECTIONS Atlanta is reached by I–20 east and west, and by I–75 or I–85 north and south. It is 149 miles from Birmingham, 249 miles from Charlotte, 252 miles from Nashville, 112 miles from Chattanooga, and 144 miles from Greenville, South Carolina.

PUBLIC TRANSPORTATION Atlanta is the hub city for Delta, and is served by virtually every airline as well as by Amtrak.

ACCOMMODATIONS   All are considerably less expensive on weekend packages. *Downtown: Ritz Carlton Downtown,* 181 Peachtree Street, 30303, 659–0400 or 800–241–3333, EE; *Hyatt Regency,* 266 Peachtree Street N.E., Peachtree Center, 30303, 577–1234, EE; *Westin Peachtree Plaza,* Peachtree Street at International Boulevard, 30343, 659–1400, EE; *Suite Hotel Underground,* Peachtree and Alabama streets, 30303, 223–5555, E-EE; *Omni at CNN Center,* 100 CNN Center, 30335, 659–0000, EE; *Comfort Inn Downtown,* 101 International Road, 30303, 524–5555, M-E; *Days Inn Downtown,* 300 Spring Street, 30308, 523–1144, M-E; *Inn at the Peachtrees,* 330 West Peachtree Street N.W., 30308, 577–6970, M ● *Buckhead: Ritz Carlton Buckhead,* 3434 Peachtree Road N.E., 30326, 237–2700 or 800–241–3333, EE; *Swissotel,* 3391 Peachtree Road, N.E., 30326, 365–0065, or 800–253–1397, EE; *Hotel Nikko,* 3300 Peachtree Road, N.E., 30305, 365–8100 or 800-NIKKO-US, EE; *Embassy Suites,* 3285 Peachtree Road, 30305, 261–7733, E-EE; *Days Hotel at Lenox,* 3377 Peachtree Road, 30326, 264–1111, M; *Holiday Inn Buckhead,* 3340 Peachtree Road N.E., 30026, 231–1234, M ● *Stone Mountain: Stone Mountain Inn,* Box 778, Stone Mountain, 30086, 800–277–0007, M ● *Evergreen Conference Center and Resort,* Stone Mountain, 30086, 800–722–1000, E. *Inns: Ansley Inn,* 253 15th Street N.E., 30309, 872–9000, E-EE, CP; *Shellmont,* 821 Piedmont Avenue N.E., 872–9290, M, CP; *Bed and Breakfast Atlanta,* 800–967–3224, registry service for bed and breakfast homes.

DINING   *The Abbey,* 163 Ponce de Leon Avenue N.E., Midtown, 876–8831, vaulted ceilings in a former church, M-E ● *Bones,* 3130 Piedmont Road N.E., Buckhead, 237–2663, wood paneling, fireplace, E-EE ● *Buckhead Diner,* 3073 Piedmont Road, 262–3336, trendy choice, I-M ● *Chops,* 70 West Paces Ferry Road, Buckhead, 262–2675, art deco scene, M-EE ● *City Grill,* 50 Hurt Plaza, Downtown, 524–2489, elegant, E ● *The Dining Room,* Ritz Carlton Buckhead (see accommodations listings above), best in town, EE ● *Hedgerose Heights Inn,* 490 East Paces Ferry Road, Buckhead, 233–7673, elegant home setting, M-E ● *Indigo Coastal Grill,* 1397 Highland Avenue, Virginia-Highlands, 876–0676, Key West ambience, Caribbean food, M ● *Lombardi's,* 94 Upper Pryor Street, Downtown, 522–6568, northern Italian, best choice in Underground Atlanta, I-M ● *The Mansion,* 179 Ponce de Leon Avenue, Midtown, 876–0727, gracious 1885 home, M-E ● *Ciboulette,* 1529 Piedmont Avenue, N.E., 874–7600, country French, rustic bistro setting, M-E ● *Deacon Burton's Grill,* 1029 Edgewood Avenue, 525–3415, funky combo TV-repair shop and restaurant with great fried chicken and the trimmings, I ●

Mary Mac's Tearoom, 224 Ponce de Leon Avenue, Midtown, 876–0727, fried chicken and fixings, I ● *103 West,* 103 West Paces Ferry Road, Buckhead, 233–5993, antiques, Victoriana, excellent food, M-EE ● *Pano & Paul's,* 1232 West Paces Ferry Road, Buckhead, 261–3662, Victorian decor, elegant, top choice, M-E ● *Peasant Uptown,* 3500 Peachtree Road N.E., Phillips Plaza, Buckhead, 261–6342, informal, courtyard settings, M ● *Pleasant Peasant,* 555 Peachtree Street N.E., Midtown, 874–3223, informal bistro, M ● *Partners,* 1399 North Highland Avenue, Virginia-Highlands, 876–8104, trendy favorite, M ● *The Restaurant,* Ritz Carlton Hotel, Downtown (see accommodations listings above), elegant, E-EE.

SIGHTSEEING *Atlanta Botanical Garden,* Peachtree Avenue at the Prado, Piedmont Park, 876–5858. Hours: Tuesday to Sunday 9 A.M. to 6 P.M., $$ ● *Atlanta History Center,* 130 West Paces Ferry Road, Buckhead, 814–4000. Hours: Monday to Saturday 9 A.M. to 5:30 P.M.; Sunday noon to 5:30 P.M.; $$$ ● *Center for Puppetry Arts,* 1004 Spring Street at 18th Street N.W., 873–3089. Hours: Monday to Saturday 9 A.M. to 4 P.M., $$ (check for performance schedules) ● *CNN Center,* One CNN Center, Marietta Street at Techwood Drive, 827–2491. Hours: Monday to Friday 10 A.M. to 5 P.M.; Saturday 10 A.M. to 4 P.M.; $$ ● *Cyclorama,* 800 Cherokee Avenue S.E., Grant Park, 624–1071. Hours: daily 9:30 A.M. to 5:30 P.M.; in winter months to 4:30 P.M.; $$ ● *Fernbank, Inc.,* 767 Clifton Road N.E., 378–0127. Includes two major buildings, woodlands, a greenhouse, and gardens. Hours: Fernbank Science Center and Planetarium, 378–0127, Monday 8:30 A.M. to 5 P.M.; Tuesday to Friday 8:30 A.M. to 10 P.M.; Saturday 9 A.M. to 5 P.M.; Sunday, 1 P.M. to 5 P.M.; free, except planetarium shows, $; *Fernbank Museum of Natural History,* Monday to Saturday, 9 A.M. to 6 P.M.; Sunday noon to 6 P.M.; $$$. *Georgia State Capitol,* Capitol Hill at Washington Street, 656–2350. Hours: Monday to Friday 9 A.M. to 5 P.M.; Saturday, 11 A.M. to 3 P.M.; Sunday 1 P.M. to 3 P.M., free. *High Museum of Art,* 1280 Peachtree Street, N.C., 892–3600. Hours: Tuesday to Saturday 10 A.M. to 5 P.M.; Sunday noon to 5 P.M.; $$ ● *Jimmy Carter Library and Museum,* 1 Copenhill, 331–0296. Hours: Monday to Saturday 9 A.M. to 4:45 P.M.; Sunday noon to 4:45 P.M.; $$ ● *Martin Luther King, Jr., Historic District,* Auburn Avenue between Jackson and Randolph streets, 524–1956. King's birthplace, church, and other sites; guided tours by National Park Service. Hours: daily 10 A.M. to 5 P.M., Labor Day through May, free. ● *New Georgia Railroad,* 1 Martin Luther King Jr. Drive S.W., 656–0768. Dinner trains and excursions; phone for schedule and rates ● *Scitrek,* 395 Piedmont Avenue, 522–5500. Hours: Tuesday to Saturday 10 A.M. to

5 P.M.; Sunday noon to 5 P.M.; $$$ ● *World of Coca-Cola*, 55 Martin Luther King Jr. Drive, 676–5151. Hours: Monday to Saturday 9 A.M. to 9:30 P.M.; Sunday noon to 6 P.M. $$ ● *Georgia's Stone Mountain Park*, Highway 78, Stone Mountain, 498–5600. Hours: June to August 10 A.M. to 9 P.M.; rest of year, 10 A.M. to 5:30 P.M.; $$ per car ● *Walking tours: Atlanta Preservation Center*, 401 Flatiron Building, 84 Peachtree Street, 522–4345. Phone for current schedule of guided tours of Atlanta neighborhoods; $$.

INFORMATION *Atlanta Convention and Visitors Bureau*, 233 Peachtree Street N.E., Suite 2000, Atlanta, GA 30303, 521–6600. *Information Centers: Peachtree Center Mall*, 231 Peachtree Street. Hours: Monday to Friday 10 A.M. to 5 P.M.; *Lenox Square*, 3393 Peachtree Road, Monday to Friday 10 A.M. to 5 P.M.; *Underground Atlanta*, 65 Upper Alabama Street, Monday to Saturday 10 A.M. to 9:30 P.M., Sunday noon to 6 P.M.

Summer

Peak Season at Roan Mountain

Rhododendrons like cool weather. Give them a mountain slope at a high elevation, and they thrive in remarkable fashion.

For spectacular proof, come to Roan Mountain State Park in Tennessee. Located astride the border with North Carolina at an elevation of 6,285 feet, the mountain is one of the highest in the Southeast and it provides the perfect growing climate for the largest natural display of rhododendron in the world, some 600 acres of purple and pink blossoms. Knockout views of the dusky ridges of the mountains are a bonus backdrop.

This glorious natural garden usually reaches its peak just in time to welcome the arrival of summer. For almost 50 years the weekend closest to June 20 has been the occasion for a celebration on both sides of the state line, featuring old-time music, Appalachian crafts, food, and all the hoopla of a gala festival.

But then this Tennessee state park is worth discovering anytime, whether you are looking for activity or beautiful serenity. Those who reserve far enough ahead to snag one of the 20 attractive cabins will enjoy a mountain setting and resort facilities that include a pool, tennis courts, and an amphitheater with a schedule of country entertainment every weekend, ranging from cloggers to storytellers to mountain music.

Ranger-guided programs of nature walks, bicycle tours, and evening adventures, such as "owl prowls," are all free. And then there are special events such as the July Fourth fireworks jamboree, an exhibition of champion cloggers, and a carnival of clowns.

Away from the activity, Roan Mountain offers breathtaking views and solitude above the clouds. Hiking is superb. Seven miles of trails from a quarter-mile to four miles in length meander through the park. Some ascend to highland peaks; others follow the mountain streams and the Doe River. One of the most popular stretches of the Appalachian Trail crosses Roan High Knob, the highest point in the park.

The view at the top hasn't changed much since Dr. Elisha Mitchell described it in 1836: "The most beautiful of all the high mountains . . . the top of the Roan may be described as a vast meadow without a tree to obstruct . . . with Carolina at the feet on one side and Tennessee on the other, and a green ocean of mountains rising in tremendous billows immediately around."

Dr. Mitchell, incidentally, is the scientist who measured and established that the highest peak east of the Rockies was located not in

New Hampshire, as had been thought, but in North Carolina, where that mountain and a county are named for him.

The Roan summit area is now administered by the U.S. Forest Service, which maintains picnic areas, hiking and interpretive trails, and scenic overlooks, all accessible by car.

A world of wildflowers also awaits walkers. Roan Mountain has long drawn botanists for its rich varieties of plants. In the last century, Dr. Asa Gray, considered the father of American botany, called Roan "without doubt the most beautiful mountain east of the Rockies."

One of the most interesting sights in the park is the Dave Miller Homestead, where you'll visit the past when you meet Frank Miller, Dave's grandson, who was born and raised in this very house. Miller shares memories of growing up and taking over the farm when his father died in 1924. The barn, chicken house, smokehouse, and root cellar of the original farm remain, telling of a time when isolated mountain families were self-sufficient, using lye soap made from ashes and medicines made with herbs and plants.

Since the park cabins go fast and preference is given to week-long stays in summer, you may have to stay elsewhere in the area and enjoy the park activities as a day visitor. In Tennessee, the best bet is Jonesborough, about 45 minutes northwest. This is the oldest town in the state, and it is a charmer. Read more about it on pages 149–54.

Or you can go through the park and over the mountain, descending into North Carolina's Mitchell County, a drive of about 20 minutes. The North Toe River has carved out a scenic valley here between high mountains. Mount Mitchell, at 6,684 feet, is one of a dozen peaks in the area over 6,000 feet high. There's a North Carolina state park with a road to the summit of Mount Mitchell and an observation tower, if you want another peak view.

This is a relatively quiet and often overlooked part of North Carolina, but you'll find ample rewards for a visit.

Even if you've never set foot in Mitchell County, you may have had some part of it in your home. The Roan Mountain Fraser fir, with its rich needles and pungent aroma, is the king of Christmas trees, and it is grown here at more than 50 nurseries.

Mitchell County mines produce lovely gemstones, as well as significant amounts of the feldspar and quartz used to manufacture everything from mayonnaise jars to bathroom fixtures. About 95 percent of the United States' supply of ultrapure quartz used in semiconductors comes from the region.

You can actually go underground in some of the historic mines. The biggest is the North Carolina Mining Museum at Emerald Village near Little Switzerland, a town named for its scenic mountain setting. Some 45 different minerals and gems, including aquamarines, emeralds, garnets, and smoky quartz, have been found in the Emerald area. The museum is located at a mine where feldspar was the principal find, valued as an ingredient of the once-popular cleansing powder known as Bon Ami. The cavernous tunnels dug by the miners remain, along with the crushers, cable cars, and machines used to extract the feldspar.

After the tour, you can have a go at finding your own gems. You pay for a bucket of stones, then wash and sift through them at a heated indoor flume. You may not find a priceless prize, but every bucket is guaranteed to contain at least one small gem. Other area mines offer the same chance to hunt for treasures.

The Emerald Village gift shop displays gem jewelry and loose gems priced from $3 to $100. Half a dozen more gem shops in Spruce Pine sell not only jewelry but beautiful geodes, stones that have been split to reveal a colorful, mineral-lined cavity. Stop at Gems by Gemini, on Highway 226 in Spruce Pine, to see a dazzling, 702-pound amethyst geode, valued at over $14,000.

As capital of the state's mining and mineral-processing industry, Spruce Pine is the logical place for the annual summer Mineral and Gem Festival, which has been going on for over 35 years. Some 50 retail dealers set up shop in the Pinebridge Coliseum, offering everything from inexpensive clear quartz crystals to flawless gems worth thousands of dollars.

Spruce Pine itself is the commercial center of the area, not a tourist town, but it is being spruced up and has recently been discovered by retirees.

You can see gorgeous gems displayed at the Museum of North Carolina Minerals, just off the Blue Ridge Parkway in Spruce Pine. Right next door to the museum is a sample of another Mitchell County specialty, fine handcrafts. Bea Hensley and his son Mike operate a forge where they hammer out custom-designed wrought-iron chandeliers and other decorative pieces for customers all over the world. The forge is open Monday through Saturday noon.

A few miles north of the Hensley forge on N.C. route 226, the fifth generation of the appropriately named Woody family produces handmade chairs assembled without nails or glue.

Another talented local family are the Stroups, who have been handcrafting grandfather clocks since 1949. They can be found at the Stroup Hobby Shop, 102 Stroup Road in Spruce Pine.

The Penland School of Crafts in Penland, a few miles north of Spruce Pine, is renowned. It was founded more than 60 years ago by Miss Lucy Morgan, who came to the area in 1920 to help her brother Rufus run the Appalachian School, a school for mountain children supported by the Episcopal Church. Miss Morgan saw crafts as a way to help mountain women earn money, and began to revive the dying art of handweaving. More than 60 women took part in the initial project, working in their homes. Eventually a "weaving cabin" was built at the school. It now serves as a visitor center and craft store. The school has grown to offer a wide variety of classes. It is considered one of the top centers of glass art in the country.

Many former students have established permanent studios in the area. Stop at the Twisted Laurel Gallery in Spruce Pine, at 333 Locust Avenue, to see the work of 120 regional craftspeople. If you want to visit artists' studios, tucked away in the hills and hollows, stop at the Chamber of Commerce for a listing.

Among several lodgings in the area, the choicest is the chalet-style Switzerland Inn in Little Switzerland, with panoramic vistas that would do credit to the Alps. Guests have use of a spring-fed pool, tennis courts, and lovely hiking trails.

If you spend a day atop Roan Mountain State Park and a day admiring gems and exploring underground mines, there's plenty to fill a weekend, but if time allows, Little Switzerland is less than half an hour from Grandfather Mountain and Blowing Rock to the east, with some of the best scenery and highest waterfalls along the Blue Ridge Parkway on the way.

Which only goes to prove that there's no end to the beautiful sights in the Blue Ridge Mountains.

Area Codes: Roan Mountain, TN, 615; Mitchell County, NC, 704

DRIVING DIRECTIONS   Roan Mountain is on county Route 143, reached in Tennessee via U.S. 19E. From I–40 east, continue south on I–40 at the I–81 intersection. Exit at U.S. 321 east and follow it to U.S. 19E at Elizabethton. Turn south on 19E, then turn right on county Route 143 to the park. Roan Mountain is 130 miles from Knoxville.

From Atlanta and other southern points, the best route is through North Carolina. Take I–85 north to I–26 north to Asheville, follow I–240 north to U.S. 70/19 east, bearing right on 19E to Spruce Pine. Here, take state Route 226 north to Bakersville, then take state Route 261 north to state Route 143 into Roan Mountain State Park, 294 miles. Spruce Pine is 102 miles from Charlotte, 51 miles from Asheville.

ACCOMMODATIONS   *Roan Mountain State Park,* Route 1, P.O. Box 50, Roan Mountain, TN 37687, 772–3303, 20 modern cabins, I-M; weekly reservations given preference in summer • *Switzerland Inn,* P.O. Box 399, Little Switzerland, NC 28749, 800–654–4026, Chalet lodge on a mountain crest, fine views, open May to October, I-M • *Big Lynn Lodge,* P.O. Box 459, Little Switzerland, NC 28749, 765–6771 or 800–654–5232. Upscale motel-style rooms, scenic vistas, M-E • *Richmond Inn,* 101 Pine Avenue, Spruce Pine, NC 28777, 765–6993. Bed-and-breakfast home in the country, I, CP • *Pinebridge*

SUMMER at Roan Mountain

Inn, 101 Pinebridge Avenue, Spruce Pine, NC 28777, 765–5543 or 800–356–5059, former school remodeled into a hotel and conference center, I • *Fairway Inn,* 110 Henry Lane, Spruce Pine, NC 28777, bed and breakfast home near town, I, CP • For Jonesborough, TN, see pages 152–53.

DINING *Switzerland Inn* (see above), Continental fare in a room with a view, M-E • *Beam's,* Route 19E, Spruce Pine, 765–6191, Chinese food, a surprise in the mountains, but this restaurant has prospered since 1969, I • *Cedar Crest Restaurant,* 311 Locust Avenue, Spruce Pine, 765–6124, casual, family fare, I-M • *Pinebridge Meeting Place Restaurant,* Pinebridge Inn (see accommodations listings above), seafood and steaks, I-M.

SIGHTSEEING *Roan Mountain State Park,* Route 1, P.O. Box 50, Roan Mountain, TN, 37687, 772–3303. Hours: daily 8 A.M. to 8 P.M.; swimming, picnicking, hiking, tennis, many special programs; rhododendron gardens in bloom usually late May to late June; free • *Mineral and Gem Festival,* c/o Mitchell County Area Chamber of Commerce (see below), late July or early August, gem displays, jewelry-making demonstrations, mine tours. Check current dates, $$ • *Mount Mitchell State Park,* Route 128 near Little Switzerland, 675–4611, observation tower, museum, picnicking, restaurant. Hours: Daily in summer 8 A.M. to 9 P.M.; rest of year to 6 P.M.; free • *Emerald Village,* P.O. Box 98, Little Switzerland, 765–6463. Hours: in summer, daily 9 A.M. to 6 P.M.; in spring and fall, 9 A.M. to 5 P.M.; November to April, open by appointment or by chance; $$ • *Penland Gallery,* Penland School of Crafts, Penland, 765–6211. Hours: Monday to Saturday 9 A.M. to noon, 1 P.M. to 4 P.M., free • *Museum of North Carolina Minerals,* Blue Ridge Parkway Milepost 226, 765–2761. Hours: Daily 9 A.M. to 5 P.M.; closed 12 noon to 1 P.M. in winter months; free.

INFORMATION *Mitchell County Chamber of Commerce,* Route 226 and the Blue Ridge Parkway, Route 1, P.O. Box 796, Spruce Pine, NC 28777, 765–9483 or 800–227–3912.

Splendid Summers at the Shoals

The northwest corner of Alabama is a land of lakes, big bodies of blue formed by mighty dams on the Tennessee River that some have called "the Great Lakes of the South." More than 1,200 miles of shoreline offer infinite possibilities for summer fun.

The "quad cities" of Muscle Shoals, Tuscumbia, Sheffield, and Florence, situated near the banks of the Tennessee, have their own claims to fame, thanks to some special residents, past and present.

The Miracle Worker, the inspiring story of Helen Keller, has thrilled audiences on Broadway and in movie theaters everywhere, but nowhere is it quite so moving as when performed at Ivy Green, Keller's birthplace in Tuscumbia, where the real miracle occurred.

It seems appropriate that the Alabama Music Hall of Fame was established near Tuscumbia in 1990, because the area is home to still-active recording studios where the Rolling Stones, Bob Dylan, Aretha Franklin, and many others have made hit albums. Florence was the birthplace of W. C. Handy, "the father of the blues," who is saluted each August with a spirited festival.

Between the lakes and the luminaries, this is a refreshing summer getaway. Diverse history has left its legacy, as well, with sightseeing including everything from Indian mounds to an early 1800s stagecoach tavern, from antebellum plantations to a Frank Lloyd Wright home.

Florence, the largest and most interesting of the towns, and the only one on the north side of the river, was the site of an Indian settlement and trading post until 1818, when a group of wealthy land developers established a town, naming it for the home city of a young Italian who was brought from Florence to lay out the streets.

The city's growth was not thanks to its river. The site overlooked dangerous rocky shoals that made the Tennessee impassable for barge traffic. So notorious were these hazards that the entire area became known as Muscle Shoals.

The government tried to build a canal around the shoals in 1836, but it was inoperable within a year. Soon after, the first railroad west of the Virginia mountains came chugging into town and made river transportation less important. Florence quickly developed into a trading and educational center.

In 1855, Wesleyan University was founded. General Sherman used the school building as his headquarters in 1865. In 1872 it became part of the first college for teacher training south of the Mason-Dixon Line, and the first coeducational college in the South. It is now known as the University of North Alabama.

When President Woodrow Wilson finally began the construction of a dam on the Tennessee in 1918, it was not for navigation but as a wartime project intended to generate power to make munitions. Completed in 1925, Wilson Dam—137 feet tall and 4,542 feet long—was the highest dam in the world. Though munitions were no longer needed, the dam would tame the treacherous shoals forever. Wilson became the first of a chain of nine dams built along the Tennessee River from Alabama to Kentucky, improving river navigation and providing hydroelectric power for industry that has greatly aided regional development.

The main navigation lock at Wilson Dam is one of the highest single-lift locks in the world. When a ship enters the lock, it is raised or lowered as much as 100 feet in order to navigate the river safely. The lock holds 50 million gallons of water, which it can empty in 12 minutes. It is fascinating to watch. Visitors can drive across the dam to an overlook on top of the lock, and can also tour the turbine rooms and tunnels deep within the dam.

For a bird's-eye view of the action, take the elevator to the top of Alabama's tallest tourist attraction, the Renaissance Tower, a slim, futuristic shaft rising 500 feet above Pickwick Lake. The Top of the Shoals restaurant offers panoramic views of the dam and the two lakes it formed. Wilson Lake stretches for 15 miles upriver to Wheeler Dam, while Pickwick Lake, fed by the spillwaters below the dam, runs for 52 miles to Pickwick Dam in Tennessee. Exhibits in the tower tell more about the work of the TVA.

Wheeler Dam, named for Confederate General "Fightin' Joe" Wheeler, who later represented the Tennessee Valley in Congress, has in turn formed its own 74-mile lake. Joe Wheeler State Park, on 3,400 wooded acres around the dam, has an attractive lodge with 75 guest rooms, each with a balcony overlooking Wheeler Lake. The park offers tennis, golf, and a marina with boat rentals in season.

All three lakes provide prime fishing. Pickwick, in particular, is famous for smallmouth bass. The Chamber of Commerce of the Shoals offers a free pamphlet with detailed fishing information, regulations, and tips.

When you're not busy with the dam or its lakes, you'll find Florence a city filled with lovely homes, almost 100 included in four historic districts. Court Street, the attractive main street of town, has some of the finest dwellings, such as Wakefield, an 1825 brick house patterned after George Washington's ancestral home, and the 1857 Governor O'Neal home, named for the family that produced two Alabama governors.

Courtview, the grand 1855 Greek Revival house at the north end, turned the street into a dead end. Beyond it, farther up the hill, are the handsome, columned brick buildings of the University of North Alabama.

One of Florence's oldest structures, Pope's Tavern, is one block from Court on a street that used to be called Military Road because it was the most direct route from Nashville to New Orleans. During the Civil War the house was used as a hospital for both Union and Confederate soldiers. In 1874 it became a private home, and remained in one family until it was purchased by the City of Florence in 1965. Now furnished as a tavern once again, it is the site of an annual Frontier Day celebration the first weekend in June that includes demonstrations of arts and crafts, storytelling, and music by members of the Shoals Dulcimer Society.

Long before Pope's Tavern or the rest of the town existed, this area was inhabited by Native Americans known as Mound Builders. Huge ceremonial mounds that may once have had temples on their summits are monuments to this ancient past in many Southern locations. The mound on South Court Street is the largest in the Tennessee Valley. Tools and artifacts found in and around the mound are displayed at the Indian Mound and Museum. Some artifacts date back 10,000 years.

Two later Florence homes are not to be missed. The Rosenbaum House is the oldest Frank Lloyd Wright house in the United States still occupied by its original owners. Designed in 1939–40 of cypress, glass, and brick, it is one of only 26 Usonian houses that Wright developed as prototypes for residences that the average American family could afford. A tour is all the more meaningful because Mrs. Rosenbaum herself takes visitors through.

The hand-hewn log cabin where William Christopher Handy was born in 1873 has been restored to tell the story of a remarkable musician, the son and grandson of ministers, who left the expected family path to follow his own star. His musical education came partly from singing classes in Florence's black public school, and partly from listening to the spirituals and melodies he heard along the river. Handy left home at 18, but floundered until, at the age of 38, he wrote a campaign song for "Boss" E. H. Crump, mayor of Memphis. It became the classic "Memphis Blues," and the rest is musical history. During his lifetime, Handy wrote more than 150 secular and sacred songs, including the universally known "St. Louis Blues."

Adjoining the cabin is a museum with the most complete collection of Handy's personal papers and artifacts, including his famous trumpet, his piano, and handwritten sheet music, including braille compositions he wrote after losing his sight.

Handy is one of many Alabama-born musicians who are honored at the Alabama Music Hall of Fame, a lavish facility where you can walk through a giant jukebox that plays songs by Alabama performers; see wax figures of Nat "King" Cole and Hank Williams, Sr.; board the tour bus used by the group Alabama; admire costumes worn by Lionel Richie; and hear music from the world's largest guitar. Included are exhibits about the recording studios that continue to bring many musical stars to the area. If you want your own hit record as a souvenir, the Music Hall of Fame offers a recording studio complete with taped backup music, and you can take your cassette home with you.

Tuscumbia also boasts one of the finest antebellum homes in the state, Belle Mont, built in 1828 as an outstanding example of Palladian architecture, perhaps inspired by Thomas Jefferson's Monticello.

But the most memorable home in Tuscumbia is the far more modest 1820 white clapboard house known as Ivy Green, where Helen Keller was born, on June 27, 1880. When she was 19 months old, the healthy child was stricken with a severe illness that left her blind and deaf. The miracle wrought by teacher Anne Sullivan, who penetrated Helen's silence to enable her to learn and communicate, revealed a remarkably gifted child. In 1904, with Sullivan still at her side, Helen Keller graduated cum laude from Radcliffe College, and went on to become one of history's most courageous and admired women. She dedicated her life to improving conditions for the blind and deaf, writing and lecturing in more than 25 countries on five continents.

The home is still as it was when Helen lived here, as is the cottage that was first a playhouse, then the place where Anne Sullivan tamed and taught the half-wild child. Each is filled with Miss Keller's personal mementos, including her original braille typewriter. The well pump where Helen spoke her first word, "water," remains in its original location as well.

William Gibson's *The Miracle Worker,* which tells the story of Helen Keller and Anne Sullivan, is performed at Ivy Green by a talented local cast who obviously relish their roles. The first performance each year is in June during the Helen Keller Festival, a week-long event celebrating Tuscumbia's most famous native. A parade, entertainment, arts and crafts, tours of historic sites, puppet shows, and many other special activities take place during the week. It is a unique celebration for a most unique woman—and one more reason to set your sights on Alabama's Shoals.

Area Code: 205

DRIVING DIRECTIONS The quad cities are off U.S. 43/Ala. route 17. To reach the Shoals area from Atlanta, take I–20 west to I–65 north, then Ala. Route 20/U.S. 72A west to U.S. 43, 232 miles. From Birmingham, take I–65 north and follow directions above, 119 miles; from Nashville, I–65 south, then as above, 177 miles.

ACCOMMODATIONS *Wood Avenue Inn,* 658 North Wood Avenue, Florence 35630, an 1880 Victorian bed-and-breakfast home, I-M,

CP • *Key West Inn,* 1800 Highway 72, Tuscumbia 35674, 383–0700 or 800–833–0555, an attractive motel complex, I, CP • *Holiday Inn,* 4900 Hatch Boulevard, Sheffield 35660, 381–4710, lavish indoor pool area, I-M • *Ramada Inn,* 4205 Hatch Boulevard, Sheffield 35660, 381–3743, I • *Comfort Inn,* 400 South Court Street, Florence 35630, 760–8888, I • *Best Western Executive Inn,* 504 South Court Street, Florence 35630, 766–2331, I • *Joe Wheeler Resort Hotel,* off U.S. 72, 25 miles east of Florence, 247–5461; reservations 800-ALA-PARK, hotel or cabins, I.

DINING   *Dale's Restaurant,* Mitchell Boulevard, U.S. 72 and 43, Florence, 766–4961, steaks are the specialty, I-E • *Top of the Shoals,* 1 Hightower Place, Florence, 766–3200, lunch, dinner, Sunday brunch, unbeatable view, I-M • *Court Street Cafe,* Mobile and Seminary streets, 767–4300, informal, I • *Fisherman's Resort,* Ala. route 101 just south of Wheeler Dam, Town Creek, 685–2094, keep driving through the trailer park for the freshest fish around, I • *Cafe Continental,* 4001 Jackson Highway, Sheffield, 383–2233, intimate, attractive, I-E • *George's Steak Pit,* 1206 Jackson Highway, Sheffield, 381–1531, M-E.

SIGHTSEEING   *Ivy Green,* 300 West North Commons, Tuscumbia, 383–4066. Hours: Monday to Saturday 8:30 A.M. to 4 P.M.; Sunday 1 P.M. to 4 P.M.; $$; *The Miracle Worker* is performed on the grounds six weekends from mid-June to July • *Alabama Music Hall of Fame,* U.S. 72 West, Tuscumbia, 381–4417 or 800–239-AMHF. Hours: Monday to Saturday 10 A.M. to 6 P.M.; Sunday 1 P.M. to 5 P.M.; $$$ • *Renaissance Tower,* 1 Hightower Place, off East Union Street, Florence, 764–5900. Hours: Monday to Saturday 9:30 A.M. to 5:30 P.M.; Sunday noon to 5 P.M. • *Stanley and Mildred Rosenbaum House,* 601 Riverview Drive, Florence, 764–5274. Hours: by appointment, $$$. • *Indian Mound and Museum,* South Court Street, Florence, 760–6379. Hours: Tuesday through Saturday 10 A.M. to 4 P.M., $ • *W. C. Handy Museum,* 620 West College Street, Florence, 760–6434. Hours: Tuesday to Saturday 9 A.M. to 12 noon and 1 P.M. to 4 P.M., $ • *Pope's Tavern,* 203 Hermitage Drive, Florence, 760–6439. Hours: Tuesday to Saturday 10 A.M. to 4 P.M., $ • *Kennedy Douglass Center for the Arts,* 217 East Tuscaloosa Street, Florence, 760–6379. Hours: Monday to Friday 9 A.M. to 4 P.M., free • *Belle Mont,* 111 Jefferson Avenue, Muscle Shoals, 383–2865. Hours: Sunday 1 P.M. to 5 P.M. or by appointment, 381–5052 • *Tennessee Valley Art Center,* 511 North Water Street, Tuscumbia, 383–0533. Hours: Monday to Friday 1 P.M. to 9 P.M.; Sunday 2 P.M. to 5 P.M.; free • *Joe*

Wheeler State Park, off U.S. 72, 25 miles east of Florence, 247–5461. Hours: daylight hours, $.

INFORMATION   *Chamber of Commerce of the Shoals,* Tourism Division, 104 South Pine Street, Florence, AL 35630, 764–4661 • *Colbert County Tourism and Convention Bureau,* U.S. 72 West, P.O. Box 440, Tuscumbia, AL 35674, 383–0783.

Basking on the Outer Banks

Whether you like your beaches sociable or solitary, you're going to love the Outer Banks of North Carolina. These 80 miles of barrier islands boast the most magnificent shores in the Southeast (if not the nation), and they offer infinite variety in mood. With a little advance guidance, you're sure to find your own place in the sun.

It is true that the location is somewhat remote, and there are no superhighways to make the driving easy, but this is a destination no beach lover should pass by. If you live too far away to drive for a weekend, come for a week—or take a plane.

Most people arriving from the south by car come via U.S. 64 across Roanoke Island, which lies in Roanoke Sound between the mainland and Bodie Island, the central part of the Outer Banks.

Roanoke is the site of a unique bit of history. The British, under Sir Walter Raleigh, established a colony here over 400 years ago, long before the landing at Jamestown, Virginia. But the 116 men, women, and children of the settlement disappeared without explanation. Their story is re-created in the outdoor pageant "The Lost Colony," presented each summer in the town of Manteo. It is the nation's oldest and longest-running outdoor drama.

The theater adjoins Fort Raleigh National Historic Site, where the tale of the ill-fated colonists is told in exhibits. Lovely Elizabethan gardens have been planted here in memory of the lost settlers. Plan to spend time in Manteo when you take a break from the beach. Besides the sights, this is a delightful town on a picturesque marina. Moored at the dock is the *Elizabeth II,* a 69-foot, square-rigged sailing ship representative of the kind of ship Raleigh might have sailed on in the sixteenth century. And the local branch of the state aquarium is a safe haven on a rainy day. Some of Manteo's lodgings are so inviting, you might even be tempted to stay.

But if you want to be on the beach, continue across the bridge to

Bodie Island, arriving in the community of Nags Head. Finding your way on Bodie is simple; there are only two main roads, N.C. route 12, known as Beach Road, near the ocean, and BR 158, in the center of the island. On the other side of the narrow peninsula, accessible via side roads, is Pamlico Sound, protected waters for sailing, canoeing, and other water sports.

North of Nags Head lie the communities of Kill Devil Hills and Kitty Hawk. Little other than signs differentiate these towns. Shops, restaurants, miniature golf, and other typical beach amusements run nonstop along the center highway, and the beaches are almost completely lined with weathered cottages and low-rise motels. These are fine for families and others who enjoy company at the beach. The motels are standard, with no particular standouts; those listed on pages 87–88 are newer or seem better values.

Two major sights are in this area. The Wright Brothers National Memorial in Kill Devil Hills has a replica of Orville and Wilbur Wright's first successful flying machine, in a museum near the hill where they launched it on December 17, 1903.

They're still launching things at Jockey Ridge State Park in Nags Head, but this time it is hang gliders that soar from the highest natural sand dune in the eastern United States. They're great fun to watch, and if you're tempted, Kitty Hawk Kites offers expert instruction, teaching some 2,000 people each year how to fly through the air.

The abovementioned sand dune is one of eight mammoth dunes in the area formed by shifting winds, a sandscape that looks more like the Sahara than the South. The height of the largest dune varies from 110 to 140 feet, depending on weather conditions. Kids of all ages love climbing these huge sand piles and sliding down.

Though it is convenient to Virginia and the Norfolk airport, the northernmost end of Bodie was the last part to be developed because of its past proximity to Norfolk military bases and bomb testing. Recently this has become the most exclusive preserve on the island, rapidly building up with developments of large, very expensive summer homes, some costing a million dollars or more.

Follow N.C. Route 12 north to the town of Duck, and you'll find the area's best shops, particularly in the wooded Scarborough Faire complex. Waterfront Shops, with a walkway on the water, is another attractive enclave.

Continue on N.C. Route 12 past the 7,000-acre Audubon preserve and the lineup of developments under construction, and just as the paving ends, look to the left and you'll see the red brick Corolla Lighthouse, built in 1875. This is one of a set of lighthouses along the Outer Banks dating from the 1870s, built to warn seamen away from the treacherous shoals along the coast. Some are painted in striking black and white patterns. Photographs of these landmarks are sold just about everywhere, and visiting camera buffs invariably go out of their way to shoot a set for themselves. The adjoining lightkeeper's house at Corolla has been restored recently.

Signs along the road to the lighthouse mark the Currituck Wild Horse Sanctuary, which has been established to protect the few remaining horses that used to roam here before houses and the highway began usurping their land. The mustangs are descendants of horses brought by the first English settlers.

Just north of Duck is the pick of Outer Banks lodgings, the Sanderling Inn. Though it was built in 1985, the weathered gray wood and the porches are in the style of summer homes of the 1890s. With an 1899 lifesaving station converted to serve as the dining room, the inn is tastefully at home in its surroundings. Guests here enjoy five miles of private beaches as well as a pool and a health club. Only a true escapist would quibble about the lovely homes spaced among the dunes along the beach.

Such purists are advised to turn south when they arrive on Bodie Island, following N.C. route 12 past the horizontally striped Bodie Lighthouse (with a detour for a photo, of course) and the busy marina and fishing center at Oregon Inlet to Hatteras Island. You may want to return to this marina for sportfishing; it is home to the largest fishing fleet on the coast.

Once you cross the bridge over the inlet to Hatteras, you're in the heart of the National Seashore, which has been protected since 1953. Suddenly there's little development in sight, and almost nobody is on the beach. For many people, this is what the Outer Banks are all about. The Seashore stretches for 70 miles across the end of Bodie, the whole length of Hatteras, and on to Ocracoke Island, which can be reached only via ferry.

On Hatteras, you'll first pass Pea Island National Wildlife Refuge, whose nature trails and observation platforms are popular spots with bird and wildlife watchers and wildflower enthusiasts.

Next along the road are a few surviving early U.S. lifesaving stations. The Chicamacomico Station, established in 1874, is one of the oldest. Exhibits remind visitors of the daring rescues that have been made off the treacherous shoals and surf of Hatteras Island, and demonstrations of the old techniques are sometimes given. Check the schedules.

Small villages along the road, such as Rodanthe, Salvo, and Hatteras, were allowed to remain because they existed before the National Seashore was declared. Beach worshipers and fishermen occupy most of the widely spaced, low-key motels.

The only thing resembling a crowd on Hatteras is the group usually found taking pictures around the diagonally striped Hatteras Lighthouse, at 208 feet the tallest in the country. It warns ships away from the perils of Diamond Shoals, waters that became known as the "Graveyard of the Atlantic." More than 600 ships have sunk here, victims of shallow shoals, storms, and war.

Heavy storms in 1992 shifted sands and currents, uncovering some of the shipwrecks, which are now visible from shore. Look for the *Laura A. Barnes* at Coquina Beach, three miles north of Oregon Inlet, and the Civil War transport *Oriental,* which can be seen at low tide near the Pea Island National Wildlife Refuge comfort station.

These same storms washed away major portions of the dunes, and some of the huge sandbags used to build a wall against the ocean's surges may still be in evidence. It is a tug-of-war that has gone on for centuries, with storms pulling relentlessly at the exposed shoreline.

At the very end of Hatteras, drive aboard the car ferry for the free 12-mile, 30-minute ride to Ocracoke Island. As soon as you head out to sea and sniff the fresh salt air, the feeling of freedom grows. Ocracoke's 17 miles of beach are the kind of wide, dune-backed, deserted sands that beach lovers dream about. Some areas have lifeguards in attendance, while others are completely deserted, places where there is no one but you, the sun, and the sea.

Ocracoke's deep inlet made it suitable early on as a port for oceangoing vessels. The North Carolina Colonial Assembly recognized the settlement in 1715 and officially proclaimed it a town in 1735.

Not only commercial seamen were attracted here. The secluded location made it a favorite haunt of the infamous pirate Blackbeard, who was killed off Ocracoke in a hand-to-hand battle and then beheaded. Some believe Blackbeard's buried treasure remains on the island.

The ferry pulls into the docks at Silver Lake, a natural harbor on the southern side of the island shared by yachts and fishing boats. The dominant building is a 1942 coast guard station. In the distance is the Ocracoke Lighthouse, dating to 1823, one of the oldest still in use on the Atlantic coast.

The entire village is on the National Register of Historic Places and is so picturesque that color sketches of the harbor, painted on weathered boards, are the best-selling island souvenir. Some 100 cottages built between the 1880s and 1930s remain.

A walk around the island yields many discoveries. Stop at the Ocracoke Preservation Society Information Center for a brochure to guide you. Some of the roads are still unpaved. At the end of sandy Howard Lane is Village Craftsmen, the best place to find local crafts. It is owned by Philip Howard, whose island ancestors go back several generations. You'll see the name again in town on Howard's Pub, a popular watering hole known for its original concoction, the Ocracoke Oyster Shooter.

There are over 80 small cemeteries on the island, maintained by families like the Howards, whose ancestors can be traced through the intriguing epitaphs on the headstones.

The British Cemetery, near Northern Pond, is unique. It is the burial ground of four British sailors whose bodies washed ashore, casualties of a battle with a German submarine in 1942. With the Union Jack flying proudly, it is a tiny bit of official British soil in the United States.

Ocracoke's small remaining herd of about two dozen ponies, known as Banker horses, also descendants of horses brought by the first settlers, can be seen on the road near the beach at the Ocracoke Pony Pen, where they have been brought together to be protected and properly fed.

The classic lodging on Ocracoke is the white, balconied Island Inn, a no-frills former 1901 Odd Fellows lodge restored in traditional island style. Berkeley Center is a pleasant alternative, though it lacks water views.

No reservations are needed for the ferry back to reality. Though the schedule says the boats leave every 30 minutes, ferries often run every 15 minutes during peak times, so while there is sometimes a line waiting to board, you'll not have to wait too long.

There's only one problem—you'll never want to leave.

Area Code: 919

DRIVING DIRECTIONS   The Outer Banks are approached via U.S. 64/264 east or via U.S. 158 from the north. Nags Head is about 200 miles from Raleigh-Durham.

PUBLIC TRANSPORTATION   The closest large airports are Raleigh-Durham or Norfolk, Va., about a two-hour drive. Dare County Regional Airport, on Roanoke Island, has commuter service from Norfolk; phone 473–2600 for current information. Limousine and van service is also available from Norfolk. From the south, a toll ferry brings motorists from Cedar Island, near Morehead City, to Ocracoke. Phone 225–3551 for schedules and rates.

ACCOMMODATIONS   *Sanderling Inn Resort,* Route 12, S.R. Box 319Y, Duck 27949, 261–4111, EE, CP ● *The Islander Motel,* Route 12, Nags Head 27959, small property, pool, all rooms oceanfront, M ● *Comfort Inn,* Route 12, Nags Head, 27959, 480–2600, pool, M-E ● *Days Inn Oceanfront,* Route 12, Nags Head, 27959, 441–7211, attractive lobby, pool, refrigerators, M-E ● *Cape Hatteras Motel,* P.O. Box 939, Buxton 27920, pool, tennis, rooms, and efficiencies, M; cottages, E ● *Comfort Inn,* Hatteras Island, 27943, 995–6100 or 800–228–5150, newly built, pool, refrigerators, M, CP ● *Durant Station,* P.O. Box 266, Hatteras 27943, motel attached to 1878 lifesaving station, pool, I-M; apartments in lifesaving station, I-M ● *Island Inn,* P.O. Box 9, Ocracoke 27960, 928–4351, I-M ● *Berkley*

Center, P.O. Box 220, Ocracoke 27960, 928–5911, warm country-inn feel, pine-paneled walls, no views but nice grounds, easy walk to the harbor, I, CP • *Pirate's Quay Hotel,* P.O. Box 526, Ocracoke 27960, 928–1921, new, suites with views, E • *Crews Inn,* P.O. Box 460, Ocracoke 27960, typical modest island home turned bed-and-breakfast, I, CP • *Tranquil House Inn,* Manteo 27954, 473–1404 or 800–458–7069, attractive rooms on the harbor, M-EE, CP • *Roanoke Island Inn,* 305 Fernando Street, Manteo 27954, 473–5511, wonderful island house, tasteful furnishings, M, CP • *Cottage rentals:* Contact Chamber of Commerce for realtor listings.

DINING Seafood is the specialty everywhere unless otherwise noted. *Blue Point Bar and Grill,* The Waterfront Shops, Duck, 261–8090, M-E • *Elizabeth's Cafe and Winery,* Scarborough Faire, Duck, M-E • *Sanderling Inn Resort,* (see above), M-E • *Kelly's Restaurant and Tavern,* U.S. 158, Nags Head, 441–4116, M • *Owens' Restaurant,* Beach Road, 441–7309, Nags Head, M • *Penguin Isle,* U.S. 158, Nags Head, 441–2637, M-E • *Waves Edge Restaurant,* Waves, Hatteras Island, 987–2100, I-M • *The Froggy Dog,* Avon, Hatteras Island, 995–4106, I-M • *Clara's Seafood Grill,* on the waterfront, Roanoke Island, 473–1727, M • *Queen Anne's Revenge,* Old Wharf Road, Wanchese, Roanoke Island, 473–5466, hidden gem, M-EE • *Island Inn,* Ocracoke (see accommodations listings above), M • *The Back Porch,* Ocracoke Village, 928–6401, M-E • *Capt. Ben's Restaurant,* Ocracoke Village, 928–4741, M-E • *Pony Island Restaurant,* Ocracoke Village, 928–5701, casual, I-M.

SIGHTSEEING *Cape Hatteras National Seashore,* N.C. route 12, Bodie, Hatteras, and Ocracoke islands, 473–2111. Visitor centers at Whalebone Junction near U.S. 64, Bodie Island; Oregon Inlet, Bodie Island; and Hatteras Lighthouse, Cape Hatteras. Guided walks, activities, evening programs held at all locations, mid-June through early September; check current schedules. Hours: 9 A.M. to 6 P.M., free • *Pea Island National Wildlife Refuge,* Hatteras Island, 987–2394. Hours: daily, dawn to dusk. Visitor station hours: weekdays 9 A.M. to 4 P.M.; check for times of guided bird walks and children's programs; free • *Wright Brothers National Memorial,* U.S. 158, Kill Devil Hills, 441–7430. Hours: June 15 to Labor Day, daily 9 A.M. to 7 P.M.; rest of year to 5 P.M.; $ • *Jockey's Ridge State Park,* off U.S. 158 bypass, 441–7132. Hours: June to August, 8 A.M. to 9 P.M.; April, May, and September, 8 A.M. to 8 P.M.; March and October, 8 A.M. to 7 P.M.; November to February, 8 A.M. to 6 P.M.; free • *Chicamacomico*

Lifesaving Station, N.C. route 12, Rodanthe, 987–2203. Hours: Memorial Day to Labor Day, Tuesday, Thursday, Saturday, 11 A.M. to 5 P.M.; check for off-season hours; free ● *Cape Hatteras Lighthouse,* N.C. route 12, Hatteras Island, 995–4474. Lighthouse closed to public. Keeper's House hours: Memorial Day to Labor Day, daily 9 A.M. to 6 P.M.; rest of year 9 A.M. to 5 P.M.; free ● *Hatteras-Ocracoke Ferry,* 928–3841. Hours: April 1 to October 31, from Hatteras 5 A.M., 6 A.M., on the half hour from 7 A.M. to 6:30 P.M., then 8 P.M., 10 P.M., and midnight. From Ocracoke: 5 A.M., 6 A.M., 7 A.M., on the half hour from 8 A.M. to 7:30 P.M., then 9 P.M., 11 P.M.; rest of year, usually hourly service, best to check current hours; free ● *Fort Raleigh National Historic Site,* U.S. 64/264, Roanoke Island, 473–5772. Visitor Center hours: Monday to Saturday 9 A.M. to 8 P.M.; Sunday 9 A.M. to 6 P.M.; free ● *The Lost Colony,* Waterside Theater, 473–3414. Hours: mid-June through August, 8:30 P.M.; all seats by reservation; $$$$; behind-the-scenes tours, $$ ● *Elizabethan Gardens,* 473–3234. Hours: daily 9 A.M. to 5 P.M.; closed weekends in December and January; $$ ● *Elizabeth II State Historic Site,* on the harbor, Manteo, 473–1144, replica of sixteenth-century sailing ship. Hours: April to October, Tuesday to Sunday 10 A.M. to 6 P.M.; rest of year, 10 A.M. to 4 P.M.; $$ ● *North Carolina Aquarium,* Airport Road off U.S. 64/264, Roanoke Island. Hours: Monday to Saturday 9 A.M. to 5 P.M.; Sunday from 1 P.M.; free.

SPORTS *Kitty Hawk Sports,* three locations: Nags Head, 441–6800; Duck, 261–8770; Cape Hatteras, 995–5000; kayaking, windsurfing, sailing ● *Kitty Hawk Kites,* 441–4124 or 800–334–4777; locations in Nags Head, Duck, Corolla; hang gliding, paragliding instruction, rollerblade rentals, kites, workshops in juggling, paper airplane making ● *Barrier Island Sailing Center,* Duck, 261–7100, sailboats, catamarans, sailboards ● *Waterworks Inc.,* Nags Head Causeway, 441–8875, fishing trips, parasailing, boat rentals, sailboat and canoe rentals, windsurfing lessons ● *Oregon Inlet Fishing Center,* Oregon Inlet, Bodie, sportfishing trips, boat rentals ● *Miss Hatteras,* 986–2365, daily fishing trips, evening cruises ● *On Ocracoke Island: Ocracoke Outdoors,* Ship's Timber Bed & Breakfast, 928–4061, windsurfing, kayaking, sailing, biking, rentals and lessons; *Ride the Wind,* kayak rentals, lessons, guided tours, sailboats, 928–6311; *Scarborough's Bicycle Rental,* 928–4271; Fishing charters: *Drum Stick,* Capt. David Nagel, 928–5351; *The Outlaw,* Capt. Woody Outlaw, 928–4851; *Rascal,* Capt. Norman Miller, 928–6111.

INFORMATION *Outer Banks Chamber of Commerce,* Corner of Ocean Bay Boulevard and Bustain Street, P.O. Box 1757, Kill Devil

Hill, NC 27948, 441-8144 • *Dare County Tourist Bureau,* Route 64 and Budleigh Street, P.O. Box 399, Manteo, NC 27954, 473-2138.

On Top of the World in Georgia

When Georgians want to escape the summer heat, they know just where to go. Northeast Georgia is "where spring spends the summer," according to the slogan of Rabun County, which occupies a big, scenic corner of the region. It's an apt description, since the average temperature in August is 76 degrees.

The state's highest elevations account for the breezes as well as the beauty. Adding to the scenery are four lakes, rushing rivers, waterfalls, and 1,000-foot-deep Tallulah Gorge. Much of the terrain is part of the Chattahoochee National Forest, preserved cool and green forever.

This is great country, whether you want to sit back and admire the scenery or be active outdoors. Hikers, golfers, and fishermen are in their glory. For river rafters, the ultimate challenge is the Chattooga, a National Wild and Scenic River, whose roaring rapids became famous as the location for the movie *Deliverance.* At its toughest, it is the steepest river in the East. Several companies offer guided tours, including calmer stretches for the less adventurous.

This is also a happy hunting ground for crafts and folk art, with wonderful galleries beckoning at every turn. The region's Appalachian heritage is celebrated at the annual Georgia Mountain Fair, and in one of the South's most unique entertainments, the moving musical called *The Reach of Song.* This colorful drama celebrating the history and poetry of the mountains has been declared Georgia's "Official Historic Drama."

The first difficult decision is choosing a home base. One possibility is to stay on the western rim of the region, in Hiawassee, at the attractive Fieldstone Inn on the shores of Lake Chatuge. Guests enjoy a pool, tennis court, fishing dock, and marina, with rental boats right on the premises.

A stay here puts you five minutes away from the Georgia Mountain Fairgrounds, where *The Reach of Song* is performed each night from early June through July. The changes in the mountains, seen through the life and works of native writer and farmer Byron Herbert Reece, form the theme of the show. The cast of 35 to 40 is made up of both professionals and local residents, ranging in age from seven to 78.

Later in the summer, the Fairgrounds hosts the big 10-day Mountain Fair, with more than 60 artisans showing off old-time crafts from woodcarving and candlemaking to moonshine stilling. Midway rides, mountain heritage booths, and a daily schedule of bluegrass music and country artists keep everyone busy and happy.

Hikers will also find Hiawassee a handy location. Follow Georgia route 75 south of town and go west on Georgia route 180 for the turn-off to Brasstown Bald, at 4,784 feet the state's highest mountain. The 360-degree views from the visitor center and observation tower at the summit take in four states. A steep, paved half-mile trail leads from the parking lot to the top. If you'd rather not make the trek, a shuttle bus will do it for you for a small fee.

Clayton, a charming little mountain town that is the seat of Rabun County, offers more variety for dining and lodging and better shopping. The 30-mile drive east on U.S. 76 from Hiawassee to Clayton is one of the loveliest in the state, dipping and curving into even more dramatic mountain scenery.

On this road is Timpson Creek Gallery, overflowing with Southern folk art, both painted and handmade twig furniture, and country treasures in a variety of media.

Clayton has its own not-to-be-missed folk art and contemporary crafts, found at the Main Street Gallery. Antiquers also will be happy in this area. Shops begin on Main Street and continue north on U.S. 441 for the seven miles through Mountain City and into Dillard.

As you drive north, watch for the small museum of Appalachian artifacts on U.S. 441 that is headquarters for Foxfire, the well-known educational experiment that encourages active learning.

A bit farther north, you can admire the handwoven items and other handwork at Rabun Gap Crafts, operated by the Rabun Gap–Nacoochee School. The weaving is done on shop looms, and visitors are welcome to watch.

You are in the midst of one of the most beautiful sections of the Georgia mountains. Just off the main highway, in Mountain City, is Blackrock Mountain State Park, cloud-high astride the Eastern Continental Divide at 3,640 feet. Named for its sheer cliffs of dark granite, this is Georgia's highest park. On the right day, you can see 80-mile vistas of the southern Appalachians.

Also beckoning are prize hiking trails. A complete "Trail Guide to the Chattahoochee-Oconee National Forests," with detailed directions to each trail, is available free from the Tallulah Ranger District office in Clayton. The Northeast Georgia Mountain Travel Association publishes a pamphlet detailing where to find waterfalls.

If you're not a hiker, you can get some idea of the Chattooga River's majesty by driving east on U.S. 76. Just after you cross the bridge into South Carolina, there's a parking area and a short trail to outcroppings with fine views of the Bull Sluice Rapids.

The scenery continues to the south on U.S. 441. Right off the highway is Tallulah Falls, the legendary gorge whose waters have been harnessed for hydroelectric power. To take advantage of the lake formed by the Tallulah Falls dam, the Georgia Power Company has created Terrora Park, 300 acres with a swimming area, sand beach, tennis courts, hiking trails, a playground, and tables for picnicking beside the lake. The park includes hiking trails and a paved walkway to an overlook for the gorge.

Crafts also are still very much part of the picture. The Co-op Craft Store at Tallulah Falls is a showcase for more than 100 members who produce everything from stained glass to stuffed toys. A bit farther south is Lofty Branch Art & Craft Village, a complex of artists and craftspeople who work and sell in their own studios as well as displaying their wares in a group gallery.

The gallery that takes the prize for scenery is the Mark of the Potter, housed in a converted gristmill beside the Soque River on Georgia route 197, 10 miles north of Clarkesville. The mill is a national historic landmark. Potter Jay Bucek makes and sells his own pottery here, and shows work by 45 other Southeastern craftspeople.

Buy Bucek's book, *Something's Cookin' in the Mountains,* for recipes plus tips on where to find the kind of hidden beauty spots and meet special local people that only a longtime resident can know. Among other places, he will steer you down the road to the Batesville General Store for lunch and their famous biscuits, followed by a browse through the homemade gifts.

Lodgings are choice throughout the region. In Clayton, the English Manor Inn consists of seven balconied buildings on seven acres, with a swimming pool and attractive grounds. Rooms have period furnishings, kitchens, and some fireplaces.

A few miles north in Mountain City, the York House will delight inn lovers. Tucked away in a valley with mountain views, the expansive 1896 country house is just the place to sit in a rocker on the porch and savor the scenery.

Accommodations at Dillard House are of the standard motel or cottage variety, but facilities include a pool, a tennis court, and stables, and you're just a stroll away from the Southern, family-style, all-you-can-eat meals that have kept folks coming for almost a century. Other members of the Dillard family run various motel accommodations in town, as well as Chalet Village, which offers individual units with fireplaces. Farther north, at Sky Valley condominium resort, 18 holes of golf, a pool, and tennis courts beckon, surrounded by Blue Ridge Mountain peaks. In winter, Sky Valley offers Georgia's only skiing.

Other excellent choices await south of Clayton. The Lake Rabun Hotel, a mountain lodge on the banks of the lake, has been a quaint, rustic favorite since 1922. The Barn is another option, a onetime dairy barn converted into a small, inviting bed-and-breakfast home across the road from the lake.

You can see by the walled entrances and iron gates that Lake Rabun was a wealthy estate area earlier in this century. The unspoiled lake has remained quite private, used mainly by those whose homes remain. Rabun Beach provides picnic and swimming areas in a quiet spot amid the mountain laurel.

There's more hiking here, and more of those waterfalls. The Rabun Beach trail follows and occasionally crosses the waters of Joe Branch. Near the end is Angel Falls, and for those willing to do a little climbing, Panther Falls awaits upstream. Minnehaha Falls, one of the most beautiful in the area, is reached via the half-mile Fall Branch Trail. To get to the trail, go past the Rabun Beach Recreation Area for a mile, turn left, cross the bridge, and follow Bear Gap Road around the lake for 1.6 miles.

My favorite of all the area lodgings is below Lake Rabun, far off the highway on an unpaved road. Glen-Ella Springs, a resort since 1890, is on the National Register of Historic Places. It has been restored with a perfect mix of old-fashioned charm and modern comforts, an effort that won an award from the Georgia Trust for Historic Preservation. A pool and sun deck beckon outside on 17 acres of lawns and meadows, perennial and herb gardens. The dining room is renowned in the region.

If you can't decide where to stay, that may be all to the good. It means you can return for fall color, cozy winter hideaways, and wildflowers in the spring. There's beauty and fun whenever you come to this special section of the mountains.

Area Code: 706

DRIVING DIRECTIONS   Clayton is at the intersection of U.S. 441 and U.S. 76. From Atlanta, take I–85 north to the junction with U.S. 441 north, 116 miles. It is 95 miles from Asheville, 155 miles from Charlotte, 155 miles from Chattanooga, and 56 miles from Greenville, S.C. Hiawassee is 30 miles west of Clayton on U.S. 76. To go directly from Atlanta, take I–85 north, branching into I–985 to Gainesville exit 67. Turn left onto U.S. 129 to Cleveland. Go halfway around the square in Cleveland and follow signs for Ga. route 75. Proceed on Route 75 until it merges with U.S. 76, and continue north.

ACCOMMODATIONS   *Fieldstone Inn,* U.S. 76, Hiawassee 30546, 896–4128 or 800–545–3408, M ● *English Manor Inns,* Highway 76E, Clayton 30525, 800–782–5780, I-M ● *York House,* off U.S. 441, Mountain City 30562, 746–2068 or 800–231–YORK, I, CP ● *Dillard House,* U.S. 441, Dillard, 30537, 746–5348 or 800–541–0671, motel *rooms, I-M; suites, M-E; cottages, M-EE* ● *Chalet Village,* Dillard Best Western, U.S. 441, Dillard 30537, 746–5321, I-EE ● *Sky Valley Resort,* P.O. Box 39, Dillard 30537, 746–5301 or 800–262–8259, condominium units, E-EE ● *Lake Rabun Hotel,* Lake Rabun Road, Lakemont 30552, 782–4946, I ● *Barn Inn,* Highway 1, Lakemont 30552, 782–5094, I, CP ● *Glen-Ella Springs,* Bear Gap Road, Highway 3, Box 3304, Clarkesville 30523, 754–7295 or 800–552–3479, M-EE ● For listings of cabins, contact the Rabun County Chamber of Commerce.

DINING *Fieldstone Inn* (see accommodations listings above), steaks are the specialty, lake views, I-M ● *The Stockton House,* Warwoman Road, Clayton, 782–6175, light and airy, American menu, mountain views, I-M ● *Stonebrook,* U.S. 441, Clayton, 782–6789, luncheon buffet, standard dinner menu, lunch, I, dinner, I-M ● *Green Shutters,* Main Street, Clayton, 728–3342, Southern cooking, family style, I ● *Chik'n Coop,* Clayton, 782–3437, fried chicken is only the start, Italian buffet Friday night, I ● *Dillard House* (see above), famous family-style feasts, reservations strongly advised, lunch, I, dinner, M ● *Glen-Ella Springs* (see above), highly recommended, M ● *LaPrade's,* Highway 197 North, Lake Burton, Clarkesville, 947–3312, Southern family style, in business since 1925, open April through November, I.

SIGHTSEEING *The Reach of Song,* Georgia Mountain Fairground, U.S. 76 West, Hiawassee, 800–262-SONG. Hours: early June through July, Tuesday to Saturday 8 P.M., general admission, $$$; reserved seats, $$$$ ● *Georgia Mountain Fair,* P.O. Box 444, Hiawassee, 30546, 896–4191. Nine days in mid-August; phone for current dates; $$$ ● *Brasstown Bald,* off Ga. route 180 south of Hiawassee, 896–2556. Hours: Memorial Day to October, weekends in early spring, daily 10 A.M. to 5:30 P.M., free ● *Foxfire Appalachian Museum,* U.S. 441, Mountain City, 746–5828. Hours: April to October, Monday to Saturday 9 A.M. to 4 P.M.; rest of year, closed Saturday; free ● *Black Rock Mountain State Park,* U.S. 441, Mountain City, 746–2141. Hours: daily 7 A.M. to 10 P.M.; office hours, 8 A.M. to 5 P.M.; parking fee, $ ● *Moccasin Creek State Park,* Ga. route 197, Clarkesville, 947–3194. Hours: daily 7 A.M. to 10 P.M.; office hours, 8 A.M. to 5 P.M.; parking fee, $ ● *Terrora Park and Visitor Center,* U.S. 441 South, Lakemont, 754–3276. Hours: park, daily, daylight hours; visitor center, Monday to Saturday 9 A.M. to 5 P.M.; Sunday 1 P.M. to 5 P.M.; free.

SPORTS *Hiking information: Tallulah Ranger District,* Checher/Savannah Street, P.O. Box 438, Clayton 30525, 782–3320; or contact

Forest Supervisor, 508 Oak Street N.W., Gainesville, GA 30501, 536–0541; hiking maps are also available at Rabun Chamber of Commerce ● *Guided hikes: Real Rabun,* 782–5014 ● *Whitewater rafting: Nantahala Outdoor Center,* 782–4812 or 800–232–7238 for reservations; *Wildwater Ltd.,* 800–451–9972; *Southeastern Expeditions,* 800–868–7238 ● *Horseback riding: Dillard House Stables,* 746–5348; *Smokey Mountain Stables,* 782–5836; *Tut's Stables,* 782–6218.

INFORMATION   *Rabun County Chamber of Commerce,* U.S. 441, Clayton, 782–4812 ● *Northeast Georgia Mountain Travel Association,* P.O. Box 464, Gainesville 30503, 535–5757.

Hitting the High Spots in Upcountry

Pendleton, South Carolina, is a town with personality.

The village green is picture perfect, and the entire town, which dates to 1790, is on the National Register of Historic Places.

However, the restaurants occupying some of the quaint buildings around the green are the first clue that this community of 3,300 is not your typical, sleepy small Southern town. Take a peek at the menus— Italian, Caribbean, Mennonite, Southern, Continental—and a sandwich shop that advertises 75 varieties.

Now look around town a little. Check out the art deco movie theater, recently renovated to present stage plays by the Clemson Little Theater. Visit the town baker, who hails from England, and the local innkeepers, who moved here from St. Louis. Stop in at the goat farm, whose cheeses are becoming legendary, and call on one of the many talented artisans who have made Pendleton a center for crafts. The two big craft fairs held on the green in spring and fall bring crowds of 40,000.

You're beginning to get the picture. Pendleton is a little bit sophisticated, a little bit offbeat—and a lot of fun to visit. To make things even better, it is just five miles from the campus of Clemson (which accounts for much of the sophistication), and is located in the state's "Upcountry," the hilly northwest corner that is home to six state parks, five lakes, a wild and scenic river, and a national forest.

One possible plan is to divide Saturday between Pendleton and Clemson, and save Sunday for scenery.

The best place to get your bearings is the Pendleton District Historical and Recreational Commission, located in the former Hunter's Store, an 1850 brick building across from the village green. A center for the region, it offers scads of brochures, cassette-tape tours, and exhibits of local art and crafts. The office is open weekdays only, so if you can't get to town on Friday, write ahead for the local walking-tour guide.

You'll learn that this portion of South Carolina belonged to the Cherokee Indians until they chose the wrong side in the American Revolution. The South Carolina militia marched in and wreaked such havoc in Cherokee country that the Indians sued for peace and gave their land to the state. After the war, settlers were attracted by the fertile land, and in 1789, Pendleton County was established, named for a Revolutionary War hero. The next year the town was formed as the county seat. Later the growing district was divided into three counties.

Early farming settlers were soon joined by wealthy, well-educated Lowcountry families who built summer homes in the cooler Upcountry. Two of the finer homes are now house museums. Woodburn, circa 1830, was built by prominent South Carolinian Charles Cotsworth Pinckney. Ashtabula, an 1820s home, was occupied by five respected families over the years.

Farmers Hall, the town's centerpiece, went up on the site of the old courthouse after the district was divided. It was in the second-floor meeting hall that Thomas Green Clemson first advocated the need for a state agricultural college, today's Clemson University. Members of the hall also included Clemson's father-in-law, John C. Calhoun, vice-president of the United States.

The ground floor of the hall is now a popular restaurant serving Southern dishes and legendary sour-cream drop biscuits.

The rest of the town tour takes in the 1819 St. Paul's Episcopal Church and many homes dating from the first half of the nineteenth century, all still privately owned and occupied. Mi Casa, at 430 South Mechanic Street, was the home of Mrs. John C. Calhoun after her husband's death.

Take time for a leisurely stroll on the blocks around the green, looking into the small antique, gift, and craft shops along the way.

It's definitely worth the drive of about a mile into the country to find the Central Road workshop and showroom of talented potter Rob Gentry. Phone 646–9622 for driving directions.

The Duke Street Gallery, at 109 Duke Street, off Mechanic Street about a mile north of the square, is another highly recommended shop. The gallery represents 60 contemporary artists, including jewelers, woodworkers, and toymakers.

It is just a five-minute drive from Pendleton to the campus of

Clemson, an unusually interesting campus because of the history associated with the site. The South Carolina Botanical Garden, part of the campus, is also a good reason for the trip.

Start at the University Visitors Center in Tillman Hall, easily recognized by its clock tower. Here you can join a guided tour or pick up information for your own tour.

Clemson is located on land that was once the plantation of John C. Calhoun, South Carolina's most eminent early statesman, who spent the last 25 years of his life here.

His son-in-law, Thomas Clemson, inherited the Fort Hill house and land after his wife's death. He had long been interested in agriculture, and, in 1888, he bequeathed the 814-acre plantation and a considerable sum of money to establish a scientific and agricultural college.

Clemson College opened formally in 1893 with 4,465 students. It was an all-male military school until 1955, when women were admitted and the focus of the school changed. In 1964 it became a university in recognition of the expanded academic offerings and research pursuits. It would no doubt please Clemson to know that the agricultural, engineering, and architectural schools are highly respected. He might share the pride of the avid fans who root for the Clemson Tigers football team, known for their orange "paw" symbol, which is generously painted around the campus.

The house at Fort Hill was built during the late Federal and early Greek Revival periods, and is characteristic of Upcountry South Carolina plantation design. On the grounds are a reconstructed kitchen near the west wing, Calhoun's office, and a restored springhouse on the north lawn. Most of the furnishings are original Calhoun and Clemson family pieces.

Another historic home open for tours is Hanover House, built in 1716 in the Lowcountry. It was moved and reconstructed here by the School of Architecture in the 1940s as a house museum, interpreting the lifestyle of South Carolina's rice, indigo, and cotton planters.

The South Carolina Botanical Garden got its start in the late 1950s, when a small portion of the Fort Hill estate was set aside to preserve a nineteenth-century camellia collection. It has grown to 256 acres, rich with camellias, native wildflowers, and daffodils, and an arboretum with over 1,000 species of trees. Miles of trails wind through the native woodlands and gardens.

Depending on your time and interests, there are many other worthwhile sights on campus. The Thurmond Institute Building includes the Graem Yates Collection of Presidential Portraits and special exhibits from the University Library's extensive rare-book collection. Changing art exhibits can be seen at the Rudolph E. Lee Gallery, and the Livestock Arena is a showplace for horse and livestock shows.

No one should miss a visit to the Agricultural Produce Sales Center in Newman Hall for their famous rich ice cream. Also for sale are milk, eggs, meat, and delicious Clemson blue cheese.

The 1840 Liberty Hall Inn in Pendleton is the only inn in the area, and it is a beauty, a comfortable, antique-filled home with a wide-railed, two-tiered porch, complete with rockers. The dining room serves some of the best meals in town.

If there's no room at the inn, consider a motel in Clemson or lodgings in one of the state parks within a half hour's drive. The Schell Haus, opposite the entrance to Table Rock State Park, is another wonderful choice, beautifully furnished and with grand views from the porch.

Come Sunday, get ready for the best of South Carolina's Upcountry. Follow U.S. 76 west and turn north on S.C. route 11, the Cherokee Foothills Scenic Highway, which stretches for nearly 130 miles. Along the way are scenic lookouts and access to many magnificent state parks. The road is flanked by orchards, and in summer, many stands offer fresh-picked peaches from local farms.

One of the newest parks, Devils Fork on Lake Jocassee, opened in 1991 in cooperation with the Duke Power Company. Located three miles from the main road on U.S. 25, it is a favorite spot for fishing, boating, and swimming. The 20 cabins overlooking the lake would do credit to a luxury resort. Understandably, they go fast, so plan ahead if you want to try one.

Table Rock State Park is the most striking of the parks, with deep forest set against the massive formation that inspired the name, a slice of granite 3,157 feet high. At the bottom of the mountain is the Table Rock Reservoir, a picturesque lake that provides water for Greenville County. The park offers swimming, rental canoes and boats, carpet golf, and a nature center. The rustic log buildings here, Civilian Conservation Corps projects from the 1930s, include a restaurant that serves up sensational views with lunch and dinner. The cabins are far more basic than those at Devils Fork, but they offer the necessary comforts and supreme privacy.

This park, whose entrance is right on S.C. route 11, affords the best hiking in the region, from easy nature trails to treks to the top of Table Rock and nearby Pinnacle Mountain. The rugged and beautiful Foothills Trail across the ridge of the mountains also passes through the park.

For dramatic views, however, the prize goes to Caesars Head State Park. Take the turnoff north on U.S. 276 and wind your way to the top escarpment, 3,266 feet high, for a truly spectacular panorama, taking in Table Rock and Pinnacle mountains and many more-distant peaks of the Blue Ridge chain.

You can enjoy this view at the overlook without any effort, but only those energetic enough to tackle a two-mile trail will get to see Raven Cliff Falls, one of the highest waterfalls in the Eastern states.

Those who want to tackle the Chattooga, one of the Park Service's system of Wild and Scenic Rivers, will find outfitters happy to oblige.

If the unthinkable happens and it rains, all is not lost. Just take a drive east to Greenville, where there are several art galleries and an attractive small museum in the heart of the nicely refurbished downtown. It's worth the drive just to see the Yagoto Nippon Center, built in the traditional architectural style of early Japan and containing a rock garden that is a replica of a famous garden in Kyoto. The center, which includes an exquisite (albeit expensive) Japanese restaurant, was built by a Japanese businessman as thanks to the community. It hosts classes with Furman University, offering language, cooking, ikebana flower arrangement, and the study of Japanese lifestyle and business practices. Totally unexpected in the hills of South Carolina, the center is one more welcome Upcountry surprise.

Area Code: 803

DRIVING DIRECTIONS   Pendleton is reached via U.S. 76 off I–85. It is about 120 miles from Atlanta, 118 miles from Charlotte. Clemson is four miles farther north via U.S. 76 or S.C. Route 187.

ACCOMMODATIONS   *Liberty Hall Inn,* 621 South Mechanic Street, one-half mile south of the green, Pendleton 29670, 646–7500, I, CP ● *Comfort Inn,* 1305 Tiger Boulevard, Clemson 29631, 653–3600, motel, M ● *Schell Haus,* Highway 11, Pickens 29671, 878–0078, delightful inn, convenient to state parks, M, CP ● *Devils Fork State Park,* 161 Holcombe Circle, Salem 29676, 944–2639, luxury cabins, M-E ● *Table Rock State Park,* 246 Table Rock State Park Road, Pickens 26971, 878–9813, rustic cabins, I.

DINING   *Farmers Hall Restaurant,* on the green, Pendleton, 646–7014, lunch Tuesday to Saturday, I; dinner Friday and Saturday, M ● *Liberty Hall Inn* (see above), M ● *Pendleton House,* 203 East Main Street, Pendleton, 646–7795, warm home setting, M ● *The Lazy Islander,* across from the green, Pendleton, 646–7672, Caribbean, raw bar and grill, I-M ● *Bravo's On-the-Square,* across from the green, Pendleton, 646–8687, Italian, wood-fired pizza, I ● *The Dutch Oven,* 1 Mechanic Street, bountiful Mennonite buffets, lunch only, I ● *Just Barbecue,* 1410 Cherry Street, Pendleton, 646–3674, live country-western and bluegrass music, I ● *Calhoun Corners,* 103 Clemson Street, Clemson, 654–7490, campus favorite, I-E ● *Table Rock State Park Restaurant,* East Gate, Table Rock State Park, dinner year-round, Sunday lunch buffet, I; lunches served May through October, I ● *Aunt Sue's,* Highway 11, 2 miles east of Table Rock State Park, 878–4366,

April through November, rustic decor, views, part of a small shopping complex, I ● *Yagoto Nippon Center,* 500 Congaree Road, Greenville, 288–8471, traditional Japanese cuisine, extraordinary setting, E-EE.

SIGHTSEEING *Ashtabula Plantation,* S.C. Route 88 East, Pendleton, 646–3847. Hours: April to October, Sunday 2 P.M. to 6 P.M., $$ ● *Woodburn Plantation,* U.S. 76 west of town, Pendleton, 646–3655. Hours: April to October, Sunday 2 P.M. to 6 P.M., $$ ● *Pendleton Playhouse,* 402 South Mechanic Street, Pendleton, 654–1131. Check for current productions ● *Clemson University,* Visitors Center, 103 Tillman Hall, 656–4789. Hours: Monday to Friday 8 A.M. to 5 P.M. year-round; also March to November, Saturday 10 A.M. to 4 P.M., Sunday 2 P.M. to 5 P.M.; guided tours Monday through Saturday 10 A.M. and 2 P.M., Sunday at 2 P.M. when classes are in session; at other times, Monday through Friday 2 P.M. Campus sights include *Fort Hill,* 656–2475. Hours: Monday to Saturday 10 A.M. to 5 P.M., Sunday 2 P.M. to 5 P.M., donation; *Hanover House,* 656–2241. Hours: Saturday 10 A.M. to 5 P.M., Sunday 2 P.M. to 5 P.M., donation; *Graem Yates Collection of Presidential Portraits and Special Library Collections,* Strom Thurmond Institute Building, 656–4700. Hours: Monday to Friday 8 A.M. to 4:30 P.M., free; *Rudolph E. Lee Gallery,* Lee Hall (College of Architecture), 656–3081. Hours: Monday to Friday 9 A.M. to 4:30 P.M., Sunday 2 P.M. to 5 P.M., free.; *Clemson University Botanical Garden,* 656–4964. Hours: daily 8 A.M. to dusk, free; *Agricultural Sales Center,* Hours: Monday to Saturday 9 A.M. to 9 P.M., Sunday 1 P.M. to 9 P.M. ● *Devils Fork State Park,* 161 Holcombe Circle, Salem, 944–2639. Hours: Park open daylight hours; office Monday to Friday 9 A.M. to 5 P.M.; Saturday and Sunday 11 A.M. to noon, 4 P.M. to 5 P.M.; parking fee in season, $ ● *Table Rock State Park,* 246 Table Rock State Park Road, Pickens 26971, 878–9813. Hours: park open daylight hours; office hours Monday to Friday 9 A.M. to 5 P.M.; weekends 11 A.M. to noon, 4 P.M. to 5 P.M.; parking fee in season, $ ● *Caesars Head State Park,* 8155 Geer Highway, Cleveland, 836–6115. Hours: daily 9 A.M. to 5 P.M., parking fee in season, $ ● *Whitewater rafting on the Chatooga River: Nantahala Outdoor Center,* 800–232–7238; *Wildwater, Ltd.,* 800–451–9972.

INFORMATION *Pendleton District Historical and Recreational Commission,* 125 East Queen Street, P.O. Box 565, Pendleton, SC 29670, 646–3782.

Blazing Trails Near Cherokee

There's something mystical about the Smoky Mountains. The long, dusky ridges that the Cherokee people called "Place of Blue Smoke" are among the world's oldest mountains, rounded and softened by the ages, and bathed in a perpetual hazy mist that clings to the peaks and fills the valleys.

The tiers roll out into the distance like waves cresting in a lofty ocean, shifting in mood and color with every change in the light. They are equally beautiful outlined by the golden sun or shrouded in wispy fog. No matter how many times you see these mountains, they never look exactly the same.

This is part of the fascination that has made Great Smoky Mountains National Park the most visited of all U.S. national parks, enjoyed by nearly 9 million people each year, twice the number recorded at any other park.

Though it gets crowded in summer, this is the best season for families, with many special activities that children enjoy, including the Junior Ranger program geared to ages five to 12.

The North Carolina entrance to the park, at Cherokee, adds another dimension to a visit—the chance to learn about the Cherokee Indians, who were the first to live on this land.

It must be said, however, that the modern town of Cherokee has little appeal. It has become overrun with tacky shops selling bogus Indian crafts that have nothing to do with the Cherokees. See the important sights and get out fast.

Far better places to stay are in Maggie Valley, 15 miles to the east, which has its share of touristy attractions but is still a great improvement over Cherokee, or in quieter Bryson City, 10 miles to the west.

The Swag, a superb rustic inn outside of Maggie Valley, is as close as you'll get to a private mountain, set all by itself on a mile-high mountaintop. Guests at Cattaloochee Ranch are also 5,000 feet up, with peerless views and the chance to see the scenery on horseback.

Wherever you stay, spend an evening in Maggie Valley at the Stompin' Ground, where the real flavor of mountain living is provided by the enthusiastic locals who come to clog up a storm every night. The Maggie Valley Opry House is the place to hear bluegrass music.

When you are ready for Great Smoky Mountains National Park, head for the Oconaluftee Visitor Center at the Cherokee entrance. Here you can pick up a map and a copy of the *Smokies Guide,* the official park newspaper, which lists all current ranger-guided activities. It will help you plan your day. Among the choices are guided nature walks and hikes to see waterfalls and other scenic areas, storytelling, and talks about many phases of the park as well as about Cherokee history and culture. Nights bring campfires, slide shows, mountain music, and early-evening nature walks.

Though it includes the highest mountain range in the East and protects the last remnant of the southern Appalachian forest, establishing this 550,000-acre sanctuary was a struggle. The terrain was occupied by hundreds of small farmers and a handful of large timber companies, none of whom were anxious to leave. Congress signed a bill establishing a park in 1926, but since the government was not allowed to buy land for national park use, private money was needed. The states of Tennessee and North Carolina, early competitors to host the park, settled on a location straddling both states, and each contributed $2 million to get things rolling. Private groups and individuals, including many schoolchildren, helped raise another $5 million, and that sum was matched by the Laura Spellman Rockefeller Memorial Fund. Those living on the land were allowed to stay under lifetime leases. Franklin Roosevelt finally dedicated the park in 1934.

Seeing the sights by car is easy but slow, since there is only one main roadway through the park. Newfound Gap Road, running 35 miles from Cherokee to the Tennessee border, provides lookouts with fabulous views all along the way. About midway along the road is the turnoff for the most dramatic vista of all, from Clingmans Dome, where you are atop a ridge 6,642 feet high. Pick a clear day for this visit, since the Dome is often enveloped in fog.

To fully appreciate the beauty of the forests, mountains, and streams around you, get out and walk. Though there's plenty of challenge for hardy hikers, you don't have to go far to share the scenery. Watch along the main road, and you'll see signs marking "Quiet Walkways." These are short walks planned as samplers.

There are several easy, self-guiding nature trails as well, under a mile round trip. The Cove Hardwood Trail, just inside the entrance to the Chimney Tops Picnic Area off Newfound Gap Road, leads to the big trees of a splendid old-growth forest.

In summer, the high-altitude trails off Clingmans Dome Road are rich in wildflowers. One of the best routes is along the Appalachian Trail, where half an hour's stroll in either direction will show you some of the splendid display. Pamphlets with maps, available at the visitor center, detail walks and hikes and pinpoint waterfalls throughout the park.

Horseback riding is another wonderful way to appreciate the scenery. There are five stables located in the park.

On the trails you may catch a glimpse of some of the diverse plant and animal life in these forests.

If you become intrigued with the flora and fauna and want to know more, check the programs at the nonprofit Great Smoky Mountains Institute at Tremont, where there are weekend and three-day field courses in viewing wildlife, forests, and streams and special plants such as mushrooms or ferns. The Institute also offers backpacking trips, photo workshops, and family camp programs, all of which include tuition, meals, and lodging at minimal fees.

Some sections of the park will take you back in time to see how early settlers lived. Oconaluftee Pioneer Homestead, adjacent to the visitor center near Cherokee, offers short talks and tours on weekends at 2:30 and 3:30 P.M., focusing on the early days. Often there are living-history demonstrations of old-time skills, and just down the road, at Mingus Mill, you can see corn being ground by a water-powered gristmill.

More perspective on pioneer days can be found at the Cades Cove section of the park in Tennessee, about a 55-mile drive from Cherokee. Traditional chores are demonstrated, such as spinning, weaving, blacksmithing, and turning sorghum into molasses, and there are many special events, such as quilt shows. Read more about Cades Cove on pages 138–43.

Be sure to save an afternoon for Cherokee, going past the tacky main street to find the authentic and very worthwhile attractions. A good start is the Museum of the Cherokee Indian, where you'll learn about this once proud and powerful nation. The tribes were forced to abandon their ancestral homeland for the long trek to Oklahoma in 1838, along what has become known as the Trail of Tears. But one band hid in the North Carolina hills, refusing to obey the government edict. They lived as fugitives for many years, but in 1889, by then 1,000 strong, they were given official permission to establish the Qualla Indian Reservation just south of what is now the southern entrance to the national park. Some 4,500 descendants occupy the reservation today.

The Oconaluftee Indian Village is a living-history lesson for children and grownups alike. Cherokees in period dress demonstrate skills passed down through the generations, such as finger weaving, pottery, and basketmaking, and traditional male occupations such as flint chipping, dugout canoe carving, and blowgun hunting.

The log cabins are typical of what homes here might have been like in the eighteenth century. One of the highlights of the village is the re-created seven-sided council house, where you learn about the culture and rituals that have been handed down over the generations.

Another recommended stop in town is the Qualla Arts and Crafts Mutual, an Indian-owned and -operated cooperative primarily responsible for keeping the arts and crafts of the Eastern Band of the Cherokees alive. The offerings, from 300 artisans, range from black pottery to patterned baskets, and from woodcarvings to stone sculptures.

You may want to remain into the evening to learn the story of the Cherokee struggle for survival, movingly told in the musical drama *Unto These Hills.* It is performed in an outdoor amphitheater from mid-June to August.

One last outing that should not be missed is a drive on the Blue Ridge Parkway, which snakes its way heaven-high across the crest of the southern Appalachians for 470 miles, from the Great Smoky Mountains National Park entrance at Cherokee to the Shenandoah National Park in Virginia.

An engineering marvel that took 50 years to complete, the parkway provides an eagle's-eye view of the ridges away from the crowds found within the park. Driving its winding course is a delight. There's not one commercial sign in sight, only lush greenery and wildflowers. The speed limit is a relaxing 35 miles per hour, and lots of overlooks are perfectly placed to allow you to pull off and gaze at the mountains or take a woodland walk whenever the spirit moves you.

From Cherokee, the parkway leads east to the Balsam Mountain area of the park, and then crosses U.S. 19 at Soco Gap for the turnoff to Maggie Valley. But stay on for a while and you'll come to Waterrock Knob and a fabulous panorama of the Smokies from 5,718 feet.

When you've had enough driving, loop back to your home base, knowing you've just experienced one of the most remarkable roads in the world.

Museum Area Code: 704

DRIVING DIRECTIONS   Cherokee, the North Carolina entrance to Great Smoky Mountains National Park, is located at the intersection of U.S. 19 and U.S. 441. From Atlanta, take I–85 north to the junction with U.S. 441 north, 181 miles. From the east, take I–40 to the U.S. 19 exit, near Waynesville. The park can also be reached via the Blue Ridge Parkway. Cherokee is 162 miles from Charlotte, 50 miles from Asheville.

ACCOMMODATIONS   *Cataloochee Ranch,* Fie Top Road, Route 1, P.O. Box 500F, Maggie Valley 28751, 926–1401 or 800–868–1401, comfortable ranch in a grand setting, tennis, pool, riding, EE, MAP ● *The Swag,* Route 2, Box 280A, Waynesville (5 miles from Maggie Valley) 28786, 926–0430, superb rustic inn, beautiful country decor, heavenly mountaintop location, late May through October, EE, AP ● *Smokey Shadows Lodge,* off Fie Top Road, Maggie Valley 28751, 926–0001, rustic, informal log lodge, 4,500 feet high, I, CP ● *Abbey Inn,* 1739 Soco Road, Highway 19, Maggie Valley 28751, 926–1188 or 800–545–5853, motel with a view, some kitchenettes, good bet for families, I ● *Hemlock Inn,* off U.S. 19, Bryson City 28713, 488–3885, log lodge, cottages on very attractive hilltop grounds with views, open April to December, E, MAP ● *Maggie Valley Resort and Country*

Club, Highways 276 and 19, Maggie Valley 28751, 926–1616 or 800–438–3861, deluxe resort with golf, tennis, pool, EE, MAP • *Fryemont Inn,* Fryemont Road, P.O. Box 459, Bryson City 28713, 488–2159, rustic inn on the National Register of Historic Places, chestnut-paneled rooms, views, M, MAP • *Randolph House,* Fryemont Road, P.O. Box 816, Bryson City 28713, 488–3472, 1895 mansion, also on National Register, April to October, E, MAP • *Folkestone Inn,* 767 West Deep Creek Road, Bryson City 28713, 488–2730, chalet-style bed-and-breakfast inn, walking distance to Deep Creek Campground entrance of the park and many hiking trails, I-M, CP.

DINING *Maggie Valley Resort and Country Club* (see above), Maggie Valley's best, window walls for views, M-E • *J. Arthur's,* 801 Saco Road, Maggie Valley, 926–1817, rambling loft dining room, good for families, known for gorgonzola cheese salad, I-M • *Smokey Shadows Lodge* (see above), by reservation only, full dinner, M • *The Swag* (see above), by reservation only, full dinner, EE.

SIGHTSEEING *Great Smoky Mountains National Park,* 107 Park Headquarters Road, Gatlinburg, TN 37738 615–436–1200 • *Oconaluftee Visitor Center,* 150 U.S. 441 North, Cherokee, NC, 497–9246. Hours: daily 8 A.M. to 7 P.M. in summer; earlier closing rest of year; free • *Park Horseback Riding: Smokemont Riding Stable,* near Smokemont Campground, 497–2373; *McCarter's Riding Stable,* near Tennessee park headquarters on Newfound Gap Road, 615–436–5354. For other Tennessee stables, ask at nearest park visitor center • *Oconaluftee Indian Village,* U.S. 441 North, Cherokee, 497–2315. Hours: mid-May to late October, daily 9 A.M. to 5:30 P.M. Guided tours, $$$ • *Unto These Hills,* Mountainside Theater, U.S. 441 North, Cherokee, 497–2111. Hours: mid-June to late August, daily 8:30 P.M., $$$ • *Museum of the Cherokee Indian,* U.S. 441 North, Cherokee, 497–3481. Hours: mid-June through August, Monday to Saturday 9 A.M. to 8 P.M.; Sunday 9 A.M. to 5 P.M.; rest of year, daily 9 A.M. to 5 P.M., $$.

INFORMATION *Maggie Valley Chamber of Commerce,* P.O. Box 87, Maggie Valley, NC 28751, 926–1686 or 800–334–9036 • *Cherokee Visitor Center,* P.O. Box 460, Cherokee, NC 28719, 497–9195 or 800–334–9036.

Beach Bounty in Alabama

Are there beaches in Alabama? You betcha. Just west of Florida's better-known Gulf Coast is a 32-mile strand with the kind of soft sand and balmy breezes beach lovers dream about. The scene comes complete with sandpipers, starfish, and sea shells. Because the sand is 99 percent quartz crystal, it is as fine as powder and a shade of white that positively dazzles in the sunlight.

Though more people every year are discovering L.A. (that's "lower Alabama"), it remains less well known than its Florida counterpart, and is, therefore, less crowded and lower-key. Pick the kind of beach retreat you prefer, from low-rise motel to comfortable condo, resort hotel to lodge or cabin in a state park. Families will find their fill of amusements to keep the kids happy, but couples who prefer peace and solitude can find that as well. And there's interesting territory to explore not far away, on the eastern shore of Mobile Bay and at historic Fort Morgan to the west.

It isn't surprising that the coast was something of a secret until recently. In 1933, when a canal was cut through to create a section of the Intracoastal Waterway, the beach area actually became an island. The only way to get there was via barge, ferry, or, eventually, a swing-span bridge. It was not until 1972 that a bridge over the waterway linked the beaches to the rest of the state and families began coming in earnest, building modest vacation cottages on pilings. A bridge also made the connection eastward to Florida.

Then, just as things were looking up, ferocious hurricane Frederic blew into town in 1979 and the beach was swept clean. The dunes were flattened, as were most of the buildings. The ironic silver lining to the devastation was that Gulf Shores was suddenly in the news, and the word was out that Alabama had a coastline. Investors soon arrived, new building began, and the area has prospered ever since, drawing both vacationers and retirees.

Most people these days arrive via Alabama route 59 from the north, driving past shopping centers and eating places to reach the western end of the community of Gulf Shores, where it intersects with Alabama route 182, the road paralleling the beaches.

A left turn on 182 leads past rows of motels, Gulf State Park, Romar Beach, and finally to the second major shoreline community, Orange Beach, the boating center of the coast because of its access to the Gulf of Mexico. Marinas such as Perdido Pass and Orange Beach offer boat charters, fishing expeditions, and rentals of pontoon boats, jet skis, or sailboats.

One unique outing is on the 50-foot sailboat *Daedalus,* which goes out shrimping, often with an escort of dolphins. Nets are cast while you

sail, and as the catch is sorted out, the sweet, fresh shrimp
to be enjoyed on the spot.

Fishermen enjoy a choice of legendary Gulf catch
bluefish, speckled trout, and Spanish mackerel, or fresh
on 395,000 acres of lakes, back bays, and inlets. Marina docks
bait-and-tackle shops are the best sources of information on what's
biting where.

Most people stay in motels or resorts right on the beach, but for
those who do not, there is a public beach six miles west of Alabama
route 59, and parking and swimming are free at the Perdido Point
Beach in Orange Beach.

Gulf State Park Resort also has two and a half miles of superb open
beach. This state-owned 6,000-acre playground is a popular convention site and family resort, with tennis courts, an 18-hole golf
course, a marina, and nature and biking trails. The park is booked
solid in season, so make plans well ahead of time if you want to stay
here.

The park has carefully preserved its marshes and wetlands, but
there's even more flora and fauna to be seen at the Bon Secour Wildlife
Refuge, west of Gulf Shores. Here are nearly four miles of undeveloped
beach and 4,000 acres of dunes, wetlands, and pine-oak forests. It is a
protected area for indigenous plants and animals, especially endangered
species such as loggerhead turtles and American alligators. This is also
a bird-watching paradise. More than 120 species of birds have been
spotted during spring and fall migrations.

Families looking for splashier diversions might head for Waterville,
USA, which has lots of exciting water slides and a 500,000-gallon
wave pool that generates three-foot waves. The complex also includes
miniature golf, go-carts, and other summer recreational favorites.

Zooland Animal Park should also please the kids. The nicely planted
16-acre park is home to more than 200 exotic animals, from alligators
to zebras.

In Orange Beach, the Main Street amusement mall for kids has a
host of diversions, including a billiard parlor, a skating rink, video
games, kiddie rides, a teen dance club, mini-speedboats, go-carts, and
a skateboard run.

Interesting sightseeing can be found in several directions. At the
western tip of the coast, on Alabama route 180, running parallel to
route 182, is Fort Morgan, the star-shaped massive brick 1817 fortress
that guarded the entrance to Mobile Bay.

It was here in 1864 that Union Admiral David Farragut, annoyed at
his fleet's lack of progress against Confederate forces guarding the
harbor, was said to have uttered the legendary words, "Damn the
torpedoes. Full speed ahead." More than 3,000 cannonballs were fired
in a 19-day siege before the fort finally fell, and the last major
Confederate Gulf defense was lost in one of the key naval battles of the

Civil War. A reenactment of the battle takes place every year on the fourth weekend in October.

Visitors are free to climb the steps into the fortress, where cannons still stand at the ready, and to wander through its many arches. The nearby Mobile Bay Light, built in 1885, is one of only three remaining lighthouses along the Alabama coast. The Mobile Bay Ferry leaves from near Fort Morgan on á 30-minute trip to the Civil War–era Fort Gaines on Dauphin Island, with a nice view of the Gulf en route.

For those who prefer bargains to battles, heading north on Alabama route 59 toward Foley brings you to a shopper's mecca, the Riviera Centre, with some 70 outlet stores. Foley itself will interest antiquers. There are three malls with well over 100 dealers, including the Gas Works, where 70 of those dealers can be found in an art deco building.

Turn west on U.S. 98 before you get to Foley to explore the many pleasures of the eastern shore of Mobile Bay.

The most famous stop is Point Clear and the Grand Hotel, which has stood on its superb secluded site surrounded by water since 1847. You could easily spend a weekend or more enjoying the facilities of this top-class resort, but for now consider it a choice spot for lunch, and plan your schedule accordingly.

The first 40-room hotel, known as the Point Clear, was a glittering gathering place for antebellum Southern society. It was christened the Grand after being rebuilt in 1875 following a fire. The heart-of-pine flooring and the frame of the original Grand were used when the hotel was rebuilt again in 1941.

Taken over by Marriott in 1981, the main building retains its architecture and charm—the weathered wood and faded brick, the octagonal, wood-paneled lobby, and the brick fireplace that soars three stories high. Swimming, boating, riding, tennis, golf—name it and you'll find it here—but nothing tops a simple stroll to Julep Point to gaze out at the water, water everywhere. At night, when there's dancing on this terrace under the stars, it's pure magic.

About a mile below the Grand Hotel is a place guaranteed to please your sweet tooth. Punta Clara Kitchen is a family-owned business in an 1897 house, a mini-museum of Victoriana where you can watch fudge, pralines, and chocolates being made by hand.

The next stop to the north is the attractive little town of Fairhope, an art colony set on a bluff above the bay. The Eastern Shore Art Center, one of the state's best, exhibits works in all media in its attractive galleries, and holds an outdoor art show during the town's big arts-and-crafts fair the third weekend in March each year. More than 200 artists participate in this major event, which celebrated its fortieth birthday in 1992.

Interesting art and crafts can be found year-round in the 80 or so shops within about four blocks on flower-festooned Fairhope Avenue.

Seafood lovers should hurry to Fairhope during Jubilee, which

marks a late-summer phenomenon in which a su~
the seawater drives such bottom-dwelling cre~
and shrimp toward the shore. When the wor~
coming in, everyone for miles around arriv~
hand.

Fairhope has several small bed-and-breakfasts, a~
mark for a return visit, when you can continue explor~
surprises such as the lavish Byzantine-style Greek Orthoo~
the Greek community of Malbis, or the American Sport Art ~
on the campus of the U.S. Sports Academy in Daphne, a gra~
school offering master's degrees in sports science for coaches, fitnes~
experts, and others involved in athletics.

With so much to recommend it, who knows? Lower Alabama may
one day be as famous as the L.A. on that other coast.

Area Code: 334

DRIVING DIRECTIONS   Routes I–10 from east or west and I–65
from the north connect with Ala. Route 59 south, which ends in Ala.
route 182, the beach road in Gulf Shores. From Atlanta, take I–85 west
to I–65 south, 353 miles. From Birmingham, follow I–65 south, 274
miles.

PUBLIC TRANSPORTATION   Gulf Shores is located 34 miles
west of Pensacola, Florida, and 48 miles east of Mobile. Car rentals are
available at both airports.

ACCOMMODATIONS   (Rates given are for summer; all are lower
off-season.) *Perdido Beach Hilton,* 2720 Perdido Beach Boulevard,
Orange Beach 36561, 981–9811, the class of the coast, private beach,
first-class facilities, and fine dining, many weekend packages, E-EE •
Gulf Shores Plantation Resort, Route 180, P.O. Box 1299, Gulf Shores
36547, 540–2291 or 800–554–0344, condo resort with beach, boats,
outdoor and indoor pools, tennis, fitness center, M-EE • *Gulf State
Park Resort Hotel,* Gulf State Park, Route 182, Gulf Shores 36547,
948-GULF or 800–544-GULF, state-operated lodge on beach, resort
facilities, M • *Holiday Inn,* Route 182, P.O. Box 417, Gulf Shores
36547, 948–6191, best of the oceanfront motels, lighted tennis, pool,
M-E • *Quality Inn Beachside,* Highway 182 West, P.O. Box 1013,
Gulf Shores 36547, 948–6874 or 800–844–6913, indoor pool, E • *Best
Western on the Beach,* Route 182, P.O. Box 481, Gulf Shores 36542,
948–2711 or 800–788–4557, M-E • *Romar House,* 23500 Perdido
Beach Boulevard, Orange Beach 36561, 981–6156 or 800–48-

MAR, art deco–style bed-and-breakfast inn, no children under 12, E, CP • *Marriot's Grand Hotel,* Point Clear 36564, 990–6300 or 00–544–9933, lavish resort, E-EE • *Fairhope Bed & Breakfast Inns: Away at the Bay,* 557 North Mobile Street, Fairhope 36532, 928–9725, I, CP; *Doc and Dawn's,* 3245 De Le Mare, Fairhope 36532, 928–0253, a private cottage in a garden, M, CP; *Marcella's,* 114 Fairhope Avenue, Fairhope 36532, 928–9212, I, CP; *Mershon Court,* 203 Fairhope Avenue, Fairhope 36532, 928–7398, swimming pool, I, CP.

DINING *Voyagers,* Perdido Beach Hilton (see above), Continental, best in the area, E • *Perdido Pass,* 27501 Perdido Beach Boulevard, Orange Beach, 981–6312, on the water, seafood, mesquite grill, M • *Zeke's Landing,* 16619 Perdido Beach Boulevard, Orange Beach, 981–4001, on the harbor, seafood, Sunday jazz brunch, I-E • *Hemingway's Dockside,* Orange Beach Marina, 981–9791, Cajun, marina views, I-M • *Original Oyster House,* Alabama 59 at Bayou Village, 948–2445, the name says it, I-M • *Sea N Suds,* Young's by the Sea Motel, East Beach Boulevard, Gulf Shores, 968–7893, restaurant and oyster bar on the pier, I • *Coconut Willies,* Routes 59 and 180, Gulf Shores, 948–7145, local seafood, great gumbo, I-M • *Mikee's Seafood,* 1st Street East at 2nd Avenue East, 948–6452, I-M • *Kirkland's Hitching Post,* Route 59, 968–5041, western ambience, barbecue, steaks, seafood, I-M • *Crabby Pete's,* Fort Morgan Road and Route 59, Gulf Shores, 968–4811, live crabs, local seafood, I-M • *Pink Pony Pub,* Highway 59, Gulf Shores, 948–6371, burgers and beer, liveliest local gathering spot, casual, I-M • *Hazel's Nook,* corner of Ala. routes 59 and 180, 968–7065, breakfast standout, don't miss the biscuits and gravy, I • *Yardarm Restaurant,* on the pier, Fairhope, 928–8322, informal, I • *Old Bay Steamer,* Fairhope Avenue, Fairhope, 928–5714, steamed and grilled seafood, fun atmosphere, I-E • *Marriott's Grand Hotel* (see above), choices include Grand Dining Room, formal, Continental menu, E; *Magnolia Room,* more intimate room, bay views, seafood specialties and New Orleans cuisine, E.

SIGHTSEEING *Gulf State Park,* Ala. Route 182, Gulf Shores, 948–7275. Hours: 8 A.M. to sunset, parking, $ • *Bon Secour National Wildlife Refuge,* Route 280, Gulf Shores, 968–8623. Hours: daily, daylight hours, free • *Waterville, USA,* Ala. Route 59, Gulf Shores, 968–2106. Hours: Memorial Day to Labor Day, 10 A.M. to 8 P.M., $$$$ • *Zooland Animal Park,* Ala. route 59, Gulf Shores, 968–6731. Hours: Memorial Day to Labor Day, 9 A.M. to 7 P.M.; rest of year, hours vary, best to call; $$ • *Fort Morgan State Historical Park,* Ala. Route 180,

Gulf Shores, 540–7125. Hours: daily 9 A.M. to 5 P.M., $ ● *Eastern Shore Art Center*, 401 Oak Street, Fairhope, 928–2228. Hours: Tuesday to Saturday 10 A.M. to 4 P.M.; Sunday, 2 P.M. to 5 P.M.; free ● *American Sport Art Museum*, U.S. Sports Academy, Dahne, 626–3303. Hours: Monday to Friday 10 A.M. to 2 P.M., free ● *Fine Arts Museum of the South*, 4850 Museum Drive, Langan Park, 343–2667. Hours: Tuesday to Sunday 10 A.M. to 5 P.M., free.

SPORTS *Sailing cruises* (phone for current schedules, rates): *Island Sailing Center*, 26201 Perdido Beach Boulevard, Orange Beach, 981–9706; *Daedalus*, Pirate's Cove, Elberta, 986–7018; *Three's Company*, Bear Point Marina, 952–7630 ● *Golf: Gulf State Park*, 968–2366; *Gulf Shores Golf and Country Club*, 968–7366; *Lakeview Golf Club*, 943–8000; *Cotton Creek Golf Course*, Foley, 968–4622 ● *Horseback riding: Beach Rides*, Ala. route 180, near Fort Morgan, 800–824–2104; in state, 800–554–0344 ● *Balloon Rides:* Gulf View Balloon Company, 949–7440.

INFORMATION *Alabama Gulf Coast Convention & Visitors Bureau*, Ala. route 59, P.O. Drawer 457, Gulf Shores, AL 36547, 968–7511 ● *Fairhope Chamber of Commerce*, Fairhope Avenue, 928–6387.

Hidden Treasures Near Monteagle

Monteagle Mountain is part of the lofty Cumberland Plateau that runs across the width of Tennessee like a gentle wall, forming the scenic western boundary of the Tennessee Valley. The hills loom unexpectedly for motorists humming along I–24 between Nashville and Chattanooga, and then disappear. Many travelers speed right by, never suspecting the treasures awaiting atop the ridge.

For example, pass through the stone gates of the Monteagle Assembly, and you've stepped into a storybook Victorian world of quaint wooden cottages with wide porches, lush shrubbery and flowers. On the heavily wooded grounds are gazebos, narrow, winding walking paths, and wooden trestle bridges across scenic ravines.

Five miles to the south are the Gothic stone buildings of the University of the South—an architectural replica of England's Oxford

University—in the matching stone town of Sewanee. The 200-acre campus is a place for hiking as well as a picture-book setting for a fine summer music festival, and a writer's conference with public lectures by famous authors.

Outdoors lovers who want room to roam will find 12,000 acres of untouched mountain wilderness in the South Cumberland State Recreation Area. This scenic land is laced with majestic waterfalls tumbling over rocky cliffs, with deep gorges carved into the sandstone by mountain streams.

The Monteagle Assembly, founded in 1882, was modeled after the Chautauqua Institute in New York State, originators of the popular nineteenth-century notion of combining Sunday-school teacher training with a broader program of education, entertainment, and recreation. The 900-foot elevation of the plateau made it a perfect escape for families seeking a cool summer retreat.

Soon known as "the Chautauqua of the South," Monteagle's nondenominational program quickly caught on. A giant tent meeting grew into a permanent community. Picturesque bridges were built to span the natural gorges and ravines. Eventually there were 162 gingerbread cottages on the 96-acre grounds, in addition to dining rooms and indoor meeting facilities. The entire complex is on the National Register of Historic Places.

Over 100 years after its founding, the colony is still going strong, with members from 20 states. While today's eight-week program still has a strong religious component, it offers topics as varied as floral design, historic preservation, health, nature, photography, travel, books, and the arts. Sports, concerts, and guided hikes are also part of the agenda.

Monteagle used to be only for cottage owners and their friends, but that changed in recent years, when two inns opened in historic cottages. Guests are entitled to attend programs and to use the swimming pool and tennis courts. The inns are open year-round, offering access to the very private and very scenic grounds.

The Adams Edgeworth Inn, a quaint 1896 Victorian with a railed, wraparound porch, is a haven of charm, a combination of period antiques and artful sophistication. Walls are adorned with the owners' impressive collection of more than 100 paintings. Rooms have antique beds, some of them four-posters, with covers that range from fluffy comforters to hand-embroidered Pakistani cashmere blankets. Some have fireplaces.

North Gate Lodge is far more modest, but the former 1890s boardinghouse is pleasant and the rates are quite reasonable.

The University of the South, founded by the Episcopal Church in 1857, is one of the loveliest schools in the South. One of the special sights on the Gothic campus is the Du Pont Library, which houses a collection of rare books and manuscripts. Another is the All Saints'

Chapel, a campus landmark boasting an ivy-covered tower containing a 65-bell carillon, one of the largest sets of bells in the world. Carillon concerts are held most Sunday afternoons.

The chapel is often a setting for all-brass concerts during the Sewanee Summer Music Festival. The highly regarded festival is in its third decade of presenting classical orchestra and chamber concerts in Guerry Hall. Student ensembles also give concerts outdoors on Guerry Garth.

A more recent addition is the Sewanee Writers' Conference, funded by the estate of the late Tennessee Williams. This series of workshops in fiction, poetry, and playwriting brings outstanding speakers whose lectures are often open to the public. Recent participants were novelist William Styron and poet Richard Wilbur. The last week of the conference often coincides with the Music Festival concerts, a double helping of the arts.

The campus, covering 10,000 acres at an elevation of 2,000 feet, is a nature lover's delight, with mountain overlooks, hiking trails, waterfalls, and caves. The University View, at the end of Tennessee Avenue, is marked by a 40-foot marble cross. On a clear day it offers views as far as 80 miles along the Highland Rim. One of the favorite spots for watching sunsets is Morgan's Steep, a stone shelf on the edge of the Cumberland Plateau.

Two miles south of the campus is Sewanee Natural Bridge, a 25-foot sandstone arch overlooking Lost Cove. Keep driving south and you'll come to the Carter State Natural Area, a 140-acre tract that includes the Lost Cove Caves.

This is one of the nine sections of the South Cumberland State Recreation Area, which is scattered across 100 square miles of south-central Tennessee. Closer to Tracy City on U.S. 41 is Foster Falls Small Wild Area, featuring 60-foot falls with the largest volume of water of any cascade in the South. The grounds are open for swimming, hiking, and picnicking.

The Fiery Gizzard Hiking Trail winds around the cliffs to connect this area with the Grundy Forest State Natural Area, whose features include Sycamore Falls at the bottom of Fiery Gizzard Gorge, and the striking geological formations known as Chimney Rocks.

For hiking information and maps, stop at the Visitors Center on U.S. 41 between Monteagle and Tracy Springs. Drive into Tracy Springs to satisfy your sweet tooth at the Dutch Maid Bakery, Tennessee's oldest, run by the Baggenstoss family since 1902.

The inspiring surroundings of the region have attracted many craftspeople, whose work can be seen in their studios or in local shops. Watch for their signs along the highway. A major event each year is the Mountain Market, held on the first weekend in August at the Monteagle Elementary School. It features regional arts and crafts, plus exhibits from over 200 exhibitors from 15 other states.

Restaurants in the area are nothing fancy, but Jim Oliver's rustic Smoke House draws people from miles around for country ham and hickory-smoked bacon. Guests consume more than a million flaky biscuits each year.

There's a different taste awaiting next door at the Monteagle Winery, the largest in the state.

An even more potent lure can be found about half an hour's drive to the west in Lynchburg, the home of the man who is arguably the best-known Tennessean. Jasper Newton "Jack" Daniel founded the nation's oldest registered distillery in his hometown in 1866. It is now a historic landmark. Visitors are taken on a tour that includes the seven-story barrelhouse, where the aging whiskey is stored, and the charcoal-mellowing vats, where the whiskey is filtered for smoothness.

If you're going to Lynchburg, be sure to make reservations in advance for the bountiful midday, family-style dinner at Miss Mary Bobo's Boarding House, a town tradition since 1908. It's another Southern classic.

Area Code: 615

DRIVING DIRECTIONS   Monteagle is off I–24, exit 134. It is 170 miles from Atlanta, 90 miles from Nashville, 50 miles from Chattanooga, and 190 miles from Birmingham.

ACCOMMODATIONS   *Adams Edgeworth Inn,* Monteagle Assembly, Monteagle 37356, 924–2669, rooms, I-M, CP; suites, E-EE, CP ● *North Gate Lodge,* Monteagle Assembly, Monteagle 37356, 924–2799, I, CP ● *Jim Oliver's Smoke House Motor Lodge,* Routes 64 and 41A, Monteagle 37356, 924–2268 or 800–241–1740, motel and cabins, I-E ● *Country Inn,* Box 188, Monteagle 37356, 924–2221, motel, I ● *Clouds Rise Farm,* Rattlesnake Spring Road, Sewanee 37375, 598–0993, bed-and-breakfast near the campus, E-EE, CP.

DINING   *Jim Oliver's Smoke House Restaurant* (see above), known for smoked meats, homemade jams, country breakfasts, bountiful buffets, I ● *Lockhart's Family Restaurant,* 212 Main Street, Monteagle, 924–2233, informal, barbeque, ribs, I ● *4 Seasons,* Midway Road, Sewanee, 598–5544, catfish, chicken, and shrimp buffets, I ● For lunch or light meals near the Sewanee campus, all I: *Sundae's,* next to campus bookstore, sandwiches, light dinners, homemade ice cream; *City Cafe,* some Oriental dishes; *Shenanigan's,* sandwiches and pizza ● *Miss Bobo's Boarding House,* Main Street, Lynchburg, 759–7394, reservations required, I.

SIGHTSEEING *Monteagle Assembly,* P.O. Box 307, Monteagle 37356, 924–2286, eight weeks of programming each summer, mid-June to early August; write for information ● *University of the South,* Sewanee, 598–1000, free guided tours Monday to Friday 10 A.M. and 2 P.M.; from the Admissions Office ● *University of the South, Sewanee Summer Music Festival,* Sewanee Summer Music Center, University of the South, 735 University Avenue, Sewanee, 598–1225, concerts from late June to early August; check for current schedules ● *South Cumberland Recreation Area,* Route 1, Box 2196, Monteagle 37356, 924–2980 (for maps and information, go to the Visitor Center, U.S. 41 East, between Monteagle and Tracy City), free ● *Monteagle Mountain Market,* Monteagle Elementary School, first weekend in August, sponsored by Town of Monteagle, Monteagle school PTA, and Monteagle Assembly Woman's Association; check with the Town Hall or the Assembly for dates ● *Monteagle Wine Cellars,* off I–24, exit 134, 924–2120. Hours: Monday to Saturday 8 A.M. to dark; Sunday 12 noon to 5 P.M.; free ● *Jack Daniel Distillery,* Tenn. route 25, Lynchburg (from Monteagle, pick up U.S. 64 and follow off the mountain to Winchester, continuing to Tenn. route 50; take Tenn. route 50 to Tenn. route 55 into Lynchburg), 759–4221. Hours: daily 8 A.M. to 4 P.M., free.

INFORMATION *Town of Monteagle,* Town Hall, College Street, P.O. Box 127, Monteagle, TN 37356, 924–2265.

Making the Rounds in Alabama

They've been making tracks in eastern Alabama for a long time. First it was the Creek Indians, then General Andrew Jackson coming through in the early 1800s. Tracks of early settlers were made in the photogenic covered bridges of this wooded region, where you'll also find some of the loveliest wilderness hiking and scenic driving in the state.

Nowadays, things are speeding up. Talladega, site of one of the old covered bridges, is also home to the speedway that has gone into the record books as the fastest auto-racing track in the world.

Anniston merits first place as a base for exploring the region because it boasts two prize inns. The Victoria, an 1888 showplace complete with turrets and a wraparound veranda, was occupied by three prominent Anniston families before it was transformed into a country inn and restaurant in 1985. There are three grand period suites in the main building and 44 new units with old-fashioned decor and modern amenities located in an addition across the courtyard. The dining room, done in formal Victorian fashion, is highly recommended.

The second choice, the Noble-McCaa Butler House, circa 1887, was occupied by members of the town's founding Noble family for over 100 years and is also on the National Register of Historic Places.

You'll see at once that Anniston is an unusually attractive small town. It was born when two industrialists, Samuel Noble and Daniel Tyler, established textile mills and blast furnaces in 1872, in an effort to bolster the Southern economy after the Civil War. They brought in the noted New York architect Stanford White to lay out a model company town, with wide streets and grand churches. It was named "Annie's Town" for Tyler's wife, Annie, and remained a private company town until 1883.

Many of the original churches and homes remain, along the stately divided boulevard called Quintard Avenue and in the Tyler Hill historic district on East Sixth Street, which peaks at a square surrounded by Victorian homes from the late 1880s.

Not to be missed is the interior of St. Michael and All Angels Episcopal Church, at the corner of 18th Street and Cobb Avenue. The church was built for the foundry workers in 1888 by Noble, who is buried near the entrance. Masons from his native Cornwall were brought to do the outside stonework, and the 95-foot altar of white Carrara marble was shipped from Italy. The glowing stained-glass windows include a Madonna and Child by Louis Comfort Tiffany.

This city's special pride is its Museum of Natural History, housing a remarkable collection that would do credit to a metropolis many times the size of Anniston. The modern building is divided into halls with varying themes.

The Ornithology Hall holds one of the most remarkable bird collections anywhere. Assembled by William Werner, a well-known nineteenth-century naturalist, it includes over 600 kinds of North American birds in their natural habitats, with authentic nests and eggs.

The African Hall is home to more than 100 creatures shown in correct habitats.

The Underground World exhibit, a replica of an Alabama cave, is complete with cool, damp air, pools, stalactites, stalagmites, and simulated resident bats, snakes, and salamanders.

Since 1917, Anniston's economy has been bolstered by Fort McClellan, once one of the nation's largest military bases, but now greatly reduced owing to recent military cutbacks. Located five miles outside town, it was headquarters for the U.S. Army Chemical Corps and Military Police regiments. Each service maintained a museum on the grounds. Another museum traces the history of the Women's Army Corps. The future of the base and its museums was uncertain when this was written, so phone before visiting.

Nature and art lovers should pay a visit to the Wren's Nest, a gallery exhibiting paintings, prints, and sculptures of wildlife and other subjects by Larry K. Martin. The gallery is located in the 100-year-old carriage house of the Victoria Inn.

Antiquers will want to head just south of Anniston to Oxford and the Olde Mill Antique Mall, a converted century-old cotton mill with two floors housing 150 dealers offering just about every kind of collectible imaginable. Eight former homes of mill workers nearby are now shops offering everything from candy to quilts.

Oxford is also where you can see one of the early covered bridges, the Coldwater Bridge in Oxford Lake Park, off U.S. 78.

If you prefer scenery to shopping, drive south from Anniston on U.S. 431 and watch as the road winds higher and higher until you reach Cheaha State Park. This peaceful, 2,500-acre preserve offers picnicking, boating, and swimming in a mountain lake, and the chance to climb a rustic rock tower for the view from 2,407 feet up, the highest point in the state. The big windows in the park restaurant offer their own sweeping vistas.

The park is within the Talladega National Forest, and opens to the Cheaha Wilderness Area, the southernmost extension of the Appalachians and a glorious place for a hike. The almost completed Pinjote Trail System traverses the highest terrain in the state for nearly 100 miles. It is a prize route along the edges of rock bluffs, through forested coves, and beside rocky streams. There are several entry points—in the park, at the Coleman Lake Recreation Area to the north, and in the Friendship community to the south.

One of the state's best auto routes, the Talladega Scenic Drive, begins one mile southwest of Cheaha and ends on U.S. 78 near Heflin. There are many magnificent vistas, such as that which may be seen from the rocky escarpment of Sherman Cliff. During foliage season, it is a heavenly drive.

Cheaha offers a lodge and cabins and is a fine place for a weekend stay among the tall trees, if you reserve early enough to get one of the popular accommodations.

Another option is Talladega, where you can stay at the Oakwood, the columned home built in 1847 by the town's first mayor. It is the perfect picture of a Southern mansion, with high ceilings, tall windows, and a graceful staircase.

Talladega was officially founded in 1834, but the local history goes back farther. The site was part of the Jackson Trace, the first wagon road through the Creek Indian nation, built by Andrew Jackson and his army of Tennessee volunteers. A monument located a block from Courthouse Square marks the Big Spring where the Indian village of

Talladega was defeated by Jackson in the Creek War of 1813. The city grew up later around this same spring.

Though the town square is no longer the thriving trading center of the past, the 1836 brick courthouse still stands proud, the oldest in continuous use in Alabama, and there are many other historic structures in town. The Silk Stocking Historic District, south of the square, includes many homes dating from the 1820s. Markers on the lawns give the owners and dates of the most significant houses. East South Street is especially fine.

Another important local site is Talladega College, founded in 1867 by two former slaves. Still predominantly black, it was the first college in the state open to all races, and many landmark buildings can be seen on the oak-lined campus.

Another school of interest is the Alabama Institute for the Deaf and Blind, one of the country's most comprehensive institutions of its kind. Two buildings, Grace Hall and Jemison House, are over 100 years old, and Manning Hall, the administration building, dates from 1850.

Talladega boasts one of the state's oldest covered bridges, the Waldo Bridge, six miles south of town on Alabama route 77. This truss-type bridge dates from around 1858. The surrounding area is now a pioneer park that includes Riddle's Grist Mill and a log cabin of about the same vintage as the bridge.

To see how the pace of life has picked up since horse-and-buggy days, head for the Talladega Superspeedway. Built in the late 1960s, this is the site of the state's largest sports events—the Winston 500 Race, held the first Sunday in May, and the DieHard 500, the final major NASCAR Winston Cup stock car competition of the season, usually the last Saturday in July. Qualifying rounds begin on the Thursday before the big races.

Both events are nationally televised and regularly sell out the 83,000-seat stands. Tickets go on sale far in advance, and hotel rooms are sold out for miles around.

Whenever you visit Talladega, you can relive some of the great races at the International Motorsports Hall of Fame, which is filled with famous stock cars, Indy cars, and drag racers. Exhibits range from the 1935 *Bluebird,* brought from England by Sir Malcolm Campbell to triumph at Daytona Beach, to the 1985 Ford Thunderbird driven by Bill Elliot when he established the record for the fastest 500-mile race ever run—186.288 miles per hour.

From Talladega, head south on Alabama route 21 and connect with Alabama route 76 to reach a unique eastern Alabama attraction, De Soto Caverns Park.

The park's vast onyx cave has a colorful history. It was discovered in 1540 by the Spanish explorer Hernando de Soto, who camped nearby during his quest for the Fountain of Youth. The Creek Indians considered it a holy place, the birthplace of their ancestors. It became the first officially recorded cave in the United States in 1796, when Benjamin Hawkins, the superintendent of Indian tribes in the region, wrote to President George Washington describing its beauty.

The cave was used by the Confederates to mine saltpeter for gunpowder during the Civil War, and it was notorious during Prohibition as a speakeasy well out of sight of the authorities.

Today it is a major state tourist attraction. Its history is entertainingly narrated by the pleasant guides, who also point out the eerie formations created by the dripping of mineral-rich waters. The grand finale is a sound-and-light show complete with leaping waters, presented inside the cave's best-known feature, the great onyx cathedral, a space higher than a 12-story building.

In the park outside the cave await such family amusements as a playground, a maze in the form of a wooden stockade, and the chance to pan for gemstones and gold.

On the way to the cave, you will pass the Kymulga Covered Bridge, which spans Talladega Creek. It was one of four under construction at the start of the Civil War, and was the only one to escape burning by the Union army. It is on the National Register of Historic Places.

The adjoining three-and-a-half-story mill was built in the 1860s by slave labor, and was restored in 1988. On a guided tour, you can watch corn being ground. The mill and bridge are part of a 78-acre park with the largest stand of white oak trees east of the Mississippi and a giant sugarberry tree. It's yet another place where history and scenery meet in eastern Alabama.

Area Code: 205

DRIVING DIRECTIONS   Anniston is on U.S. 431, just north of I–20. From Atlanta, follow I–20 west, 87 miles; from Birmingham, take I–20 east, 66 miles. Talladega is 24 miles south via Ala. route 21.

ACCOMMODATIONS   *The Victoria,* 1604 Quintard Avenue, Anniston 36201, 236–0503, I-M, CP ● *Noble-McCaa-Butler House,* 1025 Fairmont Avenue, Anniston 36201, 236–1791, M, CP ● *Oakwood Bed and Breakfast,* 715 East North Street, Talladega, 35160, 362–0662, an 1847 Federal home near courthouse square, I, CP ● *Cheaha Mountain Lodge,* Cheaha State Park, P.O. Box 546, Lineville 38266, 488–5115 or 800-ALA-PARK, lodge, I; rustic cottages, I; modern cottages, M.

DINING   *The Victoria* (see above), M ● *Annistonian,* 1709 Noble, 236–5156, German and American specialties, I-E ● *Morrison's Cafeteria,* 700 South Quintard Avenue, Quintard Mall, Oxford, 831–

7470, branch of the popular cafeteria chain, reliable and reasonable, I
• *Cheaha Mountain Lodge* (see above), go for the views, I • *Red's Catfish Cabin*, Ala. route 49, south of Cheaha Park, Lineville, 354–7705, catfish and all the trimmings, I.

SIGHTSEEING   *Cheaha State Park*, Ala. Route 49, off U.S. 431, 29 miles south of Anniston, P.O. Box 546, Lineville, 488–5111. Hours: daily, daylight hours, parking fee, $ • *Anniston Museum of Natural History*, 4301 McClellan Boulevard, Anniston, 237–6766. Hours: Tuesday to Friday 9 A.M. to 5 P.M.; Saturday 10 A.M. to 5 P.M.; Sunday 1 P.M. to 5 P.M.; $$ • *Fort McClellan Museums*, Ala. route 21, Anniston (phone to check status before visiting): *Military Police Corps Regimental Museum*, 848–3511; *U.S. Army Chemical Corps Regimental Museum*, 848–3355; *Women's Army Corps Museum*, 848–3512. Hours: All open Monday to Friday 8 A.M. to 4 P.M.; Saturday and Sunday by appointment; free • *International Motorsports Hall of Fame*, Speedway Boulevard off I–20, exit 173, Talladega, 362–5002. Hours: daily 9 A.M. to 5 P.M., $$ • *Talladega Superspeedway*, P.O. Box 777, Talladega 35160, off I–20, exit 173, 362–9064; check for current schedules and ticket information • *De Soto Caverns Park*, De Soto Caverns Parkway off Ala. route 21, Childersburg, 378–7252. Hours: April to September, Monday to Saturday 9 A.M. to 5:30 P.M., Sunday 12:30 P.M. to 5:30 P.M.; rest of year, to 5 P.M.; $$; cave plus other attractions, $$$.

INFORMATION   *Calhoun County Chamber of Commerce*, 801 Noble Street, P.O. Box 1087, Anniston, AL 36202, 237–3536 • *Greater Talladega Chamber of Commerce*, 210 East Street South, P.O. Drawer A, Talladega, AL 35160, 362–9075.

Heaven High in Highlands

Highlands, North Carolina, is the closest to heaven you can get without leaving this world behind.

The highest town east of the Mississippi River, perched at an altitude of over 4,118 feet at the southern tip of the Blue Ridge Mountains, this pinch of paradise is a world apart, surrounded by more than a million acres of the Nantahala National Forest. In every direction, roads wind toward stunning views, mirror lakes, and walking paths on trails lined with rhododendron and pine. More than 200 waterfalls tumble through these hills.

Cool and green in summer, Highlands and the whole region become an autumn fantasy when the nights grow cool and the foliage turns to gorgeous gold, orange, and russet red.

Oddly enough, a resort town was not what the Northern founding fathers, Samuel Truman Kelsey and Clinton Carter Hutchinson, had in mind when they bought up property in 1875. Fresh from completing the town of Hutchinson, Kansas, they were looking to the Southeast for a business center. When they checked out the topography, however, they had to settle for a mountain retreat instead. By 1883 they had cut 40 miles of road out of the native forest, incorporated a town of 300 residents, and were advertising Highlands across the Southeast as a health retreat whose climate and fresh air had rejuvenating powers.

Highlands quickly became a favorite hideaway for wealthy Southerners, as it has remained for well over a century. Many have summer homes on the grounds of the exclusive Highlands Country Club, founded in 1929 around a Donald Ross golf course. Their support has helped spawn many activities, including a summer playhouse now well past its fiftieth season, a chamber music festival, and a forum on international affairs.

Lately the town has also become a popular retirement community and has been attracting tourists, along with Floridians escaping the heat, swelling the population of 2,000 to 20,000 in summer. But compared to most places, the two-block Main Street is still delightfully unspoiled—no fast food, no gewgaw souvenirs, no bright lights. And the encircling mountains ensure that Highlands will never grow too large.

There are plenty of shops, to be sure, but they are upscale emporiums where browsing is a joy. Downtown remains so compact that none of the Main Street shops even bother about storefront numbers. Their wares range from English antiques to Japanese porcelains to Appalachian quilts, all in the best of taste. Southern Hands carries as fine an assemblage of regional crafts as you'll see anywhere.

There's just a smattering of sightseeing in town. The Bascom-Louise Gallery, inside the Hudson Library, showcases regional artists, and there's a botanical garden right behind the local nature center.

The Scottish heritage of this region is also reflected in an annual Scottish Tartans Festival in mid-September, and in the Wee Shoppe at the edge of town, on U.S. 64, which sells all kinds of British Isles imports, from tartans to teas.

You can easily find a place to stay right on Main Street, within easy range of all the shopping. Two old-timers, the 1880 Highlands Inn and its sister across the street, the 1878 Old Edwards Inn, have been nicely restored and refurbished.

Since mountain views are what Highlands is all about, an even better bet is just a few blocks up the hill. Colonial Pines is a delightful bed-and-breakfast inn, cozy and welcoming, with a big wide porch affording nonstop mountain views. The requisite rockers are waiting for you.

One of the most spectacular views around is from the Skyline Lodge, on a mountaintop four miles from town. The 1920s lodge, designed by Frank Lloyd Wright, is made of native granite and has enormous windows to take in the mind-boggling vistas. Rooms here are less unusual—in fact, they're downright motelish. But there's a pool and tennis courts and the panoramas from the ceiling-high dining-room windows are dazzling.

It's necessary to get out and about to appreciate the beauty that can be seen only on a drive and/or a walk outside of town.

Begin by driving to the end of East Main Street as it turns into Horse Cove Road. If you feel like taking a 20-minute hike, stop at the Highlands Nature Center on Horse Cove Road and take the path to Sunset Rock, overlooking the town.

Come back to the road, and you'll wind around some 37 curves before you come to the cove itself. A very short detour onto Wilson Gap Road will give you a view of Highlands' venerable Giant Poplar, said to be one of the three largest poplars in the nation. Then continue on Horse Cove Road until you come to a fork in the road. On the right will be Bull Pen Road, a gravel road leading to an outlook on the Chattooga, a national wild and scenic river. Go left on Whiteside Cove Road, and you'll pass the world's smallest post office, Grimshaw's. There are magnificent views along this drive of Whiteside Mountain, striking for its steep sheer cliffs.

You can double back the way you came and enjoy the scenery from a different perspective or continue on Whiteside Cove Road to N.C. route 107 south of Cashiers, turning left onto U.S. 64 west to get back to Highlands.

Another scenic drive awaits on N.C. route 106 south from Highlands toward Dillard, Georgia. Look for a turnoff in about three miles to the dirt road leading to Glen Falls, a series of three large falls, each dropping 60 feet into the Overflow Creek in Blue Valley. About a half-mile farther on route 106 is the Blue Valley Overlook, a spot where the mountains seem to go on forever.

Just a half-mile farther on is a picturesque shopping stop, the Lick Log Mill Store, an 1851 log cabin in a lavish garden setting, filled with folk art and other nice country things.

For a veritable feast of waterfalls, head west from Highlands on U.S. 64/28 toward Franklin along the Cullasaja River Gorge. You'll be riding beside a river that ripples over rapids and cascades into a series of dramatic falls, all within sight of the road. Among these are Bridal Veil Falls, which you can drive under in your car, and Dry Falls, so named because you can walk behind the falls without getting wet.

Before you get to Franklin, watch for Buck Creek Road on the right, connecting U.S. 64 west with 64 east toward Cashiers. The Buck Creek community is in a basin surrounded by hardwoods, a brilliant sight in the fall. The road continues east in a series of sharp curves between thickly wooded hillsides until the trees open again at Cowee Gap for an awe-inspiring view of Whiteside Mountain.

The drive from Highlands to Cashiers is ten miles, and if you arrive in time for lunch, both the Market Basket and Cornucopia will serve you nicely—or prepare takeout picnics to allow you to continue your scenic drive.

The next stop is Whitewater Falls, the highest waterfall in the East, about 20 minutes from Cashiers. Take N.C. route 107 south for about 13 miles, and at the Whitewater Falls sign, turn left onto S.C. route 130 into South Carolina; continue to the stop sign and turn left onto Whitewater Road, route 1171, for one mile. When you see the Whitewater Falls sign, turn right into the parking area and take an easy walk of five to ten minutes to an overlook and view of the two-level, 411-foot falls, spuming as they crash onto the rocks.

The energetic will find trails to the top and bottom of the falls. For more national forest hiking trails, ask for a brochure at the information center in either Highlands or Cashiers.

The shops of Cashiers are scattered along the sides of the highway. The town lacks the quaint main street or the surrounding mountains of Highlands, but there is no shortage of exceptional lodgings nearby.

High Hampton Inn and Country Club, set on 1,400 acres, 3,600 feet high amid the mountains, is a determinedly old-fashioned resort with rockers on the porch and huge, four-sided fireplaces inside, where guests gather to enjoy hot soup at noon or afternoon tea. Rooms in the main house or in the 19 cottages around the grounds are simply furnished with mountain pine pieces made on the premises, chenille bedspreads, and rag rugs.

This remains the kind of place where guests play at croquet and lawn bowling, and where they swim in the lake, not a pool. It is also the site of a spectacular golf course with Chimney Top and Rock Mountain standing guard. The island eighth green, beneath Rock Mountain, is a classic. Seven tennis courts, boating, sailing, fly-fishing and instruction, and guided walks to scenic areas are among the multitude of activities. Considering the amenities and the three bountiful meals plus afternoon tea, rates here are surprisingly reasonable.

Those who prefer a more intimate setting will appreciate the Millstone Inn, a rustic, shingled home built in the 1930s atop a shady knoll some 3,500 feet high. Views of Whiteside Mountain can be seen from many of the pine-paneled bedrooms as well as from the picture window of the commodious, beamed living room, which takes up most of one of the two wings of the house. The autumn views are so spectacular that some people book a year in advance.

A few miles away is the Innisfree Inn on Lake Glenville, a new "old Victorian," built in classic style in 1989. The most popular room here is Victoria's Suite, where the whirlpool for two is surrounded by windows with a mountain view.

Whether you take your views from the whirlpool or a car window, a front porch or a hiking trail, you'll surely agree that Highlands and its neighbors are heavenly places to be.

Area Code: 704

DRIVING DIRECTIONS   Highlands is at the intersection of U.S. 64 and N.C. Routes 28 and 106. It is 140 miles from Atlanta, 65 miles from Asheville, 180 miles from Columbia, S.C., 150 miles from Knoxville, and 160 miles from Charlotte. From Atlanta, take I–85 north, exit at I–985 Gainesville, which becomes Ga. Route 365. Continue to U.S. 23/441 north to Dillard, then follow Ga. Route 246, which becomes N.C. Route 106 at the North Carolina state line, and continue to Highlands.

ACCOMMODATIONS   *Highlands Inn,* 526–9380, and *Old Edwards Inn,* 526–5036, same owner, both on Main Street, P.O. Box 1030, Highlands 28741, I-M, CP ● *Colonial Pines Inn,* Hickory Street, Highlands 28741, 526–2060, best of the small inns, convenient, charming, private, great mountain views from the big porch, M, CP ● *Phelps House,* Main Street, Highlands 28741, 526–2590, old-fashioned inn circa 1885, I, CP ● *Highlands Suite Hotel,* Main Street, Highlands 28741, 526–4502 or 800–221–5078, all the amenities, E-EE, CP ● *The Laurels,* Horse Cove Road, Highlands 28741, 526–2091, cozy bed-and-breakfast home in scenic section, open May through October, I, CP ● *Lakeside Bed and Breakfast,* Highway 64 West, Highlands 18741, 526–4498, overlooking Lake Sequoyah, open April 1 to December 1, I, CP ● *Skyline Lodge,* P.O. Box 630, Highlands 28741, 526–2121, secluded mountaintop, stunning lodge, motel-style rooms, pool, tennis, M ● *Millstone Inn,* Highway 64 West, P.O. Box 949, Cashiers 28717, 743–2737, M-E, CP ● *High Hampton Inn and Country Club,* 640 Hampton Road, Cashiers 28717, 243–2411 or 800–334–2551, superb resort, rustic lodge, all sports, open April through November, EE, AP ● *Innisfree Inn,* Highway 107, P.O. Box 469, Glenville 28736, romantic Victorian ambience, E-EE, CP.

DINING   *On the Verandah,* Highway 64 West, Highlands, 526–2338, scenic spot overlooking Lake Sequoyah, talented chef-owner,

best in town, M-E; also Sunday champagne brunch with jazz, M ●
Frog and Owl Cafe, Buck Creek Road, 10 miles from town, 526–5500,
gourmet food in a restored gristmill, intimate, E-EE ● *Hildegard's,*
Main Street, Highlands, 526–3807, German specialties, long established, E ● *Central House,* Old Edwards Inn (see above), country
decor, many seafood specialties, M-E ● *Paoletti's,* Main Street,
526–4906, Italian, M-E ● *Phelps House* (see above), homemade
family-style dinners, I ● *Top of the Mountain,* Skyline Lodge (see
above), M-E ● *Cornucopia,* Highway 107 South, Cashiers, 743–3750,
quaint 1892 building, sandwiches for lunch, gourmet fare for dinner,
I-M ● *Carolina Smokehouse,* Highway 64 West, Cashiers, 743–3200,
best pit barbecue around, I.

SIGHTSEEING *Bascom-Louise Gallery,* East Main Street (Horse
Cove Road), 526–4949. Hours: Monday to Wednesday and Friday, 10
A.M. to 5 P.M.; Saturday 10 A.M. to 1 P.M. Free.

INFORMATION *Highlands Chamber of Commerce,* Town Hall,
P.O. Box 404, Highlands, NC 28741, 526–2112 ● *Cashiers Chamber
of Commerce,* P.O. Box 238-A, Cashiers, NC 28717, 743–5941.

A Golden Glow in Georgia

When the sun casts its glow on the sands and the marshes, it is easy to
understand why Georgia's offshore islands have been dubbed the
Golden Isles.

Located about an hour south of Savannah, these beautiful barrier
islands are a perfect escape, offering sports and beaches galore, set
among unspoiled marshes and woodlands of moss-hung live oaks,
pines, and palmettos.

But there is a lure here beyond recreation, a special mystique from
the golden glow and dreamy feel imparted by the ever-present marshes
and the romance of the past. Jekyll and St. Simons, the two most
visited islands, have equal charm but very distinct personalities shaped
by their histories. Whichever you choose, make time to visit the other.

Jekyll Island was once the very private province of some of
America's most prominent families. For many years this remained
plantation country, with sea-island cotton as the major crop. But the
Civil War ended the plantation era, and the island's canny owners
conceived the idea of selling it as a hunting retreat for wealthy
Northerners.

In 1887 the Jekyll Island Club was formed, with a limit of 100 shares of stock. Members purchased the island for the then-exorbitant amount of $125,000. For the next 55 years it was the exclusive domain of millionaires. Families such as the Goulds, Astors, Rockefellers, Morgans, and Pulitzers were among the first to build 20-room summer "cottages," arriving by yacht and taking their meals together in the ornate Victorian clubhouse, where some members also preferred to stay. Their homes were deliberately kept simple, but life was not without its comforts. The club was a Victorian vision with a five-story turreted tower, a gourmet kitchen, a wine cellar, and a croquet lawn. Armies of servants were boated ashore.

In the early years, club activities included hunting, horseback and carriage rides, and picnics. In later years, golf and tennis were added.

They not only played here, but made a bit of history. President William McKinley planned his reelection campaign on the island in 1899. In 1910, J. P. Morgan assembled the nabobs of the banking industry for a secret meeting that plotted the Federal Reserve Act. The first transcontinental telephone call was made from Jekyll when Theodore Vail, a Bell executive and later president of AT&T, made simultaneous contact with Woodrow Wilson at the White House, Alexander Graham Bell in New York, and one of Bell's aides in San Francisco.

Although the Depression and World War II took their toll on this way of life, it can still be seen and experienced. In 1946 the state of Georgia took possession of Jekyll Island, connecting it to the rest of the world by a causeway and opening its beaches, woodlands, and marshes as a tranquil refuge for all. The grand Victorian clubhouse has been restored to the tune of $20 million as the Jekyll Island Club Hotel, and you can still play indoor tennis on the court that J. P. Morgan built for himself in 1929.

The entire 240-acre Jekyll Island Club preserve has been declared a National Historic Landmark. The Jekyll Island Museum, which maintains 25 of the original buildings, offers trolley tours of the complex, as well as visits inside the remaining grand cottages and Faith Chapel, the small church that was adorned with two stained glass windows by Louis Comfort Tiffany. Goodyear Cottage includes a gallery of Southern art and a museum shop.

The guest rooms at the Jekyll Island Club are beautifully furnished in reproduction antiques, and some rooms have fireplaces and balconies. Those who prefer to be on the beach will find a lineup of hotel-motels along the 10-mile strand at the other side of the island. Things are much livelier here, with such child-pleasing diversions as miniature golf, a water park with a wave pool, and a waterskiing center on a man-made lake. The local recreation department runs a day camp for children ages 4 to 12.

The first golf course, constructed in 1898, now has company. With

63 holes of golf, Jekyll is Georgia's largest public golf resort. The Oleander course, known for its bunkers, is the toughest. Also available are a 13-court tennis complex and a fitness center. Where millionaires' yachts used to dock, you can now board boats for deep-sea fishing or scuba diving.

Not to worry, however, if you want to get away from all this activity. Since only one-third of the island is allowed to be developed, much of the center remains pristine, reserved for quiet outings on the 20 miles of biking and walking paths that meander among twisted live oaks trailing wispy scarves of moss.

St. Simons Island, with its charming Colonial village, is becoming a popular art colony and upscale retirement haven as well as a resort town. Although it is more built up than Jekyll, it still has managed to retain open spaces and its own romantic history.

It was in 1736 that 4,477 men and 72 women and children arrived from Savannah to build a fort to protect the new colony of Georgia. Known as Fort Frederica, it was here that Spanish invaders from Florida were ousted for good at the Battle of Bloody Marsh in 1742. The fort is now maintained by the National Park Service, and the foundations of many of the original dwellings have been excavated.

Lovely Christ Church, erected in 1886 to replace an earlier structure destroyed by British troops, housed the congregation originally founded by John and Charles Wesley, Anglican missionaries who came to Georgia with Oglethorpe and subsequently returned to England to found the Methodist Church. Christ Church was built by the Rev. Anson G. P. Dodge, Jr., as a memorial to his wife, Ellen, who died during their honeymoon trip. Their tale is one of the romantic St. Simons legends retold in the books of local novelist Eugenia Price.

Wandering around town, shoppers will find treasures in the boutiques and galleries along Frederica Road and in the village. At the end of Mallery Street in the village are a fishing pier and a waterfront park, pleasant places to linger. It is exactly 129 steps to the top of the nearby 1872 lighthouse, a climb that yields sweeping views of the islands. The lighthouse replaces one of America's oldest, destroyed by Union troops in the Civil War. The old lightkeeper's cottage now houses a Museum of Coastal History.

St. Simons has many championship golf courses, including some on the grounds of former plantations, with picturesque ruins as unexpected hazards. Sea Palms Golf & Tennis Resort offers access to 37 holes of golf and 12 tennis courts, and has its own private beach club. The King and Prince Beach Resort is for those who prefer to be directly on the water. Guests here have privileges at the Hampton Club golf course.

Two of the best courses are among the famed 54 holes of golf that belong to The Cloister, a five-star resort located on Sea Island, across a causeway from St. Simons. Developed in the 1920s, The Cloister remains a genteel world apart, a moss-draped, Spanish-style retreat with the best of everything. It is one of the most outstanding resorts in the South.

Many miles of St. Simons's beaches are open to the public and have been renewed after a rousing local battle about whether this would damage the ecosystem. There is no dispute about the surrounding wetlands that inspired poet Sidney Lanier to write about "The Marshes of Glynn" in the 1870s; they remain untouched. Guided nature walks and salt marsh boat tours are available.

The marshes are protected by law because of their ecological importance as a buffer preventing erosion, as a nesting ground for all manner of sea birds, and as a rich spawning ground for the delicious shrimp found on island menus.

One of the best excursions from the Golden Isles is a trip to the deep, dark, and mysterious waters of Okefenokee Swamp. The closest gateway is the less-visited east entrance to the Wildlife Refuge at Folkston. Facilities here include hiking trails for swamp viewing, a 50-foot observation tower overlooking the Okefenokee, and a 4,000-foot boardwalk into the swamp. The best fun is actually getting out on the water. Suwannee Canal Recreational Concession offers rental canoes or guided boat trips for gliding among the cypress trees, a wonderful chance to pay your respects to the 'gators lazing in the sun or floating along like logs with gleaming eyes. You'll also get close-up views of the open "prairies" dotted with floating vegetation so massed it almost seems solid. Great blue herons and other magnificent birds love these habitats; bring your binoculars and a camera and be forewarned—no matter how much film you bring, it probably won't be enough.

Area Code: 912

DRIVING DIRECTIONS   St. Simons, Sea Island, and Jekyll Island are situated on Georgia's southeast Atlantic coast. From north or south, they can be reached via U.S. 17, the Golden Isles Parkway, off I–95, or drivers coming from Savannah can follow more scenic U.S. 17 all the way. From Atlanta, follow I–75 south to Macon, then I–16 east toward Savannah and I–95 south to Brunswick. Signs point the way to Jekyll and St. Simons, about 300 miles.

PUBLIC TRANSPORTATION   The closest airports are Savannah, about 75 miles north, and Jacksonville, Florida, 65 miles south.

ACCOMMODATIONS   *Jekyll Island Club Hotel, A Radisson Resort,* 371 Riverview Drive, Jekyll Island 31527, 635–2600 or 800–333–3333, M-EE • *Clarion Resort Buccaneer,* 85 South

Beachview Drive, Jekyll Island 31527, 635–2261 or 800-CLARION, oceanfront, M-EE ● *Comfort Inn Island Suites,* 711 North Beachview Drive, Jekyll Island 31527, 635–2211 or 800–228–5150, M-EE ● *Villas by the Sea,* 1175 North Beachview Drive, Jekyll Island 31527, 635–2521 or 800–841–6262 outside Georgia, condominium hotel with 1- to 3-bedroom apartments, I-EE ● *Sea Palms Golf & Tennis Resort,* 5445 Frederica Road, St. Simons 31522, 638–3351 or 800–841–6268, rooms M, one-bedroom condos E, offers access to 37 holes of golf and 12 tennis courts ● *The King and Prince Beach Resort,* 201 Arnold Road, St. Simons 31522, 638–3631 or 800–342–0212, M-EE ● *The Cloister,* Sea Island 31561, 800-SEA-ISLAND, EE-AP ● *Sea Gate Inn,* 1014 Ocean Boulevard, St. Simons 31522, 638–8661, motel with waterfront section, I-E ● *Days Inn,* 1701 Frederica Road, St. Simons 31522, 634–0660, good value, I, CP.

DINING *Grand Dining Room,* Jekyll Island Club (see above), wonderful setting, good food, M-E ● *Blackbeard's,* 200 North Beachview Drive, Jekyll Island, 636–3522, seafood, ocean views, outdoor dining, I-E ● *Jekyll Wharf,* Riverview Road at the pier, Jekyll Island, 635–3000, informal, chowder, burgers, screened porch for watching boats come and go, I ● *Blanche's Courtyard,* 440 Kings Way, St. Simons, 638–3030, Victoriana and gaslights, M ● *Alfonza's Old Plantation Supper Club,* Harrington Lane off Frederica Road, St. Simons, 638–9883, tabby walls, checkered tablecloths, soul food and seafood, gospel singing on Thursday and Saturday, M-E ● *Emmeline & Hessie,* 100 Marina Drive, Golden Isles Marina, St. Simons, 638–9084, seafood, views, I-M ● *Spanky's,* Golden Isles Marina, St. Simons, 638–0918, more seafood and sea views, I-M ● *Crab Trap,* 1209 Ocean Boulevard, St. Simons, 638–2047, very informal, I ● *The Cloister* (see above), elegant, jackets required, EE prix-fixe.

SIGHTSEEING *Jekyll Island Club Historic District Tours,* from Museum Orientation Center, Stable Road, 635–2762. Hours: daily tours; times vary, phone for current hours, $$$ ● *Fort Frederica,* off Frederica Road, St. Simons. Hours: daily 9 A.M. to 5 P.M. $ ● *Christ Church,* off Frederica Road near the fort, St. Simons, 638–8683. Hours: daily 2 P.M. to 5 P.M. in summer; rest of year, 1 P.M. to 4 P.M. ● *Museum of Coastal History,* 101 12th Street, St. Simons, 638–4666. Hours: Tuesday to Saturday 10 A.M. to 5 P.M.; Sunday from 1:30 P.M.; $ ● *Okefenokee National Wildlife Refuge,* east entrance, Suwannee Canal Recreational Concession, Inc., Route 121, 8 miles south of Folkston, 496–3331. Guided boat tours, one hour, $$$, two hours, $$$$, night boats, $$$$. Also canoe and bicycle rentals.

ACTIVITIES *Summer Waves Water Park,* South Riverview Drive, Jekyll Island, 635–2074. Hours: late May to early September, Sunday to Thursday 10 A.M. to 6 P.M.; Friday and Saturday to 8 P.M.; July Saturdays to 9 P.M.; $$$ • *Jekyll Island Nature Walks,* held year-round, led by docents of University of Georgia Marine Extension Service; phone 635–2232 for current schedules • *Deep Sea Fishing, Sightseeing Cruises, Scuba Diving: Jekyll Historic Marina,* 635–2891 • *Sailboats, Bicycles, Windsurfing:* Rentals and lessons at *Barry's Beach Service,* Jekyll Inn, Jekyll Island, and King and Prince Beach Hotel Beach Club, St. Simons, 638–8053; *Yankee Bream,* 511 Marsh Villa Road, St. Simons, 638–3214, cruises for fishing, birding, or touring marshes. Phone for schedules.

INFORMATION *Jekyll Island Convention & Visitors Bureau,* P.O. Box 3186, Jekyll Island, GA 31520, 800–342–1042; outside Georgia, 800–841–6586 • *St. Simons Island Chamber of Commerce,* Neptune Park, St. Simons Island, GA 31522, 638–9014 • *Brunswick & The Golden Isles Visitors Bureau,* 4 Glynn Avenue, Brunswick, GA 31520, 264–5337.

Fall

Price Lake, near Blowing Rock. Photo courtesy of North Carolina Travel and Tourism Div.

Lolling About the Lowcountry

If you arrive for the first time and somehow feel you've been here before, that's not unusual. Beaufort, South Carolina, is familiar to anyone who has seen the movies filmed here, such as *The Big Chill*, Pat Conroy's *The Great Santini*, and *The Prince of Tides*. The small town where Pat Conroy grew up and taught is quintessential Lowcountry—ancient oaks overhung with moss, a river meandering by, inlets and boats everywhere.

Though it is tranquil today, Beaufort (pronounced *Bew-fort*) has had an active history. Seven flags have flown here since the first Spanish explorers came in 1520. The town was officially founded in 1711, and by the nineteenth century was described as the wealthiest, most aristocratic and cultivated city of its size in America, the queen of the Sea Islands. The streets are lined with the gracious homes once occupied by plantation owners who grew rich growing indigo, sea-island cotton, and rice, and built fine residences in town, with wraparound porches and wide balconies facing the river.

The town endured four years of Northern occupation during the Civil War, but while many homes were confiscated, few were destroyed. Prosperity returned in this century. The United States Marine base at Parris Island was established nearby during World War I, and in 1958 a major shipping terminal was opened. Tourists began coming as early as the 1960s, and the movies filmed here have greatly increased their numbers.

There's very good reason to come. The whole center of Beaufort is a historic district, still looking much as it did in the nineteenth century. There are 90 historic homes and buildings, some dating from the early 1700s. Luckily, the town was unharmed by Hurricane Hugo, which wreaked such havoc on Charleston, just an hour to the north. So the shady, towering, moss-hung oaks remain.

Check into one of the fine homes now serving as inns, and take a stroll. Guided walking tours are offered, as well as tours in horse-drawn carriages, which seem right at home on Beaufort's streets. But the town is small and it's easy enough to wander on your own, at a slow pace in keeping with the languid aura of the town and allowing the time to admire the homes and gardens. Walking-tour leaflets are available at the chamber of commerce office.

Bay is the main street, running parallel to Port Royal Bay and rimmed by a seven-acre waterfront park. Several local restaurants open to the park and face the bay, which runs into the Beaufort River, part of the Intracoastal Waterway.

They treasure tradition here even in cuisine, which features traditional Lowcountry specialties such as she-crab soup, shrimp and grits, oyster stew, and red rice.

Two grand homes on Bay Street have been restored by the Historic Beaufort Foundation, and are open to the public. The antique-filled George Parsons Elliot House Museum, an 1840 Greek Revival antebellum home, provides a glimpse of gracious Lowcountry living.

The Federal-style John Mark Verdier House is even older, built by a wealthy merchant in 1790, and now restored and furnished in keeping with that period. The Marquis de Lafayette was entertained here in 1825. Less welcome were the Union forces who occupied the home from 1861 to 1865. The first floor is now headquarters for the Historic Beaufort Foundation.

Continue right to the end of Bay Street, turn left on New Street, and you'll come to the 1717 Thomas Hepworth House, the oldest in town. Go right on Craven, left on East, and right again on Federal to Pinckney Street and the Old Point section, facing the river.

The finest homes are here on the Point, on Pinckney, Hancock, and Short streets. Tidalholm, at the very end of Hancock, is the house that was featured in both *The Big Chill* and *The Great Santini*. Built in 1850 by James Fripp, it was one of the many homes sold at auction by the Federal government during the 1860s. In this case, the house was bought by a sympathetic Frenchman who returned it to the Fripp family.

One of the oldest homes is the 1720 Hext House, known as Riverview, on Pinckney between Hancock and Baynard.

These are private homes, but if you plan your visit for mid-October, when the Historic Beaufort Foundation sponsors its Fall Tour of Homes and Plantations, you'll be able to go inside for an intriguing look at the hospitality of today and yesterday.

Come back toward the water on Carteret Street, and at the corner of Craven Street you'll see the Arsenal. Built of brick and tabby in 1795 and rebuilt in 1852, it housed the Beaufort Volunteer Artillery, one of the oldest military units in America. It is now a museum whose exhibits are donated or loaned by local citizens. They cover a wide range, from Indian arrowheads and tools to costumes of the 1800s and Civil War weapons.

At the corner of Craven and Church streets is the Milton Maxey House, known as "Secession House," built around 1813 on a tabby foundation dating from 1724. It belonged to the prominent Rhett family, and it was here that the first Ordinance of Secession, taking South Carolina out of the Union, was drawn up.

Turn right on Church to St. Helena Episcopal Church, dating from 1724. This, too, was a Civil War hospital, and churchyard gravestones were brought inside to be used as operating tables.

Owing to the large number of war casualties, Abraham Lincoln established a National Cemetery outside Beaufort in 1863 as a resting place for Union soldiers. Located on U.S. 21, it includes the graves of 9,000 Union soldiers and 122 Confederates.

Turn left on King Street for three blocks, then left again on Monson and back toward the water to see a final cluster of fine early homes at the other end of Bay Street. These include the 1785 Edward Barnwell House, used as Union headquarters; the 1811 James Joyner Smith House, the residence used by the Union's commanding general; Leverett House, a pre-Revolutionary home moved to this location from St. Helena Island around 1850; the 1786 Thomas Fuller House, also known as Tabby Manse; and the William Elliott House, called the Anchorage, another pre-revolutionary home now extensively remodeled as a restaurant. At this point you are across from the chamber of commerce office where you began.

Beaufort is located on Port Royal Island, and is surrounded by dozens of other islands, large and small. One of the best ways to see them is aboard a sightseeing boat on the Beaufort River, which also allows stops for shell collecting and beachcombing.

You'll also get a sense of the terrain when you drive on U.S. 21, known as Sea Island Parkway, across the bridge to Lady's Island and past a series of inlets and islets, some so small you hardly know you've gone from one island to another.

Lady's Island is of interest mainly for seafood restaurants on the water. Next comes St. Helena Island, and fascinating bits of history at Penn Center and Frogmore.

This was plantation country, but the planters of St. Helena abandoned their property and fled inland as Union troops neared. A group of abolitionists inaugurated the Port Royal experiment for the benefit of the 10,000 blacks who remained, providing newly freed slaves with opportunities for education and self-sufficiency. In 1862, two female missionaries from the North established the first local school for black children, in a building shipped from Philadelphia that was dubbed the Penn School. The school continued to operate for nearly a century, graduating its last class in 1953. It was then renamed Penn Center and dedicated to a new purpose—to provide services related to health care and community enrichment for the islanders. Martin Luther King, Jr., and other black leaders met here to plan their 1963 march on Washington and their 1965 march in Selma, Alabama.

Penn Center, a national historic landmark, is now short of funds and has an uncertain future. Most recently it was used by Peace Corps volunteers in training for assignments overseas. You can see the original buildings as well as the brick church just across the road, built in 1855 with steep stairs to a balcony where slaves were relegated. The church became the spiritual center for the Penn School, and is still in use.

In these communities, where boats were the only means of transportation in early days, residents remained isolated, and many old traditions are still preserved. The Gullah dialect spoken by slaves from Africa can be heard today among their descendants. Old superstitions, such as buying charms and amulets from witch doctors to ward off evil spirits, also remain.

The center of black magic traditionally was Frogmore, the tiny community on U.S. 21, just past the turnoff to Penn Center. This was the home turf of Dr. Buzzard, the king of the witch doctors. Frogmore also has its own famous dish, Frogmore stew, an old island recipe combining sausage, shrimp, crabs, tomatoes, and corn boiled in beer. Visitors come to hear Gullah spoken, to sample the stew—and, who knows, maybe to banish hexes. The Gullah Festival, held each Memorial Day weekend in Beaufort, celebrates the old heritage with crafts, dancing, singing, storytelling, and games.

Frogmore Frolics, an art gallery showing work by local artists, and the Red Piano Too Gallery, with eclectic folk art, antiques, primitive art, and jewelry, are two interesting stops on U.S. 21 in Frogmore.

Beyond St. Helena, a bridge leads to Hunting Island, the largest of a group of islands that once were hunting preserves for wealthy planters. The island is now a state park, with a lighthouse whose steep spiral stairs lead to a dazzling view. The park offers wildlife "browsing areas" for spotting animals, boardwalks over the salt marshes, and four miles of beach.

Across the next bridge is Fripp Island, now entirely a privately owned resort, where homes and villas can be rented to enjoy the uncrowded beach, golf course, and tennis courts.

Returning on U.S. 21, make a left turn on S.C. route 802 across the McTeer Memorial Bridge, and you're on the way to Parris Island, the base where recruits are toughened into U.S. Marines. Some 20,000 men and 2,000 women complete their rigorous training here each year. Curious visitors arrive at the rate of 100,000 a year, and they are welcome.

But if you are expecting a stark boot camp, think again. Like most of the Lowcountry islands, Parris offers history spanning 450 years, natural beauty, water views, and beaches. When complimented on the beauty of the island, however, the marine on duty at the information center smiled and said, "Yeah, visitors call it paradise. We call it hell."

The reason becomes clear when you see the recruits drilling on the parade grounds or tackling the "confidence course," a formidable obstacle course of logs, cables, pipe, and rope that makes for a supreme test of coordination and endurance. The most challenging of the 11 obstacles are known as the "dirty name" and the "slide for life."

The printed driving tour, available at the gate, leads to all the major sights on a 15-mile loop past historic buildings, barracks, training grounds, and the section where women have been quartered since becoming part of the corps in 1949. Down the palmetto-lined main road are two famous statues. "Iron Mike," erected in 1924 to honor marines who lost their lives in World War I, has become the symbol of the marines. A replica of the Iwo Jima Monument in Arlington, Virginia, commemorates the heroic flag-raising on Mount Suribachi in 1945. It is an enduring symbol of the U.S. victory in World War II.

In the Parris Island Museum are displays on island and Marine history, vintage Marine Corps uniforms and weapons, and a display explaining the training process, including a model of the infamous confidence course.

Despite the trials they may have endured here, many ex-marines return to retire in the Lowcountry. That's not really too surprising. This is an area that is hard to resist.

Area Code: 803

DRIVING DIRECTIONS Beaufort is between Charleston and Hilton Head, a short drive off I–95. It is 266 miles from Atlanta, 262 miles from Charlotte. Approaching on I–95 from the north, take exit 8 and S.C. route 170; from the south, take exit 33 and U.S. 21, U.S. 17 is the scenic route from Charleston, 69 miles; S.C. route 70 leads to Hilton Head, 43 miles.

ACCOMMODATIONS *Rhett House,* 1009 Craven Street, Beaufort 29901, 524–9030, elegant antebellum home, antiques, gardens, best in town, M-EE, CP ● *Two Suns Inn,* 1705 Bay Street, Beaufort 29901, 522–1122, comfortable inn in a 1912 home, M, CP ● *Old Point Inn,* 212 New Street, Beaufort 29901, 524–3177, an 1898 Victorian in a historic district, I-M, CP ● *Trescot Inn,* 500 Washington Street, Beaufort 29901, 522–8552, a 140-year-old home moved to its present site after the Civil War, I-M, CP ● *Bay Street Inn,* 601 Bay Street, Beaufort 29902, 524–7720, an 1852 home with two-tiered verandas, river views, M, CP ● *Hunting Island State Park,* 1775 Sea Island Parkway, St. Helena, 19920, 838–2011, rustic cabins, some with fireplaces, some oceanfront, I-M.

DINING *Anchorage House,* 1103 Bay Street, 524–9392, a 1765 mansion with period furnishings, candlelight, Lowcountry and Continental menu, M-E ● *Wilkop's White Hall Inn,* Bay Street, 524–0382, overlooking Beaufort River, good for sunset watching, M-E ● *Bananas,* 910 Bay Street, fun spot on the waterfront, 522–0910, I-M ● *Gullah House,* 761 Sea Island Parkway (U.S. 21), St. Helena Island,

and *Old Bay Marketplace*, Bay Street, Beaufort, both 838–2402, traditional Lowcountry dishes, I-M • *Gadsby's Tavern,* 822 Bay Street, Beaufort, 525–1800, informal, outdoor terrace, I-M • *Terry V's Lady's Island Seafood Restaurant*, U.S. 21, next to Lady's Island Marina, 525–1011, seafood and river views, I-M.

SIGHTSEEING   *Historic Beaufort Foundation House Museums*, all 524–6334: *Elliot House,* 1001 Bay Street; hours, February through December, Monday to Friday 11 A.M. to 3 P.M., $$; *Verdier House,* 801 Bay Street; hours, February through December, Tuesday to Saturday 11 A.M. to 4 P.M., $$ • *Beaufort Museum (The Arsenal)*, 713 Craven Street, 525–7471; hours: Monday to Friday 10 A.M. to 12 noon, 2 P.M. to 5 P.M.; Saturday 10 A.M. to 12 noon; donation • *Beaufort Walking Tours,* 525–9292. Hours: departs from park behind Beaufort Visitor Center, Monday to Friday 10 A.M., 1 P.M., 3 P.M., 5 P.M.; Saturday 10 A.M., 12 noon, 3 P.M., and 4 P.M.; Sunday 1 P.M., 3 P.M., 5 P.M., weather permitting; $$ • *Carriage Tours of Beaufort*, Beaufort Visitor Center, 1006 Bay Street, 524–3163. Hours: daily 9 A.M. to 4 P.M., 45-minute ride, $$$ • *Beaufort River Cruises*, daily from Port Royal Landing Marina, 525–1174; phone for current schedules and rates • *Hunting Island State Park,* 1775 Sea Island Parkway, St. Helena Island, 838–2011. Hours: daily 6 A.M. to 9 P.M., parking fee, $$ • *Parris Island Marine Corps Recruit Depot,* off S.C. route 802; Museum, 525–2951. Hours: daily 10 A.M. to 4:30 P.M., free.

INFORMATION   Greater Beaufort Chamber of Commerce, 106 Bay Street, P.O. Box 910, Beaufort, SC 29901, 524–3163.

On the Peaceful Side of the Smokies

For those who love the beauty of the Smokies, but not the crowds and commercialism, Townsend, Tennessee, is a tonic. Though it is one of the three main entrances to the park, this town, population 350, is anything but touristy—no wall-to-wall gift shops, no chain restaurants, nary a discount outlet.

One reason that Townsend has escaped buildup is that the gateway here doesn't lead into the heavily trafficked main park road. It's easy enough to get to the park for a visit, but from this home base you are convenient to beautiful areas that many visitors miss, for example, the 4,000-acre, mountain-rimmed valley called Cades Cove and the Little River Gorge. You can also find scenic drives and hiking trails guaranteed to be traffic-free even at the height of fall color season.

U.S. 321, the main artery through Townsend, links with heavily wooded Scenic Highway 73, into the park. Bear right at the intersection, and you'll soon spy the green meadows of Cades Cove. In early Appalachian days, "cove" was another word for "valley," and this one is ringed by surrounding mountains.

This was frontier country in 1820, when it was acquired by the state of Tennessee from the Cherokee Indians. In 1850, the population of settlers peaked at 685, comprising 137 families, each an almost self-contained economic unit.

The population began to dwindle as families eventually moved farther west in search of newer and more fertile frontiers. Many members of the community moved out when the national park was established in the late 1920s, leaving their homes, churches, and mill behind.

The 11-mile driving tour of the cove on a one-way loop shows the original lifestyle in the valley. The historic structures include a working gristmill, a variety of barns, three churches, and a wonderful collection of log homes. There are 17 stops on the driving loop; only the visitor center and blacksmith shop are not historic structures. All the other buildings were assembled here after removal from other places in the park.

The Gregg-Cable House, built in 1879, may have been the first frame house in the community. It served as a store, boardinghouse, and private residence, and remained in the family until Aunt Becky Cable died, in 1940.

The cantilever barn, a building style that originated centuries ago in Europe, was used frequently in eastern Tennessee. The loft could hold several tons of hay, and the large overhead protected many head of cattle plus farm equipment. There were no posts to get in the way.

Half-hour walking tours of the historic community are given by park rangers, and there are living-history demonstrations at the gristmill area. Special programs at the homes and churches tell about how the first settlers lived and worshipped.

Cades Cove makes for an excellent bicycle tour, with time to savor the scenery. Horseback riding is available from the Cades Cove Riding Stables, which also give hayrides in the Cove in season.

The favorite hike from the Loop Road is to Abrams Falls, one of the largest waterfalls in the park, reached via a moderate five-mile round-trip trek.

For trails outside the park, in the Townsend area, ask for the hiking brochure at the town's visitor center. They also offer a guide to bicycle trails, both in and out of the park.

If you turn left instead of right at the junction near the park entrance, you will be taking a scenic drive along the Little River Gorge and looking upstream at the rapids. The gorge road was constructed on the bed of railroad tracks once used in the logging operations that built the town of Townsend early in this century. It takes about 45 minutes from Townsend along this road to reach the Sugarlands Visitor Center, south of Gatlinburg.

Along the way you will see Indian Head, also known as Great Stone Face, a large rock overhanging the highway, carved by some celestial sculptor into the likeness of the face of an Indian. Meigs Falls are also visible from the highway, across from the spot where Meigs Creek empties into the river. Take a break to see Laurel Falls, one of the most visited in the park, reached via an easy, paved mile-and-a-quarter walk.

East of Fighting Gap Creek, watch for Maloney Point and an excellent view of the Sugarlands Valley and 6,593-foot Mount LeConte, the highest peak in Tennessee.

Past the Sugarland Visitor Center, Little River Road feeds into the Roaring Fork Motor Nature Trail, a pleasant, albeit steep and curvy, drive through five miles of young forest and past aging pioneer structures. You can pick up a self-guiding booklet at the road entrance. Much of the drive follows the rapid descent of the creek. Water cascades down the moss-covered rocks in a noisy froth that tells you why the falls were named "roaring."

From here you can turn right on U.S. 441 to check out the shops in Gatlinburg, or go left to join the rest of the leaf-lookers on Newfound Gap Road, the main park road.

If you prefer more-private drives to admire the foliage, there are two prime routes off the Cades Cove Loop Road. About a third of the way along the 11-mile loop, a sharp right turn takes you onto Rich Mountain Road, a well-maintained, one-way gravel road. It presents panoramic views of Cades Cove, and is a favorite spot for photographers. If you are energetic, it is a moderate 8.5-mile round-trip hike to the top.

The road leads to the Dry Valley area near Tuckaleechee Caverns, and to U.S. 321 in Townsend. Take a break underground to visit the cavern, a one-mile walk along an underground stream with lots of stalactites and stalagmites in eerie shapes on all sides.

A longer detour from the Loop Road is the right turn just past the Cable Mill area to Parsons Branch Road, another gravel road, which follows the Little Tennessee River on its route to the North Carolina state line. You'll have a close-up view of the trees in their autumn finery on the way to Calderwood Lake and Dam, where there are fine vistas of Shuckstack, a 4,000-foot peak at the southern end of the park.

The road descends to U.S. 129, where a right turn takes you to the Chilhowee Dam and Lake, with easy access for fishing and boating.

Highway 129 continues across the mouth of Abrams Creek, at 857 feet the lowest point in Great Smoky Mountains National Park.

To complete your foliage route, at Chilhowee, turn right again to the Foothills Parkway. Eventually this parkway will stretch for 72 miles north, ending at I–40, and will offer dramatic Smokies vistas. The plan, approved by Congress in 1944, has been slow to be realized, but the 17-mile section from U.S. 129 to U.S. 321 at Walland is complete, and it is noted for its autumn views.

When you turn right, back to Townsend, on U.S. 321 at Walland, you are at the turnoff to West Millers Cove Road and the most elegant lodging on the Tennessee side of the Smokies, The Inn at Blackberry Farm. It is hard to imagine a more scenic view than the ridges of the mountains seen across the green lawns from the inn's terrace. The rambling stone-and-shingle house is on 1,100 secluded acres offering mountain trails and trout streams to please hikers, joggers, cyclists, and anglers. Tennis, swimming, and lawn games complete the picture.

The inn's sitting room has the ambience of an English country house, and the 25 guest rooms are decorated with rich English florals and antiques. Rates include three sumptuous meals.

If you prefer something a bit more modest, there's an equally delightful choice high on a ridge in Townsend, with equally spectacular views of Rich Mountain. The Richmont Inn is built in the shape of a classic cantilever barn, and furnished simply and tastefully, with an appreciation of the area and its history. Each room is named for a prominent Appalachian settler, and decorated appropriately. Most have fireplaces, some have spa-tubs, and several offer private balconies for savoring the view.

The inn is in the Laurel Valley vacation-home development, which includes a golf course with lovely views. Homes and condos may be rented for a weekend or a week. At the top of the hill is a restaurant with its own view. Townsend dining reflects the town—no frills, but plenty of variety.

An excellent option for families is Pioneer Cabins and Guest Farm, vacation log cabins with full kitchens, set on 41 secluded acres. The grounds include a pond for fishing and boating, hiking trails, a petting farm, and a pick-it-yourself vegetable garden.

There are other cabin colonies in the area, and particularly pleasant motels in town, with lovely garden landscaping. In fact, Townsend offers everything you might expect for a fall mountain outing—except the crowds.

Area Code: 615

DRIVING DIRECTIONS   Townsend is located on U.S. 321, about 32 miles south of Knoxville. From I–40 at Knoxville, take U.S. 441 south to U.S. 321. From southern points, Townsend can be reached on a scenic route via U.S. 411 to U.S. 129 to U.S. 321 south, or by taking I–75 past Chattanooga to the Lenoir City exit to U.S. 321 south. It is 213 miles from Atlanta, 197 miles from Nashville.

PUBLIC TRANSPORTATION   Townsend is about a 45-minute drive from Knoxville's McGee Tyson Airport.

ACCOMMODATIONS   *The Inn at Blackberry Farm,* 1471 West Millers Cove, Walland 37886, 800–862–7610, EE, AP ● *Richmont Inn,* 550 Country Club Drive, Laurel Valley, Townsend 37882, 448–6751, M-E, CP ● *Pioneer Cabins and Guest Farm,* P.O. Box 297, Townsend 37882, 448–6100 or 800–621–9751, M ● *Laurel Valley,* c/o White Oak Realty, P.O. Box 247, Townsend 37882, 448–6697, private homes and villas, one night, E, two nights or more, M ● *Valley View Lodge,* Highway 321, P.O. Box 148, Townsend 37882, 800–292–4844 out of state, 800–882–3341 in Tennessee, motel, I ● *Highland Manor Motel,* Highway 321, P.O. Box 242, Townsend 37882, 800–321–0286, I.

DINING   *Kinzel House,* 7002 East Lamar Alexander Parkway (U.S. 321), Townsend, 448–9075, excellent chef, buffets Friday and Sunday, I-M ● *Laurel Valley Restaurant,* Laurel Valley Resort, 448–9534, informal ambience, lovely setting and views, I ● *Hearth and Kettle,* Highway 321, Townsend, 448–6059, Southern country cooking, I ● *Timbers,* 8123 Lamar Alexander Parkway (U.S. 321), 448–6838, prime ribs are the specialty, I-M.

SIGHTSEEING   *Great Smoky Mountain National Park,* 107 Park Headquarters Road, Gatlinburg, 436–1200. Hours: Cades Cove Visitor Center, daily 9 A.M. to 7 P.M. in summer; to 6 P.M. spring and fall; 8:30 A.M. to 4:30 P.M. rest of year; free ● *Tuckaleechee Caverns,* off U.S. 321, Townsend. Hours: April 1 to October 31, 9 A.M. to 6 P.M.; late March and early November, 10 A.M. to 5 P.M.; closed rest of year; $$$.

SPORTS   *Bicycle rentals: Cades Cove Bike Shop,* Cades Cove, 448–9311 ● *Golf: Laurel Valley Golf Course,* 720 Country Club Drive, 448–6690; phone for fees and tee times ● *Horseback riding and hayrides: Cades Cove Stables,* 4035 Lamar Alexander Parkway,

Townsend, 448–6286; *Davy Crockett Stables,* Highway 73, Townsend, 448–6411.

INFORMATION   Smoky Mountain Visitors Bureau, c/o Townsend Visitors Center, 7906 East Lamar Alexander Parkway (U.S. 321), Townsend, TN 37882, 448–6134.

Making History in Georgia

The peaceful villages and rural farmland in southwestern Georgia don't seem to be places where historic events would take place—but sometimes looks are deceiving.

Andersonville, just a dot on the map, became the site of the most notorious Confederate prison of the Civil War era, a place where more than 12,000 Union prisoners perished.

Plains is a town to restore your faith in the American dream. Who could have predicted that this isolated hamlet, population 650, would have produced the first president to come from the South since the Civil War? Or become a tourist attraction that draws thousands of visitors each year?

Near the little town of Lumpkin, the 1850 village of Westville is unique in Georgia, a remarkably realistic re-creation of a nineteenth-century village. Much of this is lively history that will keep you entertained as you learn.

While you're in the neighborhood, you can take a look at Providence Canyon, Georgia's own wondrous "Little Grand Canyon." And you might wind things up in Columbus, a city that has nicely preserved its past.

Proper headquarters for your historic weekend is the lavishly restored 1892 Windsor Hotel in Americus, less than ten miles from Plains to the southwest and Andersonville to the northeast. If you prefer cozier quarters, there are several bed-and-breakfast inns in town and nearby.

Founded in 1832 as the county seat, Americus prospered both before and after the Civil War from the abundant surrounding cotton fields and from its position as a railroad center. The town has preserved many of the best of its antebellum and turn-of-the-century buildings. Pick up a local driving tour and admire the Victorian homes on Church Street and Rees Park, the earlier structures on Taylor Street, and the mix of periods on Lee and College streets.

Downtown, a major building boom occurred in the prosperous 1880s and 1890s. The old wooden buildings were replaced with grand brick structures such as the Glover Opera House and the courthouse with its imposing clock tower.

The queen of them all was the Windsor Hotel, known as the crown jewel of South Georgia in the days when it hosted elaborate balls. When the Windsor reopened in 1991, with the brick towers and turrets, golden oak woodwork and soaring atrium lobby as grand as ever, it sparked the further downtown revitalization now taking place.

Jimmy Carter, a young politician from neighboring Plains, got his political start representing Americus and Sumter County in the Georgia legislature. The Carter Library, on the Georgia Southwestern College campus, offers photos, a film, and lots of Carter memorabilia.

When you've had a look around Americus, take the short drive to Andersonville. It is a sobering experience to tour the grounds of what was officially known as Camp Sumter and realize the harsh reality of this place, now a serene field of green. The 12-minute slide program at the visitor center will help you to understand what took place here.

Stone columns mark the line once formed by stockade posts at this largest of the Confederate military prisons, built in 1864. During the prison's 14 months of existence, more than 45,000 Union soldiers were crowded into these inadequate stockades, without trees for shade and no shelter except their own clothing, scraps of tenting, and loose lumber.

Food was scarce for both captors and captured. Thousands died from disease, malnutrition, polluted water, or exposure. Photos of the bone-thin prisoners released at the end of the war remind one of the concentration-camp survivors of World War II. The commander of the camp, Henry Wirz, was tried and executed after the war.

The Andersonville National Historic Site, which includes a National Cemetery where soldiers from both sides are buried, today serves as a memorial to all Americans ever held as prisoners of war. A museum explains the role of prisoner-of-war camps in history and commemorates the sacrifice of Americans who lost their lives in such camps.

The village of Andersonville, the terminal where prisoners arrived by train, began to revive as visitors came to the prison site, and it has been restored to look much like the town that existed a century ago. The old depot is now a welcome center and museum, and the little log church remains. Civil War buffs will want to see the wealth of memorabilia at the Drummer Boy Civil War Museum.

The town park, five shady acres, boasts a living pioneer farm area with log cabins, animals, and a sugarcane mill and syrup kettle. The Andersonville Guild, which is responsible for much of the restoration, also sponsors two historic fairs in this park that bring thousands to town every year. An antiques fair takes place over Memorial Day weekend. The Historic Fair, held the first full weekend in October, is the big event, offering dozens of old-time artisans working at their traditional crafts, plus square dancers, cloggers, and military bands. During this fall weekend, you can see large-scale mock skirmishes between Confederate and Union troops.

One last worthwhile stop in Andersonville is the 1833 Trebor Plantation, once one of the largest and most prosperous in the area. It has remained in the same family for five generations. The gracious Greek Revival main house and more than a dozen outbuildings are in varying stages of restoration.

If you come back to Americus for the night, the best bet for dinner is the Windsor Hotel's handsome dining room. Or, if you're up for a drive of about 25 miles, head for Lake Blackshear and the Daphne Lodge, specializing in game dishes and good ol' catfish dinners. The biscuits here are famous.

When you make your way to Plains, you'll find a town as unpretentious as its most famous resident. Stop at the National Park Service temporary headquarters in the town train station.

This is the spot that Carter made his hometown headquarters, where he was greeted by crowds of neighbors whenever he came home, no matter what the hour. It was here that he returned after his election as the nation's thirty-ninth president, bringing tears to the eyes of his friends and shedding a few tears himself.

At the visitor center, you can watch a film about Carter's rise to national prominence and take a picture tour of his Plains home, narrated by none other than Jimmy and Rosalynn Carter, both attired in blue jeans. The unpretentious former president sounds like any proud do-it-yourselfer when he points out the shelves and bed he built for his daughter Amy.

You can take a ranger-guided walking tour of Plains, buy a self-guided tour booklet, or rent a cassette to take you around town, but it's more fun to sign up for the tours offered from B.J.'s Pitt Stop, the gas station that used to belong to Billy Carter, the president's late brother. The guides give you all the local gossip when they show you the sights, assuring you that the Carters were not the richest folks in town and telling you who was. They'll point out Rosalynn's mother if she happens to be on her porch, and show you the public housing where the couple and their three children lived when they returned to Plains in 1953 after Jimmy Carter's naval service. Then they'll show you the house the Carters rented in 1955, known as the "haunted house" for the many tales of its ghosts.

The present Carter home is not open to tours, but if you happen to arrive when they are in town, you are welcome to attend Sunday school at the Maranatha Baptist Church, where President and Mrs. Carter both teach. You might also spot them having a meal at the Kountry Korner, the local dining spot.

Downtown you'll likely find cousin Hugh Carter in his dusty store filled with antiques and Carter memorabilia, and you can take the obligatory snapshot down the street in front of the giant smiling peanut.

Plains is small—you can see everything in less than two hours—but you won't soon forget it.

From Plains, it's about a 26-mile drive to Lumpkin, a pretty little town boasting a classic square. Stop for a look at the Singer Company, Georgia's oldest hardware store, established in 1838 by Johann George Singer, a German immigrant, and still operated by his great-great-grandson.

Nearby is Westville, an outdoor museum on 58 acres re-creating a village straight out of the 1850s. The buildings here are authentic, from farmhouse to town house, from church to carriage shelter, brought from nearby areas and reassembled as a town.

The residents in each house or strolling along the unpaved paths of the village wear properly old-fashioned clothing, including ruffled bonnets and broad-brimmed hats to keep off the sun. As you walk around, you'll likely see an elderly craftsman making baskets, hear the clang of the blacksmith's hammer, and smell the gingerbread and biscuits cooking on the stove and in the fireplace. It's all wonderfully realistic.

It's only seven miles west of Lumpkin on Georgia route 39C to reach Providence Canyon State Conservation Park, where multicolored layers of soil form Georgia's "Little Grand Canyon." The chasm is vast, the colors are fantastic, and the wild azaleas and wildflowers growing in the protected canyon make for a scene of rare natural beauty. The park provides picnic grounds and three miles of hiking trails if you want to stay awhile.

A fine way to wind up the weekend is to come back east to Lumpkin and take Georgia route 27/U.S. 280 north about 31 miles to Columbus.

Columbus was a planned city, established in 1828 on the banks of the Chattahoochee River. The home of many mills and the Columbus Iron Works, which manufactured cannons and gunboats during the Civil War, the city has preserved many of its early buildings in a 26-block National Register Historic District, which can be seen in a short, pleasant drive.

For some award-winning examples of preservation, go along the river to see the old iron works, now a striking Convention and Trade Center, and over to Front Avenue, on the edge of the historic district, where an abandoned mill has been converted into a most unusual Hilton Hotel.

Ride along Broadway to view the city's attractively restored Victorian homes. Don't miss the Springer Opera House on Tenth Street at First Avenue, an 1871 beauty that has been restored to its Victorian splendor and is once again presenting plays on its stage. It is now the official State Theater of Georgia.

If you have the time, the Historic Columbus Foundation offers guided walking tours of several historic properties. Military buffs may want to make a stop at the only Confederate Naval Museum, where remains of two warships are on display, or take in the National Infantry Museum at Fort Benning, a march across time with the American infantry from the 1750s to the present.

A short visit to the handsome Columbus Museum will tell you more about the development of the entire Chattahoochee valley.

The museum's excellent film about the city boasts about the barbecue that is Columbus's pride. Taste a sample at one of the locations of Country's Barbecue, and you'll see why they brag.

Or perhaps you'd rather wind up a weekend of history with another bit of the past, at Bludau's at the 1839 Goetchius House. Thanks to philanthropist J. W. Woodruff (one of the Coca-Cola Woodruffs), the New Orleans–style mansion was saved and moved to a new site in the lower Broadway historic district. The elegantly restored interior is now a series of dining rooms with an equally elegant Continental menu.

Area Code: 912

DRIVING DIRECTIONS Americus is at the intersection of U.S. 19 and Ga. Route 27, about 28 miles west of I–75. From Atlanta, the most direct route is south on U.S. 19, or take I–75 and turn west on Ga. Route 27, 130 miles. From Americus to Plains, drive 9 miles west on Ga. Route 27; continue on Ga. Route 27 another 26 miles to Lumpkin. From Lumpkin to Columbus, follow U.S. 27/Ga. Route 1 north into U.S. 280 North, 31 miles. Returning from Columbus to Atlanta, take I–185 into I–85 North, 123 miles. Birmingham is 114 miles from Columbus via U.S. 280, about another 66 miles to Americus.

ACCOMMODATIONS *Windsor Hotel,* Americus 31709, 924–1555, I-M ● *Cottage Inn,* Macon Road, P.O. Box 488, Americus 31709, 924–9316, antebellum raised cottage, I, CP ● *Merriwood Country Inn,* Mask Road, Americus 31709, 924–4992, rustic homestead in the country, I, CP ● *Morris Manor,* 425 Timberlane Drive, Americus 31709, 924–4884, Georgian Colonial, rural setting, I, CP ● *New Land Bed & Breakfast,* Highway 19 north, Americus 31709, 928–9620, two log cabins on the outskirts of town, I, CP ● *A Place Away Cottage,* 110 Oglethorpe Street, Andersonville 31711, 924–1044, quaint private cottage, I, CP ● *Plains Bed & Breakfast Inn,* 100 West Church Street, Plains 31780, 824–7252, Victorian home, I, CP ● *Columbus Hilton,* 400 Front Avenue, Columbus 31901, 706–324–1800, restored nineteenth-century mill, pool, M-E.

DINING *Windsor Hotel* (see above), I-E ● *Sheppard House,* 411 Tripp Street, Americus, 924–8756, come for lunch buffet and barbecue, closes at 5:30 P.M., I ● *Daphne Lodge,* Highway 280, Lake Blackshear (25 miles east of Americus), 273–2596, country lodge serving quail, rabbit, fried catfish, I-M ● *Country's Barbecue,* 313 Mercury Drive, Columbus, 563–7604. Other locations: *Country's North,* Main Street Village, Hamilton Road at Weems Road, 660–1415; *Country's on Broad,* 1329 Broadway, 596–8910, all with delicious barbecue, all I ● *Kountry Korner,* Highway 280, Plains, 824–7467, breakfast, lunch, dinners Friday and Saturday, I ● *Bludau's Goetchius House,* 405 Broadway, Columbus, 324–4863, 1839 antebellum mansion, Continental menu, M-EE ● *McKinley's,* 2041A Auburn Avenue, Cross Country Plaza, Columbus, 563–4488, American, casual, I-M.

SIGHTSEEING *Andersonville National Historic Site,* Ga. route 49, Andersonville, 924–0343. Hours: park, daily 8 A.M. to 5 P.M.; museum, daily 8:30 A.M. to 5 P.M.; free ● *Andersonville Historic Fair,* c/o Andersonville Guild, P.O. Box 6, Andersonville 31711, 924–2558. Crafts demonstration, music, dancing, and mock Civil War battles, held first weekend in October; check for current information ● *Drummer Boy Civil War Museum,* Andersonville Village, 924–2558. Hours: spring through fall, Tuesday to Saturday 10 A.M. to 4 P.M., $$ ● *Jimmy Carter National Historic Site,* Railroad Depot, U.S. 280, Plains, 824–3413. Hours: daily 9 A.M. to 5 P.M., free ● *Trebor Plantation,* P.O. Box 25, Andersonville, 924–6886. Hours: Wednesday to Monday 10 A.M. to 5 P.M. $$ ● *Providence Canyon State Conservation Park,* Ga. route 39C, Lumpkin, 838–6202. Hours: mid-April to mid-September, daily 7 A.M. to 9 P.M.; rest of year to 6 P.M.; office hours, 8 A.M. to 5 P.M.; parking fee, $ ● *Westville Village,* Troutman Road off Ga. Route 27, Westville, 838–6310. Hours: Tuesday to Saturday 10 A.M. to 5 P.M.; Sunday 1 P.M. to 5 P.M.; $$$ ● *Columbus Museum,* 1251 Wynnton Road, 649–0713. Hours: Tuesday to Saturday 10 A.M. to 5 P.M.; Sunday 1 P.M. to 5 P.M.; free ● *Heritage Corner Tours,* 700 Broadway, Columbus, 322–3181. Hours: tours given Monday to Friday 11 A.M. and 3 P.M.; Saturday at 1 P.M.; $ ● *Confederate Naval Museum,* 202 Fourth Street, Columbus, 327–9798. Hours: Tuesday to Friday 10 A.M. to 5 P.M.; Saturday and Sunday 1 P.M. to 5 P.M.; donation ● *National Infantry Museum,* Building 396, Baltzell Avenue, Fort Benning, 545–2958. Hours: Monday to Friday 8 A.M. to 4:30 P.M.; Saturday and Sunday 12:30 P.M. to 4:30 P.M.; free.

Telling Tales in Jonesborough

Storytellers are spellbinders. The skill of an actor, the wit of a comedian, and warmth that either might envy—these are the tools of the trade of a talented teller, who knows how to stir the imagination, to send you into gales of laughter—and move you to tears.

If you have not experienced the joy of a tale told by a master, make haste next October to Jonesborough, Tennessee, where the nation's best tellers gather for the National Storytelling Festival, a nonstop marathon of verbal treasure.

As the oldest town in Tennessee and the first in the state to be listed on the National Register of Historic Places, tiny Jonesborough, population 3,100, is the perfect setting.

Storytellers have been with us as long as there have been children to plead "Tell me a story," but the art waned after the invention of the printing press and was almost lost in the pat scripts and canned laughter of the television age.

A Jonesborough journalist, Jimmy Neil Smith, was inspired when he heard someone telling tales on the radio one fateful day over 20 years ago. The storytelling festival he first put together in 1972 in the high school gym and on a haywagon in front of the Jonesborough Town Hall was the first full-fledged gathering of its kind.

Today the festival attracts more than 10,000 visitors each year, and has spearheaded a national revival of storytelling.

If you are attending for the first time, you'll find six giant tents set up around the town, each one big enough to hold about 1,000 people. One is devoted entirely to family programs, making this a great weekend with the kids.

Begin your visit with the purchase of a ticket at the visitor center and a look at the schedule. During the day, three tellers perform per hour in each tent, followed by a half-hour break. In the evening, eight or nine tellers take turns. There's also an extra ghost-story session in Mill Spring Park on Friday and Saturday nights, lit by spooky lantern light. One ticket gives admittance to all the tents, so you can take your tales in small or massive doses, as you please.

All of the 80-plus performers are stars of the storytelling circuit, but there are superstars among them, so if the names are not familiar to you, talk to people around you to discover the standouts. You can also check the resource sales tent to see which names have the most records and books to their credit.

In any event, you'll want to spend some time in the resource tent. The big selection of books, records, and tapes gathered here from many sources is unmatched, and it is a major lure for many who come to the festival. The sales tent, like the festival, is sponsored by the National Association for the Preservation and Perpetuation of Storytelling (NAPPS), an organization based in Jonesborough and dedicated to fostering storytelling in classrooms, libraries, and local gatherings.

When you've zeroed in on a few tellers you want to hear, find them on the schedule and take a seat in the tent where they will perform. Do this long before the appointed hour, to be sure of getting a seat; if you wait until the session begins, you'll be left standing in the rear. The pleasure you'll reap from those who perform while you are waiting makes the time go fast. Young or old, mountain man or city sophisticate, each brings something unique and personal to the art, leaving listeners enriched.

If you see that Donald Davis is appearing, grab a seat in a hurry. A native of the Southern Appalachians and a retired minister, Davis spins wonderful tales of the trials of growing up, of imperious grandmothers and mischievous but well-meaning boys, stories that never fail to spark recognition and warm laughter.

Bearded Jay O'Callahan of Marshfield, Massachusetts, is another extraordinary teller, who livens his performances with sound, rhythm, and movement. He has been heard on National Public Radio and has won awards for his recordings.

The possibilities go on and on. North Carolinian Jackie Torrence is famous for her tales of growing up on the farm. Kathryn Windham not only collects and tells ghost stories, but is said to have a resident ghost in her home in Selma, Alabama. Mary Hamilton will surely enchant you with her hilarious tall tales, told with such conviction, you can't be quite sure whether they are too tall to be true.

Ray Hicks, a western North Carolina potato farmer and jack-of-all-mountain-trades, is considered the patriarch of traditional storytelling in America, and Doc McConnell does his turn in the form of an old-time medicine show.

The scheduling allows plenty of time to wander around Jonesborough. If this town's buildings could speak, they would tell marvelous stories of their own. The town came within two votes of becoming the capital of America's fourteenth state, which would have been known as Franklin.

This was the frontier country of legends. Daniel Boone helped open up the territory, and Davy Crockett was born down the road. In 1779 the first township was staked out in what was then part of North Carolina, and named in honor of a state assemblyman, Willie Jones. Later, North Carolina ceded her western land, including Jonesborough, to the new federal government. Congress did not respond immediately, so the people set up their own government, forming the state of Franklin, with Jonesborough as capital and John Sevier as governor.

Franklin was expected to be officially named the first new state since the original 13 colonies, but it received only seven of the needed nine votes, supposedly because two delegates known to favor admission were absent when the vote was taken. So Franklin disappeared into Tennessee, which, in 1796, finally became the nation's sixteenth state.

Jonesborough prospered anyway as a major stopping place for pioneers moving westward. The citizens built railroads and published newspapers, including the nation's first antislavery periodicals. Andrew Jackson lived here for a time, practicing law and presiding in the courthouse. Andrew Johnson was a neighbor. Frontiersmen often came into town to pay their taxes in beaver skins.

But recent events had not been kind to the town. When Interstate 81 ignored Jonesborough, and malls in Johnson City began to hurt business on Main Street, stores began to close and buildings fell into disrepair. Realizing that their best hope for the future lay in the past, town leaders developed a plan to restore historic Main Street, hoping to build an economy based on tourism.

Special events such as Historic Jonesborough Days, held annually around the Fourth of July holiday, began to draw people. But it was the Storytelling Festival that put Jonesborough firmly on the map. The large, modern visitor center on the edge of town is a sign of the new prosperity. This is where you can pick up a printed walking tour to guide you around the tiny town. The building also includes a museum chronicling the local history.

Most of the sights are right on Main Street. Cradled between hills, the four-block heart of town is paved with brick and cobblestone and crammed with history. The look is still very much nineteenth-century. Electric wires have been buried, and street lights resemble old-fashioned gas lamps. The architecture, which might be called "frontier-colonial," is a mix of brick, clapboard, and hand-hewn logs.

The Chester Inn, dating from the 1790s, is the oldest frame structure in town. It has hosted Presidents Jackson, Polk, and Johnson, and it was nearby that Jackson once helped fight a fire while wearing only his nightshirt. The building is now owned by the state of Tennessee and is the home of NAPPS.

The Christopher Taylor House, a circa–1778 two-story log house, was rescued from a lonely field outside town as the keystone of the town's restoration effort. Andrew Jackson boarded here during his stay in town. It was in Jonesborough that Jackson was admitted to the bar and later presided as a judge. The site of the town's original courthouse, dating from 1779, was occupied in 1913 by an imposing new towered courthouse with a massive clock.

The Greek Revival Presbyterian church, built in the 1840s, retains its original pulpit, pews, and slave gallery. Many homes from the 1830s and 1840s are also pointed out on the tour.

Behind many old façades are galleries and gift shops. The Old Town

Hall houses more than 30 merchants selling antiques, crafts, clothing, and toys. The Salt House, where salt was rationed in the 1840s, holds specialty shops. The Keene Gallery features art by East Tennessee artists in a restored 1879 wooden commercial building, while the Jonesborough Trading Company offers regional books and a coffee and pastry shop in an 1871 setting. The Jonesborough Antique Mart brims with collectibles in 50 minishops.

During the festival, food is served at outdoor stands, but otherwise choices are limited in Jonesborough. Other than fast food, there is only one choice for dinner, but it is exceptional. The Parson's Table, housed in the soaring spaces of an 1874 Gothic church, is filled with Victoriana and charm. The menu is French, and the Sunday buffet, known as the Seventh Day Feast, brings crowds from miles around.

If you take the time for an afternoon's drive, more history beckons all around the area. About 15 minutes west, off U.S. 11E, is the Davy Crockett Birthplace State Historic Park on the Nolichuckey River, with a restoration of the cabin where the famed frontiersman was born. Another 15 minutes farther west, in Greeneville, is the home of Andrew Johnson, a national historic site, as well as the quaint stone buildings of Tusculom, Tennessee's oldest college, and the state's oldest jail, dating to 1804.

Head north to Rogersville to see the oldest original courthouse still in use in Tennessee, dating from 1836, and the oldest continuously operating hotel in the state, the 1824 Hale Springs Inn.

Like Jonesborough, Greeneville and Rogersville are towns that have beautifully preserved the look of the past. They supply pictures; the words of the storytellers bring them to life.

Area Code: 615

DRIVING DIRECTIONS   Jonesborough is located on U.S. 11E in eastern Tennessee, about 95 miles east of Knoxville and 6 miles southwest of Johnson City. It is reached via I–81. From Atlanta, take I–75 north to I–40 east, which merges into I–81. Continue to exit 23, U.S. 11E, at Bulls Gap, about 325 miles.

PUBLIC TRANSPORTATION   Tri-City Regional Airport, serving Johnson City, is 25 minutes from Jonesborough.

ACCOMMODATIONS   Jonesborough inns are very small and fill up far in advance for the Storytelling Festival, when rates may be slightly higher than usual. Alternatives are the motels and hotels in Johnson City, where early reservations are also advised. *Hawley House,* 114 East Woodrow Avenue, Jonesborough 37659, 753–8869, quaint eighteenth-century log-and-frame home, folk art, best in town, I-M, CP ● *Jonesborough Bed and Breakfast,* Woodrow and South Cherokee streets, Jonesborough 37659, 753–9223, 1848 home, antiques, I, CP ● *Countryside Bed and Breakfast,* 131 Taylor Road, Jonesborough 37659, 753–3252 or 753–3832, country home, pool, I, CP ● *Aiken-Brow House,* 104 Third Avenue South, Jonesborough 37659, 753–9440, 1850s Victorian with gazebo, Victorian decor, I, CP ● *Bugaboo Bed and Breakfast,* 211 Semore Drive, Jonesborough 37659, 753–9345, pleasant country home 1 mile from town, I-M, CP ● *Garden Plaza,* 211 Mockingbird Lane, Johnson City 37601, 929–2000, motor hotel, I-M ● *Holiday Inn,* 2406 Roan Street, Johnson City 37601, 282–2161, I ● *Sheraton Plaza,* 101 West Springbrook Drive, Johnson City 37602, 282–4611, hotel, M ● *Fairfield Inn by Marriott,* 207 East Mountcastle, Johnson City 37601, 282–3335, motel, I ● *Rodeway Inn,* 2312 Brown's Mill Road, Johnson City 37601, 282–2211, motel, I ● *Super 8 Motel,* 108 Wesley, Johnson City 37601, 929–2000, I ● *Big Spring Inn,* 315 North Main Street, Greeneville 37743, 638–2917, I-M, CP ● *Hale Springs Inn,* 110 West Main Street, Rogersville 37857, 272–5171, state's oldest inn, I, CP.

DINING *The Parson's Table,* 102 Woodrow Avenue, Jonesborough, 753–8002, delightful setting in a nineteenth-century church, French fare, lunch and dinner, I-E ● *Firehouse,* 327 West Walnut, Johnson City, 929–7377, converted 1930s firehouse, ribs are the specialty, I ● *Peerless Steak House,* 2531 Roan Street, Johnson City, 282–2351, seafood and steaks, I-E.

SIGHTSEEING *National Storytelling Festival,* National Association for the Preservation and Perpetuation of Storytelling, P.O. Box 309, Jonesborough, 753–2171 or 800–952–8392. Three-day event held the first weekend in October. Phone for current information ● *Jonesborough History Museum,* 117 Boone Street, 753–9775. Hours: Monday to Friday 8 A.M. to 5 P.M.; Saturday and Sunday 10 A.M. to 5 P.M.; $ ● *Davy Crockett Birthplace State Park,* off U.S. 11E, Limestone, 257–2167. Hours: museum and visitor center, daily 8 A.M. to 4:30 P.M.; historical cabin 8 A.M. to 10 P.M. in season; free ● *Andrew Johnson National Historic Site,* visitor center, Depot and College streets, Greeneville, 638–3551. Hours: daily 9 A.M. to 5 P.M.; visitor center free; homestead $.

INFORMATION *Historic Jonesborough Visitors Center,* 117 Boone Street, P.O. Box 375-E, Jonesborough, TN 37659, 753–5961 ●

Northeast Tennessee Tourism Council, P.O. Box 375, Jonesborough, TN 37659, 753–4188, or 800–468–6882 outside TN.

 # Autumn Leafing in Alabama

Mention Lookout Mountain and many people think of Tennessee, but in Alabama they know better. The peak known by this name may rise above Chattanooga; the range of which it is a part may touch on Georgia; but most of this 100-mile-long mountain ridge lies squarely in Alabama's northeastern corner, where it provides one of the Southeast's most spectacular fall foliage routes.

The Lookout Mountain Parkway, between Gadsden and Mentone, runs across the crests of the Southern Appalachian foothills, with autumn color in full glory on all sides. Those who want a closer view can take a break along part of the 76-mile hiking trail that parallels the parkway.

If you plan a leaf-watching tour, you can also take in a variety of sights and pleasures along the way. Natural wonders beckon, ranging from underground lakes to dramatic canyons. Country music fans can visit the hometown and museum of the group Alabama; golfers can tee off on a mountaintop course in the clouds; riders can visit a scenic dude ranch; and shoppers can go wild at the state's biggest flea market and largest outlet mall.

The southern end of the parkway begins in Gadsden, where you can start things off nicely with a ride on the riverboat *Alabama Princess*, along the scenic Coosa River. Special fall color cruises are scheduled in late October and early November.

Gadsden's pride is Noccalula Falls, cascading 90 feet down into a beautiful ravine. According to legend, an Indian princess, heartbroken because her father disapproved of the man she loved, plunged to her death here on her wedding day rather than go through with a dreaded arranged marriage. Her bereaved father named the falls in her memory. A statue of the young girl stands near the waterfall.

The falls are just one part of a town park that includes extensive botanical gardens with over 25,000 azaleas, a pioneer village, miniature train rides, picnic areas, hiking trails, miniature golf, and a children's playground.

Though the best lodgings and scenery await farther north, shoppers might choose to stay in Gadsden on Friday night in order to beat the crowds headed for Boaz, 19 miles north via U.S. 431. This is one of the South's largest outlet centers, with more than 140 stores.

If you're more intrigued with the kind of bargains to be found at a giant flea market, you can join the hunt a few miles north on Highway 22 in Collinsville, where Trade Day brings out 1,000 vendors selling crafts, clothing, furniture, fresh produce, plants, animals, and—you name it. This Saturday outdoor event has been a tradition since the early 1900s.

Should you be in this area on Sunday, the Mountain Top Flea Market goes into action in Attalla, on U.S. 278 just outside Gadsden. A little bit of everything is for sale on this 970-acre site. It's the state's biggest flea-market event.

If you're looking for beauty rather than bargains, the Lookout Mountain Parkway, county road 89, beckons out of Gadsden.

Turn right on Alabama route 176 at Dogtown for an awe-inspiring sight, the Little River Canyon, one of the deepest gorges in the eastern United States. A 22-mile paved drive follows the steep, wooded wall of the canyon north to the river's source, with many overlooks for marveling at the sheer drop below. The river feeds into 60-foot Little River Falls, at the junction of the rim road and Alabama Route 35.

The scenery gets even more spectacular as you work your way up. The river begins at a natural spring on top of the mountain, where it wanders a bit, then tumbles through the rocks and crashes down more than 100 feet over De Soto Falls. The water is so clear you can see fish swimming several feet below the surface.

The beauty of Little River Canyon is protected in a 15,000-acre federal preserve that includes the 5,000 acres of Alabama's De Soto State Park, a wonderful place to stay or to visit. The park offers 20 miles of hiking trails, tennis courts, a pool, and lawn games. The 25-room stone-and-log lodge has a good restaurant and a big country porch, complete with rockers. Accommodations are available in the lodge, or in 22 chalets and rustic cabins on the grounds, most with fireplaces for cool fall evenings.

Detour farther north, above Groveoak, to discover a hidden treasure, Buck's Pocket State Park, a rugged and secluded spot in a natural pocket of the Appalachian chain. This is a nature lover's dream, with a picnic area offering vistas into the pocket below. It is said that state politicians who lose on Election Day retreat to isolated Buck's Pocket the day after to weep and wail, out of public view.

When you're ready for a touch of town with your country, head for Fort Payne, best known as the home of the wildly successful country music group Alabama. Three of the four members of the group are natives and the band was born here, so it is for sentimental reasons that the Alabama Fan Club and Museum is located nearby. An audiovisual presentation tells the story of the group, and giant photos, awards, and lots of memorabilia trace their careers.

Alabama members still have homes in Fort Payne, and they appear in person each year for the June Jam Week Festival, a fund-raiser for the community that brings big-name musicians and lots of excitement to town.

Fort Payne's other attractions include the 1891 stone train depot, richly adorned with turrets and arches. It is now a museum filled with local history exhibits. The Fort Payne Opera House, built in 1889, was described then as "the most convenient and handsome opera house in the state." Nicely restored, it is the oldest theater in Alabama still in use.

This region has its share of scenery underground, as well as above. Sequoyah Caverns is renowned for its "Looking Glass Lakes," reflecting the otherworldly cave formations for a double measure of eerie beauty. Outdoor attractions at the cave include deer, peacocks, streams full of rainbow trout, and a herd of American bison.

Farther north is another cave that is now a national monument. Excavations show that Stone Age men took shelter in Russell Cave some 9,000 years ago. The site, a limestone chamber 210 feet long and 107 feet wide, was discovered in 1953, and archaeologists have found records of continuous human habitation from 7,000 B.C. to about 1,000 A.D. After a self-guided tour of the shelter, you can stop at the visitor center to see prehistoric tools and artifacts found during excavation.

The final stop on the Alabama portion of the Lookout Mountain Parkway is the tiny town of Mentone, perched on the mountain rim 1,000 feet above the valley. The lush, wooded terrain has made it a longtime favorite area for summer camps.

Interesting shops now fill some of Mentone's weathered buildings. In the old Hitching Post, where square dances used to be held upstairs, you'll find Gourdies, with imaginative gourd dolls, and Crow's Nest Antiques. This is the unofficial town welcome center, with information about what's going on.

Mentone has also developed into a center for crafts. The town is filled with artisans showing their wares during the Mentone Fall Colorfest, the third week in October, timed for the peak fall color.

Mentone has two other unexpected attractions, both owned by the same family. Above town is the Cloudmont Ski and Golf Resort—that's right, ski. When the weather is cold enough for snow-making, this is Alabama's one and only ski area. In balmier seasons you can play golf here in the clouds, teeing off from a formation of rocks.

The latest adjunct to Cloudmont is the Shady Grove Dude and Guest Ranch, set on 1,000 acres with 100 miles of hiking trails and many miles of rivers and wilderness for other adventures. Guests enjoy horseback and wagon rides and western-style square dancing.

From Mentone, it's an easy drive to the end of the parkway through Georgia (where you can detour for spectacular scenery at Cloudland Canyon State Park) and into Chattanooga. Or, having now seen the beauty of Alabama's Lookout Mountain Parkway, you may just want to turn around and do it all again.

Area Code: 205

DRIVING DIRECTIONS   The Lookout Mountain Parkway, Ala. route 89, runs from Gadsden to Chattanooga, with Mentone the last stop in Alabama. Gadsden is at the intersection of I–759 and U.S. 411, three miles off I–59, exit 188. From Birmingham, follow via I–59 north, 60 miles. From Atlanta, follow I–20 west to I–59, 112 miles. Gadsden is 90 miles south of Chattanooga via I–59, or about 100 miles on the Lookout Mountain Parkway.

ACCOMMODATIONS   *De Soto State Park,* Route 1, P.O. Box 205, Fort Payne 35967, 845–5380 or 800-ALA-PARK, I ● *Mentone Inn Bed and Breakfast,* P.O. Box 284, Mentone 35984, 634–4836, stone-and-wood 1927 lodge, spacious, pine paneling, big porches, open April through November, I, CP ● *Cloudmont Ski and Golf Resort,* Lookout Mountain Parkway, Mentone 35984, 634–4344, chalets, I ● *Shady Grove Dude Ranch,* Alpine Road, Mentone, c/o Cloudmont, 634–4344, I ● *Humble House,* Route 1, Box 304, Valley Head (8 miles south of Mentone) 35989, 635–6682, bed-and-breakfast home with 2 guest rooms, great valley views, I, CP ● *Woodhaven,* Route 2, P.O. Box 10A, Lowry Road, Valley Head 35989, 635–6438, turn-of-the-century manor house on a working farm, fireplaces in guest rooms, children welcome, I, CP ● *Days Inn,* 1600 Rainbow Drive, Gadsden 35901, 543–1105, I ● *Holiday Inn,* 801 Cleveland Avenue, Attala 35954, 538–7861, I ● *Best Western Fort Payne,* 1828 Gault Avenue North, Fort Payne 35967, 845–0481, I ● *Days Inn,* P.O. Box 655, Fort Payne 35967, 845–2085, I.

DINING   *Cragsmere Manna,* Lookout Mountain Parkway, Mentone, 634–4677, nineteenth-century home on the mountain's rim, varied menu, I-M ● *Kountry Chef* (Dessies' Place), Mentone, 634–4232, Southern country cooking, famous for catfish, I ● *Log Cabin Deli,* Mentone, 634–4560, quaint, popular, oldest building in town, sandwiches, salads, lunch and dinner, I ● *De Soto State Park* (see above), good food, views, generous Sunday buffet, I ● *White Palace Cafe,* 504 Broad Street, Gadsden, 547–016, local landmark, I-M ● *Top O' The River,* 1606 Rainbow Drive, Gadsden, 547–9817, family style, catfish, cornbread and all the fixings, I ● To see where the mountain folks gather, have breakfast at the Tiger Inn in Valley Head.

SIGHTSEEING *Noccalula Falls Park,* 1500 Noccalula Road, Gadsden, 549–4663. Hours: daily 8 A.M. to dusk, $ ● *Alabama Princess Riverboat,* P.O. Box 1892, Gadsden, 549–1111; check current schedules, rates ● *De Soto State Park,* Route 1, P.O. Box 205, Fort Payne, 845–0051. Hours: daily 7 A.M. to dusk, $ ● *Buck's Pocket State Park,* Route 1, P.O. Box 36, Groveoak, 659–2000. Hours: 7 A.M. to dusk, $ ● *Alabama Fan Club Museum,* 201 Glenn Avenue South, Fort Payne, 845–1646. Hours: Monday to Saturday 8 A.M. to 5 P.M.; Sunday 1 P.M. to 6 P.M. $$$ ● *Depot Museum,* Fifth Street Northeast, Fort Payne, 845–5714. Hours: Monday, Wednesday, and Friday 10 A.M. to 4 P.M.; Sunday 2 to 4 P.M.; free ● *Sequoyah Caverns,* Route 1, off I–59, 6 miles north of Valley Head, 635–6423. Hours: March 1 to December, daily 8:30 A.M. to 5 P.M.; January and February, weekends only; $$$ ● *Russell Cave National Monument,* Highway 75, Bridgeport, 495–2672. Hours: daily 8 A.M. to 5 P.M., free ● *Cloudmont Ski and Golf Resort,* Box 435, County Road 89, Mentone, 634–4344, 18-hole golf course, tennis, fishing, hiking, swimming. Check current fees ● *Shady Grove Ranch,* off Highway 117, Mentone, c/o Cloudmont, 634–4344 or 634–3841, guided trail rides and wagon rides. Check current schedules and rates.

INFORMATION *Alabama Mountain Lakes Tourist Association,* 201 North Street, P.O. Box 1075, Moorsville, AL 354649, 350–3500 or 800–648–5381 ● *DeKalb County Tourist Association,* 2201 J. Gault Avenue North, Fort Payne, 845–3957 ● *Gadsden-Etowah Tourism Board, Inc.,* 1058 Rainbow Drive, P.O. Box 8367, Gadsden, AL 35902, 549–0351.

A Taste of Fall Near Ellijay

Ellijay, Georgia, is a small town, but in autumn it takes on a big title: Apple Capital of Georgia.

Some 400,000 bushels of apples—60 percent of the state's crop—are grown in the Ellijay/Gilmer County region.

In autumn, both roadside stands and the big "apple houses" overflow with a dozen different varieties of fresh-picked fruit, not to mention cider, apple butter, apple fritters, apple turnovers, apple pies, and just about every good thing you can think of made from fall's favorite crop.

Of course, there's an apple festival, held on the second and third weekends of October. By nice coincidence, that overlaps the Columbus Day weekend date for the big, lively Praters Mill Country Fair, located not too many miles away in Dalton, a town also known for its carpet bargains. Two more attractions in the neighborhood are Jasper, where the famous Georgia marble is mined, and Blue Ridge, where a mini-Williamsburg is taking shape. Add a backdrop of lakes, rivers, and misty mountains aglow in autumn hues, and you can pack a peck of pleasures into the long weekend.

Make your first stop the Gilmer County Chamber of Commerce in the old-fashioned town square in Ellijay, where you can pick up a driving-tour map of the apple orchards.

The square itself makes for rewarding browsing through antique and gift shops. Gilmer County's imposing 1900 courthouse is worth a tour, and the Gilmer Arts and Heritage Association, housed in a historic home on Broad Street, often has interesting art exhibits.

If you come for the Apple Festival, head for the fairgrounds south of town on old U.S. 5, where you'll find apple exhibits, arts and crafts, and lots of good home cooking.

Golfers will be glad to know that Ellijay offers an 18-hole scenic golf course. One of the problems in conquering the mountain topography was figuring out how golf carts would climb the hills, a dilemma that was solved by cutting tunnels into the mountainside so that golfers could traverse from hole to hole.

A dozen of the 20 or so orchards in the area are clustered along Georgia route 52 east of Ellijay. Route 515 south of town has more choices, including Panorama Orchards, one of the biggest and most complete of the apple houses. It is one of many orchards where you are welcome to pick your own apples.

Like most of the orchards, this one has been family owned and operated for generations; the Stembridge family established the business in 1927.

The apple selection includes not only familiar varieties like Delicious and McIntosh, but many that never make it to the ordinary grocery store, apples with names like Yates and Arkansas Black, some 20 varieties in all. Free samples in the apple house let you decide on your favorites.

In the apple house, a viewing window lets you watch the bakers at work in the kitchen—and just wait until you taste their fried apple pies! A unique feature at Panorama is an observation window that lets you see some of the packing operations and cider making that go on behind the scenes.

When you've loaded your goodies into the car, head north to Blue Ridge and you've moved into Fannin County. National forest makes up more than 40 percent of the land in this county, making it a great place for hiking along the Appalachian Trail and other well-known paths such as Duncan Ridge and Rich Mountain.

The visitor center, in the old railroad depot, will provide you with detailed scenic driving tours into the mountains and countryside around town. Ask for Tour One, a one-to-two-hour backroad circuit that runs part way along the Toccoa River and includes views of Deep Gap, the Lake Blue Ridge Recreation Area, and Springer Mountain. The route passes not only scenery but bits of history, such as old gristmills and pioneer log homes.

A highly recommended short detour from Blue Ridge is Forge Mill Crossing, a shopping and dining complex in Morganton, on Georgia route 60, six miles east of town. Here, the Windy Ridge Gallery features work by artisans who live and work within a 40-mile radius. The shops also include an antique store, a candy emporium with tempting hand-made chocolates, and one of the best restaurants in this part of Georgia. Patrons line up here for the mountain trout and lemon chess pie.

By far the most unusual place in Blue Ridge is Merchants Hope, north of town, where a local resident is creating a working colonial village, including faithful reproductions of properties in Williamsburg, Virginia. Gardens from formal plantings to herb gardens contain plants known to have grown here in the eighteenth century. They also include the only maze garden in Georgia.

A duplicate of the stately, twin-chimneyed Wythe House of Williamsburg was built here of handmade bricks. Tours of the house also include outbuildings such as the kitchen, storehouse, stable, office, and smokehouse, as well as the gardens.

The Merchants Hope Inn is a reproduction of Williamsburg's Wetherburn Tavern, accurate down to the hinges and nails. The candlelit rooms are furnished with antiques and reproductions, and servers in colonial dress offer traditional early American dishes, from meat pies to Virginia Smithfield ham with raisin sauce. Those who want to live in the past will find rooms available on the second floor.

Drive over to Dalton for a bit of history that is Georgia's own. Just before the turn of the century, a young Dalton girl named Catherine Evans saw a hand-tufted bedspread she liked and copied it, selling her work for $2.50. It was much admired, and she began teaching other ladies in town how to tuft. Soon a cottage industry was booming. Highway 41, from Chattanooga to Atlanta, became known as "Peacock Alley" for the rows of colorful spreads hanging on clotheslines along the route, many adorned with a colorful peacock with its feathers displayed across the spread.

The story of this unique cottage industry is told in a fascinating little museum run by the local historical society in an 1890 building called Crown Gardens and Archives. The structure was once the office of the Crown Cotton Mills, the town's first textile manufacturer. Some of the early spreads are displayed here. There's also a room devoted to Robert

Loveman, who wrote the lyrics to the Georgia state song as well as a poem familiar to many: "It is not raining rain to me, it's raining daffodils."

The tufting techniques used for the spreads eventually were applied to carpets, and the rest is history. Dalton produces more than 200 miles of carpet every day, more than half of the world's supply, and a $5 billion business.

Those who come to Dalton to shop for carpeting can save 30 to 70 percent off retail prices at the many mill outlets. If you plan to buy carpets, it's a good idea to learn something about how to shop and what measurements you need before you make the trip. Beckler's, one of the larger outlets, offers a comprehensive free guide to buying carpet. Write to P.O. Box 9, Dalton 30722, or phone 800-BECKLER.

Carpet or not, it is definitely worth a trip to Dalton for the Prater's Mill Country Fair. The fairgrounds adjoin a three-story gristmill built in 1855 and operated continuously during and after the Civil War. It still grinds cornmeal on special occasions such as the spring and fall country fairs, when the original mill store is also open for fairgoers. These events draw some 185 artists and craftsmen to town to demonstrate their techniques and sell their wares. The festivities include mountain music and mounds of traditional Southern foods.

The story of another Georgia industry and a family dynasty founded on marble unfolds in Jasper and the neighboring hamlet of Tate. A stonecutter named Henry Fitzsimmons, who was passing through the valley in 1835, is credited with being the first to spot and mine a vein of rich marble.

The land belonged to Samuel Tate, whose family would acquire legendary wealth from the mines when Samuel's son Stephen persuaded the railroad to come into Pickens County so that the marble could be shipped out easily. For over 100 years, Georgia marble has been used for famous buildings, statues, and monuments all over the world. The incredible supply here is, in fact, estimated to be large enough to supply the world's building needs for 3,000 years.

In this area, still dominated by the 30 quarries of the Georgia Marble Company, you'll find homes with marble steps, flower beds with marble borders, and marble sidewalks. In Jasper, the high school and even the old Pickens County Jail are made of blocks of marble. Once a year, on the first weekend in October, you can visit the quarries during the annual Marble Festival.

But you can see one of the most elaborate results of the Tate fortune anytime—and even stay there if you like. Colonel Sam Tate, the eldest of Stephen's 19 children, became president of the Georgia Marble Company in 1905, and by 1924 his fortune was estimated at $165 billion. He used some of the rare Etowah pink marble from the quarry to construct a marble mansion in 1923, but he lived in his pink palace for only 12 years before he died at age 78, leaving no heirs. Nicely restored and grand once again, the Tate House is now a palatial bed-and-breakfast inn and restaurant.

Jasper also offers a far more rustic but no less appealing lodging at the Woodbridge Inn, a simple 12-room lodge overlooking the mountains. It adjoins the restaurant, whose Bavarian chef is considered by many to be the best in the mountains.

If you want to include some truly magnificent scenery in your trip, consider staying at the lodge at Amicolola State Park, 20 miles east of Ellijay. The mountain views from these modestly priced rooms are unmatched.

One final option for lodging within easy reach of Ellijay is Carters Lake, a big body of blue water 11 miles long, with 62 miles of shoreline amid the mountains. The lake was created when Carters Dam was constructed to generate hydroelectric power. The only development that has been allowed on the pristine shoreline is one small marina with motel rooms and lakeside cabins. Or, for the ultimate view of the surrounding mountain foliage, you can rent a 60-foot houseboat that sleeps up to eight, leaving the rest of the world behind and waking up to glorious views reflected in the water.

At the least, come down and rent a pontoon boat for a while. The lake is one of the loveliest of the many pleasures of the northwest mountains. And if you bring along a picnic, those tasty Ellijay apples make a perfect dessert.

Area Code: 706

DRIVING DIRECTIONS   Ellijay is located on Georgia Route 515, a continuation of I–575. Blue Ridge is to the north, Jasper to the south on the same road. Dalton is to the west, reached via Georgia Route 52. From Atlanta, take I–75 north into I–575. Near Jasper, the road changes to Georgia Route 515. Stay on this road and proceed north to Ellijay, a total trip of about 55 miles. Ellijay is about 75 miles from Chattanooga.

ACCOMMODATIONS   *Elderberry Inn,* 75 Dalton Street, Ellijay 30540, 635–2218, I, CP • *Stratford Motor Inn,* East Ellijay 30539, 726–1080 or 800–526–1258, golf packages offered, I • *Merchant's Hope Bed and Breakfast,* P.O. Box 836, Blue Ridge 30513, 632–9000, E • *Tate House,* Highway 53, Tate 30177, 735–3122 or 800–342–7515, E, CP • *Woodbridge Inn Lodge,* 411 Chambers Street, Jasper, 30143, 692–6293, I-M • *Carters Lake Marina and Resort,* Route 4, P.O. Box 41503, Chatsworth 30705, 276–4891, rooms, I; cabins, M; houseboats, EE • *Amicolola Falls State Park,* off

Ga. route 52, Dawsonville 30534, 265–8888, lodge rooms, I; suites, M; cottages, I ● *Mountain cabin rentals: Mountain Retreat*, Ellijay, 276–2992; *Blue Ridge Mountain Cabins*, Blue Ridge, 632–8999; *My Mountain*, Blue Ridge, 800–532–2007; *The Last Resort*, Blue Ridge, 632–3864.

DINING   *Country Cupboard Restaurant*, North Main Street, Ellijay, 635–7575, Southern specialties, pies and cobblers, I ● *Apple Dumpling Deli*, River Street, Ellijay, 276–1900, homemade everything including chili and apple dumplings, I ● *River Street Cafe*, River Street, Ellijay, 635–5500, more good Southern stuff, I ● *The Pink Pig*, Highway 515 North, Cherry Log (between Ellijay and Blue Ridge), 276–3311, barbecue and good, garlicky salad dressing, check out the wooden pigs on the hillside, I ● *Forge Mill Crossing Restaurant*, Forge Mill Road at Highway 76, Morganton (6 miles east of Blue Ridge), 374–5771, a regional favorite, I-M ● *Toccoa Riverside Restaurant*, Aska Road, Blue Ridge, 632–7891, casual, country cooking, scenic setting, outdoor deck on the river, I-M ● *Merchant's Hope Inn*, Highway 5, north of Blue Ridge, 632–9000, authentic colonial recipes and decor, I-M ● *Fannin Inn*, Highway 76, south of Blue Ridge, 632–2005, known for pot pies, peanut soup, I ● *Flammini's Cafe*, 1205 West Walnut Avenue, Dalton, contemporary decor, good Italian food, I-M ● *Greystone Restaurant*, 514 Church Street, Jasper, 692–5932, best in town for breakfast and lunch, I ● *Tate House* (see above), elegant surroundings, M-E ● *Woodbridge Inn* (see above), gourmet's choice, M-E.

SIGHTSEEING   *Prater's Mill Country Fair*, Prater's Mill Foundation, c/o 848 Shugart Road, Dalton, 275-MILL, held twice annually on Mother's Day and Columbus Day weekends. Phone for current hours and admission ● *Crown Gardens and Archives, Whitfield-Murray Historical Society*, 725 Chattanooga Avenue, Dalton, 278–0217. Hours: Tuesday to Friday 10 A.M. to 5 P.M.; Saturday 10 A.M. to 3 P.M., free.

SPORTS: *Horseback riding: Trail Rides*, Ellijay, 276–3900; *Hitching Post Stables*, Blue Ridge, 632–3864; *Hell's Hollow Stables*, Blue Ridge, 632–8472 ● *Whitewater rafting: Ocoee Rafting*, 800–251–4800; *White Water Express*, 325–5295; *Wildwater Ltd.*, 800–451–9972 ● *Golf: Whitepath Golf Course*, Ellijay, 726–3080 ● *Boating: Carters Lake Marina*, off Ga. route 136 (between U.S. 411 and Ga. Route 515), Chatsworth, 276–4891.

INFORMATION   *Gilmer County Chamber of Commerce,* P.O. Box 818, Ellijay, GA 30540, 635–7400 • *Fannin County Chamber of Commerce,* P.O. Box 875, Blue Ridge, GA 30513, 632–5680.

Hunting Ghosts in Georgetown

Georgetown County, South Carolina, has a population of about 46,000 according to the last count—plus a number of ghostly characters who show up often, though rarely for the census. In this Lowcountry land, called "the most haunted place in the South," people not only believe in ghosts, they swear by them.

Join the local residents paying their respects at the annual Georgetown Ghost Hunt the weekend before Halloween and you, too, may meet some of the interesting characters who haunt the county. At the very least, you'll learn a lot about ghosts, while discovering the charming old port town of Georgetown and some of the loveliest, least crowded beaches on the South Carolina coast.

The Ghost Tour takes in 11 Georgetown County sites, each replete with scary histories, strange noises, and the promise of a ghostly presence or two. Each of the haunted places provides a host to relate the legend behind the haunting.

By night, there's a drama titled "Ghosts of the Coast" and the telling of shivery ghost stories. Youngsters will find haunted houses specially built for them to explore at Huntington Beach State Park and on the Inlet Square Mall.

Anybody can tell you about the best known of Georgetown's spectral visitors. Among the favorites is Alice Flagg, known as the "Little White Lady of the Hermitage," the Hermitage being a plantation at Murrells Inlet, north of Georgetown.

Alice secretly wore around her neck a ring given to her by a forbidden lover, until her brother spied the ring and hid it away, unmoved by his sister's tears. Though she turned the house upside down searching, Alice never found her ring. Not long after, she fell ill with typhoid and died. She has often been sighted in the Hermitage garden and in her former bedroom. More than once, later owners of the house have entered a room to find it a wreck, with drawers opened and their contents scattered.

There are various theories about the identity of the man dressed all in gray, known as the "Gray Man of Pawleys Island," but there is unanimous agreement that he appears to give warning before a storm or tragedy occurs. He was sighted before the great storms of 1893 and 1916, and preceding Hurricane Hazel in 1954.

Georgetown also has its own resident in-town ghosts. There's the British soldier who once tripped on an uneven step in the house at the corner of Duke and Screven streets and tumbled to his death. Lots of people have tripped since, but none have fallen; they say that an invisible pair of gentle hands steadies them.

The state's third-oldest city, Georgetown has an interesting un-haunted past, as well. Though located at the southern end of the Grand Strand, 35 miles from Myrtle Beach, the flavor and history here are entirely different.

This could well have been the first European settlement in the United States if the Spanish colony established in 1526 had succeeded, but the settlement was ravaged by disease and the colonists perished within a year.

Two centuries later, English settlers formed Prince George Parish and in 1730 laid out the plans for Georgetown. The five surrounding rivers and their marshlands were ideal for growing first indigo and then rice. The rich plantation culture rivaled that of Charleston. By 1840 it produced nearly half of the total rice crop of the United States. Planters used some of their fortunes to build summer cottages along the beach at Pawleys Island, creating one of the first resorts on the Atlantic Coast.

The Rice Museum, upstairs in the historic Old Market Building in Georgetown, tells about the crop that accounted for the town's early glory. Some of the original plantations south of town remain to recall even more vividly the flavor of the past.

Hopsewee Plantation, built in 1740, was the birthplace of Thomas Lynch, Jr., a signer of the Declaration of Independence. This is a typical Lowcountry plantation house, with four rooms opening to a wide center hall on each floor. Special features are the graceful staircase and the hand-carved moldings in every room.

Hampton Plantation, now a state park, was built in 1735 and hosted President Washington in 1791. Its owners have included some of South Carolina's most prominent families. The rice fields and magnificent old oaks remain, and the house is under restoration.

Not far from Hampton is St. James Santee Church, an Episcopal church dating from 1768. The red brick structure still boasts the original brick columns on the portico and box pews inside.

Many more plantations still stand along the rivers where they once flourished, hidden from view except from the water. Several boat excursions go past the plantations, along sleepy waterways that have hardly been altered since the end of the plantation system after the Civil War. Boat cruises also include shelling expeditions to offshore islands.

A more recent estate is now the Bellefield Nature Center. The home was owned by presidential adviser and Wall Street wizard Bernard Baruch, who entertained many notables here, including Franklin Roosevelt and Winston Churchill. Baruch's daughter Belle left the property to the state for research in forestry and salt-marsh ecosystems. The center offers nature exhibits and films.

In this century, Georgetown's livelihood comes from its busy port, now dedicated to bulk cargo handling, and from the paper mills that are a none-too-scenic presence just outside town.

The town itself retains its early charm, and looks better than ever since a recent renovation restored Front Street and built a Harbor Walk along the Sampit River. The historic district, roughly seven blocks long and three blocks deep, makes for a wonderful stroll past some 50 significant sites, including many homes from the 1700s.

Of special note is the Prince George Winyah Episcopal Church, circa 1750, whose congregation was first established in 1721. It retains its Colonial gated pews.

The oldest house in town, the Blythe Tavern House, dates from 1737. Following its use as a tavern, it became the residence first of a surgeon in the Revolutionary War, then later of South Carolina governor Robert F. W. Allston. The eighteenth-century windows remain.

The 1740 Heriot House has several legends, from stories of resident ghosts to tales of blockade runners and bootleggers who were guided to shore by a light in the dormer windows.

The 1760 Harold Kaminski House is now open to visitors as a museum, with an outstanding collection of antiques.

A few of Georgetown's picturesque homes are now bed-and-breakfast inns. A more elaborate historic residence open to guests is farther north at Litchfield Plantation, one of the major early producers of rice. The grounds have been used for a residential development, but the original 1750 "big house" has been restored as an elegant inn.

The nearby Litchfield by the Sea resort is also on former plantation grounds, but the old buildings are gone. The new resort, with its seven-mile private beach, three golf courses, and the largest tennis complex on the Grand Strand, is one of the choicest lodgings in the area, with the bonus of many indoor facilities when the weather is uncooperative.

Pawleys Island, the oldest beach resort between North Carolina and Charleston, retains many of its eighteenth- and nineteenth-century cottages, including the Pelican Inn, the reputed home of the famous Gray Man. The narrow island is small and wonderfully private. There is only one rambling, rustic wooden inn, so most people rent cottages to enjoy the beautiful beaches.

Pawleys Island is known to many people for its hammocks. In the 1800s, a riverboat pilot named Joshua John Ward created a cotton rope hammock woven without knots and renowned for its perfect comfort and coolness. They are still handwoven, just as in the past, and are now available in natural cotton or soft-spun polyester. You can watch the weaving at the Hammock Shop, which is now part of a charming shopping and dining complex of nicely landscaped cottages under ancient oaks.

Further north on U.S. 17 is Brookgreen Gardens, famous for its statuary set amid beautiful gardens. The largest showcase for outdoor sculpture in the world and a national historic landmark, the gardens exhibit 500 sculptures, including works by artists such as Daniel Chester French, Gaston Lachaise, and Augustus Saint-Gaudens.

Brookgreen was the idea of Archer Huntington, heir to a railroad and shipbuilding fortune, and his wife, Anna, a gifted sculptor. They bought several South Carolina plantations comprising some 6,635 acres, to preserve the native plants and animals and to exhibit Anna Huntington's work. The idea expanded to include other artists who produced the representative sculpture the Huntingtons favored. No abstracts are allowed.

Anna Huntington's graceful *Diana of the Chase*, posed in the middle of a tranquil pool, is a stunning welcome to the ten-acre sculpture gardens. Though the original plantation house burned, a magnificent *allée* of 200-year-old live oaks remains, draped with silvery moss. It has become a focal point for a series of interconnected gardens with pools, ponds, and fountains, forming a butterfly-shaped background for the sculptures. Strategic plantings ensure year-round displays.

Across the road, in Huntington Beach State Park, is the brick castle, Atalaya, built in the 1930s by the Huntingtons. The park itself offers beach access and nature trails.

Georgetown County ends at Murrells Inlet, a picturesque fishing village founded in the early eighteenth century. Capt. Dick's Marina at Murrells Inlet is headquarters for deep-sea fishing expeditions as well as for nature cruises into the salt marshes. A marine biologist accompanies these educational tours, where marsh plants and animals are collected and brought on board to be seen, touched, and discussed.

The inlet has its full share of ghost stories and legends, including the tale of the famous Alice. The narrow channels were also a favorite hideout for pirates. The story of Drunken Jack is part of the pirate lore. Jack was a crewman who came ashore with his pirate captain, Blackbeard, to bury a stash of hijacked rum. Jack missed the boat while sleeping off a hangover, and when the crew returned for him some two years later, legend has it that all they found were 32 empty rum casks and Jack's bleached bones.

A restaurant named in Jack's honor is one of a slew of eating places along the inlet, making Georgetown County the seafood capital, as well as the ghost capital, of South Carolina.

Area Code: 803

DRIVING DIRECTIONS   Georgetown is at the intersection of U.S. 17 and U.S. 701 north/south and U.S. 521 from the west. It is 35 miles south of Myrtle Beach, 322 miles from Atlanta, 178 miles from Charlotte, 123 miles from Columbia. From I–95, take U.S. 521 east.

PUBLIC TRANSPORTATION   Myrtle Beach Airport is 18 miles north of Georgetown; Charleston is 60 miles south.

ACCOMMODATIONS   *530 Prince Street,* at that address, Georgetown 29440, 527–1114, gracious home in the historic district, rockers on the veranda, I, CP • *Shaw House,* 8 Cypress Court, Georgetown 29440, 546–9663, pleasant home with marsh views, I, CP • *1790 House,* 630 Highmarket Street, Georgetown 29440, 546–4821, in the historic district, I, CP • *Ashfield Manor,* 3030 South Island Road, Georgetown 29440, 546–5111, columned country house, big screened porch, I, CP • *Clarion Carriage House–Carolinian Inn,* 706 Church Street, Georgetown 29440, 546–5191, in-town motel, pool, I, CP • *Sea View Inn,* Pawleys Island 29585, 237–4253, rambling beachside guesthouse with ocean and marsh views, E–EE, AP • *Ramada Inn at Pawleys Island,* Highway 17, Pawleys Island 29585, 237–4261 or 800–553–7008, motel on a golf course, outdoor pool • *Manor House at Litchfield Plantation,* P.O. Box 290, Pawleys Island 29585, 237–9322, original 1750 plantation home, elegant, also cottages, E–EE, CP • *Litchfield-by-the-Sea Resort,* P.O. Box 320, Highway 17 North, Pawleys Island 29585, 237–3000, beach, golf, tennis, spa, and health club • *Beach rentals: Pawleys Island Realty,* 237–2431; *Dunes Realty of Litchfield,* 237–4473; *The Dieter Company,* 237–2813.

DINING   *River Room,* 801 Front Street, Georgetown, 527–4110, waterfront views, char-broiled seafood specialties, I-M • *Poogan's Porch,* Highway 17 North, Hammock Shops, Pawleys Island, 237–4949, Lowcountry cuisine, branch of Charleston restaurant, M • *Frank's Restaurant and Bar,* Highway 17 North, Pawleys Island, 237–3030, M • *Community House Restaurant,* Highway 17 South, Pawleys Island, 237–8353, Italian, M-E • *Carriage House Club at Litchfield Plantation,* 237–9322, international cuisine in mansion setting, E • *Websters,* Litchfield-by-the-Sea Resort (see above), informal, lake views, serves all three meals, I-M. *Around Murrells Inlet: Gulf Stream Cafe,* Marlin Quay, Garden City Beach, 651–8808, seafood and sunsets, M-E; *Planters Back Porch,* Highway 17, Murrells Inlet, 651–5263, springhouse of an old farm, garden dining, homemade biscuits, I-M; *Drunken Jack's,* Murrells Inlet, informal, seafood specialties, I-M; *The Captain's Restaurant,* Highway 17, Murrells Inlet, 651–2416, seafood in a quaint home, M.

SIGHTSEEING *Georgetown Ghost Hunt*, c/o Chamber of Commerce (see below). Two days of tours and special events, usually held last weekend before Halloween, $$$ ● *Rice Museum*, Old Market Building, Front and Screven streets, 546–7243. Hours: daily 9:30 A.M. to 4:30 P.M., $ ● *Hopsewee Plantation*, U.S. 17, 12 miles south of Georgetown. Hours: March through October, house tours Tuesday to Friday 10 A.M. to 5 P.M., $$; grounds open daily, $ ● *Hampton Plantation State Park*, 1950 Rutledge Road, off U.S. 17, 20 miles south, McClellanville, 546–9361. Hours: Thursday to Monday 9 A.M. to 6 P.M.; office hours, 11 A.M. to noon; mansion hours, Saturday and Sunday 1 P.M. to 4 P.M. except April 1 to Labor Day, Thursday to Monday 1 P.M. to 4 P.M. ● *Brookgreen Gardens*, U.S. 17, Murrells Inlet, 237–4218. Hours: daily 9:30 A.M. to 4:45 P.M. $$ ● *Huntington Beach State Park*, U.S. 17, 17 miles north, 237–4400, includes Atalaya mansion, open June to Labor Day, $ ● *Boat tours* (phone for current schedules and rates): *Captain Sandy's Tours*, 709 Front Street, Georgetown, 527–4106, seaport tours, ghost watches, plantation excursions, visits to Shell Island; *Island Queen*, Georgetown Landing Marina, Highway 17 Bridge, Georgetown, 527–3160, river plantation tours; *Capt. Dick's Marina*, Highway 17, Murrells Inlet, 651–3676, naturalist educational cruises, scenic cruises, and deep-sea fishing excursions ● *Miss Nell's Tours*, 546–3975, walking tours of Georgetown Historic District and downtown, phone for schedules, $$-$$$.

INFORMATION *Georgetown County Chamber of Commerce*, P.O. Box 1776, Georgetown, SC 29442, 546–8436 or 800–775–7705.

Fishing for Fun in Chattanooga

Want to hear a fish story? A real whopper? Check into what's happening along the Tennessee River in Chattanooga, Tennessee.

Time was when people passing through Chattanooga, lured by the ads on the highway, might drive up Lookout Mountain for the view and see Rock City and Ruby Falls. Downtown Chattanooga was rarely on anybody's list.

All of that changed in 1992, when derelict industrial buildings along the river were replaced by parkland and the sensational Tennessee

Aquarium. The 4,000 finny residents here attracted nearly a million and a half visitors to town even before the aquarium's first birthday in 1993. And this is just the start of a plan that is transforming the riverfront.

One thing hasn't changed. By land or by sea, October is fabulous along the scenic Tennessee River, when the wooded shore bursts into a blaze of fiery autumn hues. River cruises and train rides specially planned to see the foliage are longtime local traditions. There's even a major folk and country music festival at the scenic point of the river known as "the Grand Canyon of the Tennessee." You can get there via a riverboat ride from Chattanooga.

There couldn't be a better time to discover the changes that have made Chattanooga an increasingly popular weekend destination. The challenge is how to fit everything into one weekend. Here's a plan that might work, with a city overview the first day and foliage forays the second.

Start at the waterfront and be prepared to fall hook, line, and sinker, for this is the first major aquarium in the world devoted to freshwater life. Wait until you see the excitement they've created in this dazzling $45 million, 12-story complex, the most technologically advanced aquarium in the country. It's all the more meaningful since the river you are learning about is right outside the door.

Escalators take you to the top, beneath the pyramid-shaped glass roof, to a mountain valley like those where many of the tributaries of the river originate. This realistic scene comes complete with mountain mist, a waterfall, a woodland pool, and live creatures.

Begin your descent along the ramps, and you'll soon be looking below the surface of the water to watch the fish that live in re-creations of three natural habitats—a mountain stream, an otter pool, and a mountain sink pond, the last of these providing an especially intriguing view for fishermen, who can discover where the trout like to hang out.

The Tennessee River Gallery traces the river's history—from the days when the waters ran wild, to modern times, after the TVA controlled flooding and provided power with its system of 35 dams. Nickajack Lake represents underwater life in the body of water created by a dam, and Reelfoot Lake duplicates the waters of Tennessee's largest natural lake.

The final leg of the river's journey is the Mississippi Delta, a re-created cypress swamp whose denizens include alligators, turtles, toads, and snakes.

The aquarium is enlightening and entertaining from top to bottom. The only problem with the facility may be its popularity. To avoid overcrowding, only a certain number are admitted at one time, so come early or be prepared to be given a later entry time—not so terrible, since it will leave you time to explore some of the nearby city.

You won't have to look far to see the most dramatic changes in

Chattanooga. Ross's Landing, the park that surrounds the aquarium, has replaced the industrial clutter that once separated the city from its river. The unique design, alternating bands of colored stone and waterways, traces the stages of local history, brought to life with quotations and artifacts embedded in the walls and the pathways. The objects form a kind of treasure hunt for the kids, who can spy everything from Civil War cannonballs to arrowheads.

To see more of the newly pristine riverfront, walk out on the recently restored, century-old Walnut Street Bridge spanning the water, touted as the world's longest pedestrian bridge. Ross's Park is the start of a riverside path that will eventually run for 22 miles, offering recreation and beauty. You can see some of the results to date at the segment called Tennessee Riverpark, on the outskirts of town near Chickamauga Lake.

You can find the way to this and every other major attraction in Chattanooga with the excellent Choo Choo Scenic Drive map available from the visitors bureau.

From Ross's Park, it's a short walk uphill to the Hunter Museum, housed in the 1905 mansion of Thomas Hunter, who made a fortune by opening the first Coca-Cola bottling plant in 1898. The collection of American art is most impressive for a city this size, and it is still growing; a large modern wing was added to the mansion in the 1970s. The art includes works by Mary Cassatt, John Singer Sargent, Winslow Homer, and many others. A sculpture garden outside offers a fine view of the river.

Across the street is a quirky museum, the collection of Anna Safely Houston, who never met a piece of antique glass she didn't like. Her home displays the glassware Houston found irresistible, including 15,000 pitchers, many of which had to be hung from the ceiling to fit into the house.

The downtown shuttle in front of Ross's Park travels about 14 blocks inland to Chattanooga's best-known symbol, the Chattanooga Choo Choo. The city's grand 1909 Victorian Terminal Station has been redone as a hotel complex that is now operated by Holiday Inn. The ticket windows and passenger waiting area, beneath a lavish 85-foot dome, serve as hotel lobby and front desk. Beyond are tracks with old trains, some of them converted into narrow but nicely furnished sleeping rooms. Even if you stay in a regular hotel room, you can have dinner in the diner, visit a display of model trains, or board the Downtown Arrow for a train ride to the Tennessee Valley Railroad Museum, where railroad memorabilia and vintage locomotives and cars are displayed. The railroad runs its own excursions into the countryside.

On the way to the Choo Choo, you'll pass Warehouse Row, a renovation that converted turn-of-the-century railroad warehouses into designer outlet stores. This is not an ordinary outlet mall. The upscale names include Albert Nipon, Perry Ellis, Adrienne Vittadini, and Ralph Lauren.

On the afternoon agenda is a ride up the Lookout Mountain Incline Railway, the world's steepest passenger railway, with a grade of 72.7 percent. The mile-long ride up the mountain takes just 10 minutes and it emerges near Point Park, one of the two sections of Chickamauga and Chattanooga National Military Park.

The visitor center at the entrance gate offers an information area and an eight-minute slide orientation about the battle for Chattanooga and its importance in determining the outcome of the Civil War. Also on display is James Walker's huge 13-by–30-foot painting *The Battle Above the Clouds*.

Afterwards, walk to the ledge of the mountain and marvel at the view, an eagle's-eye perspective on city, countryside, and the Moccasin Bend in the winding Tennessee River just below. The Ochs Museum, named for onetime Chattanooga resident Adolph S. Ochs, owner-publisher of *The New York Times*, tells more about the battle that sealed the fate of the Confederacy.

When you descend from the mountain and pick up your car, you can drive across the Georgia line to the main Chickamauga Battlefield section of the park, one of the first national military parks, established by Congress in 1888. The attractive visitor center presents an excellent multimedia presentation portraying the fierce battle.

Take the seven-mile self-guided drive around the battlefield. It is maintained as closely as possible to its 1863 appearance, with monuments marking troop positions. The beauty of the setting, now meadows and woodland, is a dramatic contrast to the battlefields where blood ran so freely that Confederate General William Bates called Chickamauga a "river of death." The Chickamauga campaign cost more than 18,000 of the 66,000 Confederate troops involved; Federal losses were 16,000 out of 58,000.

Civil War buffs may also want to visit the Confederama, a three-dimensional electric map reproducing the historic terrain with more than 5,000 miniature soldiers in place. Guns flash and cannons puff real smoke as the battle action is traced.

If you prefer inns to hotel lodgings, you'll find the best of the local choices in the Lookout Mountain area, including the Chanticleer Inn, a romantic hideaway of mountain stone cottages. Two highly recommended stops are just across the Georgia border. The Gordon-Lee Mansion, an 1847 antebellum house, is a national historic site and so elegant it is open for tours. Captain's Quarters, an early 1900s home, will delight lovers of cozy Victoriana.

Back to sightseeing: If you still have time and energy, you can consider those well-advertised attractions on Lookout Mountain. Rock City is quite an amazing series of rock formations, literally a two-acre "city of rocks." The up-and-down trail, sometimes through narrow passages, is fun to follow, and the views from "Lover's Leap" are spectacular, even if they do make things corny with a Mother Goose Village and characters like Rocky the Elf.

Ruby Falls is another matter. Getting to the falls involves a long trek to the end of the cave along a narrow underground catwalk, after which the lights are dimmed and a spotlight finally hits the falls. To this visitor, the narrow stream, albeit 145 feet high, was unimpressive and not worth the long walk. The crowds don't help.

Raccoon Mountain Cave, outside the city, has no waterfall, but the tour through its Hall of Dreams and the Crystal Palace takes you to far more beautiful and unusual underground formations. If you make the trip to Raccoon Mountain, you'll find child-pleasing amusements, such as a water slide, horseback riding, and a mini–Grand Prix racetrack where you can take a turn in a racing car. The TVA maintains a storage lake at the top of the mountain, where the visitor center provides a lovely view of the Tennessee River Gorge.

Having seen as many sights as you can fit into one day, you can turn your attention to foliage tours.

The main event is the annual Fall Color Cruise and Folk Festival, held at the Shellmound Recreation Area on the edge of Nickajack Lake (the real one), at the heart of the Grand Canyon of the Tennessee River. Now past its twenty-fifth year, the festival is one of the Southeast's largest outdoor musical events. Competitions in mandolin, five-string banjo, string band, guitar, and fiddle usually take place the first weekend, vocal competitions the second. The artists who perform on five stages are a "Who's Who" of country-music superstars, and there are also cloggers and dance teams on hand. In addition, there's a food fair and the Mid-South Arts and Crafts Show, with more than 100 craftsmen and working artists.

Buses make the trip from Chattanooga, but it's more fun to come via the *Southern Belle*, an old-time riverboat with entertainment by the Riverboat Ramblers. Once you've arrived, more cruising is available on Nickajack Lake aboard the sidewheel riverboat *Chattanooga Star*.

If you prefer to see the countryside by land, board the Tennessee Autumn trains run by the Tennessee Valley Railroad, a tradition that celebrated its twenty-fifth anniversary in 1993. Day-long, 258-mile round-trip outings to Oneida pass through the wilderness of the Emory River Gorge and into the upper reaches of the Cumberland plateau, where the train crosses the 301-foot-high New River bridge. Food and a crafts show keep you occupied while the train is turned around at Oneida.

Another itinerary rumbles along the shore of Nickajack Lake to Huntsville, Alabama.

Choo-choo or cruise boat, Chattanooga is the place to make the most of autumn—and to wave a fin at the fish at the same time.

Area Code: 615

DRIVING DIRECTIONS   Chattanooga is at the intersection of I–24 and I–75. From Atlanta, follow I–75 north, about 116 miles; from Birmingham take I–59 north into I–24, 149 miles; from Nashville, follow I–24 south, 134 miles.

ACCOMMODATIONS   *Chattanooga Choo Choo Holiday Inn,* 1400 Market Street, Chattanooga 37402, 266–5000, I-M • *Radisson Read House Hotel and Suites,* Martin Luther King Boulevard at Broad Street, Chattanooga 37402, 266–4121, restored landmark, convenient location, I-E • *Comfort Hotel River Plaza,* 407 Chestnut Street, Chattanooga 37402, 756–5150, reasonably priced, within walking distance of the aquarium, I • *Days Inn Rivergate,* 901 Carter Street, Chattanooga 37402, 266–7331, budget choice near the aquarium, I • *Marriott,* 2 Carter Plaza, Chattanooga 37402, 756–0002, adjoining the city convention center, E • *Bed-and-breakfast inns: Alford House,* 2501 Lookout Mountain Parkway, Chattanooga 37409, 821–7625, I, CP; *McElhattan's Owl Hill,* 617 Scenic Highway, Chattanooga 37409, 821–2040, I, CP; *Chanticleer Inn,* 1300 Mockingbird Lane, Lookout Mountain, GA 37350, 706–820–2015, I, CP; *Gorden-Lee Mansion,* 217 Cove Road, Chickamauga, GA 30707, 706–375–4728, I-M, CP; *Captain's Quarters,* 13 Barnhardt Circle, Fort Oglethorpe, GA 30742, 706–858–0624, I-M, CP; *Hidden Hollow Resort,* Route 4, Box 1085, Chickamauga, GA 30707, 706–539–2372, rustic cabin resort, I • Chattanooga has many motels; write to the Convention and Visitors Bureau for a complete list.

DINING   *Perry's,* 1206 Market Street, 267–0007, attractive and excellent, part of the old freight depot, M-E • *212 Market,* 212 Market Street, 265–1212, contemporary decor and menu, convenient to the aquarium, lunch, I, dinner, M • *The Loft,* 328 Cherokee Boulevard, Chattanooga, 266–3601, best steaks in town, M-E • *Dinner in the Diner,* Chattanooga Choo Choo (see above), 266–5000, nostalgic and elegant, E • *Broad Street Bistro,* Radisson Read House (see above), grill specialties, big Blue Jean Brunch on Sunday, I-M • *Ashley's,* Marriott (see above), Continental, posh, E • *Mount Vernon,* 3509 Broad Street, 266–6591, longtime local standby, I-M • *The Brass Register,* 618 Georgia Avenue, 265–2175, another downtown favorite, I-M • *Narrowbridge,* 1420 Jenkins, 855–5000, dining in a gracious home, I-E • *Provino's Italian Restaurant,* South Gerrace Plaza, 899–2559, the name says it, I-M • *Vine Street Market,* 414 Vine Street,

Chattanooga, 267–0162, informal for lunch or dinner, terrific sandwiches, takeout, lunch, I, dinner, I-M ● *Buck's Pit Barbecue,* 3147 Broad Street, 267–1390, I.

SIGHTSEEING *Tennessee Aquarium,* 1 Broad Street, 265–0695. Hours: daily 10 A.M. to 6 P.M.; May 1 to Labor Day, 10:00 A.M. to 8 P.M. Friday, Saturday, Sunday; $$$ ● *Hunter Museum of Art,* 10 Bluff View at Third Street, 267–0968. Hours: Tuesday to Saturday 10 A.M. to 4:30 P.M.; Sunday 1 P.M. to 4:30 P.M.; $ ● *Houston Museum of Decorative Arts,* 201 High Street, 267–7176. Hours: Tuesday to Saturday 10 A.M. to 4:30 P.M.; Sunday 2 P.M. to 4:30 P.M.; free ● *Lookout Mountain Incline Railway,* 827 East Brow Road, Lookout Mountain, 821–4224. Hours: daily 8:30 A.M. to 6 P.M.; in summer, 8:30 A.M. to 9 P.M.; $$ one way, $$$ round trip ● *Chickamauga and Chattanooga National Military Park, Chickamauga Visitor Center,* U.S. 27, 9 miles south of Chattanooga at Chickamauga, Ga., 706–866–9241. Hours: daily 8 A.M. to 5:45 P.M.; in winter, 8 A.M. to 4:45 P.M.; Visitor Center free, multimedia presentation, $$ ● *Point Park Visitor Center,* Lookout Mountain, Chattanooga, daily 8 A.M. to dusk, free ● *Confederama Hall of History,* 3742 Tennessee Avenue, 821–2812. Hours: Monday to Saturday 9 A.M. to 5 P.M.; Sunday 12:30 P.M. to 5 P.M.; Memorial Day to Labor Day, Monday to Saturday 8:30 A.M. to 8:30 P.M., Sunday 9:30 A.M. to 8:30 P.M.; $$ ● *Rock City Gardens,* 1400 Patten Road, Lookout Mountain, GA 706–820–2531. Hours: daily 8:30 A.M. to dusk; June to Labor Day, open at 8 A.M.; $$$ ● *Ruby Falls,* Lookout Mountain, Scenic Highway, Chattanooga, 821–2544. Hours: daily 8 A.M. to 6 P.M.; Memorial Day to Labor Day, 8 A.M. to 9 P.M.; September, October, April, May, 8 A.M. to 8 P.M.; $$$ ● *Tennessee Valley Railroad,* 4119 Cromwell Road or 2200 North Chamberlain Avenue, East Chattanooga, 894–8028. Hours: June through August, daily 9:30 A.M. to 4:55 P.M.; April to May and September through early December, Saturday 9:30 A.M. to 4:55 P.M.; Sunday 12:15 P.M. to 4:55 P.M.; trains leave from both stations, phone for current schedules; $$$ ● *Raccoon Mountain Caverns,* 319 West Hills Drive, Route 4, Chattanooga, 821–9403. Hours: daily 9 A.M. to 5 P.M.; in summer, 9 A.M. to 9 P.M.; $$$ ● *Southern Belle River Cruises,* 201 Riverfront Parkway, Pier 2, 266–4488 or 800–766–2784, sightseeing, lunch, dinner, Dixieland and moonlight cruises, check current schedules and rates.

FALL FOLIAGE EVENTS (check for current dates and rates): *Fall Color Cruise and Folk Festival,* 1000 Alhambra Drive, Chattanooga 37421, 892–0223 or 800–338–3999 in Tennessee, 800–322–

3344 out of state. Folk, country, and vocal music competitions held at Shellmound Recreation Area, Nickajack Lake, two weekends in late October and early November; bus or boat transportation from Chattanooga to Shellmound via the riverboat *Southern Belle* ● *Tennessee Autumn Trains*, Tennessee Valley Railroad, 894–8028. One-day trips to Oneida, Tennessee, and Huntsville, Alabama, held weekends in late October. Check current dates and rates.

INFORMATION *Chattanooga Area Convention and Visitors Bureau*, 1001 Market Street, P.O. Box 111, Chattanooga, TN 37401, 756–8687 or 800–333–3999 in Tennessee, 800–322–3344 out of state.

Striking Gold in Dahlonega

The year was 1828, over two decades before anybody ever dreamed of heading to a place called California. It started with a deer hunter named Benjamin Parks, who stubbed his toe on a gold-laden hunk of rock. Before you could say "Get rich quick," the word was out, the prospectors came running, and America's first gold rush was on in northeast Georgia.

In 1833 the boomtown of Dahlonega was established as the seat of Lumpkin County. The town's name came from the Cherokee word *dala-nigei-i*, meaning "yellow," the color of the precious stuff that brought the town to life.

People are still coming to Dahlonega in droves, but they are after different treasures nowadays. They come to bone up on an unusual bit of history, to browse craft shops in nineteenth-century buildings around one of the prettiest squares in the state, and to stay in country inns or cozy mountain cabins.

Those who come the third week in October get a feel for the past as the town celebrates Gold Rush Days with a pioneer parade, a beard-growing contest, buckdancing, and other hijinks. More than 300 arts and crafts exhibitors gather for the occasion in the public square and the historic district.

Far from least, folks come to enjoy the wooded countryside surrounding Dahlonega, the thousands of acres of the Chattahoochee National Forest comprising a wilderness world of hills and valleys, lakes and streams, and towering waterfalls. Whether you hike the start of the Appalachian Trail, float down a lazy river, or take a scenic drive, this is one of the state's most beautiful areas in autumn—and anytime.

There's more sightseeing nearby, as well as the shops of the Alpine village of Helen, and on the way you can drop into the town of Cleveland, famous for its Babyland General Hospital, where Cabbage Patch dolls are born.

You'll learn all about the golden past at the Dahlonega Gold Museum, now occupying the columned courthouse that was built in the center of the square in the boom times of 1836. This is the oldest public building in north Georgia, and the state's second-most-visited historic site. Exhibits and a film show the history of the county and how the gold was mined and processed. Also displayed are some of the larger nuggets found, as well as coins minted locally from the gold.

By 1837, Dahlonega had its own branch of the U.S. Mint. For the next 23 years, some 1.3 million gold coins, amounting to over $6 million, were produced, with the identifying letter *D*.

The operation was closed by the Confederate States Treasury Department in 1861, when gold coinage was deemed too expensive to meet the needs of a wartime economy. According to records, the last $25,000 worth of bullion and coins was sent to Charleston to help the Confederate cause. After the war, the building and surrounding property were turned over to the school that is now North Georgia College.

The mint was destroyed by fire in 1878. The following year, Price Memorial Hall was built on the old foundation on a hill above the town. The building's tall gold steeple is the most visible site on the North Georgia campus, and a town landmark. The building houses a collection of rare Dahlonega-minted coins.

One of the most interesting ways to relive the old days is to take a tour of the Consolidated Gold Mines, through the tunnels and past the "glory hole" of the largest and most advanced gold mine ever established east of the Mississippi River. The 7,000-acre mine contained about 200 tunnels and a 120-stamp mill to pulverize the gold ore.

The Consolidated went out of business in 1907 and was abandoned until 1980, when an award-winning restoration removed over 4,000 tons of dirt and debris from the massive tunnel network that was blasted out of solid rock over 100 years ago. The knowledgeable guides who conduct the 40-minute tours are the miners who helped resurrect the operation.

When you've had your tour, you can try your own hand at panning for gold and gemstones, here or at the old Cresson Mine. It is said that there's still gold to be found—just not enough to merit the expense of commercial mining.

Incidentally, according to one Georgia guidebook, a famous phrase was coined here when Matthew Stephenson, assayer of the Dahlonega Mint, stood on the balcony of the courthouse in 1849 urging miners not to rush off to California, pointing to the ridge before him and promising, "There's millions in it." Supposedly, Mark Twain paraphrased Stephenson's words in his book *The Gilded Age,* writing, "There's gold in them thar hills."

You can buy a sample of Dahlonega gold fashioned into jewelry at the Gold Shop on the square. Gold-dipped leaves and dogwood blossoms make unusual and inexpensive souvenirs, or you can purchase a locket filled with Dahlonega gold dust.

This is just one of many interesting shops around the square, where the arcaded sidewalks and vintage buildings may remind visitors of mining towns more familiar in the West.

The Fudge Factory will tempt you with a dozen kinds of treats, but don't spoil your appetite before you visit the Smith House, an old-fashioned mountain hotel that has been serving bountiful, family-style Southern feasts of fried chicken, country ham, and all the fixings ever since Mrs. Smith began cooking for a 22-seat dining room in 1922. They serve as many as 2,000 meals on Sunday, their busiest day.

There are several other small cafés in town, and some appealing small inns, but the prize lodging by far is Mountain Top Lodge, outside of town on 40 acres among the oaks and pines, with soaring hilltop views. The rambling house is filled with warmth and wonderful country decor, antiques, and crafts.

When you are ready to inspect the autumn leaves, one excellent way to take in the splendor of this region is from the serene seat of a canoe. Appalachian Outfitters in Dahlonega offers guided trips on the Chestatee, Etowah, and Amicalola rivers, as well as rentals for those who prefer to paddle on their own. The Amicalola is a beautiful stream with steep, dramatic rock faces rising from the water's edge. It is the site of a youth hostel, ideal for those on very limited budgets.

If you prefer to see the area by car, you won't have to drive far from Dahlonega for scenic vistas. Turn at the town traffic light and follow Georgia route 60 north about 13 miles to the Chestatee Overlook. A little farther north you can take in another fine view—the Yahoola Valley—from Woody's Gap, a picnic area beneath the tall trees. The Appalachian Trail passes here, in case you want to take a walk.

Keep heading north to Suches and Woody's Lake, a mountain lake in a wonderfully picturesque setting. If you continue driving, you'll come to Lake Winfield Scott, in the heart of the Chattahoochee National Forest, go through Sosebee Cave Scenic Area, and finally arrive at Vogel State Park, one of the oldest state parks and still one of the loveliest. You can hike, fish, picnic, or play a round of miniature golf here.

Waterfalls are plentiful in this region, but none of the others match Amicalola Falls, in the state park, 18 miles west of Dahlonega on Georgia route 52. Crashing down from 729 feet, this is the highest waterfall in the eastern United States. The park's 1,020 acres include three and a half miles of nature trails. For the hardy, an eight-mile approach trail leads to Springer Mountain and the southern terminus of the Appalachian Trail, which runs north from here for 2,150 miles to Maine.

The Amicalola Park Lodge is another extraordinary place to stay. Ceiling-high picture windows take in the views in the main lobby; the mountain vistas from the bargain-priced guest rooms would cost a fortune in a resort hotel.

In fall, a must stop at the entrance to the park is Burt's Pumpkin Farm, where you can take a scenic hay ride past the pumpkin fields and pick out a big orange beauty to take home.

More waterfalls are in store if you head northeast from Dahlonega on U.S. 19.

Continue on U.S. 19 as it merges into U.S. 129, a drive of about another 11.5 miles, to reach the De Soto Falls Recreation Area, and five more waterfalls. De Soto Falls is the giant here. It cascades in three tiers, beginning on high with a 200-foot drop down a granite rock incline. You get a fine view right from U.S. 129 bordering the area.

Keep driving east on U.S. 129 and you'll soon be in Cleveland, where the Babyland General Hospital must be seen to be believed. The "nurses," dressed in spotless white, take quite seriously their job of giving life to the latest creations of Xavier Roberts, who conceived the idea of the Cabbage Patch Kids dolls. One of the newborns who are "delivered" from the cabbage patch before your eyes will likely be named for you. Needless to say, they hope you'll want to adopt the doll, or one of the dozens of others waiting in the gift shop, hoping for new homes.

Turn north on Georgia route 75 to visit another unusual mountain attraction, the old lumber town of Helen, now transformed into a Tyrolian village. The Bavarian steeples and architecture seem far from home in Georgia, but that doesn't seem to bother the swarms of tourists who eat in the German restaurants, play in the Alpine Amusement Park, and shop, shop, shop in some 200 gift shops and outlet stores. You need no guide here—you can't miss the stores.

Visit Helen from September to early October for an old-country Bavarian Oktoberfest, with oompah bands, polkas, lederhosen, and plenty of *bier*.

There's a total change of scene if you follow Georgia route 17 south of Helen and continue on Georgia route 255 into the placid Sautee and Nacoochee Valley area. Here are more authentic Georgia country inns, such as the 1837 Stovall House, with wonderful views from the big wraparound porch and an excellent dining room.

Don't miss a stop at Nora Mill in Sautee, where the water-powered millstones have been grinding grain for over 100 years. The whole-grain grits they label "Georgia Ice Cream" are truly gourmet fare.

The Old Sautee Store nearby, both country store and museum, has also been plying its trade for over 100 years.

Gourdcraft Originals, off Georgia route 255, is closer to Cleveland, and is well worth seeking out for the whimsical toys and decorative pieces created from gourds.

Get your camera ready for another waterfall wonder when you head for Anna Ruby Falls, off Georgia route 356 north of Helen. This is a double falls created by the joining of the Curtis and York creeks off Tray Mountain. An easy paved path of less than half a mile leads to the falls and a visitor center.

A 4.8-mile hiking trail connects this area to Unicoi State Park, also reached via Georgia route 356. This is one of Georgia's most complete resort parks, comprising over 1,000 acres with a handsome, modern 100-room lodge and a restaurant. Swimming, fishing, and boating on a 53-acre lake, forest trails, four lighted tennis courts, and a gift shop loaded with local crafts are among the attractions.

It's just more proof that you can still strike weekend gold in the magnificent mountains of Georgia.

Area Code: 706

DRIVING DIRECTIONS   Dahlonega is at the intersection of Ga. route 60 and U.S. 19, off Ga. route 400. From Atlanta, follow Ga. route 400 north into U.S. 19, about 71 miles.

ACCOMMODATIONS   *Mountain Top Lodge*, Route 7, P.O. Box 150, Dahlonega 30533, 864–5257, I-M, CP; deluxe rooms, E, CP • *Amicalola Falls State Park*, Highway 52, Dawsonville 30534, 265–8888 or 800–869–8420, spectacular views, lodge rooms, I; suites, M; cabins, I • *Worley Homestead Inn*, 410 West Main Street, Dahlonega 30533, 864–7002, I, CP • *Royal Guard Inn*, 203 South Park Street, Dahlonega 30533, 864–1713, I, CP • *The Smith House*, 202 South Chestatee Street, Dahlonega 30533, 864–3566, simple rooms, I • *Unicoi State Park*, Highway 356, P.O. Box 849, Helen 30545, 878–2824 or 800–869–8420, lodge and cabins, I • *Stovall House*, Highway 255 North, Sautee Valley 30571, 878–3355, M, CP • *Amicalola River Home Hostel*, Highway 53 West, Dawsonville 30534, 265–6892, rustic, shared kitchen, bring your own linens, very inexpensive, I • *Log cabins: Hatfield's Hideaway Cabins*, 864–6743; *Mountain Brook Cabin*, 864–3127; *Blue Ridge Mountain Cabins*, 747–1052; *Tanglewood Resort Cabins*, 878–3286; *Forrest Hills Resort*, 864–6456.

DINING   *The Smith House*, 202 South Chestatee Street, Dahlonega, 864–3566, bountiful Southern family-style meals, I • *Nature's Cellar*,

North Park Street, Dahlonega, 864–6829, health-food cafe, I • *Caruso's,* 113 East Main Street, Dahlonega, 864–4664, Italian, I • *Lonesome Dove,* 201 South Park Street, Dahlonega, 864–0384, steak and prime rib, I-M • *Clark's Front Porch BarBQ,* one block west of the square, Dahlonega, 864–8250, I • *The Maple Restaurant,* Amicalola Falls State Park (see above), I • *Hofbrauhaus,* 1 Main Street, Helen, 878–2248, German-Austrian, attractive decor, nice location on the river, M • *Stovall House* (see above), I • *Unicoi Restaurant,* Unicoi State Park (see above), I.

SIGHTSEEING *Dahlonega Gold Museum,* Public Square, Dahlonega, 864–2257. Hours: Monday to Saturday 9 A.M. to 5 P.M.; Sunday 10 A.M. to 5 P.M.; $ • *Consolidated Gold Mine,* Highway 19 Connector, Dahlonega, 864–8473. Hours: daily 10 A.M. to 5 P.M., last tour begins at 4 P.M., $$$ • *Babyland General Hospital,* 19 Underwood Street, Cleveland, 865–2171. Hours: Monday to Saturday 9 A.M. to 5 P.M.; Sunday 1 P.M. to 5 P.M.; free • *Amicalola Falls State Park,* Highway 52, Dawsonville, 265–8888. Hours: daily 7 A.M. to 10 P.M.; office hours, 8 A.M. to 5 P.M.; parking, $ • *Unicoi State Park,* Highway 356, Helen, 878–2824. Hours: daily 7 A.M. to 10 P.M.; office hours, 8 A.M. to 5 P.M.; parking, $ • *Gold panning: Crisson Gold Mine,* Wimpy Mill Road, Dahlonega, 864–6363; *Consolidated Gold Mine* (see above) • *Canoe trips: Appalachian Outfitters,* Highway 60 South, Dahlonega, 864–7117 or 800–426–7117 • *Raft rentals: Wild River Rafting,* Highway 53 West, Dawsonville, 265–6892.

INFORMATION *Dahlonega-Lumpkin Chamber of Commerce,* Public Square, P.O. Box 2037, Dahlonega, GA 30533, 864–3711.

A Capital Trip to Columbia

State capitals are generally good places to visit, offering historic sites and museums, plus good restaurants catering to the bigwigs who come to break bread with legislators.

College towns have different charms—scenic campuses, sports, theater groups, concerts, and a spirit of perpetual youth, evidenced in the shops, cafes, and clubs frequented by the students.

Seldom do the twain meet—except in Columbia, South Carolina. Columbia is the only Southeastern city that is home to both the state's government and its largest university. Add an exceptional zoo and the Colonial attractions of nearby Camden, including a fabled steeplechase race, and you have more than ample ingredients for a capital weekend.

One of the first planned communities in the country, Columbia was established in 1786 as a carefully chosen site for the state capital, a centrally located compromise between Lowcountry and Upcountry factions. Though the city has spread in all directions, the wide boulevards of the original plan are still evident in the heart of town, the site of both the 1855 State House and the college founded in 1801.

Since most city attractions are downtown, and the straight grid pattern makes it easy to find your way around, this is the best place to stay. The most unusual lodging and best choice is Claussens Inn, a 1928 brick building, formerly a bakery, now converted to offer oversize and very attractive rooms. It is in the Five Points district near the university, where the streets are lined with interesting shops, galleries, and restaurants. Two bed-and-breakfast homes in the historic district are also excellent choices.

Though Columbia's history goes back a long way, many of the original buildings were burned in 1865 when General Sherman's troops occupied the city, destroying an area of 84 blocks and more than 1,300 buildings. Only the university, the unfinished new State House, and the home of the French consul were spared. Most of today's stately buildings and the modern city, with its population of 112,000, have risen since that time.

A good place to begin sightseeing is at the oldest remaining site, the lovely original campus of the University of South Carolina, known as the Horseshoe. It is entered on Sumter Street between Greene and Pendleton streets. You can pick up a campus walking tour brochure at the admissions office in Lieber Hall, the first building on the right as you face the Horseshoe.

The buildings on either side of the oak-and-magnolia-rimmed green date from 1805 to 1855; all are listed on the National Register of Historic Places. A major ten-year restoration project has returned the exteriors to their 1850 appearance while modernizing the interiors for contemporary needs. Many are now used as residence halls for honor students.

The center monument honoring Jonathan Maxcy, the first president of the college, was designed by South Carolinian Robert Mills, the first prominent native-born American architect, best known for his design of the Washington Monument. Mills was instrumental in the architectural development of the college until 1840.

Among the buildings you will pass on a stroll around the Horseshoe are the beautiful 1810 Regency-style home of the president of the university, and Rutledge College, which was the only building when South Carolina College first opened its doors in 1805. Rutledge served as dorm, lecture hall, chapel, and library for 29 students. Today's campus enrollment tops 26,000, and there are some 127 campus buildings.

At the head of the Horseshoe stands the stately, columned McKissick Museum, a relatively new addition built as a library in 1940. Southern folk art, the Howard Gemstone Collection, and the Bernard Baruch Collection of Silver are among the reasons a visit is well advised.

The rest of the campus is modern, but it makes for a pleasant hour's stroll. Two buildings farther away, on Assembly Street, that you may possibly visit later in your stay are the Carolina Coliseum, where USC Gamecock basketball games are played, and the Koger Center for the Arts, where entertainment ranging from ballet to bluegrass to Broadway shows is presented. If you come in football season, you may want to be among the avid Gamecock fans who fill the stadium.

It is a short walk from the campus to the official state buildings. If you want to do more than admire them as you walk by, you'll have to come on a weekday; all are closed on weekends. An extra half-day is worth the effort for the South Carolina State House alone; it is one of the most beautiful of all state capitols, faced with Corinthian columns of blue granite outside and graced with palmettos, the official state tree, within. Begun in 1855, the domed building was still only a shell when General Sherman's men attacked the city. Metal stars on the west and southwest walls mark places that were struck by artillery shells. Inside you can watch the proceedings of the legislature from brass-railed balconies, or stroll the historic halls.

Across the street from the State House is Trinity Cathedral, a small-scale replica of England's Yorkminster Cathedral. Prominent South Carolinians, including six governors, are buried in the churchyard.

The governor's mansion was originally built as officers' quarters for Arsenal Academy. After Sherman's visit, it was the only building left on the academy grounds. It was renovated and declared the official governor's residence in 1867. Two other fine homes moved to adjacent sites are used for official guests and for state occasions.

The mansion is located in the residential Arsenal Hill Historic District of Columbia, a section considered desirable since the antebellum era for its elevation and city views. Sydney Park, a good place to see those views, was restored in 1990 on the site of a park that had been destroyed by turn-of-the-century industrialization.

More fine homes can be seen by driving along Blanding and Richland streets, areas that escaped Sherman's flames. If you must choose only one of Columbia's four historic homes, make it the Robert Mills Historic House and Park. Planned by Mills in 1823 for a prominent Columbia merchant, the columned home has an elegant main floor with curved walls, matching drawing rooms, and decorative niches typical of Mills's style.

The other museum houses include the Hampton-Preston Mansion and Garden, built from 1818 to 1835, the home of two prominent South Carolina families; and the more modest 1872 home where President Woodrow Wilson lived during the four years his father was a minister here. The 1850 Mann-Simons Cottage is of interest because it shows how free blacks lived during Columbia's antebellum period.

Allow plenty of time when you move on to the South Carolina Museum, housed in what was the world's first all-electric textile mill. The restored four-story structure is huge, and holds displays covering every facet of the Palmetto State—artistic, scientific, and historic. In the natural-history section you can touch a 30-million-year-old tooth from a giant white shark and see replicas of creatures from the Ice Age; in the history galleries you will relive the beginning of the Civil War and visit a one-room schoolhouse and vintage country store.

The local visitors bureau occupies part of the main floor, and can supply plenty of maps, brochures, and advice to make your stay more rewarding.

The State Museum is located on Gervais Street, the center of an old warehouse district known as Congaree Vista—or, more commonly, just "the Vista." It is rapidly reviving with interesting antique shops, galleries, and restaurants.

The Columbia Museum of Art may surprise you with its fine Renaissance art, contemporary graphics, and the only collection of Vietnamese art in America.

If you can manage to fit enough of the above into one day, you can start fresh the next morning at the multi-award-winning Riverbanks Zoo, the favorite public attraction in South Carolina, with nearly a million visitors a year. There's good reason for this popularity. The complex uses the latest in naturalistic exhibit techniques, such as simulated African plains where giraffes, zebras, black rhinos, and ostriches can feel at home, and a realistic re-creation of the rain forests of South America.

The real showplace is the Aquarium Reptile Complex, added in 1989, home to thousands of fish and reptiles, amphibians and invertebrates from all over the world.

Having visited with the animals at the zoo, save the rest of the afternoon to hobnob with the horsy set in Camden, 30 miles to the east via I–20. The oldest inland town in the state, dating from 1733, Camden played a vital role in the American Revolution when Lord Cornwallis took the town in 1780 and moved with his officers into the Kershaw Mansion, the finest home in town. Camden became one of the main garrisons maintained by the British in South Carolina.

A reconstruction of the Kershaw Mansion is part of Historic Camden, a colonial village to which authentic Revolutionary War era houses have been moved and preserved. The complex includes archaeological findings of the old town walls and forts used during the

British occupation in 1780–81. On the first weekend in November, cannons roar and muskets pop as the battle between the British and the Americans is reenacted during the annual Revolutionary War Field Days and Heritage Days Crafts Fair.

Pick up the guide to historic sites, at the Historic Camden shop. It will guide you to more early homes along Broad Street, the main street of town, and other avenues such as Laurens and Chewning streets, around Monument Square.

By 1802, Camden was already holding horse races. In this century, wealthy families such as the Buckleys, du Ponts, and Firestones settled into the fine nineteenth-century estates along wooded and secluded byways in the Kirkwood section—streets like Lyttleton and Greene and Kirkwood Lane—where they raised, rode, and prepared to race their thoroughbred horses. The big, graceful, 1854 home on Kirkwood called Kamschatka, for example, was bought and renovated by the late William F. Buckley, Senior. Kirkwood is one of many lanes that remain unpaved, to be easier on the horses' hooves.

Springdale Race Course, developed in the late 1920s, quickly became famous for its premier steeplechase training facilities. In 1970, local resident Marion du Pont Scott underwrote the first Colonial Cup International Steeplechase, with the first $100,000 purse ever offered in a steeplechase racing event. Mrs. Scott willed the track to the state in 1983, along with a $1 million endowment for upkeep. It is the setting for two prestigious steeplechase events each year, the very social Carolinas Cup in March and the continuation of the Colonial Cup in mid-November. The fall event is less crowded and less formal than the spring race, but no less fun. Time your visit right, and you can join the spectators enjoying an elegant lunch al fresco while they watch the top thoroughbred 'chasers in the world running for the prized gold cup. The winner of the Colonial Cup must lead the pack around a marathon course that includes 17 fences.

If you can't make the race, you can watch the polo ponies in action almost any Saturday at 2 P.M. at the Camden Polo Field. It will give you a feeling for the equestrian life that still reigns supreme in colonial Camden.

Area Code: 803

DRIVING DIRECTIONS   Columbia is at the junction of I–20, I–26, and I–77. From Atlanta, follow I–20 east, 215 miles. From Charlotte, take I–77 south, 92 miles.

PUBLIC TRANSPORTATION   Columbia is served by seven airlines as well as Amtrak trains and Greyhound buses.

ACCOMMODATIONS *Claussen's Inn,* 2003 Greene Street, Columbia 29205, 765–0440 or 800–622–3382, M, CP • *Richland Street Bed & Breakfast,* 1425 Richland Street, Columbia 20201, 779–7001, a Victorian charmer, M-E, CP • *Chestnut Cottage,* 1718 Hampton Street, Columbia 29201, 256–1718, historic cottage, M, CP • *Whitney Hotel,* Devine and Woodrow streets, Columbia 29205, 252–0845 all suites, near Five Points, M • *Downtown hotels: Best Western Governor's House Hotel,* 1301 Main Street, Columbia 29201, 779–7790, I; *Columbia Marriott,* 1200 Hampton Street, Columbia 29201, 771–7000, M-E; *Holiday Inn Coliseum at USC,* 630 Assembly Street, Columbia 29201, 799–7800, I • *Greenleaf Inn,* 1308–10 Broad Street, Camden 29020, 800–437–5874, two nineteenth-century homes, I • *The Carriage House,* 1413 Lyttleton Street, Camden, 29020, 432–2430, delightful little 1840 raised cottage with antiques and an English garden, I, CP • *Bloomsbury,* 1707 Lyttleton Street, Camden 29020, 432–9714, 1850 Greek Revival showplace, M, CP.

DINING *Garibaldi's,* 2013 Greene Street, Five Points, Columbia, 771–8888, art deco decor, excellent Italian, I-M • *Harper's,* 700 Harden Street, Five Points, 252–2222, casual, popular, hickory-wood grill, I-M • *Goatfeathers,* 1017 Devine Street, Five Points, 771–9194, coffee bar and casual restaurant serving until 2 A.M., adjoins bookstore, I • *Columbia's Restaurant,* AT&T Building, Gervais and Assembly streets, Columbia, 779–1989, cosmopolitan air, downtown favorite, grill specialties, M • *Hennessy's Restaurant,* Main and Blanding streets, Columbia, 799–8280, varied menu, Cajun to crab cakes, M • *Key West Grill and Raw Bar,* 1736 Bush River Road (at I–20), Columbia, 772–0000, tropical decor, seafood and light fare, I-M • *Al's Upstairs Italian Restaurant,* 304 Meeting Street, Columbia, 794–7404, intimate dining rooms, popular, reservations advised, M • *Richard's Fine Southern Cuisine,* 936 Gervais Street, Columbia, 799–3071, I-E • For hearty, inexpensive Southern country cooking, look for *Lizard's Thicket,* with 14 locations all around town • *The Paddock House,* 514 Rutledge Street, Camden, 432–3222, renovated livery stable, pub, and formal dining room, lunch, I, dinner, M.

SIGHTSEEING *South Carolina State Museum,* 301 Gervais Street, Columbia, 737–4595. Hours: Monday to Saturday 10 A.M. to 5 P.M.; Sunday 1 P.M. to 5 P.M.; $$ • *South Carolina State House,* Main and Gervais streets, Columbia, 734–2430. Hours: tours every half hour Monday to Friday, 9 A.M. to noon and 1 P.M. to 4 P.M., free • *University of South Carolina,* information from Admissions Office, Lieber

College, the Horseshoe, Sumter Street between Greene and Pendleton streets, 777–7700. Hours: Monday to Friday 8:30 A.M. to 5 P.M.; free campus tours offered Monday to Friday 10 A.M. and 2 P.M.; reservations preferred • *McKissick Museum,* University of South Carolina Horseshoe, Columbia, 777–7251. Hours: Monday to Friday 9 A.M. to 4 P.M.; Saturday 10 A.M. to 5 P.M.; Sunday 1 P.M. to 5 P.M.; free • *Robert Mills Historic House and Park,* 1616 Blanding Street, Columbia, 252–1770. Hours: Tuesday to Saturday 10 A.M. to 4 P.M., Sunday 1 P.M. to 5 P.M.; $$ • *Hampton-Preston Mansion and Garden,* 1615 Blanding Street, Columbia, 252–1770. Hours: Tuesday to Saturday 10 A.M. to 4 P.M.; Sunday 1 P.M. to 5 P.M.; $$ • *Woodrow Wilson Boyhood Home,* 1705 Hampton Street, Columbia, 252–1770. Hours: Tuesday to Saturday 10 A.M. to 4 P.M.; Sunday 1 P.M. to 5 P.M.; $$ • *Columbia Museum of Art,* Bull and Senate streets, Columbia, 799–2810. Hours: Tuesday to Friday 10 A.M. to 5 P.M.; Saturday and Sunday 12:30 P.M. to 5 P.M.; free, except for Gibbes Planetarium shows, Saturday and Sunday at 2, 3, and 4 P.M., $ • *South Carolina Confederate Relic Room and Museum,* 920 Sumter Street at Pendleton, Columbia, 734–9813. Hours: Monday to Friday 8:30 A.M. to 5 P.M., free • *Riverbanks Zoological Park,* off I–126 west of downtown, Greystone Boulevard Exit, P.O. Box 1060, Columbia, 779–8730. Hours: daily 9 A.M. to 4 P.M.; summer weekends 9 A.M. to 5 P.M.; $$ • *Koger Center for the Arts,* University of South Carolina, 701 Assembly and Greene streets, 777–5113. Wide variety of performances; check current schedules • *Historic Camden,* U.S. 521, Camden, 432–9841. Hours: Tuesday to Saturday 10 A.M. to 5 P.M.; Sunday 1 P.M. to 5 P.M.; $$ • *Steeplechase races: Springdale Course,* Camden, 432–6513. Phone for dates of future Carolina and Colonial Cup events.

INFORMATION *Greater Columbia Convention and Visitors Bureau,* P.O. Box 15, State Museum Building, Columbia, SC 29202, 254–0479; *Kershaw County Chamber of Commerce,* 724 Broad Street, Camden, SC 29210, 432–2525.

Rounding the Triangle in North Carolina

North Carolina's Research Triangle may be best known for business, but it holds a triple helping of treats for visitors. Raleigh, Durham, and Chapel Hill, the points of the triangle, are only minutes apart and share the thickly wooded, green countryside of the state's rolling central Piedmont. Yet each town has a distinct history and personality.

Each boasts a major university, making them sports rivals, especially on the basketball court. The great Michael Jordan polished his skills at Chapel Hill, and Duke's Blue Devils play to sellout crowds in Durham from November to March.

Although each city alone could pleasantly occupy a weekend, because of their proximity most visitors try to combine them in a single trip. At the least, schedule a long weekend; you won't regret the time.

The first decision is where to stay. Each city offers an abundance of lodgings, but this vote goes to the lively ambience of Chapel Hill, a small, sophisticated community dominated by the campus of the University of North Carolina.

If you can afford the tab, the prime place in the entire triangle is eight miles south of town. The Fearrington House, a member of the prestigious Relais & Chateau group, is adjacent to the shopping village of a posh residential community. It offers elegantly furnished rooms and suites, a charming garden, and a dining room whose prix-fixe dinners get raves.

Chapel Hill's chief attraction is the 700-acre campus of the oldest state university in the country. It runs along Franklin Street, the city's main thoroughfare.

Founded in 1795, UNC was the only public institution granting college degrees in the eighteenth century. Among many distinguished graduates is President James Polk. A tour of the central campus is offered every afternoon from the visitor center at the west entrance of the Morehead Building. Some limited metered parking is available next to the building, but safer bets are the town lots at the intersections of Rosemary and Columbia or Rosemary and Franklin streets.

To explore on your own, ask at the visitor center for a self-guided tour brochure. Within Morehead, be sure to step into the domed and columned rotunda. It contains an impressive art collection including Rembrandt Peale portraits of George and Martha Washington. The adjoining planetarium offers science exhibits as well as planetarium shows.

The printed tour will lead you around the old campus and some of its landmarks. These include Old East, the first campus building, still used as a residence hall; the Morehead-Patterson Bell Tower, which chimes to call students to class ten minutes before each hour; and the Old Well, where students once dipped water from an oaken bucket. Virtually the only source of water for over a century, the well is now encased by columns and a dome, and is the symbol of the university.

Allow time for the Wilson Library, whose gracious reading rooms and ornately carved ceilings have been nicely restored. Another recommended stop is the Ackland Art Museum, whose holdings include paintings by Delacroix, Rubens, and Degas, and rare Oriental art.

The campus includes an arboretum, its best-known feature a 200-foot wisteria arbor. The North Carolina Botanical Garden is another fine place for a change of pace on a pleasant day.

When you are ready for worldly diversions, the low brick buildings along Franklin Street are filled with shops, and the restored Carr Mill in Carrboro, just west of town along Greensboro Street, offers a variety of tempting stores and restaurants. Check at the ArtsCenter in Carrboro for theater and concert performances.

Quite a different scene awaits in Raleigh. A modern city of 208,000 that celebrated its two hundredth birthday in 1992, Raleigh has managed to keep intact most of the green squares from the original city plan. Stop at the Capital Area Visitor Center for a free map pointing out city sights.

A tour almost has to begin with the stately Greek Revival–style 1840 state capitol building. Except for the offices of the governor and lieutenant governor, the work of government is now carried on elsewhere, but the original state senate and house chambers have been restored to their appearance from 1840 to 1865, complete to the desks and chairs created originally by William Thompson, a Raleigh cabinetmaker.

Also in the neighborhood are two major state collections. The North Carolina Museum of History reflects progress from the Stone Age to the Space Age. A wide variety of displays, ranging from native plants and animals to fossils and the skeleton of a 55-foot whale, fill the North Carolina Museum of Natural Sciences, which is due to move into a new $31 million building by 1995.

The nearby Governor's Mansion is an 1891 Queen Anne Victorian beauty with a magnificent ornate interior that rates a tour if you are in town when the building is open to the public. The mansion adjoins Oakwood, one of the city's oldest neighborhoods, a nice place for a walk to admire more Victorian homes.

Another neighborhood highly recommended for a visit is Raleigh's revitalized City Market, a 1914 produce district of cobbled streets and tin-roofed buildings that has been transformed into the city's Arts District, with boutiques, cafés, and several small galleries. Artspace, a strikingly renovated one-time Ford showroom at the corner of Blount and Davie, includes a gallery and 23 studios where artists both work and sell.

Raleigh's historic highlight is Mordecai House, a columned home dating back to 1785 and occupied by the same prominent family for five generations. Their original furnishings, including a fascinating library, remain. The grounds boast an herb garden and the tiny frame cabin that was the birthplace of Carolina-born President Andrew Johnson, moved here from its original site on Fayetteville Street.

The highway known as the Beltway divides downtown and its older neighborhoods from the city's newer suburban areas. Beyond the Beltway lies a major attraction, the North Carolina Museum of Art. The $15 million contemporary showplace, designed by Edward Durell Stone, is beautifully set on 140 parklike acres. European paintings from 1300 to 1800, including 71 paintings from the important Samuel H. Kress collection; American nineteenth-century art; and an exceptional gallery of Jewish ceremonial art are strengths of the museum.

There's a pleasant sense of calm in Durham, where the downtown loop and Main Street are lined with vintage buildings dating from the 1890s to the 1930s. The whole area has been declared a historic district.

The sign at the city limits, "Welcome to Durham, City of Medicine," tells you that this is a place known for its many hospitals, the extensive facilities of the Duke Medical Center, and the presence of more than 300 medical and health-related companies in the community.

But you can't be in town for long without being aware of another industry that formed the city—the processing of tobacco. Civil War troops were the first to discover the excellent properties of North Carolina "brightleaf" tobacco, an acquired taste that remained with them after the war. Tobacco factories, past and present, are very much in evidence around town, marked by their many brick chimneys. One former factory has been converted into a popular center for dining and shopping known as Brightleaf Square.

"Bull Durham," the title of a popular movie a few years ago, became the city's nickname thanks to the Blackwell Tobacco Company, the first factory in town, whose symbol was inspired by the bull on the Coleman's mustard jar. The original Bull Durham Factory still stands at 201 West Pettigrew Street.

By the time James B. Duke founded the American Tobacco Company in 1890, incorporating Blackwell and four other large producers, the bull was one of the best-known trademarks in the world, spawning the term "bull pen" and the expression "shooting the bull," inspired by the habits of those who chewed tobacco.

Durham residents, incidentally, are great fans of the Durham Bulls, the class-A baseball team featured in the movie. The team is getting a larger stadium to hold the crowds. The snorting bull mascot seen in the film will definitely be moved to the new ballpark.

It's fun to start Durham sightseeing by visiting the original Duke homestead, where you can see the humble 1852 farm where Washington Duke first grew and packed pouches of tobacco. A small museum traces the growth of the now controversial industry.

Then head for Durham's proudest sight, the magnificent campus that resulted from tobacco profits. The original East Campus, established in 1892 as Trinity College, acquired many of its red brick Georgian buildings and the grassy quadrangle when it was rebuilt and renamed Duke University in 1924.

Duke came into its full glory when the Gothic Revival West Campus was built between 1924 and 1938, emerging as one of the most beautiful American colleges thanks to the generous endowment from James B. Duke, Washington's son.

A statue of James Duke stands in front of the magnificent chapel that he specified to be the dominant feature of the campus. The chapel, which seats 1,470, is rich with statuary and stained glass and boasts a 120-foot bell tower. The 50-bell carillon can be heard at the end of each day. A concert on the 5,000-pipe Benjamin N. Duke Memorial Organ is held every weekday at 12:30 P.M. Free concerts and performances are also sometimes held in the 55-acre Sarah P. Duke Gardens, a beautiful blending of formal terraced landscaping and woodland surroundings. Four miles of *allées*, walks, and pathways lead past lawns, native wildflowers, an Asiatic arboretum, and formal plantings.

The 6,800-acre Research Triangle Park, set in the pine groves just outside Durham, is a unique partnership between business and academia that merits a driving tour. The Burroughs Wellcome Building, designed by Paul Rudolph, is the acknowledged architectural showpiece of the vast complex, but the park includes many other innovative designs. The breakthroughs resulting from Triangle research run the gamut from Astroturf to AZT.

If children are along, Durham has some special attractions including the hands-on exhibits at the expanding North Carolina Museum of Life and Science and the working gristmill at West Point on the Eno Park. The park offers guided nature walks as well as demonstrations of old-time crafts such as blacksmithing, weaving, spinning, and angora goat shearing.

Whatever your age and interests, you'll find plenty of pleasures in the Triangle, distinct diversions almost equally divided between the towns.

Area Code: 919

DRIVING DIRECTIONS The Research Triangle cities are reached via I–40 from east and west, I–85 and I–70 from north and south. From

Atlanta or Charlotte to Chapel Hill, the southwest corner of the triangle, follow I–85 north to I–40 southeast, and turn south on U.S. 15/501; it is 356 miles from Atlanta, 135 miles from Charlotte. Continue past the Chapel Hill exit on I–40 into U.S. 64 for exits to Raleigh, the southeast corner. For Durham, the top of the triangle, stay on I–85 and watch for exits. Distances between triangle cities: Chapel Hill is 12 miles from Durham, 28 miles from Raleigh; the distance from Raleigh to Durham is 23 miles.

PUBLIC TRANSPORTATION   Raleigh-Durham airport, 13 miles from Chapel Hill, is a hub for American Airlines, and is served by most major carriers. The Triangle area is also served by Amtrak.

ACCOMMODATIONS   *Fearrington House,* 2000 Fearrington Village Center, Pittsboro (8 miles south of Chapel Hill) 28312, 542–2121, E-EE, CP • *Carolina Inn,* 211 Pittsboro Street, Chapel Hill 27514, 333–2001 or 800–962–8519, campus standby, I-M • *Sienna Hotel,* 1505 East Franklin Street, Chapel Hill 27514, 929–4000, luxury hotel, E • *Omni Europa,* 1 Europa Drive, Chapel Hill 27514, 968–4900, hotel with tennis, health club, M • *Best Western University Inn,* Highway 54, Chapel Hill, 27514, 932–3000, upscale motel adjoining golf course, golf and tennis privileges, I-M • *Oakwood Inn,* 411 North Bloodworth Street, Raleigh 27604, 832–9712, I-E, CP • *Radisson Plaza Hotel,* 20 Fayetteville Street, Downtown Plaza, Raleigh 27601, 834–9900 or 800–333–3333, convenient in-town location, M • *Washington Duke Inn and Golf Club,* 3001 Cameron Boulevard, Durham 27706, 490–0999 or 800–443–3853, adjoining Duke campus, best in town, E-EE • *Hilton,* 3800 Hillsborough Road, Durham 27705, 383–8033 or 800-HILTONS, pool, attractive landscaping, M • *Omni Durham,* 201 Foster Street, Durham 27701, 683–6664 or 800-THE OMNI, central location adjoining Royall Center for the Arts, M • *Arrowhead Inn,* 106 Mason Road, Durham 27712, 477–8430, 1775 colonial home just outside town, I-E, CP • For lists of many other area hotels and motels, write to respective chambers of commerce.

DINING   *Fearrington House* (see above), elegant, prix-fixe, EE • *Crook's Corner,* 610 West Franklin Street, Chapel Hill, 929–7643, casual, delicious and creative Southern cuisine, M • *Pyewacket,* 431 West Franklin Street, Chapel Hill, 929–0297, varied menu, veranda, I-M • *411 West,* 411 West Franklin Street, 967–2782, cozy Italian café, I-M • *Il Palio,* Sienna Hotel (see above), gourmet Italian, M-E • *Aurora,* Highway 64 at 200 North Greensboro Street, Carr Mill,

Carrboro (1 mile west of Chapel Hill), 942–2400, casual, in a restored mill, M ● *Angus Barn*, Highway 70 West at Airport Road, Raleigh, 781–2444, the local favorite, rustic ambience, thick steaks, prize-winning wine list, M-EE ● *42nd Street Oyster Bar*, West Jones and West streets, Raleigh, 831–2811, seafood, I-E ● *Winston's Grille*, 6401 Falls of the Neuse Road, Raleigh, 790–0700, casual, open grill, I-M ● *Big Ed's City Market Restaurant*, 220 Wolfe Street, Raleigh, 869–9909, breakfast and lunch, down-home Southern cooking, I ● *Magnolia Grill*, 1002 Ninth Street, Durham, 286–3609, creative sauces and presentation, M-E ● *Crescent Cafe*, 317 West Main Street, Durham, 688–5685, Cajun, Creole, Southern Italy I-M ● *Taverna Nikos*, Brightleaf Square, Durham, 682–0043, good Greek food in attractive, airy surroundings, M ● *Bakatsias,* 1821 Hillandale Road, Durham, 383–8502, elegant continental, M-E ● *Fairview,* Washington Duke Inn and Golf Club (see above), elegant dining overlooking the golf course, E-EE ● *Bullock's,* 3330 Wortham Street, Durham, 383–3211, no frills, great barbecue, lunch or very early dinner—they close at 7 P.M., I.

SIGHTSEEING *University of North Carolina at Chapel Hill,* 962–2211. Visitor Center, Morehead Building, off East Franklin Street, 962–1630. Hours: Monday to Friday 10 A.M. to 5 P.M.; guided tours daily, 2:15 P.M.; free ● *Ackland Art Museum*, Columbia Street at Franklin, UNC campus, Chapel Hill, 966–5736. Hours: Wednesday to Friday noon to 3 P.M.; Saturday 10 A.M. to 5 P.M.; Sunday 1 P.M. to 5 P.M.; free ● *Morehead Planetarium*, East Franklin Street, UNC campus, Chapel Hill, 549–6863. Hours: art and science exhibits, Sunday to Friday 12:30 P.M. to 5 P.M. and 6:30 to 9:30 P.M., free. Planetarium shows, mid-June to Labor Day, daily 1 P.M., 3 P.M., 8 P.M.; rest of year, Monday to Friday 8 P.M.; Saturday and Sunday 1 P.M., 3 P.M., 8 P.M., $$ ● *North Carolina Botanical Garden,* Mason Farm Road off U.S. 15/501, Chapel Hill, 362–0522. Hours: mid-March to mid-November, daily 8 A.M. to 5 P.M.; rest of year, Monday to Friday 8 A.M. to 5 P.M.; free ● *ArtsCenter,* 300G East Main Street, Carrboro, 929–1787. Check for current programs ● *Duke University,* Durham, 684–8111. East Campus, entrance on Main Street just past Buchanan Boulevard; West Campus, entrance on Chapel Drive off Duke University Road; tours for prospective students leave Monday to Friday 11:30 A.M. and 2 P.M., from Undergraduate Admissions, 2138 Campus Drive, West Campus. ● *Duke University Chapel,* West Campus, 684–2572. Hours: September to May, daily 8 A.M. to 11 P.M.; rest of year, daily 8 A.M. to 8 P.M.; free ● *Sarah Duke Gardens,* West Campus, 684–3698. Hours: daily 8 A.M. to dusk, free ● *Duke University Museum of Art,* East Campus, 684–5135. Hours: Tuesday to Friday 9 A.M. to 5 P.M.; Saturday 11 A.M.

to 2 P.M.; Sunday 2 P.M. to 5 P.M.; free • *Royall Center for the Arts,* 120 Morris Street, Durham, 560–2787. Hours: Monday to Saturday 9 A.M. to 9 P.M.; Sunday 1 P.M. to 9 P.M. • *Duke Homestead State Historic Site and Tobacco Museum,* 2828 Duke Homestead Road, Durham, 477– 5498. Hours: April to October, Monday to Saturday 9 A.M. to 5 P.M., Sunday 1 P.M. to 5 P.M.; rest of year, Monday to Saturday 10 A.M. to 4 P.M., Sunday 1 P.M. to 4 P.M.; free • *North Carolina Museum of Life and Science,* 433 Murray Avenue, Durham, 220–5429. Hours: Monday to Saturday 10 A.M. to 5 P.M., Sunday 1 P.M. to 5 P.M.; Memorial Day to Labor Day, to 6 P.M.; $$ • *West Point on the Eno,* Roxboro Road, Durham, 471–1623. Hours: park open daily 8 A.M. to dusk; visitor center and blacksmith shop, March to December, Saturday and Sunday 1 P.M. to 4 P.M.; free • *North Carolina Museum of Art,* 2110 Blue Ridge Road, Raleigh, 833–1935. Hours: Tuesday to Saturday 9 A.M. to 5 P.M.; Sunday 11 A.M. to 6 P.M.; free • *North Carolina State Capitol,* Capitol Square, Raleigh 733–4994. Hours: Monday to Friday 8 A.M. to 5 P.M.; Saturday 9 A.M. to 5 P.M.; free • *Mordecai Historic Park,* 1 Mimosa Street, Raleigh, 834–4844. Hours: March 1 to mid-December, Tuesday to Friday 10 A.M. to 3 P.M.; Saturday and Sunday 1:30 P.M. to 3:30 P.M.; $$ • *North Carolina Museum of History,* 109 East Jones Street, 733–3894 (museum is moving to new quarters; check address). Hours: Tuesday to Saturday 9 A.M. to 5 P.M.; Sunday 1 P.M. to 6 P.M.; free.

INFORMATION *Chapel Hill–Carrboro Chamber of Commerce,* P.O. Box 2897, Chapel Hill, NC 27514, 967–7075 • *Durham Convention and Visitors Bureau,* 101 East Morgan Street, Durham, NC 27701, 687–2722; *Raleigh Convention and Visitors Bureau,* 225 Hillsborough Street, Suite 400, P.O. Box 1879, Raleigh, NC 27602, 834–5900 • *Capital Area Visitor Center,* 301 North Blount Street, Raleigh, 733–3456.

Counting Columns Near Athens

Though it is best known as the home of the University of Georgia, Athens, Georgia, has another claim to fame. Set on a hill beside the Oconee River, lush with towering oaks and leafy magnolias and filled with fine homes, Athens is the first stop on Georgia's Antebellum Trail, a swath of land missed by Yankee troops who devastated so much of the state. Stately columned mansions welcome visitors to the gracious past all the way from Athens to Macon. When you've seen one set of columns, you haven't quite seen them all, because each stop has quite a different personality.

The town and its school are the perfect starting points for exploring the northern end of the trail, offering history, art, the state botanical gardens, and a sports hall to delight Georgia Bulldog fans. Not far away are two unique places to watch crafts in the making, and a state park that can add golf and boating to the agenda.

The picturesque campus that is the centerpiece of the city was one of the country's first chartered state universities. It was established on this site in 1801, the same year Athens was founded. Many well-to-do families moved to town early in the nineteenth century to send their sons to the university, accounting for the handsome homes that abound today. A number of these homes are now occupied by campus fraternities and sororities, but whatever may go on behind the stately columns, the appearance is still classic Old South.

So is the campus. Walk through the nineteenth-century arch at Broad Street and College Avenue to the quadrangle of the Old North Campus, and feel the tradition all around you. Circling the green are venerable buildings that include the Old College (1805), Waddel Hall (1821), and Demosthenian Hall (1824). The 1832 chapel and Phi Kappa Hall, built in 1834, are beautiful examples of Greek Revival architecture.

One small brick building on the quadrangle houses the Georgia Museum of Art, the state's official art showcase. The exhibit space can accommodate only a fraction of the museum's 5,000 works of art, but whatever is on display is worth seeing. Expansion is planned, so perhaps by the time you read this, the museum will have more rooms to display its treasures.

The Founders Memorial Garden on the campus was planned as a memorial to the founders of the Athens Ladies Garden Club, the oldest garden club in the nation, formed in 1891. With its meandering flagstone walkways, slate walls, trickling fountain, and precision-cut boxwood garden, it makes for a delightful stroll.

A camellia garden surrounds the 1857 brick home that is the present headquarters for the Garden Club. Built as a residence for professors, it is now a house-museum furnished with antiques. A special feature is the ballroom that was added in 1865.

Sports fans won't want to miss Butts-Mehre Heritage Hall, where they can relive the greatest moments in Georgia sports history. The polished red granite and glass building was built with private donations and named for two past coaching greats, Wally Butts and Harry Mehre. The third and fourth floors are a salute to Georgia sports, especially the "Dawgs." There are national championship trophies and tributes to stars of yesterday, including Heisman trophy winners from Frankie

Sinkwich to Herschel Walker. Videos replay memorable moments from the past.

Downtown begins on Broad Street just opposite the campus gate, and has its full quota of lively cafés filled with students. The central area has been declared a historic district and has its own interesting structures, such as the 1855 First Presbyterian Church, the art deco Georgia Theater, and the 1904 City Hall, a Beaux Arts building set on the highest point in town.

In front of City Hall is what is believed to be the world's only double-barreled cannon, one of the more curious relics of the War Between the States. It was invented in 1863, but unfortunately failed to fulfill its mission of firing two balls simultaneously.

The other curiosity invariably pointed out to visitors is the oak tree that stands in a square at Dearing and Finley streets, known as "the tree that owns itself." In appreciation of the tree's beauty and sheltering shade, the owner deeded the huge tree possession of itself and all the land within eight feet around it. When the tree was destroyed by a storm in 1942, one of its acorns was planted, and the descendant of the original planting now stands in the space.

For a sampling of Athens's avenues of lovely, white-columned homes, just drive along Prince Avenue. Lumpkin House, at number 248, is an 1843 Greek Revival mansion that belonged to the first chief justice of the Supreme Court of Georgia. At 570 is the home of the president of the university, guarded by 14 Corinthian columns on the front and sides, and facing a five-acre garden.

The Taylor-Grady House, 634, was built in the 1840s. A later occupant was Henry W. Grady, an Athens native who graduated from the university in 1868 and went on to become managing editor of the *Atlanta Constitution* and a leading spokesman for the New South following the Civil War. The house has been restored and is open to visitors on weekdays.

Another historic home, the Church-Waddel-Brymby House on Dougherty Street, was built in 1820. Also beautifully restored, it serves as both a house-museum and the Athens Welcome Center.

On a fine fall day, one of the nicest places to be in Athens is the State Botanical Gardens. Located two miles from the campus, the 313-acre preserve is set in a forest along the Middle Oconee River. Five miles of walking paths take in dramatic ravines, spring-fed streams, and a variety of specialty gardens that include roses, dahlias, herbs, perennials, rhododendrons, azaleas, and daffodils. No matter what the weather, tropical displays surrounded by flowing streams and ponds await in the Conservatory. The café here is a pleasant stop for lunch.

Rock music fans should plan at least one night in Athens to sample the local music scene. As home to such nationally known groups as REM and the B–52s, the city has gained a national reputation as an innovator of "new wave" rock, and there are more than a dozen places where you can hear live music. Find out who is playing where in *The Flagpole*, the free tabloid paper found in local restaurants and hotels.

Athens has plenty of motel accommodations; some give the bonus of a free breakfast. But the choicest lodging is eight miles away, in Watkinsville. The Rivendell Bed and Breakfast Inn is a new home built in English country style and filled with antiques and art. There are striking contemporary touches such as lofty beamed ceilings, picture windows, and big stone fireplaces.

An interesting detour on a country road south of Watkinsville takes you to Happy Valley Pottery and the chance to see a thriving business housed in what were once chicken coops. Jerry and Kathy Chappelle started making pottery as a sideline while he was teaching art at the University of Georgia. The venture has been so successful that they now have assistants helping to turn out the colorful decorative wares, which can be found in craft shops nationwide. Visitors are welcome to watch the potters in action, and there's a gift shop where you can see their finished work as well as work by other artisans. Phone for driving directions if you want to make the trip.

Wind your way farther south to Rutledge for another local crafts team. The Barn Raising is run by master craftsman Paul Jones and his wife Pam, an accomplished quilter. Though the name remains, the business has outgrown its original barn quarters. Now there is a shop on the main street selling country crafts and quilts, and a workshop across the way where Paul and his staff finish wood furniture by hand, applying the patina of age to reproduction pine cabinets, tables, and chairs.

One of the smaller stops on the Antebellum Trail, "downtown" Rutledge runs for only a couple of blocks, but it is an interesting example of a community determined to upgrade. Notice the names on the 2,000 engraved bricks on the new sidewalks, each one bought by a resident for $30 to help with the repaving. Other craft and antiques shops are joining old-timers like the 75-year-old hardware store. The Yesterday Cafe, a converted turn-of-the-century drugstore, is highly recommended for a break at the sundae bar or for a meal in an old-fashioned setting that includes many vintage town photos.

From Rutledge, you are only a few miles from Madison, the next Antebellum Trail community, and one of the prettiest villages in the state. Madison prospered early in the nineteenth century as the county seat, where many wealthy cotton planters chose to build their fine town houses. The domed courthouse, a 1905 beauty, was once featured as the centerfold in a *Life* magazine article on courthouses of the South. More than 100 antebellum and Victorian homes remain in the town's historic district. The house tours held in May and December are always sellouts.

A walking-tour brochure and a taped guide to help you identify and date the houses are available at both the Chamber of Commerce and the town cultural center. As this is a small town of 3,500, a short drive or an amble are sufficient for a good sampling of the town's beauty. You can see the finest of the homes on Main Street, the Old Post Road, and Academy Street.

Worth noting is the Cornelius Vason House, at 549 Old Post Road, one of the oldest structures in town and now a private residence. It was used as a stagecoach inn on the route between Charleston and New Orleans during the period when Madison was considered the wealthiest and most aristocratic town between the two cities.

One beautiful home open to visitors is Heritage Hall, a pillared 1835 Empire-style mansion that now belongs to the Madison County Historical Society. The high ceilings, fireplaces, and typical four-over-four floor plan epitomize the antebellum era. The home is furnished with pieces from the 1830–1870 period.

Another building that can be visited is the restored 1895 Romanesque Revival–style school, now serving as the town Cultural Center, offering history displays and changing art exhibits.

The Presbyterian church, constructed in 1842 in Old English style, has a Tiffany window and a silver communion service with an interesting history. It was stolen during the Civil War, and later returned by federal order. The wrought-iron chandeliers of the 1842 Advent Episcopal Church are even older than the building. The church still has its slave gallery, now quarters for the organ and choir.

When you've counted enough columns, you may want to head for Hard Labor Creek State Park, near Rutledge. The name comes from the stream running through the park; there's disagreement over whether it was bestowed by the slaves who tilled nearby fields or by Indians who found the stream difficult to ford. Be assured that the only hard labor these days is chasing lost golf balls; the 18-hole course is known for its challenge. The park also offers hiking trails, bicycle rentals, and a lake with a swimming beach plus pedal boats and canoes for hire.

If the "Dawgs" aren't playing well this season, here's the perfect place to work off your frustration.

Area Code: 706

DRIVING DIRECTIONS   Athens is at the intersection of U.S. 78 and U.S. 441. From Atlanta, take U.S. 29 into U.S. 78, or I–85 to U.S. 441 south, 66 miles.

ACCOMMODATIONS   *Holiday Inn,* Broad and Lumpkin streets, Athens 30603, 549–4433, indoor pool, nearest to campus, I-M ● *Days Inn Downtown,* 1198 South Milledge Avenue, Athens 30601, 369–7000 or 800–325–2525, modern facility, also near campus, pool, I, CP ● *Best Western Colonial Inn,* 170 North Milledge Avenue, Athens

30601, 546–7311, good value, I, CP • *Quality Inn History Village,* 295 East Dougherty Street, Athens 30601, 546–0410 or 800–634–3862, downtown motel with historic buildings on grounds, I • *Rivendell Bed and Breakfast,* 3581 South Barnett Shoals Road, Watkinsville 30677, 769–4522, I, CP • *Burnett Place,* 317 Old Post Road, Madison 30650, 342–4034, an 1830 Federal home, I-M, CP • *Turn of the Century Victorian Bed and Breakfast,* 450 Pine Street, Madison 30650, 342–1890, the name says it, M-E, CP • *The Boat House,* 383 Porter Street, Madison 30650, 342–3061, 1850 sea captain's home on lovely grounds, I-M, CP • *Brady Inn,* 250 North Second Street, Madison 30650, 342–4400, Victorian cottage, I-M, CP.

DINING   *Trumps at the Georgian,* 247 East Washington Street, Athens, 546–6388, elegant setting, best in town, M • *Bluebird Cafe,* 493 East Clayton Street, Athens, 549–3663, eclectic ethnic and vegetarian fare, I • *Harry Bissett's New Orleans Cafe,* 279 East Broad Street, Athens, 353–7065, Cajun and Creole, I-M • *The Grill,* 171 College Avenue, 543–4770, campus favorite for burgers, etc., open 24 hours, I • *DePalma's,* 401 East Broad Street, 354–6966, Italian, I • *Charlie Williams' Pine Crest Lodge,* off Whitehall Road, Athens, 353–2606, country setting, rustic buildings, water wheel, all-you-can-eat buffet at family-style tables, a local tradition, I-M • Yesterday Cafe, 120 Fairplay Street, Rutledge, 557–9337, I • *Ye Olde Colonial Restaurant,* 108 Washington Street, Madison, 342–2211, I-M.

SIGHTSEEING   *Georgia Museum of Art,* University of Georgia, 542–3255. Hours: Monday to Saturday 9 A.M. to 5 P.M.; Sunday 1 P.M. to 5 P.M.; free • *Butts-Mehre Heritage Hall,* Pinecrest Drive and Rutherford Street, University of Georgia, Athens, 542–9094. Hours: Monday to Friday 8 A.M. to 5 P.M.; Sunday 2 P.M. to 5 P.M.; free • *Founders Memorial Garden,* 325 South Lumpkin Street, Athens, 542–3631. Hours: garden open daily, daylight hours; house museum, Monday to Friday 9 A.M. to noon, 1 P.M. to 4 P.M., free • *Taylor-Grady House,* 634 Prince Avenue, Athens, 549–8688. Hours: Monday to Friday 10 A.M. to 3:30 P.M., $$ • *Church-Waddel-Brumby House/ Athens Welcome Center,* 280 East Dougherty Street, Athens, 353–1820. Hours; Monday to Saturday 9 A.M. to 5 P.M.; Sunday 2 P.M. to 5 P.M.; free • *State Botanical Garden of Georgia,* 2450 South Milledge Avenue, Athens, 332–1244. Hours: Garden open daily 8 A.M. to dusk; Visitor Center/Conservatory, Monday to Saturday 9 A.M. to 4:30 P.M., Sunday 11:30 A.M. to 4:30 P.M.; free • *Happy Valley Pottery,* Carson-Graves Road, Watkinsville (phone for driving directions), 769–5922.

Hours: Monday to Friday 8 A.M. to 5 P.M.; Saturday 9 A.M. to 5 P.M. ●
Mockingbird Forge, U.S. 441 at Farmington, 769–7147. Hours:
variable, best to phone ● *Heritage Hall,* 277 South Main Street,
Madison, 342–9627. Hours: March to November, daily 10 A.M. to
4:30 P.M. *Madison-Morgan Cultural Center,* 434 South Main Street,
Madison, 342–4743. Hours: Tuesday to Friday 10 A.M. to 4:30 P.M.;
Saturday and Sunday 2 P.M. to 5 P.M. $.

INFORMATION *Athens Visitors Bureau*, P.O. Box 948, Athens,
GA 30603, 546–1805 ● *Madison-Morgan County Chamber of Commerce and Visitors Bureau,* 115 East Jefferson Street, Madison, GA
30650, 342–4454.

Winter

Gingerbread House, Savannah. Photo courtesy of Tourist Div., Georgia Department of Industry and Trade

Getting the Spirit
in Gatlinburg

Set in a valley ringed by high mountains, with a national park at its
front door, Gatlinburg, Tennessee, has everything going for it. Sometimes a little too much. As many as 30,000 visitors per night can invade
this town of 3,500 in peak season. The main street of town, often
clogged with traffic, is wall-to-wall with 400 shops vying for the
tourist trade.

That's why December is a wonderful time to come to town. The
crowds are small and the town is aglow with its annual Smoky
Mountain Lights show for the entire month. The main street is crowned
by 20 glittering archways of light. All around are animated displays of
lights reaching anywhere from 20 to 60 feet into the sky. They
personalize the show by creating local scenes—a 40-foot log cabin
commemorating the first houses in Gatlinburg, for example, or the
town mascot, the Gatlinbear, shown fishing on the river or making
moonshine at his still.

Sure, the jack-in-the-box popping up and the fireworks blasting off
around the American flag are a little flashy, but it's Christmas, after all,
and it's easy to get into the spirit. Besides, this is an outing guaranteed
to please the kids.

There's another good reason for a visit to Gatlinburg during the
Christmas season: shopping. There's no better place to look for
one-of-a-kind handcrafted gifts, and just down the road is Pigeon
Forge, packed with outlet-store bargains.

The crafts tradition is strong in Gatlinburg. Founded in the 1790s
and named for a nineteenth-century merchant, Radford Gatlin, the
early mountain town was so isolated that residents made their own
baskets and pottery and did their own weaving out of necessity. In
1912, Pi Beta Phi, a national sorority for women, opened the
Settlement School in town, where many mountain children received
their first real education. The school began to teach local craftspeople
how to supplement their living through a cottage crafts industry. To
provide an outlet for their wares, as well as to help support the school,
the Arrowcraft Shop was subsequently established.

Now known as the Arrowmont School of Arts and Crafts, the school
is still a highly respected teaching center located in the heart of
Gatlinburg. The Arrowcraft Shop remains, filled with quality crafts,
perfect for holiday giving.

The opening of Great Smoky Mountains National Park in 1934, with
Gatlinburg as a gateway, brought more visitors and gave a real boost
to the crafts movement. The largest group of independent artisans in

North America now lives in the scenic hills outside town. Turn east on U.S. 321 for about eight miles and you'll come to the Great Smoky Arts and Crafts Community, an eight-mile loop including over 70 working studios and galleries in quaint quarters. One of the best galleries for an overview of regional crafts is American Showcase, at 480 Buckhorn Road.

In many studios you can meet the artists. Turn left and follow Glades Road up the hill, looping back down on Buckhorn Road. Along the way, drop in on someone like Helmut Koechert, who fashions practical and beautiful things out of pewter, or Ross Markley, who turns out beautiful wooden pieces and also sells Nantucket baskets, rugs, and sculpture in his shop in Turtle Hollow. Stop into Ogle's Broom Shop, where the one-of-a-kind brooms and walking sticks made by Tammie and David Ogle have surprisingly low price tags. It's hard to imagine a pleasanter, more personal way to shop.

This is also the part of Gatlinburg where you'll find three extraordinary inns, each tucked away in a secluded spot with wide-screen mountain views. Until you've awakened in the morning and watched the mist melt off the mountaintops, you haven't really appreciated the full beauty of the Smokies.

Buckhorn Inn, in operation since 1938, is the picture of a cozy mountain escape. The big living room has beams, a massive stone fireplace, a grand piano, shelves filled with books, and large picture windows opening to a Smokies panorama. The inn offers dinner, with a changing and quite sophisticated menu, to both guests and non-guests by reservation.

Hippensteal Inn has equally stunning views but quite a different feel. The owner is noted local artist Vern Hippensteal, and the first floor is a gallery of his work. Not surprisingly, one of his favorite subjects is the mountains. The recently built inn has Victorian-style furnishings and broad verandas across each of the three floors for mountain-gazing.

The third inn, The Colonel's Lady, is a rustic and romantic hideaway with an English hostess who tells about the furnishings, which evoke the charm of an English country inn. Afternoon tea is served in the library.

Just in case you haven't checked off everyone on your Christmas list in Gatlinburg, follow Glades Road north into Bird's Creek Road, drive north through the scenic hills, and turn left at Upper Middle Creek Road toward Pigeon Forge, where there are more manufacturers' outlets than you ever imagined in one place. They offer everything from cowboy boots and clothing to sheets, towels, and Fuller brushes.

Another enjoyable stop north of town is the Apple Barn Cider Mill and General Store, where you can peek into the kitchen through a viewing window and watch apple treats in the making. The general store sells apple butter, applewood-smoked country ham and bacon, and lots of other gifts that may please someone you know.

If there's somebody really special on that list, you may want to drive a few miles farther north on U.S. 441 toward Sevierville and the newest bargain center, the Five Oaks Factory Stores, where you'll encounter such upscale names as Brooks Brothers, Lenox China, and Magnavox, brands you don't find in every outlet mall.

If you want to pick an inn closer to the bargains, Blue Mountain Mist Country Inn is just the place. Set in farm country between Pigeon Forge and Sevierville, this recently built farmhouse feels as if it has been here forever—until you see the Jacuzzis in some of the rooms.

Pigeon Forge is more shopping mall and motel strip than town, but there's a lot happening here. Dollywood, the entertainment park owned by singer Dolly Parton, is all dolled up for the season, with 500,000 twinkling lights outlining every village building and adorning festive trees.

During the Smoky Mountain Christmas celebration, usually the week before and after the holiday, Santa is on hand in his workshop to greet children and take special orders, and the whole family can climb aboard the Christmas Carol Express for a melody-filled train ride. The entertainment that is a year-round feature goes full tilt during holiday season.

Dolly also has a hand in the second major attraction in Pigeon Forge, the Dixie Stampede, a four-hour show that is part rodeo, part Deep South, featuring 32 precision-trained horses and a bevy of hoop-skirted Southern belles. A four-course dinner comes with the show. From Thanksgiving through New Year's, Christmas in Dixie is the theme.

These are the biggest and best-known of half a dozen Pigeon Forge entertainment spots with names like Smoky Mountain Jubilee, The Hee Haw Show, and Smoky Mountain Hayride. You'll see why the town advertises itself as "action packed."

Dolly Parton's interest in this area is no accident. She grew up in Sevierville, right up the road from Pigeon Forge. They've placed a handsome statue of their favorite daughter in front of the town courthouse.

This is a pleasant small mountain town, the marketing center for the surrounding farms and surprisingly free of tourist hype. Josev's, a restaurant on the second floor of a central shopping center, is a pleasant and dependable place to dine.

Winter or no, you'll not want to visit this area without a drive into the Great Smoky Mountains National Park. In the still of winter, with the throngs and the traffic gone, you can contemplate the beauty of this great park and gain new appreciation for the mountains it preserves. On a crisp, sunny winter day, there's little fog and the vistas are even wider without foliage to block the views.

It's easy to understand why this is the most visited of all the national parks.

Area Code: 615

DRIVING DIRECTIONS   Gatlinburg is on U.S. 441/321 at the gateway to Great Smoky Mountain National Park, 39 miles south of Knoxville. From I–40 at Knoxville, take U.S. 441 south. From southern points, take I–75, which merges into I–40, and turn south from I–40 at U.S. 441. It is 137 miles from Chattanooga, about 250 miles from Atlanta, 223 miles from Nashville.

ACCOMMODATIONS   *Buckhorn Inn,* 2140 Tudor Mountain Road, Gatlinburg 37738, 436–4668, M-E, CP ● *Hippensteal Inn,* Grassy Branch Road, P.O. Box 707, Gatlinburg 37738, 436–5761 or 800–527–8110, E, CP ● *The Colonel's Lady,* 1120 Tanrac Trail, Gatlinburg 37738, 436–5432, M-E, CP ● *Blue Mountain Mist Country Inn,* 1811 Pullen Road, Sevierville 37862, 428–2335 or 800–497–2335, M-E, CP.

DINING   *Buckhorn Inn* (see above), full dinner, set menu, by reservation only, E ● *Creekside Restaurant,* Highway 321-N, Gatlinburg, 436–7065, near the national park, I-M ● *The Peddler,* 113 River Road, Gatlinburg, 436–7592, cabin on the river, steak is the specialty, M-E ● *The Burning Bush,* 1151 Parkway near the park entrance, Gatlinburg, 436–4669, varied menu, M-E ● *The Wild Plum Tea Room,* 555 Buckhorn Road, Gatlinburg, 436–3808, charming log house serving lunch only; specialties include wild plum tea and plum muffins ● *Bennetts Pit Bar-B-Que,* two locations, 714 River Road, Gatlinburg, 436–2400; 2910 Parkway, Pigeon Forge, 429–2200, saucy ribs and sandwiches, I ● *Applewood Farmhouse Restaurant,* off U.S. 441, Sevierville, 453–9319, pleasant ambience, apple fritters, country ham, fried chicken, I-M ● *Five Oaks Inn,* 1625 Parkway (U.S. 441), Sevierville, 453–5994, elegant Continental menu, one of the area's best, M-E ● *Josev's,* 130 West Bruce Street, Sevierville, 428–0737, pleasant downtown setting, varied menu, dependable, I-M.

SIGHTSEEING   *Great Smoky Arts & Crafts Community,* P.O. Box 807, Gatlinburg 37738, 436–9214, call or write for a free guide to more than 70 artists and craftsmen ● *Dollywood,* U.S. 441 at Dollywood Lane, Pigeon Forge, 428–9620; best to phone for special Smoky Mountain Christmas dates and hours, $$$$ ● *Dixie Stampede,* U.S.

441, Pigeon Forge, 453–4400 or 800–356–1676; phone for "Christmas in Dixie" schedules, $$$$.

INFORMATION *Gatlinburg Chamber of Commerce,* 520 Parkway, P.O. Box 527, Gatlinburg, TN 37738, 436–4178 or 800–568–4748 ● *Pigeon Forge Department of Tourism,* 2450 Parkway (U.S. 441), P.O. Box 1390, Pigeon Forge, TN 37868, 453–8574 or 800–251–9100.

Savoring Christmas in Savannah

In the jazz clubs at City Market they sing about "Hard-Hearted Hannah"—but she's nowhere to be found in this sweet Southern city.

Savannah is a soft-spoken lady, her welcome warm and genuine, and cordial hospitality is as natural a part of things as the Spanish moss draping the live oaks in the town's green squares.

This hospitality can be sampled at its very best in December, when a beautiful city decks its halls and opens the doors to many of its finest private homes. There are parades by land and by sea, and celebrations and concerts galore in the town's historic homes, churches, and inns, each dressed in Christmas finery.

Savannah also has some unique celebrations marking the Christmas, 1864, arrival of General William Sherman and his 60,000 Union soldiers. Soldiers in authentic uniforms re-create the event at Old Fort Jackson, portraying the final hours prior to the troops' coming. Sherman's occupation is reenacted at Fort McAllister. The city had no choice but to surrender, after a coastal blockade that had brought cotton trading to a halt.

Even this infamous Yankee succumbed to Savannah's charms, and spared the city from the burning that had accompanied much of his march. He sent a now-famous telegram to President Lincoln reading, "I beg to present to you as a Christmas gift the city of Savannah . . ."

Much of Savannah still looks as it did in the 1800s, for the heart of the town is one of America's largest urban historic districts. There are more than 2,000 buildings of historic or architectural interest, many of them graceful beauties adorned with wrought-iron balconies and stairs. The buildings are all the lovelier for the greenery surrounding them, 22 landscaped squares that turn the old city into an urban garden.

It was founder James Oglethorpe who, in 1733, laid out this ingenious grid for America's first planned city—broad, straight avenues dotted with squares that served in colonial days as shady oases for peacetime socializing, and in wartime as parade grounds for militia drills. Today the squares function almost as outdoor living rooms for the families who live around them, places for friendly chats, neighborhood gatherings, and sometimes even a wedding.

A good place to get your bearings is the visitor center in the old railroad station. It includes the Savannah History Museum, with films and exhibits that bring the city's past to life. You'll find information here on the many ways to see the city on guided tours. Since the old city is compact, walking tours are especially recommended when the weather is fine, which it usually is. Though nights are cold, average December daytime highs are 62 degrees. Gray Line offers the official tours of the Historic Savannah Foundation. If you prefer a self-guided tour, pick up "Sojourn in Savannah," the official guidebook.

However you tour, you'll learn that the earliest settlement, high on a bluff overlooking the Savannah River, was intended as a defensive buffer between the English port at Charleston and the Spanish settlement in Florida, but the location, just 18 miles from the Atlantic Ocean, soon made Savannah a prominent port in its own right. The grandest homes were the mansions of cotton barons in the halcyon days before the Civil War, when bales of cotton from Georgia plantations were known as "white gold."

The stately brick Federal-style Davenport House, known for its delicate plasterwork and elliptical staircase, was the inspiration for the city's first restoration efforts. The threat to tear it down prompted a protest by local residents and the birth in 1955 of Historic Savannah, which raised money to save the home.

Historic Savannah continues to acquire properties and hold them until a preservation-minded buyer can be found. They have extended their efforts to the Victorian homes in an area beyond the original historic districts, with another 800 buildings designated as national landmarks.

The foundation's houses are only the start of lovely homes that are open for tours. The Owens-Thomas House and Museum is an urban villa, circa 1816, said to be one of the outstanding examples of Regency architecture in the United States. The Green-Meldrim House, now the parish house for St. John's Episcopal Church, was constructed in the early 1850s and served as headquarters for General Sherman during the occupation.

The Telfair Mansion, filled with opulent period rooms restored to their 1819 appearances, shows the lifestyle of a prominent family of the nineteenth century. It is also the oldest public art museum in the South, with an impressive collection of American, French, and German Impressionist paintings in the handsomest of settings.

The classical 1848 residence of Andrew Low also has a special place in history as the site where Juliette Gordon Low founded the Girl

Scouts of America in 1912. The Regency town house where Low was born has been restored and serves as the Juliette Low Center, a national program center for the Girl Scouts. Each December it joins the Owens-Thomas house in hosting a Victorian family holiday party, with caroling, parlor games, dancing, crafts, and all the trappings of Christmas past.

The King-Tisdale Cottage is now a museum telling the history of African Americans in Savannah and the Sea Islands.

As the preservation movement gained momentum, the empty brick warehouses that once stored cargo along the river were transformed into shops, restaurants, and a maritime museum known as Ships of the Sea. Cobblestoned River Street has plenty of gift shops, albeit the commercial variety, but there are interesting crafts to be seen on the First Saturday festivals held outdoors on the Rousakis Waterfront Plaza from March through December. This is also the place to board a riverboat cruise on the Savannah.

City Market is another area of shops and restaurants plus an arts center with more than a dozen studio/art galleries where you can watch work in progress.

The city specializes in antique shops, with more than two dozen in the historic district alone.

Savannah dining focuses on Southern-style seafood, including gumbos, deviled crab, and oyster stews, often accompanied by hush puppies and Savannah red rice.

Almost everyone, natives and tourists alike, visits Mrs. Wilke's Boarding House, Savannah's best-known eating place. Lunch consists of a 14-dish all-you-can-eat extravaganza. No reservations taken here—just join the line.

For late-night fun, head for the city's jazz clubs. Stop in at Hard Hearted Hannah's to hear Emma Kelly, known as "the lady of 6,000 songs," from 6 to 9 P.M., followed by cool and classical jazz. Huey's, on the bottom floor of the River Street Inn, has live Dixieland jazz on weekends.

Among Savannah's delights are the homes now serving as inns, where you can come home to polished silver at afternoon tea, cordials in the evening, and perhaps a praline on your pillow at night.

There are dozens of appealing choices, but two of special note are The Gastonian, comprising two 1868 townhouses filled with Empire and Regency antiques, and the Ballastone, an 1835 home with the city's characteristic curved wrought-iron staircase and balconies.

Whichever inn you choose, you'll be in the heart of old Savannah—and the best of the Old South.

Area Code: 912

DRIVING DIRECTIONS   Savannah is on the Georgia–South Carolina border, 17 miles inland from the Atlantic, off I–95, exit I–16 East, or I–16 coming from the west. From Atlanta, follow I–75 south to I–16 east, about 250 miles. It is 110 miles south of Charleston.

PUBLIC TRANSPORTATION   Savannah is served by several major airlines through hubs at Atlanta, Charlotte, Raleigh, and Columbia. Limo service and cabs are available from the airport, and no car is needed to get around the historic district. Amtrak and Greyhound also have terminals in the city.

ACCOMMODATIONS   Zip code for all: 31401. *Ballastone Inn,* 14 East Oglethorpe Avenue, 236–1484 or 800–822–4553, M-EE, CP ● *The Gastonian,* 220 East Gaston Street, 232–2869 or 800–322–6603, E-EE, CP ● *Magnolia Place Inn,* 503 Whitaker Street, 236–7674 or 800–238–7674, M-EE, CP ● *President's Quarters,* 225 East President Street, 233–1600 or 800–233–1776, M-EE, CP ● *Foley House Inn,* 14 West Hull Street, 232–6622 or 800–647–3708, M-EE, CP ● *Eliza Thompson House,* 5 West Jones Street, 236–3620 or 800–348–9378, M-E, CP ● *Bed and Breakfast Inn,* 117 West Gordon Street, 238–0518, best budget choice, I-M, CP ● *Inns may also be booked through two central reservations services: R.S.V.P. Savannah Bed-and-Breakfast Reservation Service,* 417 East Charlton Street, 232–7787, 800–729–7787; and *Savannah Historic Inns and Guesthouses,* 147 Bull Street, 800–262–4667 ● Hotels with charm in the historic district are *River Street Inn,* 115 East River Street, 234–6400 or 800–253–4229, M-E; and *The Mulberry,* 601 East Bay Street, 238–1200 or 800–554–5544, M-E.

DINING   *Elizabeth on 37th,* 105 East 37th Street, 236–5547, turn-of-the-century mansion, innovative Southern cuisine, tops, M-E ● *Restaurant La Toque,* 420 East Brighton Street, 238–0138, fine dining, M ● *17 Hundred 90 Inn,* 307 East President Street, 236–7122, Continental, rack of lamb a specialty, M-E ● *Garibadi's Cafe,* 315 West Congress Street, 232–7118, Italian, I-M ● *Bistro Savannah,* 309 West Congress Street, 233–6266, interesting Southern seafood dishes, I-M ● *Huey's,* 115 East River Street, 234–7385, Cajun, I ● *45 South at the Pirate's House,* 230 East Broad Street, 233–1881, longtime local favorite, E ● *River House,* 125 West River Street, 234–1900, former waterfront warehouse, casual nautical decor, M ● *Mrs. Wilke's*

Boarding House, 107 West Jones Street, 232–5997, local legend, a must for breakfast or lunch, I ● Choices around City Market: *St. Julian's Grill,* 313 West St. Julian Street, 236–0002, M ● *Hard Hearted Hannah's,* 312 West St. Julian Street, primarily a jazz club, but light meals are available, M ● *City Market Cafe,* 224 West St. Julian Street, 236–7333, I-M.

SIGHTSEEING *Christmas in Savannah.* Dozens of events beginning in November and extending through December. Write to the Visitors Bureau (see below) for a full list ● *Andrew Low House,* 329 Abercorn Street, 233–6854. Hours: Weekdays except Thursday 10:30 A.M. to 4 P.M.; Sunday from 12 noon. $$ ● *Davenport House,* 324 East State Street, 236–8097. Hours: Monday to Saturday 10 A.M. to 4:30 P.M.; Sunday from 1:30 P.M.; $$ ● *Fort McAllister Historic Site,* Spur 144 off U.S. 144, 22 miles south of Savannah. Hours: Monday to Saturday, 9 A.M. to 5 P.M.; Sunday 1 P.M. to 5:30 P.M., $ ● *Fort Pulaski National Monument,* U.S. 89, 15 miles east of Savannah, 786–5787. Hours: daily 8:30 A.M. to 5:15 P.M.; 8:30 A.M. to 6:45 P.M. in summer; $ ● Green-Meldrim Home, 1 West Macon Street, 233–3845. Hours: Tuesday to Saturday 10 A.M. to 4 P.M., $$ ● *Juliette Gordon Low Girl Scout National Center,* 142 Bull Street, 233–4501. Hours: Monday to Saturday 10 A.M. to 4 P.M.; Sunday from 12:30 P.M.; closed Wednesday and Sunday in December and January; $$ ● *King-Tisdale Cottage,* 514 Huntingdon Street, 234–8000. Hours: Monday to Friday 10 A.M. to 4:30 P.M.; weekends 1 P.M. to 4 P.M.; $ ● *Old Fort Jackson,* 1 Fort Jackson Road, 232–3945. Hours: daily 9 A.M. to 5 P.M.; in summer, 9 A.M. to 7 P.M.; $ ● *Owens-Thomas House,* 124 Abercorn Street, 233–9743. Hours: Tuesday to Saturday 10 A.M. to 4:30 P.M.; Sunday and Monday, from 2 P.M.; $$$ ● *Savannah History Museum,* 303 Martin Luther King Boulevard, 238–1779. Hours: daily 8:30 A.M. to 5 P.M., $$ ● *Ships of the Sea Museum,* 503 East River Street and 504 East Bay Street, 232–1511. Hours: daily 10 A.M. to 4 P.M., $$ ● *Telfair Academy of Arts & Sciences,* 121 Barnard Street, 232–1177. Hours: Tuesday to Saturday 10 A.M. to 5 P.M.; Sunday 1 P.M. to 5 P.M.; $$ ● *Tybee Island Lighthouse,* U.S. 80, 18 miles east of Savannah, 786–5801. Hours: April to September, daily 10 A.M. to 6 P.M.; October to March, weekdays except Tuesday, noon to 4 P.M., weekends 10 A.M. to 4 P.M.; $ ● *Riverboat cruises: Savannah Riverboat Tours,* 222 East Factors Walk, board at Hyatt Regency dock, 2 West River Street, 236–0407. Phone for schedules and reservations.

INFORMATION *Savannah Area Convention & Visitors Bureau,* 222 West Oglethorpe Avenue, P.O. Box 1628, Savannah, GA 31402,

236–0407 or 800–444-CHARM. The visitor center is located at 303 Martin Luther King Boulevard.

Season's Greetings in Asheville

It was love at first sight for George Washington Vanderbilt. The grandson of famed financier Commodore Cornelius Vanderbilt was a 25-year-old bachelor when he became enchanted with the mountain views around Asheville, North Carolina. Far from his family's palaces in Newport and points east, Vanderbilt bought up 125,000 acres surrounding Mount Pisgah and, in 1890, began to build his 285-room estate, Biltmore, still the largest private home ever constructed in the United States.

Biltmore today is a tourist attraction that greets 700,000 visitors each year. The crowds are biggest when the house is lavishly decorated for one of this country's most extraordinary Christmas tours. The tours are the star attraction of a six-week celebration throughout Asheville, which ends with a city-wide First Night festival of arts on January 31 to welcome the new year.

Not the least of Asheville's holiday lures is a host of sophisticated galleries and shops that will surely inspire your Christmas giving. The city is well known as a crafts center.

Now the largest town in western North Carolina, with a county-wide population of over 173,000, Asheville was settled by Scotch-Irish immigrants whose Appalachian culture is still evident in the regional music and crafts. But when the railroad arrived in the 1880s, Asheville was discovered by the affluent. They came to spend the summer amid the beautiful mountain surroundings and helped the town develop an unusual sophistication, as evidenced by the art films, galleries, French pastries, chocolate truffles, and California cuisine available around town. Visitors enjoy all this while still taking advantage of hiking, whitewater rafting, and the Blue Ridge Parkway, just minutes away.

Biltmore remains the city's biggest attraction. When Vanderbilt decided to build his dream house, he called on Richard Morris Hunt, one of the most prestigious architects of the day, and Frederick Law Olmsted, the father of American landscape architecture.

Hunt modeled his design on the great Renaissance chateaux of the Loire Valley, using tons of Italian marble and carloads of Indiana limestone. The house required five years and an army of stonecutters and artisans to complete.

Hunt also traveled through Europe with Vanderbilt, selecting most of the 50,000 art objects that remain today. These include artworks by Renoir, Sargent, and Whistler, furniture by Sheraton and Chippendale, a chess set and gaming table that belonged to Napoleon, fifty Persian and Oriental rugs, and eight sixteenth-century Flemish tapestries.

The house was also considered one of the most advanced of its day as it included some of Thomas Edison's first lightbulbs, central heating, a fire-alarm system, elevators, indoor plumbing for all 34 bedrooms, and a newfangled gadget called the telephone.

Olmsted's contributions to this, his last project, were a great arboretum and park, a blend of European pastoral designs and his own naturalistic style. Formal gardens, a grand three-mile approach road, and a tree-lined esplanade leading to the entrance of Biltmore House were part of the plan.

George Vanderbilt did not live long to enjoy his mansion. After his death, in 1914, a large portion of the original estate was obtained by the U.S. government, forming the nucleus for the Pisgah National Forest—a fitting development, since Vanderbilt had started the nation's first school of forestry on this land in 1898.

Biltmore Estate was inaugurated on Christmas Eve in 1895 with a lavish celebration for 200. The present-day Christmas celebrations feature re-creations of the Victorian decor of that first holiday, with the addition of lavish touches that George Vanderbilt would surely have admired.

The decorations, which the floral staff begins preparing in July, include more than 10,000 feet of evergreen roping, 1,500 poinsettias, topiary deer, 450 red velvet bows, and 130 wreaths. Rooms are aglow with 48 Christmas trees, requiring some 5,000 ornaments.

Christmas tours can be taken in the daytime or in the evening, by enchanting candlelight. Tickets can be validated for a free next-day return visit for a look at the grounds. Given the size of the house and the myriad furnishings worth a closer look, a return call is a good idea anyway.

Biltmore remains a family estate, now owned by William Amherst Vanderbilt Cecil, grandson of the builder, and proceeds from tours and sales help to maintain the house.

When you've finished your tour, Biltmore Village awaits at the entrance to the estate, with a variety of upscale shops, including the exceptional New Morning Gallery, a showcase for the best of contemporary crafts.

In addition to housing for estate workers, the picturesque village, constructed from a plan by Olmsted, has a train station and the Gothic-style All Souls Episcopal Church, the latter designed by Richard Hunt in 1896.

Asheville's second noted attraction is far more modest. It is the boyhood home of author Thomas Wolfe. The boardinghouse known as the Old Kentucky Home, run by his mother, was immortalized by Wolfe in his novel *Look Homeward, Angel.* Wolfe stayed away from his home for eight years after outraging everyone with his portrait of the town. Now he is the city's favorite native, honored with an annual celebration on his birthday in early October. The home, owned by the state, has been kept exactly as it was when Wolfe lived here, and it gives interesting insight into the author's life and work. At Christmastime the house is adorned with the kind of Victorian decorations Wolfe might have known.

Two other homes made festive for the holidays are the Vance Birthplace, home of Zebulon Vance, North Carolina's Civil War–era governor, and the Smith-McDowell House, an 1840 home where daytime tours and candlelight tours with music are offered.

The Grove Park Inn, the next stop for holiday touring, is another wonderful part of Asheville history. Constructed in 1913 on 140 acres atop Sunset Mountain, the building is now listed on the National Register of Historic Places, and has hosted many famous guests, from Woodrow Wilson to Will Rogers. The roster includes nine U.S. presidents. The hotel boasts one of the nation's outstanding collections of furnishings from the Arts and Crafts Movement, pioneered by furniture makers such as Roycrofters and Charles Stickley, and architects like Frank Lloyd Wright.

The building is a mountain masterpiece, built of rough-cut stones with natural slate floors and with a scalloped red tile roof that gives the look of a rustic fairy-tale castle. The stone-walled Great Hall is stunning, with huge wooden columns, hammered-copper light fixtures, and two ceiling-high fireplaces.

Though some of the original furniture was lost as subsequent owners sought to modernize, new owners in 1955 recognized the importance of the original inn and have carefully restored and preserved what was left. Now expanded with two new wings in harmony with the original building, Grove Park is a full-scale, four-star resort.

The inn really gets into the spirit of things at Christmas, with its own yards of garlands and beautiful floral displays. The public is invited into the Great Hall at noon Monday through Friday to join in caroling with an enthusiastic employee chorus, cheerily clad in red and capped with Santa hats. Saturdays bring visits from Santa himself, and craft demonstrations by regional artists. Evening piano concerts, candlelight caroling, and a gingerbread village and electric train display are other holiday highlights.

Grove Park is only the first of many choice lodgings in Asheville. Richmond Hill is the very picture of an elegant 1897 Queen Anne manor house, with native oak paneling, 12-foot ceilings, and a splendid staircase with hand-turned spindles as a dramatic entry to the upper floor.

More modest but no less appealing are bed-and-breakfast homes such as Cedar Crest, an 1890 Victorian not far from the Biltmore Estate, and several fine Victorian homes in the Montford Historic District, an in-town neighborhood now being rediscovered and restored. The contemporary Cairn Brae and the rustic Bridle Path Inn are for those who want a retreat in the nearby mountains surrounding Asheville. For visitors who prefer being downtown, the Haywood Park Hotel offers oversized rooms in a novel setting—a renovated department store.

When you take time to explore downtown, you'll find a surprising juxtaposition of buildings, the old mixed with the new, jarring in spots but on the whole a good sign of the rejuvenation of the city center. The city claims that it has more art deco architecture from the 1920s and 1930s than any other Southeastern city except Miami Beach. The pink-roofed City Building, at 70 Court Plaza, is the prime example.

An I. M. Pei–designed tinted glass office building seems out of place, but the new Pack Place Arts and Science Center is an important and attractive addition to downtown, providing a home for the Asheville Art Museum, a gem and mineral museum, a health museum, and a theater. Also in Pack Place is the Western North Carolina Creative Arts Hall of Fame, showing work by regional artists.

Asheville's most famous crafts group is the Southern Highland Handicraft Guild, which operates the Folk Art Center and a crafts shop on the Blue Ridge Parkway just outside town. A visit also gives the chance for a drive along the scenic parkway. The guild also has a gallery on U.S. 70 in Asheville.

More galleries and interesting small shops can be found along Biltmore Avenue, Haywood Street, and the other angled lanes that make for interesting browsing downtown. Antiquers may also want to make a foray east on I–40 to Black Mountain, where Cherry Street is loaded with shops.

You might want to note that the Chocolate Fetish, in the Haywood Park Hotel Promenade, was rated by the *Los Angeles Times* as the nation's best maker of chocolate truffles. It's a sweet idea for someone special on your shopping list.

Area Code: 704

DRIVING DIRECTIONS   Asheville is in the mountains of western North Carolina, reached via I–40, I–26, or the Blue Ridge Parkway. From Atlanta, take I–85 north past Greenville, S.C., to I–26 north, about 208 miles. Asheville is 113 miles from Charlotte via I–77 north to I–40 west, 110 miles from Knoxville via I–40 east.

PUBLIC TRANSPORTATION The Asheville Regional Airport is served by four major airlines.

ACCOMMODATIONS *Haywood Park Hotel,* One Battery Park Avenue, Asheville 28801, 252–2522 or 800–228–2522, M-E, CP ● *Grove Park Inn Resort,* 290 Macon Avenue, Asheville 28804, 252–2711 or 800–438–5800, E-EE ● *Richmond Hill Inn,* 87 Richmond Hill Drive, Asheville 28806, 252–7313, E-EE, CP ● *Cedar Crest,* 674 Biltmore Avenue, Asheville 28803, 252–1389, M-EE ● *Wright Inn,* 235 Pearson Drive, Montford, Asheville 28801, 251–0789 or 800–552–5724, M, CP ● *The Colby House,* 230 Pearson Drive, Montford, Asheville 28801, 253–5644 or 800–982–2118, M, CP ● *The Lion and the Rose,* 276 Montford Avenue, Asheville 28801, 255–7673, M, CP ● *Albemarle Inn,* 86 Edgemont Road, Montford, Asheville 18801, 255–0027, M-E, CP ● *Flint Street Inn,* 116 Flint Street, Asheville 28802, 253–6723, M, CP ● *Bridle Path Inn,* 30 Lookout Road, Asheville 28804, 252–0035, M-E, CP ● *Cairn Brae,* 217 Patton Mountain Road, Asheville 28804, 252–9219, M, CP ● *Motels near Biltmore Estate: Quality Inn-Biltmore,* 115 Hendersonville Road, Asheville 28803, 274–1800, M-E; *Forest Manor Motor Lodge,* 866 Hendersonville Road, Asheville 28893, 274–3531, pleasant wooded grounds, I-M, CP; *Howard Johnson–Biltmore,* 190 Hendersonville Road, Asheville 28803, 274–2300, I-E. There are many additional motels; write for a full list.

DINING *23 Page,* Haywood Park Hotel (see above), stylish, sophisticated menu, M-E ● *Gabrielle's,* Richmond Hill Inn (see above), lovely Victorian setting, M-E ● *Blue Ridge Dining Room,* Grove Park Inn (see above), mountain views, open breakfast to dinner, lunch, I, dinner, M-E, Sunday brunch, M ● *Windmill European Grill,* 85 Tunnel Road, 253–5285, German and many other Continental cuisines, I-M ● *The Market Place,* 20 Wall Street, 252–4162, high ceilings, pleasant ambience, fine dining, M-E ● *Cafe on the Square,* 1 Biltmore Avenue, Pack Square, 251–5565, California accent, I-M ● *Latin Quarter,* 76 Haywood Street, 252–6602, Spanish, Caribbean, Cuban, I-M ● *Blue Moon Bakery,* 60 Biltmore Avenue, Asheville, 252–6063, boulangerie/ patisserie with bistro tables for breakfast and lunch, delicious pastries, I ● *Smoky Mountain BBQ,* 20 Spruce Street, 253–4871, chopped pork and fried chicken, bluegrass band and lively clogging, I.

SIGHTSEEING *Biltmore Estate,* just north of I–40 exit 50 or 50B, Asheville; information from One North Park Square, Asheville 28801, 800–543–2961. Hours: daily 9 A.M. to 6 P.M., $$$$ ● *Christmas at Biltmore,* daily from the day after Thanksgiving to December 31, except Christmas Day. Daytime and candlelight evening tours, reservations required, available after July 1 at 255–1700 or 800–289–1895. $$$$ ● *Light Up Your Holidays Festival,* mid-November to early January, includes concerts, caroling, tours, parade, exhibits, and First Night community-wide New Year's Eve celebration; for complete printed schedule, contact Asheville Travel & Tourism Office (see below) ● *Thomas Wolfe Memorial State Historic Site,* 48 Spruce Street, 253–8304. Hours: April to October, Monday to Saturday 9 A.M. to 5 P.M.; Sunday 1 P.M. to 5 P.M.; rest of year, Tuesday to Friday 10 A.M. to 2 P.M.; weekend hours in December. $$ ● *Zebulon Vance Birthplace State Historic Site,* Reems Creek Road off U.S. 25 north, near Weaverville, 645–6706. Hours: November to March, Tuesday to Saturday 10 A.M. to 4 P.M.; Sunday 1 P.M. to 4 P.M.; rest of year, Monday to Saturday 9 A.M. to 4 P.M.; Sunday 1 P.M. to 5 P.M.; donation ● *Smith-McDowell House,* 283 Victoria Road, 253–9231. Hours: November 1 to April 30, Tuesday to Friday 10 A.M. to 2 P.M., longer hours during Christmas season, best to phone; rest of year, Tuesday to Saturday 10 A.M. to 4 P.M., Sunday 1 P.M. to 4 P.M.; $ ● *Pack Place,* 2 South Pack Square, 252–3866. Hours: Tuesday to Saturday 10 A.M. to 6 P.M., Friday 10 A.M. to 8 P.M.; Sunday 1 P.M. to 5 P.M.; one ticket admits to *Asheville Art Museum, Colburn Gem and Mineral Museum, Health Adventure,* and backstage tour of *Diana Wortham Theater*; $$$, or individual museums, $$ ● *Asheville Walking Tours,* Downtown Welcome Center, 14 Battery Park Avenue, 255–1093. Hours: Monday to Saturday 10 A.M. to 1 P.M., $$$ ● *Folk Art Center,* Blue Ridge Parkway, Milepost 382, 298–7928. Hours: daily 9 A.M. to 5 P.M., donation ● *Biltmore Homespun Shops,* Grovewood Road near Grove Park Inn, 253–7651. Hours: April to October, Monday to Saturday 9 A.M. to 5:30 P.M., Sunday 1 P.M. to 6 P.M.; rest of year, Monday to Saturday 9 A.M. to 4:30 P.M.; includes North Carolina Homespun Museum and Antique Auto Museum, free.

INFORMATION *Asheville Travel and Tourism Office,* P.O. Box 1010, Asheville, NC 28802, 258–6109 or 800–257–1300.

Having a Blast in Huntsville

Where would you go to see the Saturn V rocket that took the first Americans to the moon . . . to find out how it feels to experience the "G" forces astronauts encounter on launch and reentry . . . to buckle up for a let's-pretend mission aboard a space shuttle?

The answer is Huntsville, Alabama, the birthplace and showplace of America's space program. More than 1,500 pieces of rocket and space hardware and over 60 hands-on exhibits are part of Huntsville's out-of-this-world U.S. Space and Rocket Center.

A visit brings back the exciting days when America was making its first forays into space and reminds the visitor of Huntsville's leading role in that drama. It's also an opportunity to get acquainted with one of Alabama's most interesting cities, past, present, and future. Uncrowded March is an excellent time for a visit, especially on a weekend warm enough to take advantage of the parks and recreation that abound in and around town.

The state of Alabama was actually born in Huntsville. John Hunt, a pioneer from Tennessee, was the first to settle here, moving his family to a log home near a spring in 1805. Later, when the Huntsville land office became the place where most of the public lands in the northern part of the Alabama Territory were offered for sale, people from all over flocked here to buy parcels in the fertile Tennessee Valley. By 1818 it seemed natural to make this the temporary capital, where the first constitution for the twenty-second state was drafted, and the first governor was inaugurated.

The capital was moved to a more central location, but Huntsville continued to prosper as the processing center for cotton raised in the surrounding countryside. It flourished until the Civil War, continuing to furnish political leadership for the state. One of the largest collections of fine antebellum homes in Alabama survived the war with little harm because Huntsville became headquarters for the Federal troops in the area, and the town was spared.

It was almost a century later that this textile town of 16,000 began to change dramatically. The army needed a place to manufacture chemical weapons at the start of World War II, and 39,000 acres of cotton fields near Huntsville became the Redstone Arsenal. In 1950, Wernher von Braun and 117 other German rocket scientists were sent to Redstone to do rocket research, and the Space Age was born. The Redstone, America's first rocket, was developed here, providing the capability to launch an artificial satellite. The Redstone Arsenal was responsible for the Explorer I, sent into orbit in 1959.

In 1960, the name was changed to the Marshall Space Flight Center when space exploration was transferred from the military to the

National Aeronautics and Space Administration (NASA). The sixties were the glory years when John Glenn made his historic orbit around the earth and Neil Armstrong stepped onto the moon. Von Braun had gone back to Washington by the 1970s, but Huntsville was still in the forefront, developing the Skylab space station. It is still deeply involved in space and solar-energy projects.

The U.S. Space and Rocket Center, the world's largest space science museum, is spectacular. The space program is traced here in a lively way that invites visitors to get involved. Allow at least half a day for a visit.

You might want to start in the Spacedome Theater, where the Omnimax movie *Blue Planet* features breathtaking photography shot from hundreds of miles above the earth's surface by the crews of five Space Shuttle missions. Viewers share this ride around the earth and into the stars, with the sensation of being suspended in space.

Having sensed some of the excitement of space travel, you are ready to see what it took to launch those astronauts. Floor guides in orange space suits are strategically placed to give information and answer your questions.

Among many highlights in the big museum is the Space Shuttle orbiter mockup, built in 1977 and used to test equipment and procedures for the first shuttle launch, and the 43-foot, full-scale Hubble Space Telescope exhibit, a model of NASA's 25,000-pound telescope that has been in orbit since April 1990.

Much of the fun here comes from participatory exhibits that allow you to sit in an Apollo capsule mock-up, perform tasks with a robotic arm, and dock a Manned Maneuvering Unit. The centrifuge takes 46 people at a time on an introduction to astronaut training for the multi-G forces of launch and reentry. The shuttle Spaceliner is a make-believe voyage to dock with an orbiting space station.

The four-acre Rocket Park outside the building is the world's most comprehensive collection of rockets, including the first Saturn V built for NASA, now a National Historic Landmark.

Also outside is the $200 million Lockheed SR–71/A–12 Blackbird, the air force spy plane that set many speed and altitude records before being retired in 1990. The Blackbird is capable of flying 2,200 miles per hour, three times the speed of sound.

If you would like to tour some of the current NASA facilities where rockets were developed, where the space station *Freedom* is being designed, and where astronauts are trained, you can sign up for bus tours at the NASA Information Center in the main lobby.

If you really want to get involved in space, you can enroll in the U.S. Space Camp, a firsthand introduction to the space program that includes a simulated mission to Mars. There are week-long and weekend camps for adults and for schoolchildren, and a weekend Parent-Child Camp that is the ultimate in Space Age togetherness.

Needless to say, all of this activity has brought huge changes to Huntsville, where a quarter of the jobs are with the army or NASA. The Cummings Research Park has headquarters for many major companies working with the space programs, resulting in another 16,000 high-tech employees. The population of Huntsville has increased tenfold and the city now boasts one of the South's highest median incomes.

When you are ready to go downtown, you'll find a pleasant mix of gracious old and striking new. One way to get an overall view of things is to board the trolley that leaves from the Huntsville Depot Museum. This handcrafted replica of a 1920 trolley makes the rounds of all the main downtown sights every half hour, and you can get on and off as often as you like.

The 1860 depot has been nicely restored and offers an audiovisual presentation on the history of Huntsville, with lifelike animated figures discussing the good old days. Displays include vintage trains and a delightful operating scale model of the depot yards and its steam trains as they looked in the mid–1860s.

Downtown still centers around the old Courthouse Square, where there is history on all sides. On the west side stands the last of the original buildings of early Huntsville, the 1835 Greek Revival First Alabama Bank, which has been in continuous service since it was built. It is now known as the First National Bank of Huntsville.

On the east side is the 1845 Schiffman Building, one of the few remaining antebellum commercial structures. The actress Tallulah Bankhead was born in a second-floor apartment here in 1902.

To the south, the Harrison Brothers Hardware Store has been in business since 1897 and remains the picture of an early mercantile establishment. It has been nicely preserved and is now operated by the Historic Huntsville Foundation. Purchases are still wrapped in brown paper and tied with string.

Constitution Hall Village, commemorating Alabama's entry into the Union at the 1819 Constitutional Convention, is just south of the square on Franklin Street. Four major buildings of the period from 1805 to 1819 have been reconstructed here. Costumed interpreters bring back the days of 1819 as they take you through Constitution Hall, the Clay Building, the Boardman complex, and the Neal Residence and kitchen.

It is interesting to note that the 44 men who shaped the state's future met in a carpenter's shop. From this group would come six Alabama governors and half a dozen United States senators. Today there is a young carpenter on hand to demonstrate the woodworking skills employed in the shop before and after its brief role in history.

The city's two historic districts also begin just off the square. The Twickenham District, to the southeast, is where you can see more than sixty antebellum homes in a three-mile radius. Descendants of original owners still live in many of these homes, some of which are open for touring during the Huntsville Pilgrimage in late April, and on the Christmas Holiday House Tour held the second Saturday of December.

The 1819 Weeden House Museum, a superb example of Federal architecture, is always open to the public. It was the home of nineteenth-century poet and artist Maria Howard Weeden, and exhibits many of her paintings.

The Old Town District, to the northeast, consists mainly of residences built between 1870 and 1930, forming an attractive neighborhood of closely spaced, ornate Victorian homes. Free printed tours of both this and the Twickenham districts are available at the town information center.

The sleek new Huntsville can be seen at the Big Spring International Park, on the west side of the square. It includes the site of the spring where John Hunt founded the city in 1805. This spring is big indeed. Its fresh water, at the rate of 24 million gallons a day, comes from beneath the rocky bluff dominated by the First National Bank and flows into a lagoon surrounded by the handsome park. The landscaping includes many gifts from foreign countries, the most dramatic being the red sculptured "friendship bridge" from Japan that spans the lagoon.

Across the park is the attractive Wernher von Braun Civic Center, the town's cultural hub, with an auditorium seating 10,000, a fine small Museum of Art, and the information bureau.

If you want even more of an escape, the Huntsville–Madison County Botanical Gardens near the Space and Rocket Center is a pleasant getaway, with 35 acres of woodland paths and dogwood trails, and seasonal floral displays.

There's more nature to be found if you follow U.S. 431 east of town four miles to the top of Monte Sano, where Monte Sano State Park covers 2,140 acres, offering an abundance of trees, scenery, and scenic overlooks.

The Burritt Museum and Park, also set atop the mountain, provides its own scenic views and the chance to tour a 14-room mansion built by a prominent Huntsville physician. Historic structures here include log cabins, a blacksmith shop, a smokehouse, and a wooden church. Picnic tables and wooded trails beckon visitors.

The Madison County Nature Trail, 12 miles from downtown on Green Mountain, is another outdoor sanctuary offering wooded paths, a 16-acre lake, a covered bridge, and a wildlife sanctuary. More recreation awaits at the Madison County Lake, 105 acres including boat rentals and picnic facilities. Ditto Landing Marina south of town is the area's major access to the nearby Tennessee River.

Golfers seeking an outing need look no farther than Hampton Cove, off U.S. 431 south, where there are 54 holes of championship golf designed by Robert Trent Jones. This is the start of Alabama's Robert

Trent Jones Golf Trail, and is a top-notch public golf facility in a mountain setting.

All of which goes to show that Huntsville is state-of-the-art on earth as well as in space.

Area Code: 205

DRIVING DIRECTIONS   Huntsville is on U.S. 72, reached via I–565 off I–65. It is 101 miles north of Birmingham via I–65 north to I–565. From Atlanta, take I–20 west to I–65 north, 180 miles. From Nashville, follow I–65 south, 103 miles.

PUBLIC TRANSPORTATION   Several major airlines serve Huntsville Airport.

ACCOMMODATIONS   *Amberley Suite Hotel,* 4880 University Drive, Huntsville 35816, 837–4070 or 800–456–1578, attractive grounds, I ● *Radisson Suite Hotel,* 6000 South Memorial Parkway, Huntsville 35802, 882–9400, near Space Flight Center, M-EE ● *Huntsville Marriott,* Huntsville 35806, 5 Tranquility Base at Space Center, 830–2222, indoor/outdoor pool, E ● *Huntsville Hilton 35801,* 401 Williams Avenue, Freedom Plaza, Huntsville 35801, 533–1400, good downtown location, M ● *Holiday Inn Space Center,* 3810 University Drive, Huntsville 35816, 827–7171, I ● *Courtyard by Marriott,* 4804 University Drive, Huntsville, 35816, 837–1400, M ● *Days Inn–Huntsville Space Center,* 2201 North Memorial Parkway, Huntsville 35810, 536–7441, budget choice, I ● All hotels listed above have outdoor pools.

DINING   *Cafe Berlin,* Airport Road, Westbury Square, 880–9920, cosmopolitan menu, I-M ● *Ol' Heidelberg Cafe,* 6125 University Drive N.W., HQ Shopping Center, 922–0556, German decor and food, longtime standby, I-M ● *Fogcutter Restaurant,* 3805 University Drive N.W., 539–2121, steaks and seafood, salad bar, business lunch favorite, I-M ● *Pho's Cafe and Lounge,* 2006 Country Club Avenue, 533–5001, French, M-E ● *Greenbriar Restaurant,* I–565, Greenbriar Exit, 351–1800, barbecue, catfish, and the trimmings, I ● *Eunice's Country Kitchen,* 1004 Andrew Jackson Way, 534–9550, the place for a hearty Southern breakfast or lunch, famous biscuits, I ● *Greenbriar Bar-B-Que,* I–565 and Ala. route 20, 353–9769, best barbecue in town, I ● *Downtown choices: Twickenham Station,* 590 Williams Avenue, 539–3797, converted train car, steaks and seafood, I-E; *Village Inn on* *the Square,* 128 South Side Square, 533–9123, downtown stop for all three meals, I-M; *Bubba's,* 109 Washington, 534–3133, ribs and burgers, business crowd by day, lively sports bar at night, I-M ● *Green Bottle Grill,* Westbury Square, off south Memorial Parkway, 882–0459, fine regional cooking, best in the area, M-E

SIGHTSEEING *U.S. Space and Rocket Center,* One Tranquility Base, just off I–565/U.S. 72A, 837–3400. Hours: daily 9 A.M. to 6 P.M., extended hours in summer, $$$$ ● *Constitution Hall Village,* 404 Madison Street, 535–6565. Hours: Monday to Saturday 9 A.M. to 5 P.M., $$ ● *Huntsville Depot Museum,* 320 Church Street, 539–1860. Hours: March to December, Tuesday to Sunday $$; Depot Trolley tours, 10 A.M. to 12:30 P.M. and 1 P.M. to 4 P.M.; $ ● *Huntsville Museum of Art,* Von Braun Civic Center, 700 Monroe Street, 535–4350. Hours: Tuesday 10 A.M. to 9 P.M.; Wednesday to Friday 10 A.M. to 5 P.M.; Saturday 9 A.M. to 5 P.M.; Sunday 1 P.M. to 5 P.M.; free ● *Weeden House Museum,* 300 Gates Avenue, 536–7718. Hours: March to December, Tuesday to Sunday 1 P.M. to 4 P.M., $ ● *Burritt Museum and Park,* 3101 Burritt Drive, off U.S. 431 east, 536–2882. Hours: park, April through September 7 A.M. to 7 P.M.; rest of year to 5 P.M.; mansion, March to Thanksgiving Day, Tuesday to Sunday noon to 5 P.M.; donation ● *Huntsville–Madison County Botanical Garden,* 4747 Bob Wallace Avenue, 830–4447. Hours: Monday to Saturday 7:30 A.M. to 6:30 P.M.; Sunday 1 P.M. to 6:30 P.M. $ ● *Madison County Nature Trail,* South Shawdee Road, Green Mountain, 883–9501. Hours: daylight hours, parking fee, $ ● *Monte Sano State Park,* 5105 Nolen Avenue, off U.S. 431 East, 534–3757. Hours: daylight hours, parking, $ ● *Ditto Landing Marina,* Boat Docks Road off South Memorial Parkway, 883–9420 or 800–552–8769, picnic facilities on the Tennessee River. Hours: daylight hours, free ● *Sunbelt at Hampton Cove,* off U.S. 431 south; phone 942–1177 for Sunbelt golfing information.

INFORMATION *Huntsville Tourist Information Center,* Von Braun Civic Center, 700 Monroe Street, Huntsville, AL 35801, 551–2230 or 800–843–0468 out of state, 800–225–6819 in Ala.

Under the Spell in Charleston

You'll need no photographs to remember a visit to Charleston. This seductive charmer casts a spell that lingers long in the memory.

On the streets of the old city, it could still be the eighteenth century. Church spires remain the tallest points in the Charleston skyline. No city in America has done a better job of preserving its original homes—block after block of them, tempting visitors out to walk, to admire the graceful tiered piazzas, to peek in at the hidden gardens.

Spring is considered the prime season in Charleston, but it is also the most crowded. Since temperatures are mild most of the year, and the city is abloom in camellias in January and February, those who plan a late-winter trip will get lowest rates at inns, and have the city almost to themselves.

Simply exploring the streets of this beguiling city would make for a memorable visit, but an eventful 350-year history has left a rich sightseeing legacy, from plantations and formal gardens to museums and magnificent churches. Antiquing is choice, and water and beaches beckon on all sides. In fact, the only problem in Charleston is finding time for all the possibilities.

A carriage ride from the City Market through the historic district and along the waterfront is the traditional way to get the lay of the land and learn a bit of local lore. You'll discover that Charleston's first English settlers, in 1670, were joined the next year by pioneers from Barbados, accounting for the pastel colors and semitropical feel the city retains to this day. The lineup known as Rainbow Row, along the waterfront battery, is a favorite of local artists.

Charleston quickly prospered as a seaport. Ships sailed out carrying first furs and lumber, then rice, indigo, and cotton. They returned with fine goods from around the world, giving Charleston the reputation of a cultured "little London" in the wilds of the New World, the richest city in the South, with maritime traffic that surpassed that of Boston. America's first municipal college, museum, and formal garden were established here in the 1700s.

This was also the first planned town in the colonies, laid out with two "great streets," Market and Broad, intersecting at the Market Square. The gracious plan still stands.

Churches are plentiful, as part of the city's early sophistication resulted from its attitude of religious tolerance, which attracted a host of settlers to the "Holy City." By the end of the eighteenth century, the first Baptist church in the South and the nation's second-oldest synagogue had been established, and there were churches for French

Huguenots, Congregationalists, Scotch Presbyterians, Lutherans, Methodists, and Roman Catholics.

The lovely Colonial-style St. Michael's Episcopal Church, dating to 1761, is one of the few city churches in America that retains its original design. It was here that George Washington and the Marquis de Lafayette worshipped while in Charleston. The steeple was one of the most prominent victims of Hurricane Hugo in 1989; it should be restored by the time you visit.

Charleston is a sunnier place since Hurricane Hugo paid its unwelcome call and claimed some of the ancient, moss-draped live oaks that once formed a shady canopy. But some say this only makes it easier to see the beauty that has remained in full measure. And while many innkeepers have scrapbooks with before-and-after photos to show the storm's terrible damage, everyone reminds you that the city has recovered from worse disasters over the years—fire, plague, hurricanes, and occupation in both the Revolutionary and Civil wars.

The Civil War started at Fort Sumter, off Charleston harbor, and bombardment during the war was so heavy that by the time Union troops came in, they were greeted only by vacant houses, deserted warehouses, gardens gone to seed, and grass growing in the streets. No sooner had reconstruction gotten under way than an earthquake shook things up further in 1886. Metal earthquake rods installed in surviving homes to fortify them in case of future catastrophes are still obvious today.

All this misfortune proved a blessing in disguise. Charleston was too poor to "modernize," so her historic homes remained, shabby but unchanged, while other cities remodeled to suit the gingerbread styles of the Victorian era. Saving this irreplaceable architecture was the goal when the Preservation Society of Charleston was formed in 1920. This is the oldest community-based preservation organization in the nation. In 1931 Charleston enacted the first historic-district ordinance in the United States, and preservation fever spread.

The Festival of Houses and Gardens, held in April, and the House and Garden candlelight tours of private homes each fall, offer an inside view of some of the wonderful results.

After gaining an overview of the city via carriage, it's time to get out on foot, the only way to fully appreciate Charleston's color and charm. You can do it yourself with a printed guide available from the visitors' center, or sign up for any of several guided walking tours.

One simple route on your own is to begin at the City Market, following Meeting Street to the water, then coming back on Church Street, passing many of the city's most important sites along the way. The Market, established in 1788, was the main trading mart for the town in early days. It is now filled with shops, many quite touristy, but among the open-air vendors are ladies at work weaving the sweetgrass baskets that are a Charleston tradition, brought by the first arrivals from Africa.

Take time to stop in at the fine Gibbes Museum of Art on Meeting Street to see the work of Charleston artists like Alice Ravenel Huger Smith, whose watercolors so beautifully depict the rice plantations that produced the city's early wealth. The museum also has interesting collections of Oriental art and of miniature portraits from the eighteenth and nineteenth centuries.

In the Council Chamber of the 1801 City Hall, at the corner of Meeting and Broad streets, are many exceptional early portraits, including a Trumbull portrait of George Washington. In the shade of the post office and the federal court on the opposite corner are more ladies creating those unique baskets and wreaths.

At number 51 is one of the grandest of the homes maintained by the Preservation Society, the Nathaniel Russell House, built in 1808 and famed for its "flying staircase," spiraling upwards for three floors with no visible means of support.

Cobblestoned Tradd Street is one of many lanes that extend from river to river, lined all the way with lovely homes. Detour here or on almost any side street to admire the piazzas and the almost hidden gardens beyond.

At the end of the street are the mansions of the Battery and a park and promenade along the water. The Greek Revival style Edmonston-Alston House at 21 East Battery is one of the more ornate homes open for touring.

The waterfront continuing east of the old city walls opposite Fort Sumter, long a center for wharves and warehouses, has given way to Waterfront Park, which won the 1992 Federal Design Achievement Award. A hotel is planned for this area, continuing its upgrading.

Heading back on Church Street takes you past another home worth looking into, the 1770 Heyward-Washington House, owned by a signer of the Declaration of Independence. The walk also leads past the venerable Dock Street Theater, which began back in 1736 when this street was known as Dock Street, and finally to St. Philip's, whose cemeteries include the graves of many distinguished early South Carolinians. The greatest of them all, John Calhoun, was relegated to the west side of the street, unable to be buried in the yard next to the church because he was not a Charleston native.

Rebuilt in 1835 following a fire, St. Philip's was long known as the Lighthouse Church for the light in the steeple that once guided ships into port.

If time allows, visit the northern part of the city for the Charleston Museum, America's oldest, now in a $6 million complex loaded with clothing, furniture, silver, photos, and other memorabilia from colonial times through the Civil War, and two more fine period homes under museum supervision, the 1803 Joseph Manigault House and the 1817 Aiken-Rhett Mansion.

The museum is part of the revival of this part of town, along with the big, handsome Visitors Reception and Transportation Center in the former train depot.

A drive north on N.C. route 61 to the plantations along the Ashley River is not to be missed, but the plantations easily merit a weekend on their own. If you do want to combine them with Charleston, see "Plantation Pleasures Near Charleston," starting on page 59.

The first choices in lodgings for most visitors are the historic homes that have been converted to charming bed-and-breakfast inns. Among these, Two Meeting Street Inn is prime, a spacious and gracious 1890 Victorian mansion with Tiffany glass, elegant furnishings, and an unbeatable location facing the water. A more historic choice is the exquisite 1763 John Rutledge House Inn, one of only 15 surviving homes belonging to signers of the Constitution. Just beyond walking distance of the historic district is the Maison du Pre, circa 1804, with tasteful and cozy quarters and a delightful courtyard. Those who want to be convenient to town shopping will find two attractively furnished small hotels a few doors apart, the Queen Victoria Inn and the King's Courtyard Inn.

Dining measures up to everything else in this exceptional city. Sample some Lowcountry specialties such as Charleston's own creamy she-crab soup, best when served with a dollop of sherry, and the surprisingly delicious combination of shrimp and grits.

What to do with any remaining time in Charleston? A dozen antique stores beckon on King Street, along with scores of other shops. A boat ride to Fort Sumter, where the Civil War began, offers a tour of Charleston harbor as a bonus. Public beachfront parks await to the north on Isle of Palms and south at Folly Beach, or at the truly beautiful Beachwalker Park on Kiawah Island.

But packing a day with too many sights is almost a shame in Charleston. The nicest thing to do here is simply to stroll the old city at leisure, collecting the lovely impressions that will become permanent snapshots in your mind.

Area Code: 803

DRIVING DIRECTIONS   Charleston is located at the intersection of I–26 and U.S. 17. From Atlanta, take I–20 east to Columbia, then I–26 southeast into Charleston, about 286 miles. It is 200 miles from Charlotte, N.C., 112 miles from Columbia, S.C.

PUBLIC TRANSPORTATION   American, Delta, and USAir serve Charleston; airport shuttles and taxis bring passengers into the city, and those who stay in the center can easily manage without a car. With a car, avoid parking problems by leaving your car in the visitor center lot, 375 Meeting Street, and using shuttle service into town, leaving every 15 minutes.

ACCOMMODATIONS *Two Meeting Street,* at that address, Charleston 29401, 723–7322, glorious 1890 Victorian facing the water, top choice, M-EE, CP • *John Rutledge Inn,* 116 Broad Street, Charleston 29401, 723–7999, 1763 historic landmark, spacious and gracious rooms, EE, CP • *Maison du Pre,* 317 East Bay Street, Charleston 29401, 723–8691, or 800–662-INNS, M-EE, CP • *Loundes Grove Plantation,* 266 St. Margaret Street, Charleston 19403, 723–3530, exquisite 1786 plantation house on the river, M-EE, CP • *Less expensive choices: 1837 Bed and Breakfast/Tea Room,* 26 Wentworth Street, Charleston 29401, 723–7166, modest but pleasant, I-M, CP; *Brasington House,* 328 East Bay Street, Charleston 29401, 722–1274, M, CP; *Cannonboro Inn,* 184 Ashley Avenue, Charleston 19403, 723–8572, moderately priced but a drive from town, I-M, CP • *Convenient small hotels with inn ambience: The Anchorage Inn,* 26 Vendue Range, Charleston 29401, 723–8300 or 800–421–2952, E-EE, CP; *Queen Victoria Inn,* 208 King Street, Charleston 29401, 720–2944 or 800–933–5464, E, CP; *Kings Courtyard Inn,* 198 King Street, Charleston 29401, 723–7000, 800–845–6119, E-EE, CP.

DINING *The top 4 picks: Anson,* 12 Anson Street, 577–0551, innovative California/Thai, attractive contemporary setting, M-E; *Carolina's,* 10 Exchange Street, 724–3800, modern Carolina cuisine, M; *Magnolias,* 185 East Bay Street, 577–7771, contemporary Southern, on everybody's list of best in town, M; *Pinckney Cafe & Espresso,* 18 Pinckney Street, 577–0961, informal, funky bistro, great food, I-M • *Celia's Porta Via,* 49 Archdale Street, 722–9003, worth a bit of a drive for this neighborhood Italian winner, I-M • *82 Queen,* 82 Queen Street, 723–7591, Continental food in restored nineteenth-century townhouses, M • *Garibaldi's,* 49 South Market Street, 723–7153, attractive café for Italian and Continental food, M • *Lafayette,* 276 King Street, 723–0014, innovative French, I-M • *Louis's Charleston Grill,* 224 King Street at Charleston Place (Omni Hotel), 577–4522, formal ambience for Southern regional cuisine, jazz in the bar, M-E • *Primerose House,* 332 East Bay Street, 723–2954, charming casual cellar café, good Sunday brunch, I-M • *Saracen,* Broad Street, 723–6242, French Continental in a former 1853 bank, M • *Robert's of Charleston,* 112 North Market Street, 577–7565, a splurge for six courses, wines, songs by the owner, EE • *Arizona Bar and Grill,* 14 Chapel Street, 577–5090, Southwestern fare, fun surroundings, I • *Binh Minh,* 7685 Northwoods Blvd., North Charleston, 569–2844, authentic Vietnamese, I • *Henry's,* 54 North Market Street, 723–4363, come for happy hour and jazz • *Baker's Cafe,* 214 King Street, 577–2694, excellent downtown breakfast, brunch, or lunch choice, I.

SIGHTSEEING *Charleston Museum,* 360 Meeting Street, 722–2996. Hours: Monday to Saturday 9 A.M. to 5 P.M.; Sunday 1 P.M. to 5 P.M.; $$$. Combination ticket for museum and three historic homes that follow, $$$$: *Aiken-Rhett House,* 48 Elizabeth Street at Judith Street, 723–1159. Hours: Monday to Saturday, 10 A.M. to 5 P.M., Sunday 1 P.M. to 5 P.M., $$$; *Heyward-Washington House,* 87 Church Street, 722–0354. Hours: Monday to Saturday 10 A.M. to 5 P.M., Sunday 1 P.M. to 5 P.M., $$$; *Joseph Manigault House,* 350 Meeting Street, 723–2926. Hours: Monday to Saturday 10 A.M. to 5 P.M., Sunday 1 P.M. to 5 P.M., $$$ • *Gibbes Museum of Art,* 135 Meeting Street, 722–2706. Hours: Tuesday to Saturday 10 A.M. to 5 P.M.; Sunday and Monday 1 P.M. to 5 P.M.; $ • *Patriots Point,* Charleston Harbor, Mt. Pleasant side of Cooper River Bridge, 884–2727. Hours: daily 9 A.M. to 5 P.M.; in summer, 9 A.M. to 6 P.M.; $$$ • *Nathaniel Russell House,* 51 Meeting Street, 723–1623. Hours: Monday to Saturday 10 A.M. to 5 P.M.; Sunday 2 P.M. to 5 P.M.; guided tour, $$$; combination ticket with Edmonston-Alston house, $$$ • *Edmonston-Alston House,* 21 East Battery, 722–7171. Hours: Tuesday to Saturday 10 A.M. to 4:40 P.M.; Sunday and Monday 1:30 P.M. to 4:40 P.M.; guided tours, $$$; combination with Nathaniel Russell House, $$$ • *Walking tours* (phone for current schedules, reservations): *Architectural Walking Tours of Charleston,* 722–2345 • *Charleston Strolls,* 884–9505 • *Charleston Tea Party Walking Tour,* 577–5896 • *Historic Charleston Walking Tours,* 722–6460.

INFORMATION *Charleston Trident Convention & Visitors Bureau,* 81 Mary Street, P.O. Box 975, Charleston, SC 29401, 353–8000.

Mardi Gras Mania in Mobile

Alabama's oldest city is a mix of Southern drawl and French accent, a blend best seen in Mobile's lovely neighborhoods, where antebellum columns and fancy iron balconies stand side by side beneath the moss-draped live oak trees.

The lacy wrought-iron lends a distinct flavor, but Mobile's favorite French legacy is, without doubt, the nation's first celebration of Mardi Gras, an event repeated each year with merriment and madness for two full weeks, climaxing on the Tuesday before Lent.

Yes, the New Orleans festivities may be bigger and more famous, but they still started later, and partisans will tell you that Mobile's revelry remains number one—more manageable and, therefore, more fun. The city's mystic societies hold costume balls and lavish parades. Spectators jam the streets with hands outstretched to catch the traditional baby moon pies, beads, doubloons, tiny masks, and candies tossed out by costumed riders on board the colorful floats. Many of these riders are Mobile's most elite citizens.

There's another reason why Mobile's celebration shouldn't be missed. In this semitropical setting, Mardi Gras usually comes at the beginning of the peak blooming season at Bellingrath Gardens, one of America's great floral showplaces, located about half an hour to the south. That means you can wind up a weekend with a dazzle of flowers that will light up the rest of your spring.

Mardi Gras is a sample of the way Mobilians savor and build on their history. By some accounts, this city's first celebration dates back to 1703, just one year after the first French settlers arrived. The parades and masked participants we now associate with the holiday originated in the 1830s and 1840s as celebrations for New Year's Eve.

But it was on Fat Tuesday that festivities were revived, following a suspension during the Civil War. A lover of good times, Joseph Stillwell Cain, determined to raise the spirits of the defeated city in 1866 by holding a one-float parade on a mule-drawn coal wagon. In ensuing years, Cain found plenty of company for his celebration, and eventually a host of new mystic societies were formed, each vying to put on the best show. Cain himself established the Order of Myths, which still parades in Mobile.

Cain rests in an honored place in the historic Church Street Graveyard in downtown Mobile, with an epitaph on his headstone that reads, "Here lies old Joe Cain, the heart and soul of Mardi Gras in Mobile." When his body was moved here in 1966 from its original burying place, it wasn't long before a new tradition was born, known as "Raisin' Cain," with speeches and band music around the grave. By 1983 the crowds for this event had grown to 100,000 revelers and become what is sometimes called "the people's Mardi Gras." It is now held downtown on the Sunday preceding Mardi Gras Tuesday. The mock funeral procession includes Joe Cain's "widows," dozens of women dressed and veiled in mourning black.

This parade and two Saturday events, the coronation of King Felix and his queen and the Mystics of Time parade, are highlights of the weekend preceding Mardi Gras, in case you can't be here on Tuesday for the Comic Cowboys and Order of Myths grand parades. For the entire two-week season before Lent, the local newspapers print schedules, routes, and summaries of the float themes for the next day. If you can snag a room at the Admiral Semmes, you'll have a grand vantage point from the balcony, reserved for hotel guests. Veteran viewers say that the intersection of Government and Joachim, in front of WALA-TV, is a good spot from which to view the festivities, because of the lights set up here for television cameras.

The first Mardi Gras monarch, King Felix, the Emperor of Joy, was crowned in 1872, and purple and gold soon became the official colors used for royal robes. The costumes for the king and queen are amazingly ornate affairs. You can see some of the grandest close up at the City of Mobile Museum, where a mezzanine display shows more than a dozen gowns worn by former queens. The Staples Gallery here traces the history of Mardi Gras in Mobile.

The museum, an ornate 1872 Italianate home with two-story wrought-iron balconies typical of Mobile, follows the evolution of the city. Two special collections to note are the horse-drawn carriages of days gone by, displayed in the Rutherford Carriage Room, and the Hammel Collection of early twentieth century women's fashions.

Mobile's history is a rich one. This first permanent white settlement in Alabama was established in 1711 on the west side of the bay, a strategic spot commanding the entrances to major rivers. It became the capital of a French wilderness empire. By the 1850s, Mobile was a prosperous cotton-trading port. These were the glory years, when brokers and shippers built the town's finest homes. The Battle of Mobile Bay was a major Civil War naval engagement, but the city was occupied only briefly, in 1864.

Recovery came quickly following the war, thanks to railroads and shipbuilding. Mobile was the largest city in the state until Birmingham mushroomed near the turn of the century. The harbor is still a city mainstay. The discovery of natural gas has also brought drilling rigs to the bay.

Be forewarned that this is a city whose charms aren't immediately apparent if all you see is a commercial port and a downtown suffering from defections to the suburbs. An ambitious redevelopment plan may soon transform the downtown area, but for now it's the city neighborhoods that hold most of the attractions.

However, a good starting place to learn about the city is Fort Conde,

the centerpiece for the downtown redevelopment plans. The adminis-
trative and military center of the Louisiana Territory, the fort began in
1711 as a stockade enclosed by 14-inch cedar stakes. From 1724 to
1735, a permanent brick-and-mortar fort went up within the temporary
stockade, occupied successively by French, English, Spanish, and
American troops.

In 1820, when it was no longer needed for defense, the fortress was
blasted with gunpowder, and the rubble was used to fill in low-lying
riverfront streets. The old fort was carefully reconstructed on the
original site in 1976 with the use of drawings from French archives. It
now serves as a most unusual city welcome center, where you can pick
up current information and take a tour of the past with guides in
authentic early uniforms. Demonstrations of cannon and rifle firings
are part of the tour.

The city's oldest home, the Conde-Charlotte House, dates from 1822
and was used as a jail before it became a residence. It has been restored
and furnished in styles from the sixteenth to nineteenth centuries,
depicting the periods of Mobile's history under its five flags. An
eighteenth-century walled Spanish garden is on the grounds.

You'll see Mobile at its best along its most important and attractive
avenue, Government Street, gracefully canopied by century-old live
oak trees. Among the notable buildings along the way are the 1857
City Hall, the 1836 Presbyterian Church, the three-story 1860 Ketchum
Mansion that is now the home of Mobile's Archbishop, and the 1859
home of Confederate hero Admiral Raphael Semmes, whose statue is
also prominently displayed at Government and Royal streets. Semmes
commanded the *Alabama,* the most feared ship in the Confederate
Navy.

Government Street is one part of the Church Street East Historic
District, Mobile's second-oldest neighborhood and one of the largest
and most varied of the city's many historic districts. Though the
earliest homes were destroyed in fires in 1827 and 1839, the remaining
buildings are a catalog of American architectural styles.

Each of the historic districts has its own personality. Just north of
Government Street is a much-photographed home famous for its lavish
iron lace trim, the Richards DAR house. It was built in 1860 by a
wealthy steamboat captain. The house is part of the De Tonti Square
district, a nine-block area of flagstone sidewalks, antique gaslights, and
fine homes built when Mobile was at its affluent peak.

The Oakleigh Garden District became the city's most fashionable
address in the early 1900s, and has the finest homes from that period.
Oakleigh Mansion dates back to an even earlier time. It is the city's
most important antebellum house museum, built by slaves in raised-
cottage style in 1833 for a prominent merchant. Elegantly furnished
and known for its important early portrait collection, the house
was one of Alabama's earliest preservation projects when it was

restored in 1955. Next door is the Cox-Deasy House, a raised Creole cottage built around 1850 and a good example of a middle-class home of that time.

The Old Dauphin Way district adjacent to downtown is lined with typical Gulf Coast cottages and Victorian middle-class merchants' homes. A prominent resident of this neighborhood is the giant Duffee Oak at 1123 Caroline Avenue, the city's oldest tree, planted before America's independence and having a trunk 25 feet in circumference.

Other historic homes that can be toured include the 1855 Bragg-Mitchell Mansion, one of the grandest antebellum homes on the Gulf Coast, boasting 16 graceful fluted columns outside and a sweeping curved staircase and 15-foot ceilings within. The photogenic house is surrounded by a grove of stately live oaks.

The Carlen House Museum, on the grounds of Murphy High School, is an attractive 1842 home in Creole cottage style, displaying period fashions in clothing and home furnishings.

Mobile's Fine Arts Museum of the South has a fine collection that spans more than 200 years. Some of the highlights are American and Southern decorative arts, including ceramics, glass, and furniture. The building is in a wooded park setting near a lake.

Mobile's most popular attraction is of much later vintage. The USS *Alabama* Battleship Park has as its highlight the 680-foot massive floating fortress that earned nine battle stars in the Pacific during World War II. A self-guided tour of the ship takes you along the decks, through the engine room, the crew's sleeping quarters, and the captain's cabin, and into the gun turrets. Berthed next to the giant ship and also open to tours is the submarine USS *Drum,* veteran of 13 war missions in the Pacific.

If you want to tour the busy harbor, the excursion ship *Commander* leaves from the Battleship Park dock on 90-minute tours, with narration about the momentous battle of Mobile Bay in 1865 and other colorful tales of city history.

Mardi Gras Day is the official beginning of Mobile's Azalea Trail and Festival, with parades and carefully marked driving tours through the city's flower-filled neighborhoods for the next month. The flowers reach their peak later in March.

But you won't have to wait to see fantastic floral displays at Bellingrath Gardens. These 65 acres of beauty, patterned after the formal gardens of Europe, are lovely year-round. In late winter and early spring, camellias, the Alabama state flower, are at their peak. You can see hundreds of specimens, ranging from delicate shell pink to deep crimson. The early azaleas begin their bloom about the time that an incredible bulb display of some 90,000 daffodils, hyacinths, and tulips bursts into full splendor. Over the long blooming season, the garden shows off 250,000 azaleas representing 200 varieties.

In 1918, Walter Bellingrath, a pioneer in the Coca-Cola bottling industry, bought the property as a fishing camp. It remained a rustic retreat until his wife, Bessie, began transplanting azaleas and camellias from their Mobile garden. Seeing how plants flourished in the acid soil, Walter became interested. The couple traveled abroad to see the great gardens of Europe, and hired Mobile landscape designer George Royers to create a showplace at home.

Soon there was a gracious brick mansion overlooking the grand lawn, filled with priceless china and porcelain. The former guest house of the estate now is the Delchamps Gallery of Boehm Porcelain, which was begun with the 85-piece private collection of Mobile's Delchamps family and has grown to over 200 pieces, the largest collection in the world of the famous, exquisitely detailed porcelain birds and other figures.

Both home and gallery are part of the Bellingrath garden tour, a one-of-a-kind excursion that even Mardi Gras can't beat for color.

Area Code: 334

DRIVING DIRECTIONS Mobile is in southwestern Alabama, reached via I–10 from east or west, I–65 from the north. From Birmingham, follow I–65 south, 241 miles. From Atlanta, take I–85 west, connecting with I–65 at Montgomery, 332 miles.

ACCOMMODATIONS *Radisson Admiral Semmes Hotel,* 251 Government Street, Mobile 36602, 432–8000 or 800–333–3333, elegantly restored landmark, M-E ● *Stouffer Riverview Plaza Hotel,* 64 Water Street, Mobile 36602, 438–3719 or 800-HOTELS–1, upscale downtowner on the waterfront, attractive rooms, pool and veranda, gym, M-E ● *Malaga Inn,* 359 Church Street, Mobile 36602, 438–4701, two 1862 town houses around a patio, period furnishings, I ● *Mallory Manor,* 1104 Montauk Avenue, Mobile 36604, 432–6440, bed-and-breakfast home in historic district, I, CP.

DINING *The Pillars,* 1757 Government Street, 478–6341, restored plantation house, noted chef, best in town, M-E ● *Weichman's All Seasons,* 168 South Beltline Highway, 344–3961, antique furnishings, many fine-dining awards, M-E ● *Pier 4 Restaurant,* Battleship Parkway, Mobile, 626–6710, seafood on the bay, I-E ● *Wintzell's Oyster House,* 605 Dauphin Street, 433–1004, colorful, casual, walls covered with wit and wisdom, M ● *Ruth's Chris Steak House,* 271 Glenwood Street, 476–0516, the place for steak, M-E ● *Roussos,* 166 South Royal Street, next to the welcome center, 433–3322, seafood specialties, I-E ● *Hemingways,* 1850 Airport Boulevard, 479–3514,

Creole and Cajun, I-M • *Dick Russell's Barbecue,* Highway 90, 661–6090, ribs and meat plates, I.

SIGHTSEEING *Bellingrath Gardens,* Bellingrath Highway off I–10 or U.S. 90, Theodore, 973–2217. Hours: daily, gardens 7 A.M. to dusk, house 8 A.M. to one hour before dusk; gardens only, $$$; house and garden, $$$$ • *USS* Alabama *Battleship Park,* Battleship Parkway exit off I–10, 433–2703. Hours: daily 8 A.M. to dusk, $$ • *Alabama Cruises,* from Battleship Park dock, 433–6101. Hours vary with seasons, check current schedules; $$$ • *Carlen House,* 54 Carlen Street, 470–7768. Hours: Tuesday to Saturday 10 A.M. to 5 P.M.; Sunday 1 P.M. to 5 P.M.; free • *Conde-Charlotte Museum House,* 104 Theatre Street, 432–4722. Hours: Tuesday to Saturday 10 A.M. to 4 P.M., $$ • *Bragg-Mitchell Mansion,* 1906 Springhill Avenue, 471–6364. Hours: Monday to Friday 10 A.M. to 4 P.M.; Sunday 1 P.M. to 4 P.M.; $$ • *Fine Arts Museum of the South,* Museum Drive, Langan Park, 471–6364. Hours: Tuesday to Sunday 10 A.M. to 5 P.M., free • *Fort Conde,* 150 South Royal Street at Church Street, 434–7304. Hours: daily 8 A.M. to 5 P.M., free • *Museum of the City of Mobile,* 355 Government Street, 434–2569. Hours: Tuesday to Saturday 10 A.M. to 5 P.M.; Sunday 1 P.M. to 5 P.M.; free • *Oakleigh Mansion,* 350 Oakleigh Place, 432–1281. Hours: Monday to Saturday 10 A.M. to 4 P.M.; Sunday 1 P.M. to 4 P.M.; $$ • *Richards D.A.R. House,* 256 North Joachim Street, De Tonti Square, 434–7320. Hours: Tuesday to Saturday 10 A.M. to 4 P.M.; Sunday 1 P.M. to 4 P.M.; $$.

INFORMATION *Mobile Department of Tourism and Special Events,* c/o Mobile Visitor Welcome Center, 150 South Royal Street, Mobile, AL 36602, 434–7304 or 800–252–3862.

Making Tracks in High Country

The weather was unseasonal. The calendar said February, but the thermometer read 70 degrees, hardly a promising forecast for skiers in North Carolina's High Country. But up on the mountains they were making tracks down the hills, with jackets off, sunglasses in place. The snowmaking that works overtime to keep these slopes white had provided enough advance cover to survive a temporary blip in the temperature charts.

As long as nights stay cold, skiing is hot in the High Country. When Southern skiing arrived with the advent of mechanical snowmaking, this area quickly emerged as the center. Beech Mountain, opened in 1968, boasts the highest lift-served skiing in the eastern United States, and Sugar Mountain, which began the following year, has the highest elevation.

Near the charming little town of Blowing Rock, the smaller Appalachian Ski Mountain began even earlier, starting with one slope and a rope tow in 1962 and adding the first night skiing in the South in 1965. It is known for its French-Swiss Ski College, using European techniques to teach the sport.

Not that running a ski resort in Southern climes is easy. When the nights as well as the days stay warm, business suffers, and all these areas have tottered and actually gone into bankruptcy over the years during economic downturns. But like the skiers, they just keep coming back, and when nature cooperates they offer a skiing experience to suit every taste and ability. And there's plenty to do and see off the slopes.

Beech Mountain is the closest you'll come to an alpine village this side of the Rockies. Set at the top of the mountain at 5,505 feet, the ski slopes rise from a small complex of shops and restaurants, with an outdoor ice-skating rink for a sporting change of pace. Skiers will find 14 slopes—and a vertical drop of 830 feet. There are some slopeside condominiums at Beech, but most accommodations are located just down the hill, and include lodge-style inns as well as more condos.

There's a bit more challenge at Sugar Mountain, farther down the hill in Banner Elk. The vertical drop here is 1,200 feet, the elevation is 5,300 feet, and there are 18 slopes. Banner Elk has a couple of motels and inns, but many skiers stay in the host of condominiums surrounding the ski area. It must be said, however, that one of these is a looming high-rise building that seems very out of place in this mountain setting.

Wherever you stay while you are in Banner Elk, stop into Fred's General Mercantile Company, a modern version of a country store that seems to sell everything from soup to nuts. The soup can be ordered in the very pleasant Backside Deli, in a greenhouse setting. Fred's also includes a ski shop with rentals.

The choicest inns in this part of the mountains are seven miles from Banner Elk in Valle Crucis, a village best known as the home of the Mast General Store. This landmark from the past, established in 1883, is still complete with a pot-bellied stove, a vintage post office, and a variety of wares that keep browsers busy, from rosebud salve to birdhouses.

You can't go wrong with any of the three inns in this town. The Inn at the Taylor House is a period farmhouse decorated with tasteful antiques and works of art. The Mast Farm Inn is another farmhouse, with rockers, iron beds, quilts, and rustic accessories. Generous country dinners are served family-style. For soaring vistas, the place is Bluestone Lodge, a contemporary aerie on a mountaintop, with big picture windows and decks to take in the views. Suites here come with fireplaces or woodstoves and whirlpool baths.

Those who want the gentler slopes and the excellent instruction of Appalachian Ski Mountain will find plenty of tempting choices in Blowing Rock. The Gideon Ridge Inn is a fieldstone beauty, decorated in sophisticated good taste and set on a secluded ridge with spectacular views of the Blackberry and John's River gorges.

Resorts in the Blowing Rock area offer luxury and sports facilities. The Hound Ears Club, set on 700 acres and centered on a velvety golf course, does indeed have the aura of a private club. When the greens turn white, guests enjoy an on-site ski run with two slopes. Accommodations are in lodge rooms or condominiums, and the dining room here is one of the area's best.

Not far away is Yonahlossee Resort and Club, a heavily wooded, 140-acre resort sure to delight tennis players; the racquet club has won awards and offers three indoor tennis courts as well as a 75-foot indoor pool and racquetball courts. Outdoor attractions in season include an equestrian center and a lake for swimming and canoeing.

Chetola Resort is just outside the town of Blowing Rock; though it lacks the acreage of the other resorts, it does offer a recreation center with an indoor pool, racquetball courts, and exercise classes.

Perched at an elevation of 4,000 feet just off the Blue Ridge Parkway, the town of Blowing Rock is a strong contender for the title of prettiest town in the mountains. Main Street shops are housed in turn-of-the-century buildings made of local stone, and they offer a range of wares from antiques to crafts to folk art.

Those in search of bargains will find 30 outlet stores at the Shoppes on the Parkway, on the Highway 321 Bypass.

The Blowing Rock that inspired the town's name is a cliff above the John's River Gorge. The name comes from a believe-it-or-not natural phenomenon. The gorge forms a flume through which the northwest wind sweeps with such force that it will return light objects dropped over the cliff. The entrance to the rock and its observation deck, which has an admission charge, is closed in the winter, but there's no shortage of views if you take a spin along the Blue Ridge Parkway toward Grandfather Mountain. Many people like driving the parkway best of all in winter, when the trees' bare branches allow for distant vistas that are otherwise hidden by leaves.

From mileposts 292 to 295 you'll be in Moses Cone Park, a favorite of photographers, hikers, and horseback riders for its 25 miles of carriage roads. In warmer months, this is also headquarters for the Southern Highland Handicraft Guild Shop.

Flat Rock, at milepost 308.3, is an outcrop with a superb view of

Grandfather Mountain and the Linville Valley. A few miles farther on, you'll cross one of the most recently completed parts of the parkway, the Linville Viaduct, with views of the 90-foot Linville Falls roaring through the deepest gorge east of the Grand Canyon. A gentle half-mile trail from the parking area at milepost 316 leads to a magnificent vista of the falls and the beginning of the gorge.

The next stop is Grandfather Mountain in Linville, and a chance to challenge the mile-high, 228-foot-long Swinging Bridge that gives a lovely, albeit unsteady, view of Linville Peak. The mountainside is a park with 30 miles of nature trails and a recently built nature museum. Six natural habitats for native wildlife, including black bears, cougars, and golden eagles, allow visitors to see and photograph the animals close up.

The mountain was named by pioneers for its profile resembling a bearded face looking toward the sky. This is the summer site of one of the largest Scottish gatherings in the country, the annual Grandfather Mountain Scottish Games, a colorful event well worth a return visit.

You may want to detour into Linville for a stop at the Old Hampton Store off N.C. route 181, another classic general store, circa 1921. The gristmill here turns out delicious cornmeal and grits. This is also the home of Uncle Lee's Barbecue, serving up delicious sandwiches on sourdough buns.

At some point you'll probably want to take a stroll through Boone, a town founded in 1872, whose wood-shingled buildings, sidewalk arcades, and surrounding mountains will likely remind you of a Western town. The town is lively, thanks to the 14,000 students who attend Appalachian State University here. Shoppers will find an outpost of the Mast Store in Boone, and there's a host of local history at the Appalachian Cultural Museum, which displays everything from antique quilts to cars driven by early stock-car racers from the area. More local lore can be found in the Appalachian Heritage Museum between Boone and Blowing Rock.

N.C. route 105, south of Boone, is the road for those interested in crafts. The Artisans Gallery, about a mile from town, shows contemporary art and crafts by over 150 artists. About 7 miles farther on, in Foscoe, are two cooperatives: Hands Gallery, which shows the work of a group of local artisans, and Blue Ridge Hearthside Crafts Gallery, with 300 members. Hearthside also has a branch in Blowing Rock.

Drive a mile farther along for Creekside Galleries, a collection of fine art and contemporary crafts by regional artists. Finally, another mile ahead, is Tatum Galleries, with handcrafted traditional furniture, antiques, local pottery, and artwork.

By all means come back to Boone for the authentic mountain nightlife at Shadrack's Barbecue Barn. On weekends there's an all-you-can-eat buffet and a country-and-western band. The place is packed with local residents, ages three to 83, who come out to dance.

The clog dancing, a cross between an Irish jig and tap, is something to behold. And it's done strictly for fun, not to impress tourists. When you see the high spirits, it's hard to believe no alcoholic spirits are allowed.

Area Code: 704

DRIVING DIRECTIONS Banner Elk and Beech Mountain are on N.C. Route 184, reached via N.C. Route 105 or U.S. 221. Major highways into the area are I–77, I–40, I–85, and I–81. From Atlanta to Banner Elk, take I–85 north to U.S. 221 north, merge with N.C. Route 105 and turn left on N.C. Route 184, about 255 miles. For Blowing Rock, continue on N.C. Route 105 through Boone to U.S. 321/221 north, about 275 miles.

PUBLIC TRANSPORTATION Closest airports are Hickory, 45 miles; Tri-Cities, 75 miles; Greensboro, 100 miles; and Charlotte, 110 miles.

ACCOMMODATIONS *Beech Alpen Inn and Top of the Beech Inn,* 2 Beech Mountain Parkway, Banner Elk 28604, 387–2252, adjoining lodges, I-E, CP ● *Pinnacle Inn,* P.O. Box 1136, Banner Elk 28604, 387–4276 or 800–433–2097, condo units, indoor pool, M-E ● *Banner Elk Inn Bed and Breakfast,* P.O. Box 1953, Banner Elk 28604, 898–6223, M, CP ● *Archer's Inn,* N.C. route 184 on Beech Mountain, Route 2, P.O. Box 56A, Banner Elk 28604, 898–9004, I-M, CP ● *Gideon Ridge Inn,* P.O. Box 1929, Blowing Rock 28605, 295–3644, M-EE, CP ● *Bluestone Lodge Bed and Breakfast,* P.O. Box 736, Valle Crucis 28691, 963–5177, M-E, CP ● *The Inn at the Taylor House,* Highway 194, P.O. Box 713, Valle Crucis 38691, 963–5581, M-E, CP ● *Mast Farm Inn,* P.O. Box 704, Valle Crucis 28691, 963–5857, M-EE, MAP ● *Budget choices: Maple Lodge,* Sunset Drive, Blowing Rock 28605, 295–3311, nicely furnished in-town inn, I-M, CP; *Overlook Lodge,* P.O. Box 1327, Boone, 28607, 963–5785, rustic lodge with mountain views, I, CP ● *Resorts: Hound Ears Lodge and Club,* P.O. Box 188, Blowing Rock, 28605, 963–4321, luxury resort in mountain setting, two ski slopes, ski packages include rental equipment and lift tickets at other area slopes, golf packages in summer, EE, MAP; *Yonahlossee Resort,* Shulls Mill Road (between Boone and Blowing Rock), P.O. Box 1397, Boone 18607, 262–1222 or 800–692–1986, luxury villas, indoor and outdoor tennis, E-EE; *Chetola Resort,* North Main Street, Blowing Rock 28605, 295–5500 or 800–243–8652, indoor pool, racquetball courts, fitness center, lodge rooms, I-E, condominiums, M-EE • *Condominium rentals: Beech Mountain Slope-side Rentals,* 800–692–2061; *Beech Mountain Rentals,* 800–438–2095; *Banner Elk Beech Mountain Rentals,* 800–845–6164; *Sugar Mountain Resort Accommodations,* 800–438–4555 or 800–272–9434.

DINING *Shadrack's Barbecue Barn,* U.S. 321, Boone, 264–1737, all you can eat, live country entertainment, dancing, M • *Makoto's Japanese Steak House,* 815 Blowing Rock Road, Boone, 264–7976, tasty tableside cooking, M • *Casa Rustica,* N.C. route 105, Boone, 262–5128, Italian, homemade pasta, I-M • *Louisiana Purchase,* N.C. route 184, Banner Elk, 898–5656, Cajun and Creole, extensive wine list, M-E • *Mast Farm Inn* (see above), full dinner; M • *Hearthside Cafe at Chetola Resort* (see above), attractive, American menu, M • *The Riverwood,* U.S. 321, Blowing Rock, nouvelle American, highly rated, M-E • *The Woodlands Barbecue,* 321 Bypass, Blowing Rock, 295–3651, I • *Blowing Rock Cafe,* Sunset Drive, Blowing Rock, 295–9474, cozy, informal, serves all three meals, mountain trout is the dinner specialty, I-M • *Beech Tree Restaurant,* Beech Tree Village, Ski Beech, 387–2011, I • *Beech Alpen Inn* (see above), varied menu, I-M • *Fred's Backside Deli,* Fred's General Store, Beech Mountain Parkway, Beech Mountain, 387–4838, I.

SIGHTSEEING *Grandfather Mountain,* U.S. 221, Linville, 733–4337 or 800–468–7325, nature museum, small outdoor zoo, walking trails, mile-high swinging bridge. Hours: April 1 to Labor Day, daily 8 A.M. to 7 P.M.; rest of year, daily 8 A.M. to 5 P.M., weather permitting; $$$ • *Appalachian Heritage Museum,* U.S. 321/221 between Boone and Blowing Rock, 264–2792. Hours: October to May, daily 9 A.M. to 5 P.M.; rest of year, daily 8 A.M. to 8 P.M.; $$ • *Appalachian Cultural Museum,* off U.S. 321 at University Hall, Boone, 262–3117. Hours: Tuesday to Saturday 10 A.M. to 5 P.M.; Sunday 1 P.M. to 5 P.M.; $ • *The Blowing Rock,* off U.S. 321, Blowing Rock, 295–7111. Hours: April, May, November, daily 9 A.M. to 6 P.M.; June to October, daily 8 A.M. to 8 P.M.; $$.

SKI AREAS *Appalachian Ski Mountain,* P.O. Box 106, Blowing Rock 28605, 295–7828; French-Swiss Ski College, 800–527–7547 • *Beech Mountain Ski Resort,* P.O. Box 1118, Beech Mountain 28604, 387–2011 or 800–222–2293 in N.C., 800–438–2093 out of state • *Sugar Mountain Ski Resort,* P.O. Box 369, Banner Elk 28604, 898–4521.

INFORMATION *High Country Host,* 701 Blowing Rock Road, Boone, NC 28607, 264–1299 or 800–438–7500.

Watching the Thoroughbreds in Aiken

Champion horses have been the pride of Aiken, South Carolina, for over a century. Many thoroughbreds winter here from October to March at more than 40 local stables, training for national glory later in the year. Aiken's March "Triple Crown," the culmination of the training season, is a preview of future Derby, Preakness, and Belmont winners.

You needn't be a racing fan to enjoy these special events, and the odds are also good that you'll fall in love with the charm of Aiken, a town filled with wide, shady streets and greenery, medians planted with sweet magnolias, and grand homes in the hills around town. Some of the scenic sandy roads are left unpaved to be easy on horses' hooves. There are even equestrian stoplights at some intersections.

Aiken's name honors the first president of the South Carolina Canal and Railroad Company, William Aiken. The town's birth came about with the founding of the company in 1828 to build a railroad from Charleston to the Savannah River. The first train arrived in the newly established town in 1833. The next year, engineers laid out the present wide streets and parkways, and Aiken quickly attracted visitors.

It was the mild winter climate and the sandy soil, perfect for equestrian activities, that began drawing some of America's wealthiest families after the Civil War. They formed an exclusive Winter Colony, building enormous "cottages" where they could meet and mingle, and stables where they bred and trained fleet horses.

The social scene faded after World War II, but the Vanderbilts, Astors, Goodyears, Whitneys, and their set left behind a beautiful legacy of homes—and a tradition of winners that still holds good. Thirty-five champions grace Aiken's Thoroughbred Hall of Fame, including Kelso, the record breaker named Horse of the Year for five consecutive years in the 1960s, and Swale, who won five consecutive Belmont Stakes from 1982 to 1986.

The newest crop of soon-to-be-winners can be seen on the three successive March weekends known as the Triple Crown. The Aiken Trials show off some of the most promising thoroughbreds in the world, having their first go at racing full speed on a quarter-mile track. The Aiken Hunt Meet showcases the best of the jumpers going through their paces on a steeplechase course, where elaborate tailgate picnics on the sidelines keep everyone happy between races. The final event is harness racing at the Aiken Mile Track, where the fleetest trotters can be seen.

Even if you miss the big events, you can enjoy watching sleek steeds go through their training paces at local training tracks, or take in a Sunday polo game or one of the many horse shows where the elite of each class show their breeding. You're liable to encounter a colorful hunt heading into Hitchcock Woods almost any weekend in season, and the Aiken Driving Club takes to the roads of the historic horse districts on the second Saturday of each month, with nattily costumed drivers showing off their shiny horse-drawn carriages and carts.

The first order of business, however, is to see the lovely town and learn more about its history. One way to do this is on the Aiken Tour that leaves every Saturday morning from The Alley, the street next to the Municipal Building in the heart of town. If you can't make the tour, ask for the walking/driving tour brochure available in most local inns, and go exploring.

You might start on foot with an easily walkable loop starting from the Willcox Hotel, the *grande dame* on Colleton Avenue. The hotel dates from the early 1900s and was a gathering place for many prominent winter visitors. It is the prime place to stay in town, though there are small bed-and-breakfast inns for those who want a cozier base.

Walk away from the Willcox down Colleton for three blocks or so, then back again on the other side of the street, to admire the cottages built from 1880 to the early 1900s. The imposing house on the corner across from the hotel was owned by the Astor family of New York.

When you come back to the hotel, turn left on Newberry Street, then take a series of rights on Boundary Avenue, Laurens Street, Park Avenue, and Chesterfield Street back to Colleton. Near the corner of Boundary and Laurens is Hitchcock Woods, a lovely 1,400-acre preserve developed at the turn of the century. Currently under the protection of the Hitchcock Foundation, it is a peaceful wooded haven for both horseback riders and walkers, who equally enjoy the winding dirt paths through the tall trees.

On Thanksgiving each year, Hitchcock Woods is the site of the colorful Blessing of the Hounds, performed by a minister on horseback just before the red-jacketed riders take off on a hunt.

On Laurens Street, you'll approach the center of town. The Laurens business section suffered extensive damage from fires, the first back in 1880, but revitalization is taking place, and many of the older buildings are being restored.

Morgan Circle, across from the Municipal Building, was named for Thomas R. Morgan, who was mayor of Aiken in 1899 and 1900. The circle and its cast-iron Victorian fountain were restored in 1963 with funds contributed by residents.

Behind the municipal building is The Alley, lined with shops and cafés that are likely spots for lunch.

Now it's time for a drive up Chesterfield Street, zigzagging right on

First Avenue, left on Newberry Street, and left again on Richland Avenue to Whiskey Road, a route that takes in some important sights and some of the grandest remaining residences.

At the corner of Chesterfield and First is Joye Cottage, a simple home that was purchased in 1897 by William C. Whitney, a New York banker who expanded it into a 50-room showplace. The residence across the street was once the Whitney stables.

At the end of First, turn left onto Newberry and go beyond the serpentine walls to the Aiken County Historical Museum, housed in a wing of the palatial 1850 mansion once known as Banksia. The house has 32 rooms, 15 baths, and a full ballroom.

The museum traces Aiken history with exhibits ranging from Indian artifacts to period rooms showing the town's lavish nineteenth-century lifestyles. Also on the grounds are an 1890 one-room schoolhouse and the Ergle log cabin, dating from 1808 and furnished with pieces from the period. One popular exhibit is a 1950s drugstore, moved from nearby Dunbarton, where it was dismantled in 1952 to make way for the Savannah River Plant.

The once-secret government facility where plutonium and tritonium were produced for nuclear warheads is no longer quite so hush-hush; group tours can be arranged. It continues to influence the makeup of Aiken, which boasts more engineers and Ph.D.s than any other town of its size in America.

Behind another serpentine wall, at the corner of Whiskey Road and Dupree Place, is Hopeland, the estate of Hope and Oliver Iselen from the turn of the century until 1970, when it was willed to the city by Mrs. Iselin. Today it is a public park with a 14-acre garden incorporating the lush trees, shrubs, and flowers planted long ago by the Iselins. Two small lakes bordered with weeping willows frame a performing-arts stage where summer concerts are held.

The Iselin carriage house was renovated in 1977 by the local Jaycees as the Thoroughbred Racing Hall of Fame, honoring locally bred and trained champions, and containing exhibits of racing silks, trophies, and horse-related artwork.

Driving farther through the "horsy" part of town is a delight, a chance to see the dozens of private farms with horses and colts in the fields. Several of the farms offer riding lessons. Write to the Chamber of Commerce for The Horseman's Guide to Aiken, which contains a complete list of the area's horse farms. It will also give you names of more than a dozen equine artists who live in town.

Visitors are welcome to watch the thoroughbreds being trained. October to March is the season, but you'll have to get up early, since that's when most workouts are held. Start with breakfast at the Track Kitchen, and you'll be mingling with trainers and owners in their favorite morning gathering place.

The Aiken Training Center is considered one of the best in the world. The timed trials of the Triple Crown event are the first competitive tests under full grandstand conditions for the year's crop of spirited two- and three-year-olds. The bloodlines of the participants are a "Who's Who" of racing.

Standardbred horses for harness or sulky racing do their training at the Aiken Mile Track. This is actually one of America's oldest sports, begun when strict codes of behavior did not allow activities so frivolous as horse "racing." The horses were kept to a prescribed gait or pace as they pulled two-wheel sulkies. The trotting gait came later and had its greatest popularity in the late 1800s through the early 1900s. Dunbar Bostwick, who established this track in 1936, has been credited to a large degree for reviving interest in harness racing. Owners and drivers participate here to gain experience for their horses and to familiarize spectators with the sport.

The Aiken Hunt Meet is the first event of the steeplechasing season. This is a sport in which both horse and rider must have stamina and endurance, combining high speed and split-second timing to clear jumps and gallop long distances. The training of the horses is geared to build up lung power and the muscles of the hindquarters and shoulders. Some of the finest thoroughbreds compete here for trophies and prizes of nearly $40,000.

On any Sunday afternoon from September through November and February through July, the polo ponies compete at the Whitney Polo Field. In polo, man and horse are truly a team. The idea is to strike the ball from horseback, usually at high speed, either passing it to a teammate or hitting a scoring shot between the goalposts. Eight mounted players create quite a stir, galloping up and down the 300 yards of playing area.

Polo has been part of the winter season in Aiken since 1882, just six years after it was introduced to the United States. At one time, Aiken was the polo center of the South, with 16 fields in use. Bring a blanket or folding chairs and a picnic to get into the spirit of the fun.

If you want different kinds of sporting activity, Aiken has two public golf courses, plus tennis courts and walking trails at the Odell Weeks Recreation Center off Whiskey Road.

There is a winner's circle of things to see and do in the surrounding area, as well. The free Thoroughbred Country Touring Guide folder lists five scenic backroads tours for bicycle or auto, and more than a dozen historic homes can be seen in North Augusta, 17 miles away on the banks of the Savannah River.

Two nearby state parks offer a choice of moods. Redcliffe Plantation State Park includes the 350-acre grounds and 1850s home of Governor James Henry Hammon. Aiken State Park covers 100 acres and features four spring-fed lakes and the meandering South Edisto River, a perfect spot for picnicking, swimming, canoeing, fishing, or walking a nature trail.

Wine fanciers may want to pay a visit to Montmorenci Vineyards for free tours and tastings.

Whichever way you wander, all roads lead back to Aiken, a champion choice for a weekend.

Area Code: 803

DRIVING DIRECTIONS Aiken is located seven miles south of I–20, via S.C. Route 19 or U.S. 1. It is 163 miles east of Atlanta and 58 miles west of Columbia.

ACCOMMODATIONS *Willcox Inn,* 100 Colleton Avenue, Aiken 29801, 649–1377 or 800–368–1047, M-E, also many weekend packages ● *Newberry Inn,* 240 Newberry Street, Aiken, 29801, 649–2935, Dutch Colonial home in historic area, I, CP ● *Constantine House,* 3406 Richland Avenue, Aiken, 29801, 642–8911, stately Georgian home, I, CP ● *Annie's Inn,* P.O. Box 311, Montmorenci (5 miles east of Aiken) 29839, 649–6836, antebellum farmhouse, popovers for breakfast, I, CP ● *Rosemary & Lookaway Hall,* 804 Carolina Avenue, North Augusta 19841, 278–6222, pair of elegant turn-of-the-century mansions, high Victorian decor, M-EE, CP.

DINING *Pheasant Room,* Willcox Inn (see above), M-E ● *No. 10 Downing Street,* 241 Laurens Street, 642–9062, I-M ● *Up Your Alley,* 222 The Alley, 649–2603, seafood specials, I-M ● *Track Kitchen,* Mead Avenue near the training track, I.

SIGHTSEEING *Aiken Triple Crown,* three weekends in March featuring steeplechase, thoroughbred, and harness racing. Contact the Chamber of Commerce (see below) for current dates and information ● *Aiken Tours,* 90-minute bus tours from Aiken Municipal Building, 642–1111. Hours: Saturday 10 A.M., reservations recommended, $$$ ● *Polo Games,* Whitney Field, 648–7874. Hours: September through November and March through July, Sundays at 3 P.M., $ ● *Hopeland Gardens,* Dupree Place and Whiskey Road, 642–7630. Hours: daily 10 A.M. to sunset, free ● *Thoroughbred Racing Hall of Fame,* Hopeland Gardens, 649–7700. Hours: September to May, Tuesday to Sunday 2 P.M. to 5 P.M., free ● *Aiken County Historical Museum,* 433 Newberry Street S.W., 642–2015. Hours: Tuesday to Friday 9:30 A.M. to 4:30 P.M.; Sunday 2 P.M. to 5 P.M.; $ ● *Montmorenci Vineyards,* U.S. 78, Montmorenci, 649–4870. Hours: Monday 10 A.M. to 5 P.M.; Wednesday to Saturday 10 A.M. to 7 P.M.; free ● *Aiken State Park,* 1145 State Park

Road, Windsor, off U.S. 78, 16 miles from Aiken, 649–2857. Hours: daily, daylight hours, free ● *Redcliffe Plantation State Park,* 181 Redcliffe Road, off U.S. 278, Beech Island, 827–1472. Hours: grounds open Thursday to Monday 9 A.M. to 6 P.M., free; house tours Thursday to Saturday and Monday 10 A.M. to 3 P.M., Sunday 12 noon to 3 P.M.; $.

INFORMATION *Greater Aiken Chamber of Commerce,* 400 Laurens Street N.W., P.O. Box 892, Aiken, SC 29802, 641–1111.

Feeling the Magic in Birmingham

Birmingham may well be the South's best-kept secret. Lots of people just aren't aware of the changes, the brand-new style and spirit today, in Alabama's largest city.

The best overview of what's happening is from atop Red Mountain, gazing down from the observation deck at the base of the statue of Vulcan. This gigantic figure of the god of metalworking, forged of locally made cast iron, has presided from his lofty perch for over 50 years, a visible symbol of the steel industry that built the city.

People used to come here to see the fiery glow of the open-hearth furnaces. Now they look out on new office towers and the ever-spreading campus of the University of Alabama at Birmingham. The big steel mills are in view, but their smokestacks and furnaces are still. Environmental laws rendered them obsolete in the 1970s, and the last of the original mills that built the city shut down in the 1980s.

That could have been a death knell, but instead Birmingham reinvented itself. Now a thriving city of almost a million people, it has traded hard hats for caps and gowns and scrubs. The University and its Medical Center have experienced phenomenal growth, becoming the city's top employer. Highly educated teachers, medical researchers, and doctors are attracted from all over the country by the excellence of the UAB Medical Center and its many specialized hospitals.

The result is a more sophisticated city, with new emphasis on the arts and good living, including some very fine dining. Birmingham was included in a recent *Newsweek* list of America's best places to live and work.

It is an equally good place to visit. The city boasts the largest municipally owned museum in the South, the biggest zoo in the Southeast, one of the South's most prestigious library collections, a lovely 67-acre botanical garden, and moving remembrances of the Civil Rights struggle.

Even some of those old mills have found a new life. The Sloss Furnaces, named a national landmark, have become an industrial museum. One of the sheds serves as an amphitheater, a highly unusual backdrop for concerts and the Birmingham Jam, a summer celebration of jazz, blues, and gospel music.

Birmingham was never part of the gracious Old South. In fact, it was not founded until 1871, after the Civil War. It was dubbed "the Magic City" for the phenomenal growth that followed when it was discovered that the red rock of the surrounding mountains was actually high-grade iron ore. The steel industry that blossomed produced another nickname, "Pittsburgh of the South."

Then the magic dimmed. During the civil rights protests of the 1960s, blue-collar Birmingham became an unhappy symbol of Southern resistance to integration. As a result, the city stagnated. It was only when racial harmony was finally restored that things began to revive.

Ironically, that painful period now accounts for Birmingham's newest attraction, the $12 million Civil Rights Institute, which opened to much acclaim in November 1992. A walk through the galleries is a pilgrimage through time, from the 1920s to the present. There are vivid reminders of the barriers faced by African Americans in the South, displays of segregated lunch counters and buses, and water fountains labeled WHITE and COLORED. Multimedia displays capture the drama and the tumult of civil rights protests in the state. A bank of 1960s black-and-white TV sets plays scenes of police clad in riot gear, turning fire hoses on unarmed black demonstrators. Among the displays is the actual Birmingham jail cell of the Reverend Dr. Martin Luther King, Jr., who led many local marches. The tour ends at a life-size plaster processional depicting blacks and whites together, headed toward windows overlooking Kelly Ingram Park and the Sixteenth Street Baptist Church across the street.

The park, once the organizing point for downtown marches, was where Public Safety Commissioner "Bull" Conner attacked the marchers with police dogs and hoses, images that remain among the worst moments in the civil rights struggle.

The recently restored Sixteenth Street Baptist Church directly across the street was headquarters for many protest meetings in the early sixties. It was the only large building where blacks were permitted to assemble. The church was bombed by the Ku Klux Klan in 1963, killing four young black girls preparing for Sunday worship, deaths that horrified the world.

All of these are stops on a self-guided Birmingham Black Heritage tour. The tour also covers happier memories, such as Tuxedo Junction, a second-floor dance hall that was the social hub for the black community in the 1920s and 1930s. The name, inspired by the streetcar crossing in the Tuxedo Park neighborhood, became famous as the title of a hit song written by Birmingham-born musician Erskine Hawkins.

Athletes of all colors share the spotlight in another favorite downtown attraction, the Alabama Sports Hall of Fame. Recently ensconced in handsome expanded quarters in the Civic Center, the Hall of Fame celebrates many local heroes who are national legends. Exhibits include the trademark checkered hat belonging to the late legendary Alabama coach Paul "Bear" Bryant; the Heisman trophies won by Auburn's Pat Sullivan and Bo Jackson; golf clubs used by Hubert Green to win the U.S. Open; and memorabilia from such Alabama greats as Joe Louis, Hank Aaron, Joe Namath, Jesse Owens, and Willie Mays, to name just a few.

Though Birmingham's fans love all their sports teams, college football remains first and foremost. Every one of the 73,000 seats at Legion Field is sold out when the University of Alabama or Auburn plays here, and when those two teams play each other, the city goes berserk. Legion Field was recently chosen as the site of the Southeastern Conference championship game.

Golf also has many enthusiastic supporters here, both spectators and players. The city hosted the PGA Championships in 1984 and 1990. Two Robert Trent Jones–designed Oxmoor golf courses, high atop Little Shades Mountain, are championship caliber for public use.

The newest sport in town is the Birmingham Race Course, which presents live thoroughbred racing from May to early July.

Like many cities, Birmingham is struggling to keep its downtown area competitive with suburban shopping malls. Birmingham Green, a landscaped promenade that prettied up Twentieth Street, the main downtown artery, definitely makes things more attractive, even though some storefronts remain vacant.

The downtown blocks offer an interesting mix of architecture, from the 1925 art-deco Alabama Power Building, topped by a 22-foot golden figure of Electra, to the postmodern AmSouth tower. The restored Alabama Theater is a 1920s movie queen, with marble columns, gold leaf, and a Hall of Mirrors. The Tutwiler Hotel, built in 1914 as a luxury apartment complex, has been restored as downtown's most elegant hotel. At press time, plans were in the works to turn the empty Loveman's Department Store into a children's museum.

The enormous Jefferson-Birmingham Civic Center recently completed a $140 million expansion. It is both convention facility and cultural center. Arts venues include a concert hall that is home to the Alabama Symphony, and a theater that is headquarters for the Birmingham Children's Theater. The Coliseum arena hosts everything from ice hockey to the circus. The 771-room Sheraton, Alabama's biggest hotel, is connected to the Civic Center by a skywalk.

Not far away is the recently expanded Birmingham Museum of Art. Among its prides are Renaissance art from the Kress Collection;

American art including works by Remington, Sargent, and Mary Cassatt; African masks; Asian art; and the largest collection of Wedgwood porcelain found outside Great Britain.

The main reading room of the nearby Central Library, with its painted ceilings and murals, is one of the city's loveliest interiors. It houses the Tutwiler Collection of Southern History and Literature, a compendium of subjects from Robert E. Lee to Elvis Presley, quilts to early recipes.

Birmingham's one bit of Old South is Arlington, an antebellum mansion that predates the city. Located a mile west of town, the graceful 1840s Greek Revival mansion serves as a museum of Southern decorative arts.

You'll need a car to see Arlington as well as the rest of the sights, which are located south of downtown. Drive south on Twentieth Street to visit the sprawling 70-block UAB campus. The UAB Medical Center is recognized nationally for its work in heart surgery, kidney transplants, and many other specialties. It ranks among the nation's top 20 schools in research grants.

Next comes Five Points South, a historic neighborhood focused around a landmark circle at Twentieth Street and Highland Avenue. The city's liveliest bars and best restaurants and some intriguing shops can be found here. Cobb Lane, off Twentieth Street just above Five Points, has more shops, and a charming café serving lunch.

The intimate Pickwick Hotel, just off Five Points, is a convenient place to stay, putting you between downtown and the attractions farther south.

Head up the mountain to Vulcan Park to see the largest cast-iron statue ever made, created by Italian-born sculptor Giuseppe Moretti in 1938. An elevator whisks visitors to the observation tower at the foot of the Vulcan statue for that panoramic view of the changing city.

Another wonderful view can be had by driving along the crest of Red Mountain, especially at night, when the city lights twinkle. From Highland Avenue, take Arlington Avenue to Key Circle. At the circle, follow Argyle Road to Stratford Road overlooking the city, one of the most romantic spots in town.

Perched on the side of the mountain near Vulcan is the unusual Red Mountain Museum and Cut. The cut in the mountain clearly shows the red iron ore that spurred the city's steel industry. A one-third-mile-long, 220-foot-high walkway has been placed along the cut with interpretive geological exhibits. Inside the museum, hands-on science displays await. Nearby is the Discovery Place, a children's museum that may soon be moving to larger quarters downtown.

Continuing beyond Vulcan to the area known as "over the mountain," you'll find the zoo, where some of the rare animals in residence include white rhinoceroses and Siberian tigers. Nearby is the Botanical Garden, comprising 67 acres with thousands of different plantings and flowers. Special features include a lovely Japanese garden and a conservatory housing over 5,000 varieties of unusual plants.

Just beyond is the small, charming village of Mountain Brook, a good browsing place for shoppers. It is surrounded by one of the oldest of the city's magnificent hilly, wooded residential areas.

This is the direction in which many of the city's newer neighborhoods are spreading, resulting in suburban towns such as Hoover. Keep driving south on I–31 to see the Riverchase Galleria in Hoover, the city's poshest shopping complex, with 200 stores anchored by the attractive Wynfrey Hotel.

Many first-time visitors are surprised to discover that Birmingham is a city of hills, nestled in the wooded Appalachian foothills. This once-industrial town has always had exceptionally beautiful physical surroundings, but until recently it was like a rough-cut gem in a fine setting. Now it is becoming polished, a lively, growing metropolis of nearly 1 million people with everything to do from football to fine arts.

It's enough to make this native want to go home again.

Area Code: 205

DRIVING DIRECTIONS   Birmingham is reached by I–65, US 280, or US 31 from north and south, I–20/59 and I–459 from east and west. It is 149 miles from Atlanta, 192 miles from Nashville.

HOTELS   *Pickwick Hotel,* 1023 20th Street South, near Five Points, Birmingham 35205, 933–9555 or 800–255–7304, E ● *Mountain Brook Inn,* 28000 US 280 South, Birmingham 35223, 870–3100, M-E ● *Tutwiler Hotel,* 2100 Sixth Avenue North, Birmingham 35203, 322–2100 or 800–866-ROOM, EE ● *Sheraton Civic Center Hotel,* 901 North 21st Street, Birmingham 35203, 254–0380 or 800–325–3535, E ● *Wynfrey Hotel,* 1100 Riverchase Galleria, Birmingham 35244, 987–1600 or 800–476–7006, E-EE ● *Crown Sterling Suites,* 2300 Woodcrest Place, Birmingham 35209, 879–7400, E ● *Motels: Hampton Inn Mountain Brook,* 2731 US 280, Birmingham 35223, 870–7822 or 800-HAMPTON, motel, I, CP; *UAB University Inn,* 951 18th Street South, Birmingham 35205, 933–7700 or 800–888–5673, I ● *Howard Johnson,* 1484 Montgomery Highway, Birmingham 35216, 823–4300 or 800–654–2000, I ● For accommodations in private homes, phone *Bed and Breakfast Birmingham,* 699–9841.

DINING   (first choices are in the Highland Avenue–Five Points South area): *Highlands,* 2011 11th Avenue South, 939–1400, seafood

and jazz, M-E ● *Bottega,* 2240 Highland Avenue, 939–1000, sophisticated Italian fare, I-M ● *Baby Doe's Matchless Mine,* 2033 Golden Crest
Drive, 324–1501, mining-shack decor on the mountain with not-to-be-
missed panoramic city views, outdoor terrace, M-E ● *Dexter's,* I–280
and Hollywood Boulevard, 870–5297, informal bistro setting, grill
specialties, M ● *Tutwiler,* Tutwiler Hotel (see above), elegant decor,
Continental menu, M-E ● *John's,* 112 North 21st Street, 322–6014,
reliable downtown old-timer, I-M ● *Winston's,* Wynfrey Hotel (see
above), regional cuisine, pleasant ambience, M-E ● *For lunch: Cobb
Lane,* 1 Cobb Lane at Five Points, 933–0462, Southern charm and
specialties, I; *Irondale Cafe,* 1306 1st Avenue North, 956–5258, the
birthplace of fried green tomatoes and inspiration for the movie, I;
Browdy's, 2713 Culver Road, Mountain Brook, 879–8585, tops for deli
sandwiches, I; *Bogue's,* 3028 Clairmont Avenue, 254–9780, traditional,
bountiful Southern lunches, I ● Barbecue is big in Birmingham, with lots
of choices; my pick is *Ollie's,* 515 University Boulevard, 324–9485,
whose slogan, "World's Best Barbecue," I endorse. Others with equally
enthusiastic fans include *Costa's Bar B Que,* 3443 Lorna Road, Hoover,
823–7474; *Golden Rule,* Highway 78, Irondale, 956–2678; *Jim 'n Nicks,*
744 Clairmont, 323–7082; *Demetri's,* 1901 28th Avenue S., Home-
wood, 871–1581. All are I.

SIGHTSEEING *Alabama Sports Hall of Fame,* 1 Civic Center
Plaza, 323–6665. Hours: Monday to Friday 8 A.M. to 5 P.M.; Saturday
10 A.M. to 5 P.M.; Sunday 1 P.M. to 5 P.M.; $ ● *Arlington,* 331 Cotton
Avenue S.W., 780–5656. Hours: Tuesday to Saturday 10 A.M. to 4 P.M.;
Sunday 1 P.M. to 4 P.M.; $$ ● *Birmingham Botanical Gardens,* 2612
Lane Park Road, 879–1227. Hours: daily dawn to dusk, free ●
Birmingham Museum of Art, 2000 8th Avenue North, 254–2566.
Hours: Tuesday to Saturday 10 A.M. to 5 P.M., except Thursday to 9 P.M.;
Sunday 1 P.M. to 5 P.M.; free ● *Birmingham Zoo,* I–280, Lane Park,
879–0408. Hours: daily 9:30 A.M. to 5 P.M., $$ ● *Discovery Place of
Birmingham,* 1320 22nd Street South, 939–1176. Hours: Tuesday to
Friday 9 A.M. to 3 P.M.; Saturday 10 A.M. to 4 P.M.; Sunday 1 P.M. to
4 P.M.; check for possible new location downtown; $ ● *Red Mountain
Museum,* 1421 22nd Street South, 933–4104. Hours: Tuesday to
Saturday 10 A.M. to 4:30 P.M.; Sunday 1 P.M. to 4:30 P.M.; donation ●
Sloss Furnaces National Historical Landmark, 1st Avenue North and
32nd Street, 324–1911. Hours: Tuesday to Saturday 10 A.M. to 4 P.M.;
Sunday noon to 4 P.M.; free ● *Vulcan Statue,* Route 31 atop Red
Mountain, 328–2863. Hours: daily 8:30 A.M. to 10:30 P.M., $ ●
Alabama Ballet, Symphony, Opera Theater, Children's Theater: For

current schedules, contact Birmingham-Jefferson Civic Center, 251–4100.

Winning Ways in Augusta

Augusta, the second-oldest city in Georgia, is also the state's second-largest metropolitan area, a winning mix of old and new. No city is richer in history, but that's just the first of many reasons to visit.

The prize attractions in this "second city" include a revitalized waterfront, a remarkable collection of Southern art, great golf, and the Futurity, where Old South mingles with Old West for the liveliest cowboy event this side of the Rockies.

As if all that weren't enough, less than an hour to the west are smaller towns of picturesque charm, including Washington, a contender for the crown as Georgia's prettiest town.

To get a feel for Augusta, drive past the bland outskirts to discover the landscaped parkways, gracious homes, groves of tall pines, and lively river esplanades in the city's heart. In 1736 this became the second town marked off for settlement by General James E. Oglethorpe, who named it Augusta. An eventful history has left six distinct historic districts and many monuments.

The 50-foot granite Signer's Monument, at Greene and Gwinnett streets, commemorates Georgia's signers of the Declaration of Independence. Two of the three, Lyman Hall and George Walton, are buried here. Meadow Garden, Walton's 1791 home, has been restored and is open for tours.

After the Revolutionary War, Augusta served as the state capital from 1785 to 1795. The South's first newspaper, the still-operating *Augusta Chronicle and Herald,* began printing in 1785.

The original building of Georgia's first medical academy, completed in 1835, stands at 598 Telfair Street. The school is still in operation, and the city remains a medical center. Among other important buildings found on Telfair Street are the façade of the restored 1801 Old Government House at number 432 and the Augusta–Richmond County Museum, which includes exhibits ranging from the Revolutionary War era to a reconstructed 1930s train station.

The boyhood home of President Woodrow Wilson is located at 419 Seventh Street on the corner of Telfair, across from the First Presbyterian Church, where his father served as minister. Ware's Folly, at number 540, is a Federal-style structure built in 1818, so named because the construction price of $40,000 seemed so exorbitant at the time. It houses the Gertrude Herbert Memorial Institute of Art, an art school and gallery.

The city's second-oldest structure is the 1798 Ezekiel Harris House in the Harrisburg Historic District. It has been preserved as an example of a wealthy early merchant's home.

Also in the Harrisburg District is the first Augusta Arsenal, established in 1793 by order of General George Washington. A 176-foot-tall chimney marks the site along the Augusta Canal of the Confederate Powderworks, said to be the world's largest munitions factory of its time. The castlelike 1881 Sibley Mill on the same site resembles the old powderworks.

You can't miss the Confederate Monument in the center of town, on Broad Street between Seventh and Eighth; the marble shaft stands 72 feet high and features life-size figures of Southern heroes, including Robert E. Lee and "Stonewall" Jackson.

Another monument with an interesting tale is the Haunted Pillar at Fifth and Broad. Legend has it that a traveling minister who was not allowed to preach in the Lower Market prophesied that the building would be destroyed. Sure enough, in 1878 a tornado took down everything except this one pillar.

After the Civil War, Augusta became an industrial center for the New South. Before and after the war, it also prospered as the second-largest inland cotton market in the world, right behind Memphis. The elaborate Victorian 1886 Cotton Exchange building near the waterfront has been restored as a cotton museum and town welcome center. A 45-foot blackboard used to post daily market quotes was found intact behind a wall, still chalked with cotton and commodities prices from the early 1900s. It is the hub of the exhibit called "Cotton Pickin' Deals."

Late in the last century, the city's mild winter climate was discovered by wealthy Northerners. Drive around the Summerville Historic District, on a breezy knoll above town, to see the homes they built in what was known as the "hill section." John D. Rockefeller and Alexander Graham Bell were among the Yankees who rocked on the porch of the Partridge Inn on Walton Way, or the old Bon Air Hotel across the street.

Milledge Road is another of Summerville's wealthiest thoroughfares, lined with fine antebellum homes.

Not far away, at 2500 Walton Way, is the campus of Augusta College. Among the fine old buildings is the 1829 Payne Hall, which served as headquarters for the Augusta Arsenal. This campus is radiant in spring, when its venerable magnolias are in bloom.

Victorian homes can be found in the Old Town neighborhood, closer to downtown, where major renovation is taking place. Some of these homes now serve as welcoming inns.

One site that everyone in Augusta points to with pride is the Sacred Heart Cultural Center, an 1898 showplace of Romanesque Revival architecture with imported stained-glass windows and 15 different kinds of Byzantine brickwork.

One pleasant way to take in the historic side of Augusta is via the trolley tour that leaves from the Cotton Exchange each Saturday morning.

The Cotton Exchange borders the pride of modern Augusta, its recently transformed riverfront. The cobbled streets leading to the river, once piled high with cotton bales, are now lined with shops and cafés. Riverwalk, a landscaped park along the water, makes for delightful strolls and includes a 1,500-seat amphitheater that is used for many outdoor entertainments in summer. One end of the walk is anchored by The Shoppes of Port Royal, a retail center and condominium complex, the other end by a conference center/office complex and an elegant Radisson hotel.

On the second floor of one of those office buildings is a not-to-be-missed treasury of Southern art. The Morris Museum is an enlightening view of many facets of Southern life as seen through the artist's eye. The exhibits span the centuries, ranging from antebellum portraits to contemporary abstracts. A corridor circling all the galleries is devoted to the Southern landscape in all its beautiful forms.

Augusta's waterfront hosts many special events, including a colorful rowing regatta in late March or early April. Boat rides on the Savannah River are offered most of the year.

Spring is the season when Augusta's most famous event takes place. The city's golf heritage dates back to the post–Civil War era, when the owner of the Bon Air Hotel decided to build a nine-hole golf course. It proved so popular with his wealthy guests that the following year an 18-hole course was built on what is now the Augusta Country Club. In 1933, Bobby Jones founded the Augusta National Golf Club and held the first Masters Tournament, now a world-class attraction.

Tickets for the Masters are hard to come by, and only members can play the National, but that doesn't mean you can't play golf in Augusta. There are 11 public courses, including the Jones Creek Golf Course in nearby Evans, rated among Georgia's top public courses.

It isn't surprising that the Georgia Golf Hall of Fame was established in Augusta in 1982.

The weather is mild most of the year, which means you can often play golf in winter. But regardless of the climate, winter is the season for the city's most unusual event, the Augusta Cutting Horse Futurity, held in late January. Cutting horses are used by cowboys to separate a single cow from the safety of the herd, a maneuver that takes skill and ultimate teamwork between horse and rider. For over a decade the best professional riders have competed for speed, showing off their prowess for a purse of some $500,000 and the title of America's Greatest Cowboy.

The exciting and colorful week-long event includes a top-notch Western Art Show and a Western Expo with booths selling everything Western, from fringed suede jackets to fancy saddles and Indian jewelry.

If you have time for more sightseeing, less than an hour to the west is Washington, a beautiful small town dating to 1789 that is now a mellow mix of white antebellum columns and sturdy brick Victorian architecture. The turn-of-the-century town square, dominated by an unusual Flemish-design brick courthouse, is a classic that has been used as a setting for several movies.

Washington's most historic moment came at the end of the Civil War, when Jefferson Davis and the members of his cabinet signed the last official papers dissolving the Confederate government at the Heard House, on the site of the present courthouse. Some still believe that the remainder of the Confederate treasury, estimated at over half a million dollars in gold, was buried somewhere nearby.

A small town with a population of 4,300, Washington can be enjoyed on a brief walking or driving tour, guided with a brochure from the Chamber of Commerce. Start with a walk around the square, peeking into the old-fashioned gift shops and antique stores. Look to the left of the courthouse, in the northwest corner, to see the old jail, built in 1891 and recently restored.

Many of the finest older homes are along Robert Toombs Avenue, including the Toombs House, a 1794 pillared structure that was the home of the man known as the South's "unreconstructed rebel." Toombs, a brigadier general and secretary of state of the Confederacy, refused to take the oath of allegiance to the Union after the Civil War, remaining a rebel to the end of his days. He became a local hero, and his home is now a state historic site.

The Washington Historical Museum, housed in an 1835 structure, contains furnishings from the antebellum era and Civil War memorabilia, including a Confederate gun collection.

Another building worth a visit is the Mary Willis Library. Georgia's first free public library, founded in 1888, the ornate Victorian building boasts Tiffany stained-glass windows, charming murals of the town, and an impressive collection of rare books.

Callaway Plantation, five miles outside town, is still a working farm with a columned main house, circa 1869, outbuildings, and a barnyard full of animals. The log kitchen is often used for cooking and other demonstrations.

Several homes in the historic district are now bed-and-breakfast inns, and an even better choice awaits just outside town. Holly Ridge comprises two homes, a 1780s Colonial and an 1880s Victorian, that were moved to this site, joined, then restored to provide one inn with two distinct characters.

Another top lodging choice is 1810 West, a short drive away in Thomson. A plantation house built of heart of pine, it has five dependencies, creating a rambling inn of varying moods, tastefully decorated with antiques and offering eight fireplaces.

Thomson, the commercial center of the area, boasts a unique bit of history in the 1785 Rock House, named for its unusual building material. Tours are available; ask at the tourism center in the old railroad depot, where you can also pick up a driving tour through many nearby towns with fine period homes.

Thomson has a strong equestrian bent. The annual Belle Meade Fox Hunts, held from November to March, are renowned; you're likely to spot the red-coated riders on the outskirts of town in the Wrightsborough area.

The Classic South Steeplechase is one of many competitions held here. It's an appropriate name for a region that remains the picture of the classic South.

Area Code: 706

DRIVING DIRECTIONS   Augusta is on the eastern edge of Georgia, off I–20. From Atlanta, follow I–20 east, 145 miles; to reach Washington, take I–20 east to Ga. Route 44 north, 95 miles. From Augusta, follow I–20 west to U.S. 78 north, 45 miles.

ACCOMMODATIONS   *Partridge Inn,* 2110 Walton Way, Augusta 30904, 737–8888, restored landmark, M-E, CP ● *Oglethorpe Inn,* 836–838 Greene Street, Augusta 30901, 724–9774, pair of restored Victorian homes, M, CP ● *Clarion Telfair Inn,* 326 Greene Street, Augusta 30901, 724–3315, group of Victorian homes, pool, lighted tennis court, M-EE ● *Radisson Hotel Augusta,* 2 Tenth Street, Augusta 30901, 722–8900, elegant new hotel on the Riverwalk, M-E ● *Holiday Inn West,* 1075 Stevens Creek Road, Augusta 30907, 738–8811, I ● *Holly Ridge Country Inn,* 2221 Sandtown Road, Washington 30673, 285–2594, I, CP ● *Southern Manor Bed and Breakfast,* 412 East Robert Tombs Avenue, Washington 30673, 678–2614, I, CP ● *Water Oak Cottage,* 211 South Jefferson Street, Washington, 30673, 678–3548, I, CP ● *Wingfield Bed and Breakfast,* 512 North Alexander Avenue, Washington 30673, 678–2278, remodeled 1786 farmhouse in historic district, I-CP ● *1810 West Inn,* 254 North Seymour Drive, N.W., Thomson 30824, 595–3156, I, CP ● *Four Chimneys Bed & Breakfast,* 2316 Wire Road, Thomson 30824, 597–0220, 1800s country house, I, CP.

DINING   *Partridge Inn Restaurant,* Augusta (see above), fine dining, city's best Sunday brunch, I-M ● *Calvert's,* 475 Highland Avenue, Augusta, 738–4514, formal dining, local favorite for special occasions, I-E ● *Cotton Row Cafe,* 6 Eighth Street at Riverwalk, Augusta,

722–6901, casual café, I ● *Cotton Patch,* 816 Cotton Lane at Riverwalk, Augusta, 724–4511, New Orleans café, I ● *French Market Grille,* 425 Highland Avenue, Augusta, 737–4865, Louisiana cuisine, famous for crab cakes and peanut-butter pie, I-M ● *La Maison,* 404 Telfair Street, Augusta, 722–4805, restored home in Olde Towne, Continental, M-E ● *Le Cafe Du Teau,* 1855 Central Avenue, Augusta, 733–3505, quaint café, New Orleans–style menu, live jazz, I-M ● *Michael's,* 2860 Washington Road, Augusta, 733–2860, contemporary setting, fine dining, M-E ● *T's Restaurant,* 3416 Old Savannah Road, Augusta, 798–4245, catfish and hush puppies, oyster bar, I-M ● *Sconyers Bar-B-Que,* 2250 Sconyers Way, Augusta, 790–5411, everybody comes here, log cabin decorated with owner's pig collectibles, I ● *Another Thyme Cafe,* on the square, Washington, 678–1672, in the historic Fitzpatrick Hotel building, very informal, I ● *Plantation House,* Best Western–White Columns Motel, U.S. 78 at I–10, Thomson, 595–8000 or 800–528–1234, I-M ● *Neal's Bar-B-Que,* U.S. 78/278, Thomson, 595–2594, no atmosphere, just good food, I.

SIGHTSEEING *Augusta–Richmond County Museum,* 540 Telfair Street, Augusta, 722–8454. Hours: Tuesday to Saturday 10 A.M. to 5 P.M.; Sunday 1 P.M. to 5 P.M.; $ ● *Gertrude Herbert Institute of Art,* 506 Telfair Street, 722–5494. Hours: Tuesday to Friday 10 A.M. to 5 P.M.; Saturday 10 A.M. to 2 P.M.; $ ● *Sacred Heart Cultural Center,* 1301 Greene Street, 827–4700. Hours: Monday to Friday 9 A.M. to 5 P.M.; Saturday 10 A.M. to 1 P.M.; $ ● *Morris Museum of Art,* 1 Tenth Street, Riverfront Center, second floor, 724–7501. Hours: Tuesday to Saturday 10 A.M. to 5:30 P.M.; Sunday 1 P.M. to 5 P.M.; $ ● *Ezekiel Harris Home,* 1840 Broad Street, Augusta, 724–0436. Hours: Tuesday to Friday 1 P.M. to 4 P.M.; Saturday 10 A.M. to 1 P.M.; $ ● *Augusta Cutting Horse Futurity,* Augusta–Richmond County Civic Center, 724–2400. One week of riding competitions, Western Art Show and Expo, usually late January. Phone for current information, 823–6600 ● *Historic Augusta Guided Trolley Tours.* Ninety-minute tours leave Saturday, 10:30 A.M., from Cotton Exchange Welcome Center; phone 724–0436 for reservations by 3 P.M. the Friday before the tour, $$$ ● *Augusta Riverboat Cruises,* 1 Fifth Street, Augusta, 722–5020. Sightseeing, dinner, and entertainment cruises, February through December; phone for schedules, rates ● *Washington-Wilkes Historical Museum,* 308 East Robert Toombs Avenue, Washington, 678–2105. Hours: Tuesday to Saturday 10 A.M. to 5 P.M.; Sunday 2 P.M. to 5 P.M.; $ ● *Robert Toombs House,* 216 East Robert Toombs Avenue, Washington, 678–2226. Hours: Wednesday to Saturday 9 A.M. to 5 P.M.; Sunday 2 P.M. to 5:30 P.M.; $ ● *Callaway Plantation,* U.S. 78, Washington, 678–7060.

Hours: March 1 to December 15, Tuesday to Saturday 10 A.M. to 5 P.M.; Sunday 2 P.M. to 5 P.M.; $.

INFORMATION *Augusta Convention & Visitors Bureau,* 32 Eighth Street, Augusta, GA 30901, 823–6600 or 800–726–0243 • *Washington-Wilkes Chamber of Commerce,* 108 East Liberty Street, Washington, GA 30673, 678–2013.

Tee Time at Myrtle Beach

Everybody knows about Myrtle Beach, South Carolina, in the summer. Smack in the middle of the 60 miles of sand known as the Grand Strand, this has long been one of the busiest vacation destinations on the Atlantic seaboard. But why in the world are people now heading for the shore in winter? What makes them flock to Myrtle Beach when many people are at home by the fire?

Well, for starters, how about a round of golf? To be more precise, make that 80 rounds of golf. There are 80-plus golf courses at Myrtle Beach, enough for a game every day for over two and a half months without repeating the same course twice.

Winters are mild, with average temperatures in the fifties, and spring comes early to the South Carolina shore, so the golfing mania knows no season. Almost every area lodging entices visitors with golf galore, available in packages at bargain rates.

These rates lure not only a host of all-male foursomes, but lots of couples and families with non-golfers, who take advantage of other diversions while the fanatics are teeing off. Some hotels encourage this with special "golf widow" rates. Tennis, fishing, indoor pools, shopping, shelling, and sightseeing at one of America's loveliest outdoor sculpture gardens top the list of off-season activities, all delightfully devoid of crowds. For the kids, there's a special outing to the Waccatee Zoological Farm, to see over 100 animals from llamas to leopards.

By night, everyone can take in the lavish country-music theaters that are the newest attractions on the Myrtle Beach scene, turning it into a mini-Nashville by the sea.

Another winter bonus is the chance to see the shaggers in action. The shag is South Carolina's official dance, a Southern cousin of the lindy, replete with show-off dips, glides, and spins. It can be danced to almost any tempo, but best of all is beach music, and the preferred place is North Myrtle Beach. You can see amateurs in action almost any weekend, but the best dancers do their thing at the preliminaries for the National Shag Dance Championships in January, with winners going on to the championships in mid-March.

It might be said that Myrtle Beach's rapid development in the last few decades is making up for lost time. Separated by water from both the mainland and the Georgetown County plantation country to the south, isolated Horry County was left to the farmers and timbermen, a self-sufficient pocket cut off from development. Until the early 1900s, the beach was accessible only by ferryboat across the Waccamaw River, which is now part of the Intracoastal Waterway.

When a railroad bridge across the river made transportation easier, inland families began building summer cottages along the coast, and in 1901 the first hotel went up. A contest held by the county newspaper produced the name of Myrtle Beach, inspired by the wax myrtles growing wild along the shore.

In 1929 a group of developers built Arcady at the north end of the community, planned as a dream resort for the affluent. It included Pine Lakes, the area's first golf course; and the elegant ten-story Ocean Forest Hotel, which became the center of Myrtle Beach social life for nearly 30 years.

Modern Myrtle Beach was largely the result of Hurricane Hazel, which leveled most of the early beachfront buildings in 1954. New resorts and golf courses sprang up seemingly overnight, this time planned for families with average incomes, and development has never stopped.

The shoreline is now wall-to-wall motels and hotels, the main highway chockablock with restaurants, shopping centers, amusement parks, water slides, and elaborate miniature golf courses that vie for the most waterfalls and other extravaganzas. Property destroyed by Hurricane Hugo in 1989 was rebuilt quickly, and growth continues. It is almost essential to come off-season to see the beauty that attracted development in the first place.

The buildup is slightly less dense at North Myrtle Beach, which also boasts the widest area beaches. To the south, the towns of Surfside Beach and Garden City are mostly family cottage colonies. Murrells Inlet, favored by fishermen and seafood lovers, is the dividing line with Georgetown County, and the more secluded beaches of Litchfield and Pawleys Island beyond.

If golf is your goal, contact Myrtle Beach Golf Holiday for their big free book of golf packages. Over 100 pages thick, it includes color photos of scores of participating properties, from motels to luxury resorts, plus details of nearly 70 golf courses.

Ocean Harbour reigns supreme with golfers; it has been ranked one of the ten best courses in the world by *Golf* magazine. Other challenges are Indigo Creek, nominated as ''Best Public Golf Course for 1991'' by *Golf Digest,* and Tidewater, the 1990 choice of both magazines for best newcomer. The five Legends courses—Marsh Harbour, Oyster Bay, Heritage, Moorland, and Heathland—all are ranked in America's top 50 public courses, and a sixth should be complete by now.

Among other memorable experiences are Waterway Hills, designed by Robert Trent Jones and Rees Jones, possibly the only course in the world accessed by a glass-enclosed gondola, and the Witch, with 400 feet of bridges winding through hundreds of acres of wetlands. The Arnold Palmer courses at Myrtle Beach National also include some legendary water holes. The third hole on the North Course, a mini-island with sand traps that spell "S.C.," is probably the best-known green on the Grand Strand.

Pine Lakes, the granddaddy of the courses, still shows the Scottish influence of its architect, Robert White. Golfers are greeted by kilted starters, warmed with hot chocolate or a mimosa on the first tee, and offered clam chowder near the turn and a "crying towel" at the finish. It was on this course that *Sports Illustrated* magazine was conceived in 1954.

If tennis is your game, you'll find that courts are plentiful, 150 at last count. Tennis buffs should consider a stay at Litchfield-by-the-Sea, a 4,500-acre resort in Georgetown County, about 18 miles south of the Myrtle Beach buildup, on the site of former rice plantations. The Litchfield Racquet Club has the area's largest tennis complex, with 17 outdoor and two indoor courts. It is host to many regional and national USTA events.

The resort also offers its own three golf courses, seven miles of private beach, an indoor pool, and a fitness center, with a racquetball court and classes ranging from water aerobics to karate. If it rains, golfers can take solace at the indoor driving range, where they aim at a screen showing some of the world's most famous golfing holes.

The posh, all-suites Radisson Resort, a high-rise on 145 oceanfront acres, also offers tennis, racquetball, and a sport and health club with a pool.

There are more than 50,000 guest rooms at Myrtle Beach in every price range, including efficiencies, suites, and cottage rentals. Many are almost interchangeable motel or high-rise accommodations. Those suggested in the listings at the end of this chapter are among the choices that offer both beach access and indoor facilities for winter visitors.

When the sun goes down, Myrtle Beach really lights up these days, thanks in large part to entrepreneur Calvin Gilmore, a singer-guitarist who, in 1986, opened the first Carolina Opry at a nightclub in Surfside Beach. It proved so popular that Gilmore built a 2,200-seat palace in 1991, and has since opened two additional shows, Dixie Jubilee and Southern Country Nights. All feature comedy and music from country forties to rock and roll. A smaller competitor, the Myrtle Beach Opry, offers similar entertainment at more moderate prices.

In 1992, part-owner Dolly Parton inaugurated another $7.5 million showplace, the Dixie Stampede, a version of the Dollywood-produced spectacle on horseback that packs in crowds at Pigeon Forge, Tennessee.

The newest theater on the scene was opened in 1993 by the group Alabama, who got their first break in Myrtle Beach. Two different shows will run at their fancy showcase at Barefoot Landing, a waterfront complex that also offers 100 shops and a dozen restaurants.

By day, shoppers will find ample opportunities for their favorite sport at Barefoot Landing and all along U.S. 17. Bargain hunters should make a beeline for U.S. 501 west and Waccamaw Pottery. The original pottery outlet, now selling a huge selection of housewares and home furnishings, is adjacent to an outlet park with more than 100 brand-name factory outlets.

No one should miss a visit to Brookgreen Gardens, the main sightseeing attraction in the area, located to the south in Georgetown County. This was America's first public sculpture garden, and it is now the largest outdoor sculpture display in the world, a remarkable blend of nature and art, with over 500 sculptures set on 300 lush, landscaped acres. (Read more about the gardens and all of Georgetown County starting on page 164.

Across the road, in Huntington Beach State Park, part of the original family land holdings, is Atalaya, the Huntingtons' single-story home, inspired by Moorish watchtowers on the Spanish coast. It is unfurnished but well worth a look.

The park itself includes maritime forests, salt marshes, and sandy beaches. Like much of Myrtle Beach, it is a fine place to be on a mild winter day.

Area Code: 803

DRIVING DIRECTIONS   Myrtle Beach begins at the junction of U.S. 17 north and south with U.S. 501 from the west. From Atlanta and Columbia, follow I–20 east to Florence, then take U.S. 76 east, which merges into U.S. 501. From I–95, take the Florence exit and follow the directions above. Myrtle Beach is 354 miles from Atlanta, 174 miles from Charlotte, 143 miles from Columbia.

PUBLIC TRANSPORTATION   Myrtle Beach has its own airport; easy access and special air and car-rental rates make it easy to come for a winter weekend. Additional service is from Charleston, 70 miles south.

ACCOMMODATIONS   (All have private beach, indoor pools; I rates are usually from November to early March, higher rates in season.) *Litchfield-by-the-Sea,* P.O. Drawer 320, Pawleys Island 29585, 237–3000 or 800–845–1897, superb tennis; hotel suites, I-M; cottages, M; oceanfront cottages, M-EE ● *Radisson Resort at Kingston Plantation,* 9800 Lake Drive, Myrtle Beach 29572, 449–0006 or 800–289–4300, all-suite hotel, villas, lighted tennis courts, racquetball, lavish sport and health club room, M-EE ● *Bluewater Resort,* 2001 South Ocean Boulevard, Myrtle Beach 19578, 626–8345 or 800–845– 6994, efficiency apartments, racquetball, billiard and exercise rooms, I-E ● *The Breakers North Tower and Resort Hotel,* Oceanfront at 21st and 27th avenues North, P.O. Box 485-GHB, Myrtle Beach 29578, 626–5000 or 800–845–0688, exercise room, I-EE ● *Carolina Winds,* Oceanfront at 76th Avenue North, Myrtle Beach 29578, 449–2427 or 800–523–4027, villas with kitchens, spa, exercise and game rooms, I-EE ● *Captain's Quarters,* 901 South Ocean Boulevard, Myrtle Beach 29578, 448–1404 or 800–843–3561, rooms and efficiencies, bowling alley, I-M ● *Forest Dunes Resort,* 5511 North Ocean Boulevard, Myrtle Beach 29577, 449–0864 or 800–845–7787, suites, indoor pool, exercise and game rooms, I-E ● *Meridian Plaza,* 2310 North Ocean Boulevard, Myrtle Beach 29478, 626–4734 or 800–323–3011, suites, game and exercise room, I-E ● *Myrtle Beach Martinique,* 7100 North Ocean Boulevard, Myrtle Beach 29578, 449–4441 or 800–542–0048, sauna, exercise and game rooms; hotel rooms, I-M; efficiencies, I-E ● *Ocean Dunes/Sand Dunes Resort,* 74th Avenue North, Myrtle Beach 29572, 449–7441 or 800–845–6701, large indoor fitness center, racquetball, indoor driving range, I-E ● *Patricia Grand,* 2710 North Ocean Boulevard, 29578, 448–8453 or 800–255–4763, game room, sauna, indoor "lazy river," I-E ● *Pan American Motor Inn,* 5300 North Ocean Boulevard, Myrtle Beach 29578, 449–7411 or 800–845– 4501, rooms and efficiencies, tennis, I-M ● *Sea Mist Resort,* 1200 South Ocean Boulevard, Myrtle Beach 29577, 448–1551 or 800–732– 6478, indoor driving range, game room, I-M ● Many more choices: write to Chamber of Commerce (see below) for full hotel-motel guide or condominium-cottage guide; for a book listing golf packages at all area resorts, contact *Myrtle Beach Golf Holiday,* 609 Seaboard Street, Box 1323, Myrtle Beach 29578, 800–845–4653.

DINING *Bermuda Boat Cafe,* Barefoot Landing, U.S. 17, North Myrtle Beach, informal, Intracoastal Waterway views, M ● *The Library,* 1212 Kings Highway North, 448–4527, elegant, E ● *Parson's Table,* U.S. 17, Little River, 249–3702, award winner, stained glass, I-M ● *Sea Captain's House,* Oceanfront at 30th Avenue North, Myrtle Beach, 448–8082, restored beach house, ocean views, area favorite for all three meals, dinners, M ● *Santa Fe Station,* U.S. 17, North Myrtle

Beach, 249–3463, change-of-pace dining in a train car, I-E ● *Thoroughbreds*, 9706 North Kings Highway, 497–2636, equestrian decor, I-M ● *Webster's Fine Food and Spirits*, Litchfield-by-the-Sea (see above), informal lakeside dining, I-M ● For Murrells Inlet dining, see page 168.

SIGHTSEEING *Brookgreen Gardens*, U.S. 17, Murrells Inlet, 237–4218. Hours: daily 9:30 A.M. to 4:45 P.M., $$ ● *National Shag Dance Championship*, Studebaker's, 2000 North Kings Highway, Myrtle Beach, 626–3855 or 448–9747. Preliminaries usually in late January, championships in March; phone for current dates ● *Waccatee Zoological Farm*, 8500 Enterprise Road, 650–8500. Hours: daily 10 A.M. to 5 P.M., $$.

ENTERTAINMENT (Most shows run year-round, but schedules may be curtailed in late December and January; check all for current show times and rates.) *Alabama Theater*, Barefoot Landing, U.S. 17, Myrtle Beach, 272–1111 or 800–342-BAMA ● *Myrtle Beach Opry*, U.S. 17 and 19th Avenue North, Myrtle Beach, 448-OPRY ● *Calvin Griffith Productions*, all at 238–8888 or 800–843–6779, include *Carolina Opry*, U.S. 17 north at U.S. 17 bypass; *Dixie Jubilee*, Main Street, North Myrtle Beach; *Southern Country Nights*, U.S. 17, Surfside Beach ● *Dixie Stampede*, North Myrtle Beach, junction of U.S. 17 and U.S. 17 bypass, 497–9700.

INFORMATION *Myrtle Beach Area Chamber of Commerce*, 1301 North Kings Highway, P.O. Box 2115, Myrtle Beach, SC 29578, 626–7444 or 800–356–3016.

The Last Roundup

The Last Roundup: Southeastern Resorts

Sometimes sightseeing isn't at all what you have in mind for your weekend. There are times when the most inviting prospect may be a resort where you can stay in one place, relax and refresh, maybe play a little golf or tennis, learn a new sport, take a run around a lake, a walk in the woods, or a hike in the mountains.

Blessed with a mild climate and a spectacular range of scenery, the Southeastern states offer wonderful get-away-from-it-all resorts—by the sea, in the mountains, and in between. They come rustic and fancy, to suit every taste and budget, geared to families as well as to couples. State park resorts in many states are outstanding and are great bargains.

Many top resorts have already been mentioned in previous sections, but some just don't fit neatly into another destination. This final chapter changes the book format, moving state by state to make sure these special places are not overlooked.

Browse through this roundup, then check the index under resorts for a reminder of the other rich choices available when a one-stop getaway is what you have in mind.

ALABAMA

Less than an hour south of Birmingham, in Shelby County, is the kind of hideaway city dwellers often dream about, a rustic resort on 200 wooded acres around a 46-acre private lake. Twin Pines was designed as a conference center, but on weekends the guest rooms in the newly built log houses by the lake are perfect escapes for a mini-vacation.

While the setting is definitely country, rooms come with city comforts such as coffeemakers, refrigerators, and TV. Suites offer kitchens and fireplaces. Each guest house has a deck with rockers for admiring sunsets over the lake. Country-style meals are served in an airy dining room with a cathedral ceiling, fireplaces, and picture windows.

Besides swimming, canoeing, and fishing, the resort offers tennis, horseshoe-tossing, biking, jogging, and walking trails. Weekend package rates make this a most affordable getaway.

Even in a state filled with exceptional state resort parks, Lake Guntersville stands out. The majestic wood-and-fieldstone lodge set atop Little Mountain provides a superb view of the 66,470-acre Guntersville Reservoir, another of the beautiful Alabama lakes formed by the dam system on the Tennessee River.

Many of the lodge rooms have balconies and eye-boggling lake views. Cottages and chalets also are available on the grounds.

Water sports are the big activity here, and the lake is renowned among fishermen, but landlubbers can golf, play tennis on two lighted courts, or enjoy 20 miles of hiking trails along the park's 5,909 acres of ridge tops and in its meadows. Winter eagle-watching weekends led by park naturalists are a special treat.

GEORGIA

It's the ultimate fantasy when worldly worries close in: escape to an island where there are no cars, no commotion, and nothing but serenity. Two Georgia off-shore islands can make this fantasy come true.

Little St. Simons is a magical 10,000-acre world of unspoiled marshes, thick maritime forests, moss-draped live oaks, ponds, and seven miles of pristine beaches. It is home to deer, rabbits, 200 species of birds, alligators, and armadillos—and just 24 fortunate guests.

The island was originally purchased in 1908 by Philip Berolzheimer, head of the Eagle Pencil Company, who planned to use the cedar trees as a source of pencil wood. It proved unsuitable, but Berolzheimer fell in love with the wild beauty of Little St. Simons and kept it as a personal retreat, building a rustic hunting lodge in 1917.

The family still comes to Little St. Simons, but they opened it up to guests for the spring and fall seasons several years ago, adding two modern lodges, where each bedroom has a deck overlooking the marsh. Guests gather in the homey, memento-filled main lodge for drinks before dinner and family-style meals.

Days on the island are spent exploring the tidal marshes and creeks by canoe, beachcombing, or setting out on horseback or on foot to see birds and animals. Resident naturalists lead guided walks, or you can go off on your own. The deserted beach is a shell collector's dream come true. There are also safaris by truck to places like Murtle Pond, a prime spot for seeing alligators.

The nature is similar on Cumberland Island, but the ambience is quite different. Located farther south, near the Georgia-Florida border, the island was once a family preserve owned by Thomas Carnegie. The Carnegies lived on a lavish scale, as ruins of the old family mansions reveal.

Greyfield Inn, the only remaining island lodging, was built in 1901 for a daughter, Lucy Carnegie Ferguson, and it was opened as an inn by family descendants in the 1960s. It is still in the Carnegie family. Approached by an oak-lined drive, the house has faded from its grandest days, but high ceilings, paneling, Oriental rugs, and family heirlooms tell you that this was the province of wealth, and the air is still gracious. Dinner, for example, is served by candlelight, and jackets are suggested for gentlemen, dresses for the ladies.

There are nine guest rooms in the three-story Georgian home, only one with a private bath, and one cottage, accommodating up to six.

Some 85 percent of Cumberland is now a National Seashore, preserved forever in its unspoiled state. Visitors come over from the mainland by boat to enjoy the beach, to view the birds and the wildlife, and to enjoy the walks and talks offered by National Park rangers in season, but the isolation means the island is never crowded.

Two other Georgia resorts are convenient to Atlanta weekenders. The Lake Lanier Islands were created when the Buford Dam was built on the Chattahoochee River, forming a 1,200-acre lake with 540 miles of shoreline. The heavily forested hilltops, too high to be submerged, were developed for recreation and are now connected to the mainland by causeway. Resorts here offer just about every resort facility. Stouffer Pine Isle Resort is privately owned and is a little more posh than the Lake Lanier Islands Hotel and Golf Club, which is under the auspices of the state.

Be assured, however, that there's nothing second-rate about the attractive, modern, state-owned facility. The golf course is highly rated, sailboats and pontoon boats are for rent, and kids love the Water Park with all manner of rides and slides with names like "Triple Threat" and "Intimidator." Horseback riding, a pool, a lakeside beach, a fitness center—all of these are also available.

Chateau Elan in Braselton, Georgia, is lavish and unique. It is part winery, part exclusive spa, part golf and tennis resort, part conference center, done with all the style that money can buy. Accommodations are in the new 150-room inn and conference center, in villas near the golf course, or in the intimate spa building, where each deluxe hideaway is done to fanciful themes ranging from high-tech to Oriental, from Greek to Old South. Dining choices include an informal bistro cafe, the Golf Club House, or the very formal LeClos dining room in the winery, where there is a prix-fixe five-course dinner. An equestrian center is to be completed sometime in 1994.

NORTH CAROLINA

Imagine yourself taking a cruise around picturesque Lake Toxaway, surrounded by the dusky Blue Ridge Mountains. When you dock, you need only walk up the stone steps to find your private mansion. That's a typical afternoon scenario at the Greystone Inn. This magnificent 16,000-square-foot "cottage," rambling up six levels to accommodate its rocky terrain, was built by a Savannah heiress, Lucy Moltz, back in 1915 and is now on the National Register of Historic Places. It has become the center of a resort surrounded by 3,000 acres of wilderness, complete with the waterfalls that abound in this enchanted part of the state, about 20 miles north of Highlands.

There are 19 rooms in the main house, decorated with antique-style furnishings, canopy and brass beds, and lovely floral fabrics. An oak-paneled library, modeled after the grand library at the Biltmore Estate in Asheville, has been turned into the Presidential Suite, two stories high with huge, mullioned windows, wooden beams, and a big fireplace. A newer adjoining lodge makes up for lack of history with fireplaces, Jacuzzis, and private balconies overlooking the lake.

The resort offers a pool, six tennis courts, 18 holes of golf, a velvet-green croquet lawn, and lots of room for hiking. You can take out your own boat or join the afternoon excursions aboard the Mountain Lily II. It's a lifestyle designed to make you feel as though you've become an heiress, too.

The mood is just the opposite at Earthshine Mountain Lodge, a rustic retreat also near Lake Toxaway and set on 70 acres across a high mountain meadow. Owners Marion and Kim Boatwright designed and built the one-and-a-half-story cedar log lodge themselves, with only Kim's mother and one employee to help them. Both specialists in outdoor education, the Boatwrights were creating a dream—a place to celebrate the mountains, a center where all ages could come to appreciate and learn more about nature, to fish and hike, ride a horse, feed the family of farm animals, or test their mettle on the High Ropes course, a challenging skill akin to rock climbing.

The owners also want guests to take time to enjoy the grandeur of the mountains. The deck is equipped with rockers for contemplating the views, and the long printed list of activities ends with three R's—reading, rocking, and relaxation.

Guestrooms are small and simple, with wooden walls, quilts on the log beds, and nice touches such as tree branches as towel hooks and canning-jar lids as curtain rings. All rooms have a private bath and a loft, making them perfect for families. Children are happy here, with activities ranging from special programs such as pond exploration to horse rides in the corral, berry-picking, bread-baking, and helping with the garden and the animals.

Three miles up a steep winding road and on a site over 5,000 feet high, Cataloochee Ranch puts you at eye level with the mountains. Just 60 guests share these 1,000 acres above the Maggie Valley, another favorite haven for families. There's good hiking here, as well as tennis, trout fishing, and a swimming pool, but most guests come to enjoy the mountains on horseback, letting a trusty steed do the climbing while they enjoy the fabulous scenery.

The ranch has been in the Alexander family since 1938, and some of the guest families have been coming in successive generations for almost that long. The main ranch house was once the cattle barn, built of mud-mortared stone, and most of the original walls remain. It is furnished with big, well-worn couches and chairs, lamps made from oxen yokes, and a piano where guests often gather.

Guest rooms are in the main lodge, in seven cabins on the grounds, and in the newer Silverbell Lodge, where suites have fireplaces. Furnishings are rustic, in keeping with the setting. Meals are family-style, followed with entertainment by local musicians, who sing folk songs and teach square dancing and clogging to city folks. In winter Cataloochee offers skiing at the area that was the first for the sport in North Carolina.

Nantahala Outdoor Center doesn't exactly qualify as a resort, but it deserves mention for those who want to get out on the glorious mountain rivers. Sometimes called "The Oxford of white-water canoe schools," the center has been offering trips through the river's scenic gorge for over 20 years.

This was long before river rafting was "in," and the center has done a great deal to help the sport to grow, while expanding beyond anyone's dreams. Now an employee-owned company with 90 to 100 year-round staff members, it is the prime place in the Southeast for learning rafting. Rock climbing, mountain biking, and backpacking are also offered.

The complex is in two parts. On the river is a reception center, a day care center, a no-frills motel, a well-stocked Outfitters Store, and two informal restaurants. Up the hill is Relia's Garden, an attractive cedar chalet-style restaurant overlooking a garden growing vegetables, herbs, and flowers.

Also on the hill are cottages, dorm-style lodgings, and a small modern lodge for students who sign up for courses in canoeing, kayaking, and other sports. Baths are shared, but the accommodations are attractive and comfortable. Participants share meals, which are included in the cost. Discounts are provided if lodging is found elsewhere, and private instruction also is available.

Off North Carolina's Cape Fear coast is Bald Head Island, another private island, but one that might best be described as a live-in country club at sea. Lodgings on the 12,000-acre resort are in classy condominiums or vacation homes with every convenience, and with great privacy. Cars are not allowed on the island, but a golf cart waits in each garage to transport you from beach to golf course, croquet court to tennis court, and to the club house for an excellent dinner. The club house pool offers activities such as volleyball games and water aerobics. There are planned activities for children.

Homes dot much of the area rimming the shore, but there's plenty of untouched beauty in the island's interior and the 14 miles of unspoiled beach that remain. Bald Head is known for the loggerhead turtles who migrate to the beach each year and share their nesting rituals with turtle watchers. The Bald Head Island Conservancy conducts walks to see turtles, alligators, and numerous species of birds.

SOUTH CAROLINA

Kiawah Island Resort is living proof that you can have resort facilities without losing the integrity of the environment. Just 21 miles south of Charleston, South Carolina, this is a classic Lowcountry setting with white sand beach, marshes, and wildlife carefully preserved. The Kiawah Island Inn, a low-key, low-rise lodge, and the resort's villas are strategically tucked among the trees so as not to intrude. Views vary from ocean to forest to dune.

Whitetail deer and some 18 other species of mammals, as well as alligators, sea turtles, and 30 other kinds of reptiles and amphibians, share the island with resort guests. Some 140 species of birds have been spotted, including showy varieties such as osprey, herons, hawks, and egrets. When guests are not using sports facilities, the beach, or one of three swimming pools, a favorite pastime is "Kiawah Kollege," which includes exploring the island's flora and fauna on marsh biking tours, by canoe, and on walks accompanied by marine biologists and naturalists.

Consider the designers of the four golf courses—Gary Player, Pete Dye, and Jack Nicklaus—and you'll understand why this is a favorite resort among golfers. Two tennis clubs offer 28 hard-surface and clay courts. In summer, Kamp Kiawah offers a full-time children's program to ensure equal fun for both generations. Teen and family programs round out the agenda.

TENNESSEE

Fairfield Glade is one of the largest resorts in Tennessee, located in the scenic Cumberland Plateau region, 114 miles east of Nashville. You will not be bored here. What is there to do? Well, what about four golf courses, swimming pools, a beach, boat rentals, fishing, horseback riding, and tennis courts both indoors and out, with lights outside so you can play in the cool of the evening? Add a putting green and driving range, miniature golf, an exercise room, bikes, and dancing and entertainment at night—well, you get the idea. Accommodations are hotel-style or in villas.

There's also no shortage of fun at Tennessee's Fall Creek Falls State Resort Park in Pikeville, north of Chattanooga. This is the second largest in the state park system and its 160,000 acres offer spectacular scenery—chasms and deep river gorges, virgin forest, and, of course, the dramatic Fall Creek Falls, plunging 256 feet into a shaded pool. The park's 18-hole golf course has been listed as one of the top 20 public courses in the country. Take your pick of inn or cabins. Either way you'll have access to an Olympic-size swimming pool, hiking and biking trails, playgrounds, and a choice of dining room or snack bar.

Whichever state you choose, the range of wonderful resort facilities for weekenders will likely make you echo the old song, "That's what I like about the South."

RESORT ACCOMMODATIONS *Twin Pines Conference Center,* 9025 Twin Pines Road, Sterrett, AL 35147, 205–672–7575, E, MAP • *Lake Guntersville State Park,* Star Route 63, Box 232, Guntersville, AL 35976, 205–582–2061 or 800-LGVILLE, lodge rooms, I; suites, chalets, cottages, M • *Little St. Simons Island,* P.O. Box 1078, St. Simons Island, GA 31522, 912–638–7472, EE, AP. Open March through May, October through November. Transportation, arranged through the lodge, is by boat from St. Simons, GA, or air taxi from Savannah or Jacksonville airports • *Greyfield Inn,* Cumberland Island, GA. Mailing address: Drawer B, Fernandina Beach, FL 32034, 904–261–6408, EE, AP. Transportation is provided from Fernandina Beach, FL, via the inn's private ferry • *Lake Lanier Islands Hotel and Golf Club,* 7000 Holiday Road, Lake Lanier Islands, GA 30518, 404–945–8787 or 800–768–5253, M-E • *Stouffer PineIsle Resort,* 9000 Holiday Road, Lake Lanier Islands, GA 30518, 404–945–8921, E-EE • *Chateau Elan,* 7000 Old Winder Highway, Braselton, GA 30517, 706–441–9463 or 800–233-WINE, inn rooms, E, villas and spa rooms, EE. • *Greystone Inn,* Lake Toxaway, NC 704–966–4700 or 800–824–5766, EE • *Earthshine Mountain Lodge,* Rt. 1, Box 216-C, Lake Toxaway, NC 28747, 704–862–4207, EE, AP, or E, CP • *Cataloochee Ranch,* Rt. 1, Box 500F, Maggie Valley, NC 28751, 704–926–1401 or 800–868–1401, E-EE MAP • *Nantahala Outdoor Center,* 41 Highway 19 West, Bryson City, NC 28713, 704–488–6737. Standard courses available for weekends, and 3 to 7 days, EE per person, including instruction, equipment, shared lodging, and all meals. Motel lodgings, I; cabins, E-EE • *Bald Head Island,* P.O. Box 3069, Bald Head Island, NC 28461, 800–234–1666, condominiums and homes with golf cart, EE. Transportation via ferry from Southport, NC, 30 minutes south of Wilmington • *Kiawah Island Inn and Villas,* P.O. Box 12357, Charleston, SC 29412, 803–768–2121 or 800–845–2471 in SC, 800–654–2924 out of state, E-EE • *Fairfield Glade,* Box 1500, Fairfield Glade, TN 38557, 615–484–7521, rooms, M, villas, E • *Fall Creek Falls State Resort Park,* State Highway 30, Route 3, Pikeville, TN, 615–881–3241, I •

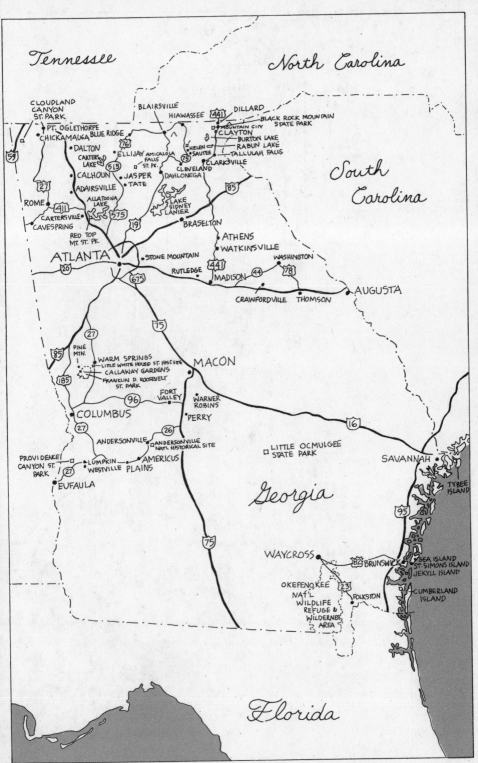

Tennessee

North Carolina

South Carolina

CLOUDLAND
CANYON
ST. PARK
PT. OGLETHORPE
CHICKAMAUGA BLUE RIDGE
59
DALTON
CARTERS
LAKE
27
CALHOUN
ADAIRSVILLE
ROME
411
CARTERSVILLE
CAVESPRING
RED TOP
MT. ST. PK.
ATLANTA
20
675

BLAIRSVILLE
HIAWASSEE 441 DILLARD
BLACK ROCK MOUNTAIN
STATE PARK
MOUNTAIN CITY
CLAYTON
HELEN BURTON LAKE
SAUTEE RABUN LAKE
TALLULAH FALLS
ELLIJAY AMICALOLA
FALLS
ST. PK.
515
JASPER
TATE
19
CLEVELAND
DAHLONEGA
CLARKSVILLE
75
LAKE
SIDNEY
LANIER
85
BRASELTON
ATHENS
WATKINSVILLE
STONE MOUNTAIN
RUTLEDGE
MADISON 44
441
WASHINGTON
78
CRAWFORDVILLE THOMSON
AUGUSTA

ALLATOONA
LAKE
575

75
27
PINE
MTN.
85
WARM SPRINGS
LITTLE WHITE HOUSE ST. HIST. SITE
CALLAWAY GARDENS
FRANKLIN D. ROOSEVELT
ST. PARK
185
MACON
96
FORT
VALLEY
WARNER
ROBINS
COLUMBUS
27
PERRY
26
ANDERSONVILLE
ANDERSONVILLE
NAT'L HISTORICAL SITE
PROVIDENCE
CANYON ST.
PARK
LUMPKIN
WESTVILLE PLAINS
27
AMERICUS
EUFAULA
LITTLE OCMULGEE
STATE PARK
16
SAVANNAH
TYBEE
ISLAND

Georgia

95

75
WAYCROSS
82 BRUNSWICK
SEA ISLAND
ST. SIMONS ISLAND
JEKYLL ISLAND
OKEFENOKEE
NAT'L
WILDLIFE
REFUGE &
WILDERNESS
AREA
23
FOLKSTON
CUMBERLAND
ISLAND

Florida

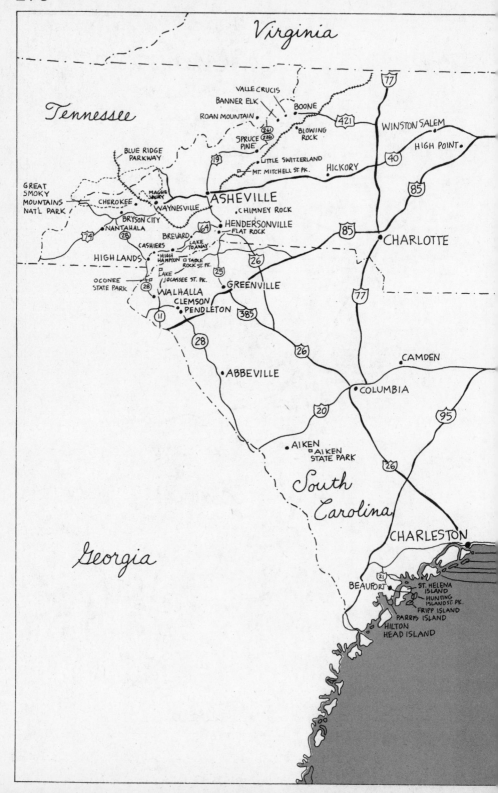

Virginia

Tennessee

VALLE CRUCIS
BANNER ELK
ROAN MOUNTAIN
BOONE
261
226
SPRUCE PINE
BLOWING ROCK
421
WINSTON SALEM
BLUE RIGE PARKWAY
40
HIGH POINT
19
LITTLE SWITZERLAND
MT. MITCHELL ST. PK.
HICKORY
GREAT SMOKY MOUNTAINS NAT'L PARK
CHEROKEE
MAGGIE VALLEY
WAYNESVILLE
ASHEVILLE
CHIMNEY ROCK
85
BRYSON CITY
26
NANTAHALA
HENDERSONVILLE
FLAT ROCK
85
CHARLOTTE
74
BREVARD
LAKE TOXAWAY
CASHIERS
HIGH HAMPTON
TABLE ROCK ST. PK.
HIGHLANDS
25
26
LAKE JOCASSEE ST. PK.
OCONEE STATE PARK
28
GREENVILLE
77
WALHALLA
CLEMSON
PENDLETON
385
11
28
26
CAMDEN
ABBEVILLE
COLUMBIA
20
95
AIKEN
AIKEN STATE PARK
26
South Carolina

CHARLESTON

Georgia

21
BEAUFORT
ST. HELENA ISLAND
HUNTING ISLAND ST. PK.
FRIPP ISLAND
PARRIS ISLAND
HILTON HEAD ISLAND

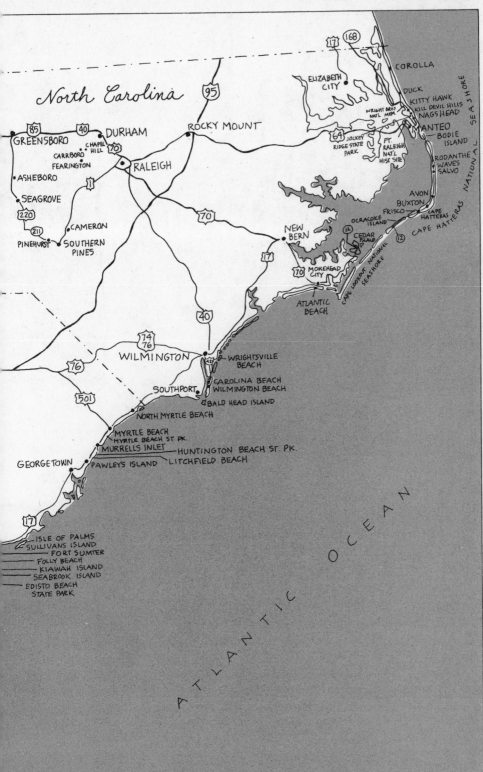

North Carolina

GREENSBORO
DURHAM
CARRBORO
CHAPEL HILL
FEARINGTON
RALEIGH
ASHEBORO
SEAGROVE
CAMERON
PINEHURST
SOUTHERN PINES
ROCKY MOUNT

ELIZABETH CITY
COROLLA
DUCK
KITTY HAWK
KILL DEVIL HILLS
WRIGHT BROS NATL MEM.
NAGS HEAD
MANTEO
BODIE ISLAND
JOCKEY RIDGE STATE PARK
FT. RALEIGH NAT'L HIST. SITE
RODANTHE
WAVES
SALVO
AVON
BUXTON
FRISCO
CAPE HATTERAS
OCRACOKE ISLAND
CAPE HATTERAS NATIONAL SEASHORE
CEDAR ISLAND

NEW BERN
MOREHEAD CITY
ATLANTIC BEACH
CAPE LOOKOUT NATIONAL SEASHORE

WILMINGTON
WRIGHTSVILLE BEACH
CAROLINA BEACH
WILMINGTON BEACH
SOUTHPORT
BALD HEAD ISLAND
NORTH MYRTLE BEACH
MYRTLE BEACH
MYRTLE BEACH ST. PK.
MURRELLS INLET
HUNTINGTON BEACH ST. PK.
GEORGETOWN
PAWLEYS ISLAND
LITCHFIELD BEACH

ISLE OF PALMS
SULLIVANS ISLAND
FORT SUMTER
FOLLY BEACH
KIAWAH ISLAND
SEABROOK ISLAND
EDISTO BEACH STATE PARK

ATLANTIC OCEAN

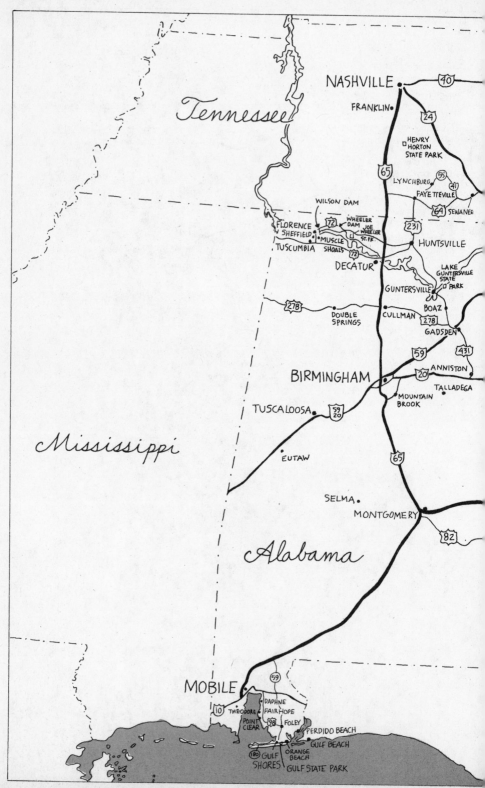

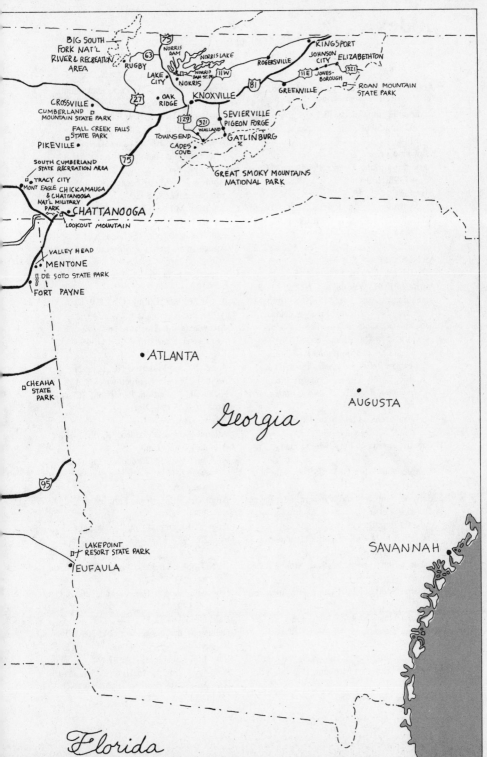

BIG SOUTH
FORK NAT'L
RIVER & RECREATION
AREA

RUGBY

63

75

NORRIS
DAM

NORRIS LAKE

ROGERSVILLE

KINGSPORT

JOHNSON
CITY

ELIZABETHTON

11E

JONES-
BOROUGH

321

ROAN MOUNTAIN
STATE PARK

LAKE
CITY

NORRIS

NORRIS
DAM ST. PK.

11W

81

GREENVILLE

CROSSVILLE

CUMBERLAND
MOUNTAIN STATE PARK

27

OAK
RIDGE

KNOXVILLE

FALL CREEK FALLS
STATE PARK

129

321

SEVIERVILLE
PIGEON FORGE

PIKEVILLE

SOUTH CUMBERLAND
STATE RECREATION AREA

75

TOWNSEND

WALLAND

GATLINBURG

CADES
COVE

TRACY CITY

MONT EAGLE

CHICKAMAUGA
& CHATTANOOGA
NAT'L MILITARY
PARK

GREAT SMOKY MOUNTAINS
NATIONAL PARK

CHATTANOOGA

LOOKOUT MOUNTAIN

VALLEY HEAD

MENTONE

DE SOTO STATE PARK

FORT PAYNE

ATLANTA

CHEAHA
STATE
PARK

Georgia

AUGUSTA

95

LAKEPOINT
RESORT STATE PARK

EUFAULA

SAVANNAH

Florida

Index